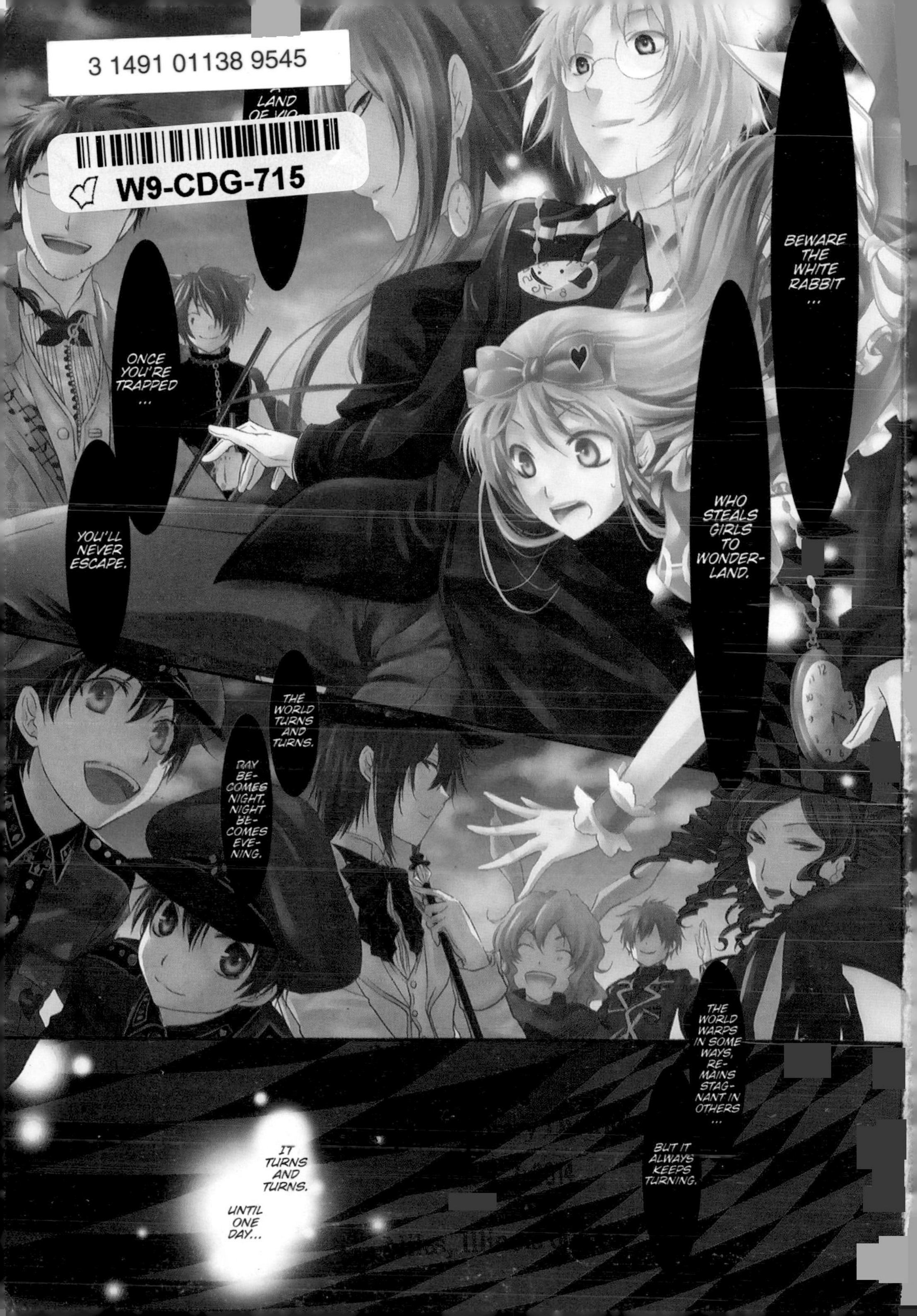
BEWARE THE WHITE RABBIT...
WHO STEALS GIRLS TO WONDER-LAND.
A LAND OF VIO-
ONCE YOU'RE TRAPPED...
YOU'LL NEVER ESCAPE.
THE WORLD TURNS AND TURNS.
DAY BE-COMES NIGHT. NIGHT BE-COMES EVE-NING.
THE WORLD WARPS IN SOME WAYS, RE-MAINS STAG-NANT IN OTHERS...
BUT IT ALWAYS KEEPS TURNING.
IT TURNS AND TURNS.
UNTIL ONE DAY...

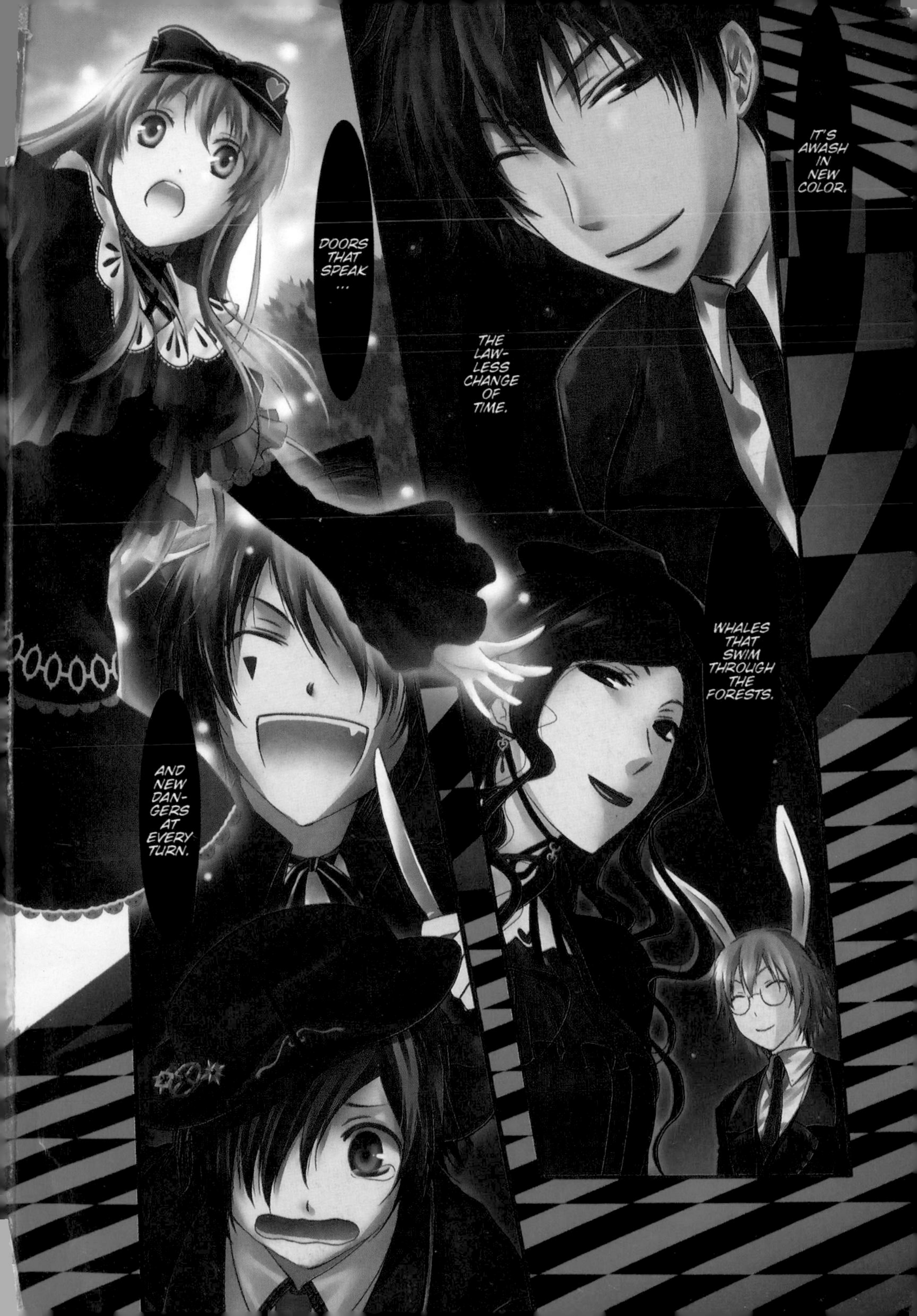
IT'S AWASH IN NEW COLOR.
DOORS THAT SPEAK...
THE LAWLESS CHANGE OF TIME.
WHALES THAT SWIM THROUGH THE FORESTS.
AND NEW DANGERS AT EVERY TURN.

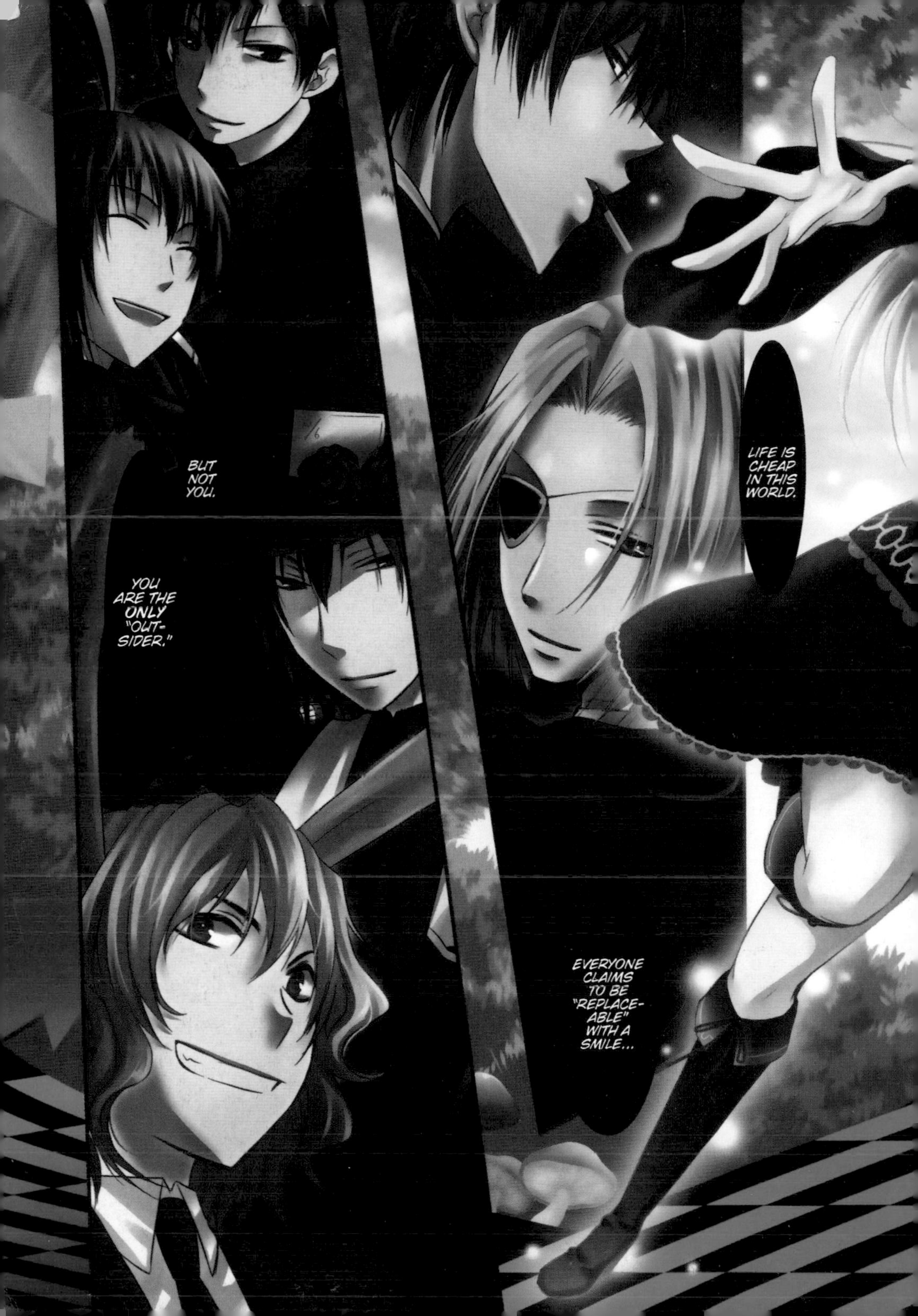
LIFE IS CHEAP IN THIS WORLD.
EVERYONE CLAIMS TO BE "REPLACE-ABLE" WITH A SMILE...
BUT NOT YOU.
YOU ARE THE ONLY "OUT-SIDER."

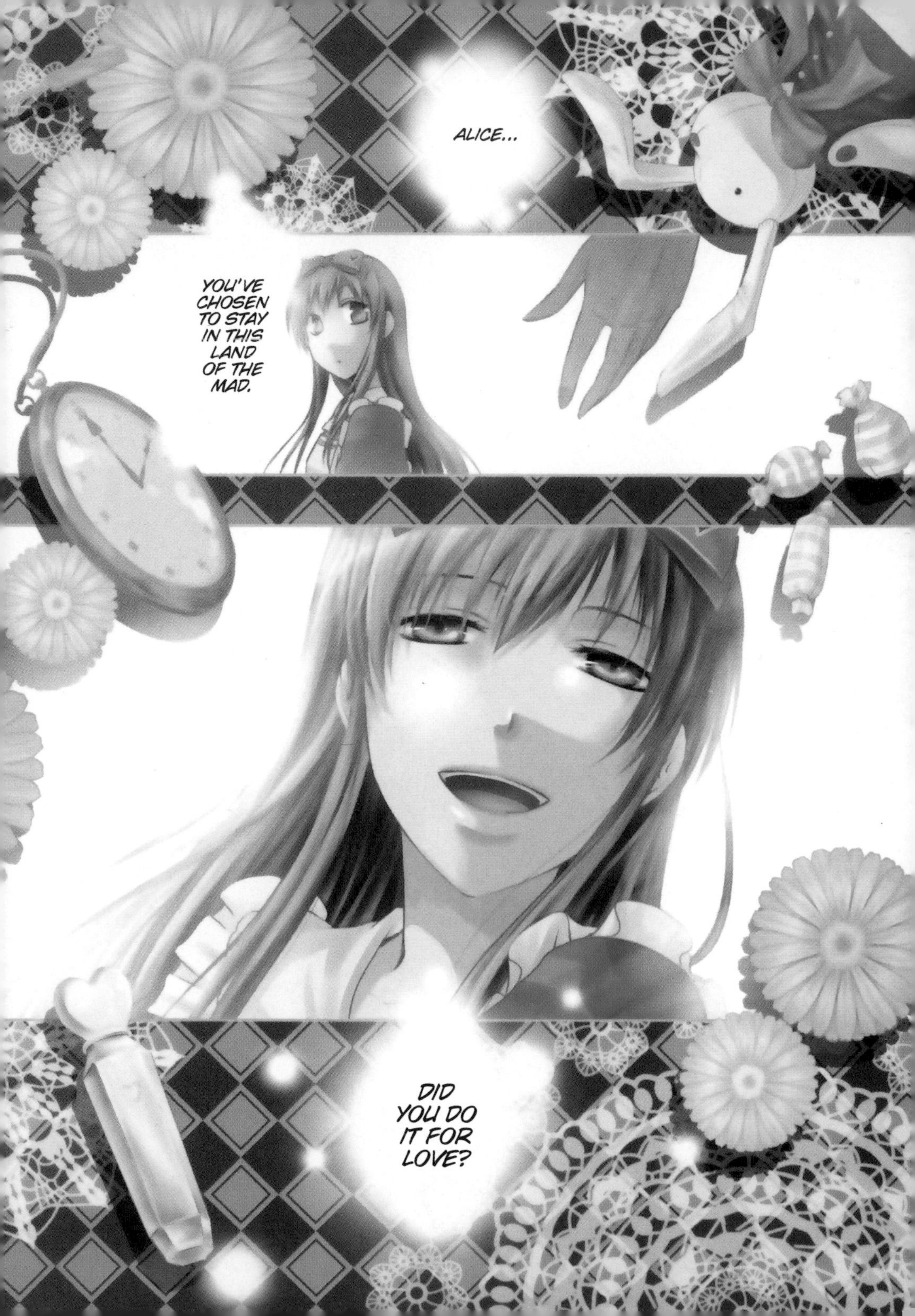
ALICE...
YOU'VE CHOSEN TO STAY IN THIS LAND OF THE MAD.
DID YOU DO IT FOR LOVE?

Alice Love Fables
~Toy Box~

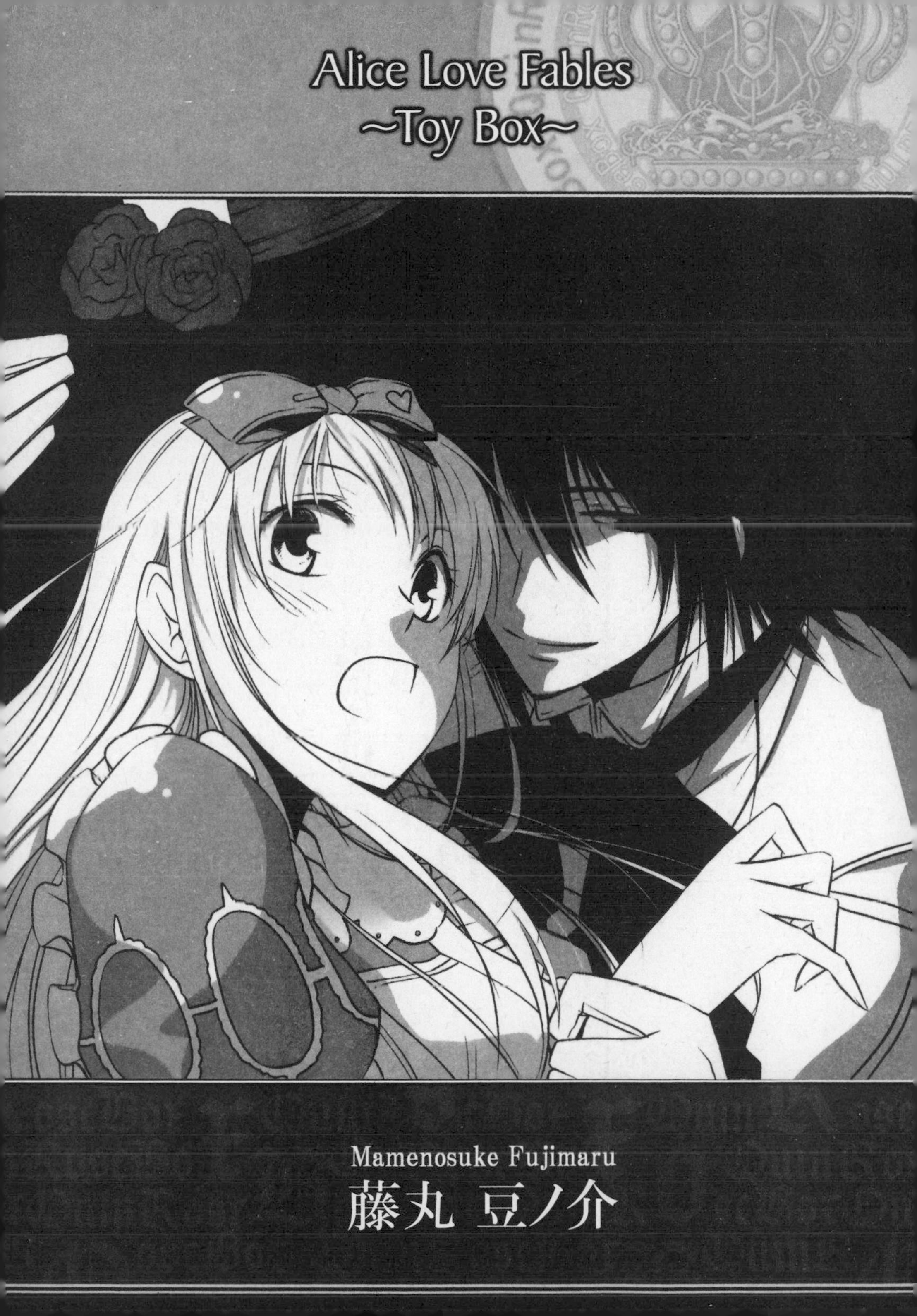

Mamenosuke Fujimaru
藤丸 豆ノ介

SEVEN SEAS ENTERTAINMENT PRESENTS

Alice Love Fables
story by QUINROSE / art by MAMENOSUKE FUJIMARU
toy box

TRANSLATION
Angela Liu

ADAPTATION
Lianne Sentar

LETTERING
Roland Amago

LAYOUT
Bambi Eloriaga-Amago

COVER DESIGN
Nicky Lim

PROOFREADER
Shanti Whitesides
Danielle King

MANAGING EDITOR
Adam Arnold

PUBLISHER
Jason DeAngelis

ALICE LOVE FABLES: TOY BOX
Copyright © Mamenosuke Fujimaru, QuinRose 2009
First published in Japan in 2009 by ICHIJINSHA Inc., Tokyo.
English translation rights arranged with ICHIJINSHA Inc., Tokyo, Japan.

Seven Seas books may be purchased in bulk for educational, business, or promotional use. For information on bulk purchases, please contact Macmillan Corporate & Premium Sales Department at 1-800-221-7945 (ext 5442) or write specialmarkets@macmillan.com.

Seven Seas and the Seven Seas logo are trademarks of Seven Seas Entertainment, LLC. All rights reserved.

ISBN: 978-1-937867-84-3

Printed in Canada

First Printing: December 2013

10 9 8 7 6 5 4 3 2 1

FOLLOW US ONLINE: www.gomanga.com

READING DIRECTIONS

This book reads from *right to left*, Japanese style. If this is your first time reading manga, you start reading from the top right panel on each page and take it from there. If you get lost, just follow the numbered diagram here. It may seem backwards at first, but you'll get the hang of it! Have fun!!

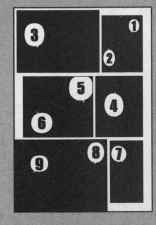

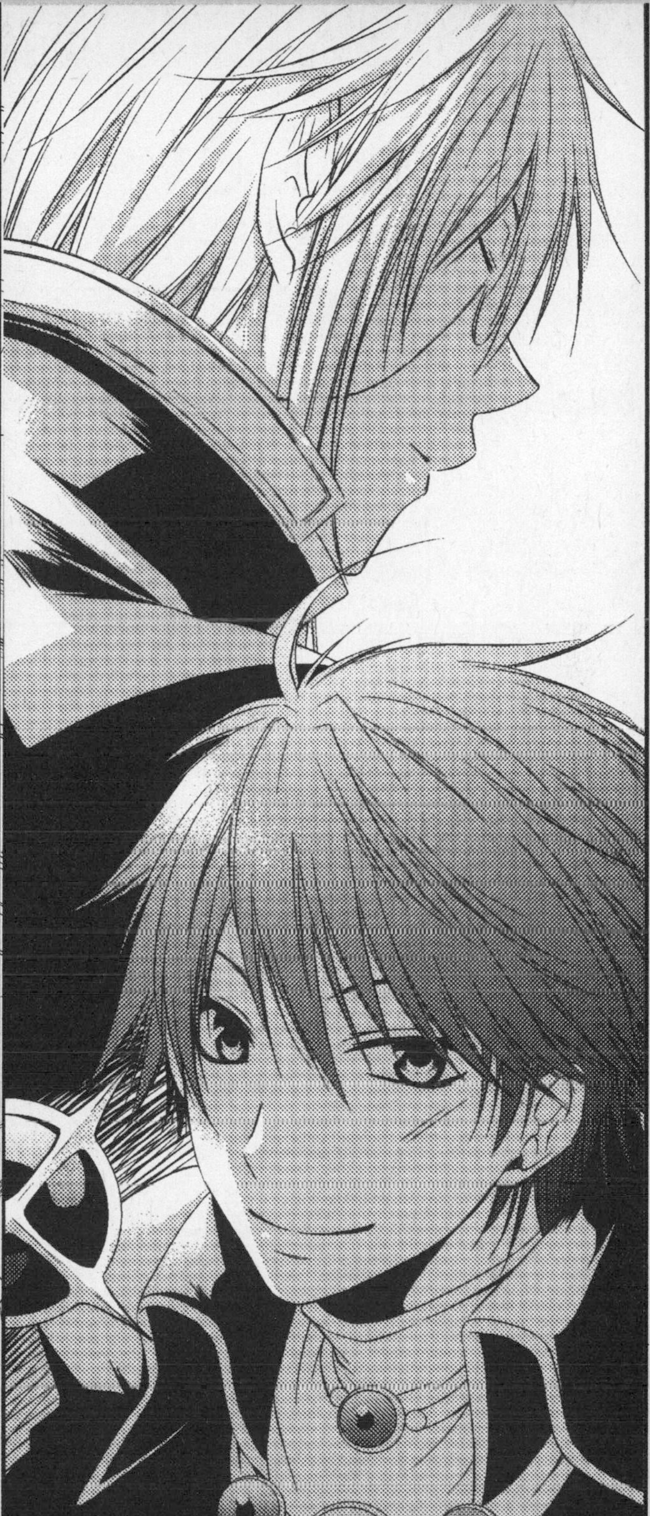

QuinRoseBox

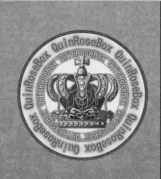

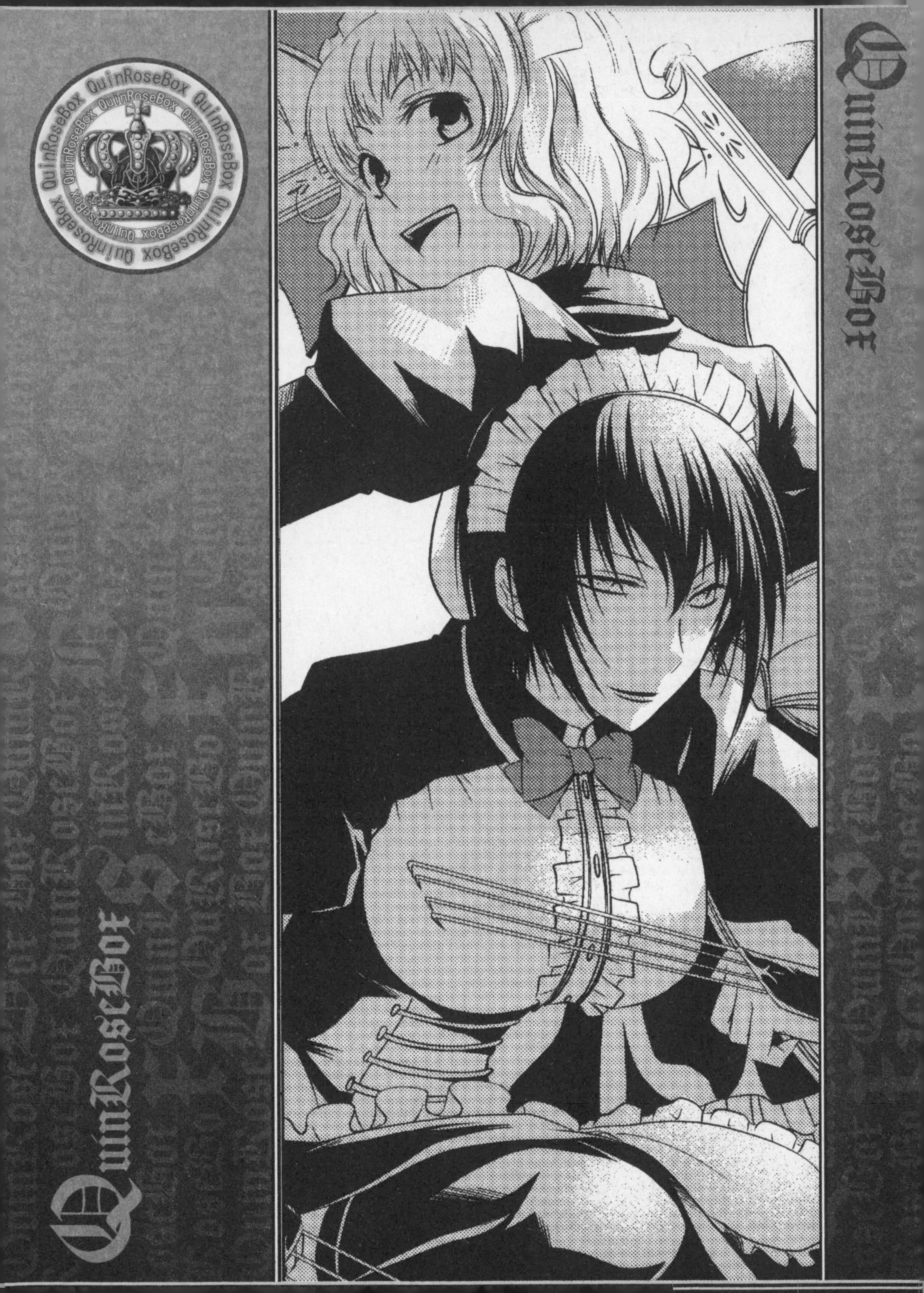
QuinRoseBox
QuinRoseBox
QuinRoseBox

Arabians Lost
アラビアンズ・ロスト
~ The engagement on desert ~

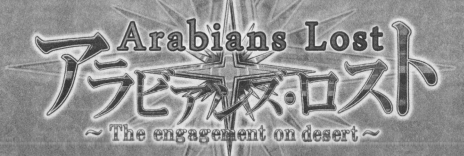

- STORY -

Aileen is the princess of Gilkatar, the great kingdom of thieves. She's the only child of her father, the revered King of Thieves.

After growing up surrounded by hoodlums and scoundrels, she dreams of a "normal" life—love, marriage, and a family that won't pick her pocket. But her doting father insists that she marry a competent man to ensure her safety...and his definition of "competent" is the exact opposite of what Aileen wants.

So she strikes a bargain with her parents—if she can gather the tremendous sum of 10,000,000G in 25 days, she'll be released from the engagement they've arranged for her.

In her quest to be "normal," Aileen didn't level up her thieving skills, but she's resourceful in other ways. The goal is (probably) possible if she dedicates her life to it. But to ensure her victory, she must strike deals with the very rogues she wished to escape...

Arabians Lost Characters Information

Aileen Olazabal
Main character.

The princess of the lawless kingdom of Gilkatar. As the only daughter of the king, she's next in line for the throne.

Curtis Nile
VA: Akira Ishida

Behind his gentle smile, Curtis is a deadly assassin who specializes in poisons. Raised in the slums, he's a master of the back roads.

Roberto Cromwell
VA: Naozumi Takahashi

The kingpin of the fast-growing casinos, Roberto is not only a powerful businessman—he's a skilled gambler (and cheater). He has insatiable ambitions.

Shark Brandon
VA: Shintaro Ohata

The young leader of a black market guild, Shark went from rags to riches, which could explain his terrible taste. Believe it or not, he's a procuring genius *and* a doctor.

Lille Sluman
VA: Anri Katsu

Aileen's kind-but-strict (mostly strict) personal tutor. He has an old leg injury; the sword he uses as a cane was a gift from Roberto. He and Roberto have been close for years.

Stuart Sink
VA: Junichi Suwabe

The heir of the mediator of the country's northern region. He's related to Tyrone, but they don't get along. He's handsome, haughty, and a stickler for cleanliness.

Tyrone Bale
VA: Katsuyuki Konishi

The heir of the mediator of the country's southern region. He's related to Stuart, but they don't get along. He's passionate, easygoing, and rather crude.

Yuu
VA: SHIGERU (AciD FLavoR)

A traveling merchant who once studied with Meissen, Yuu (name shortened for time) is a strange man with a strange way of speaking. He loves rare things and...yellow things.

Michael Faust
VA: Hikaru Midorikawa

A demon who made a contract with Meissen. He's dangerously strong, monologues a lot, and has a bad attitude. He's also strangely nervous...an unstable combination.

Meissen Hildegarde
VA: Hiro Shimono

The older brother of the main character in "Magician and Master." A friendly playboy with wanderlust, he's also a powerful wizard, searching for the truth about the world in his quest to be a sage (his words).

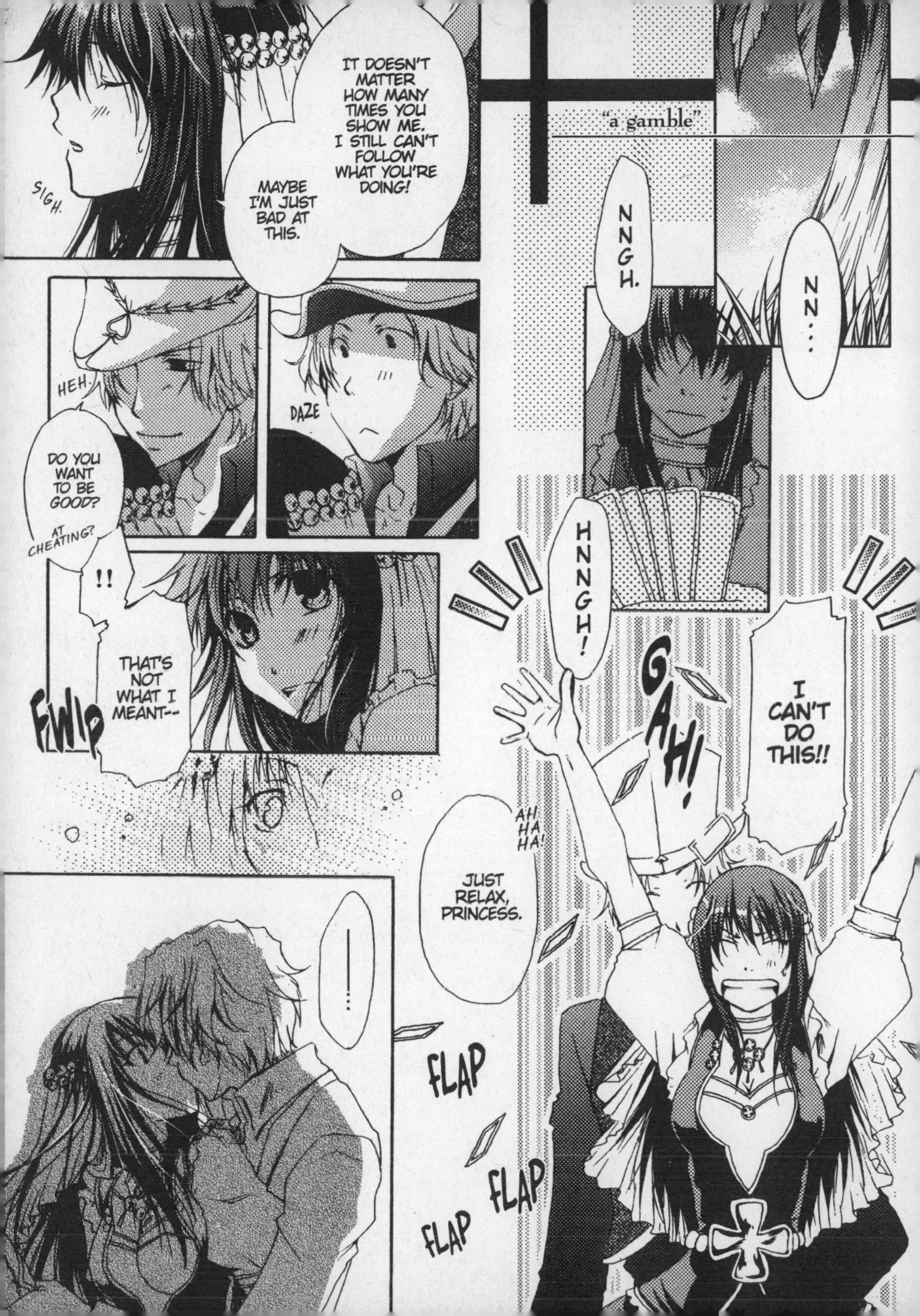
"a gamble"
NN...
NNGH.
HNNGH!
I CAN'T DO THIS!!
GAH!
AH HA HA!
JUST RELAX, PRINCESS.
SIGH.
IT DOESN'T MATTER HOW MANY TIMES YOU SHOW ME. I STILL CAN'T FOLLOW WHAT YOU'RE DOING!
MAYBE I'M JUST BAD AT THIS.
DAZE
HEH.
DO YOU WANT TO BE GOOD?
AT CHEATING?
!!
THAT'S NOT WHAT I MEANT--
FWIP
!...!
FLAP
FLAP
FLAP

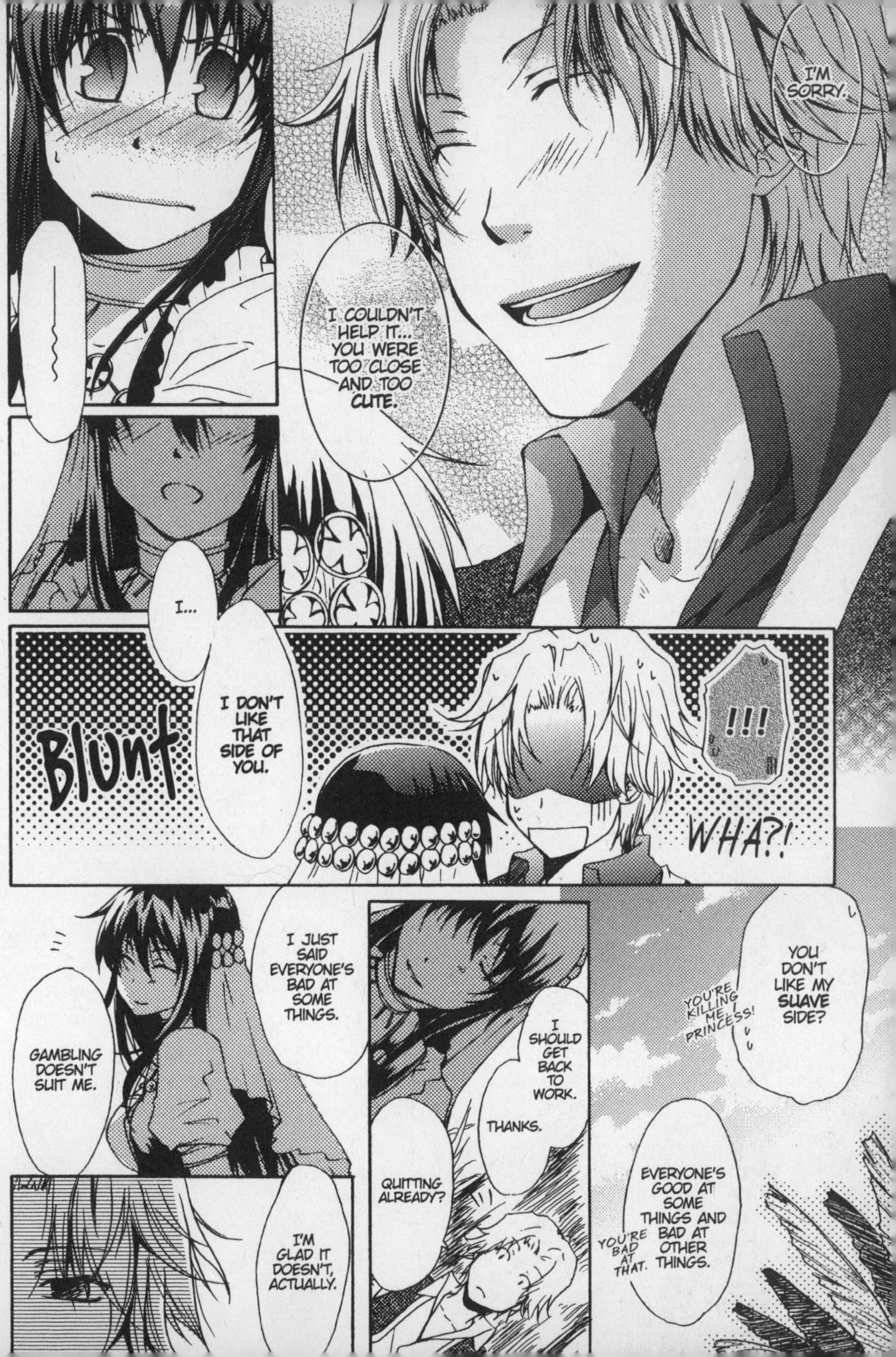
I'M SORRY.
I COULDN'T HELP IT... YOU WERE TOO CLOSE AND TOO CUTE.
I...
I DON'T LIKE THAT SIDE OF YOU.
Blunt
!!!
WHA?!
YOU DON'T LIKE MY SUAVE SIDE?
YOU'RE KILLING ME, PRINCESS!
EVERYONE'S GOOD AT SOME THINGS AND BAD AT OTHER THINGS.
YOU'RE BAD AT THAT.
I SHOULD GET BACK TO WORK.
THANKS.
QUITTING ALREADY?
I JUST SAID EVERYONE'S BAD AT SOME THINGS.
GAMBLING DOESN'T SUIT ME.
I'M GLAD IT DOESN'T, ACTUALLY.

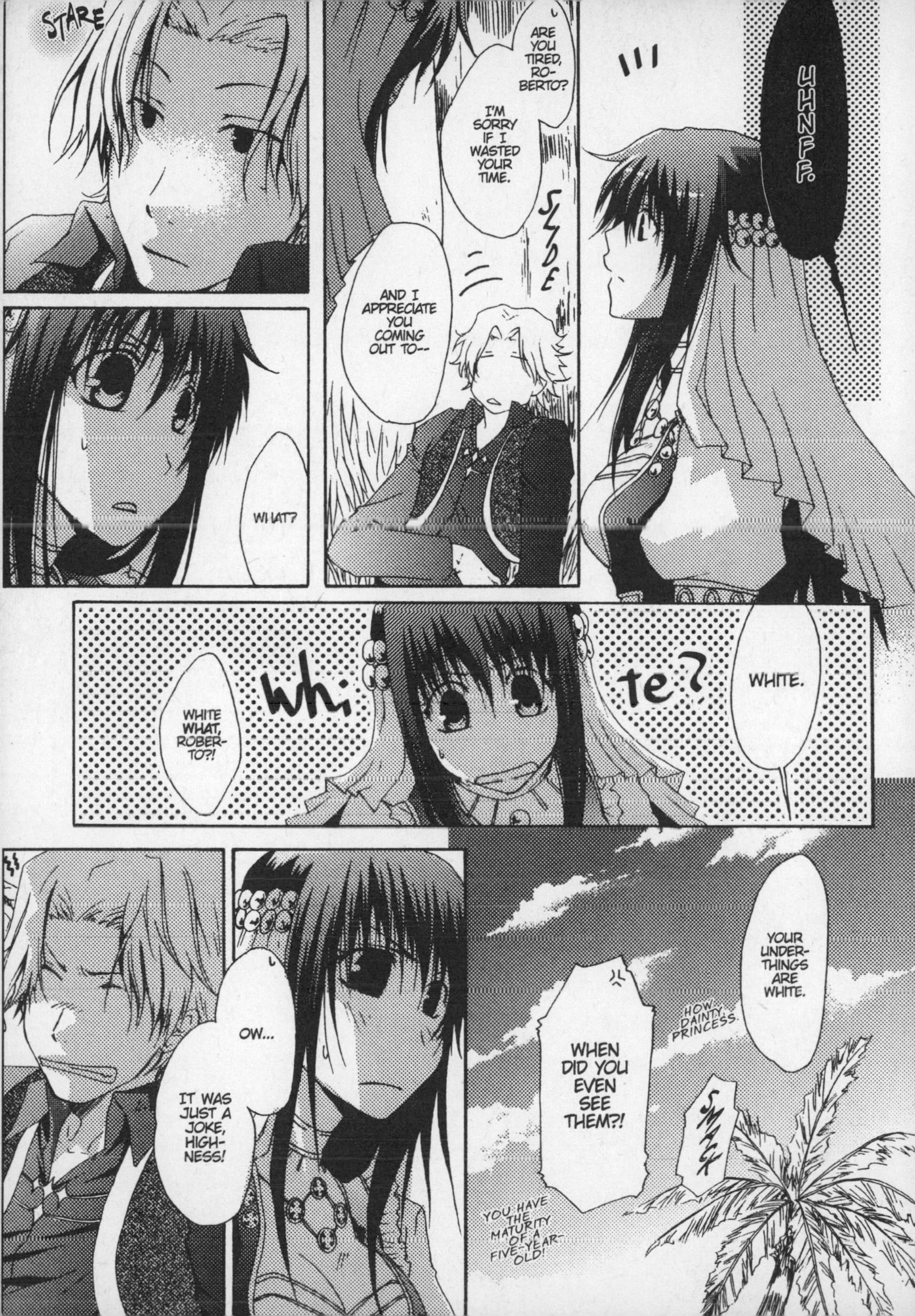
UHHNFF.
ARE YOU TIRED, RO-BERTO?
I'M SORRY IF I WASTED YOUR TIME.
SLIDE
AND I APPRECIATE YOU COMING OUT TO--
STARE
WHAT?
WHITE.
whi te?
WHITE WHAT, ROBER-TO?!
YOUR UNDER-THINGS ARE WHITE.
HOW DAINTY, PRINCESS.
WHEN DID YOU EVEN SEE THEM?!
SMACK
YOU HAVE THE MATURITY OF A FIVE-YEAR-OLD!
OW...
IT WAS JUST A JOKE, HIGH-NESS!

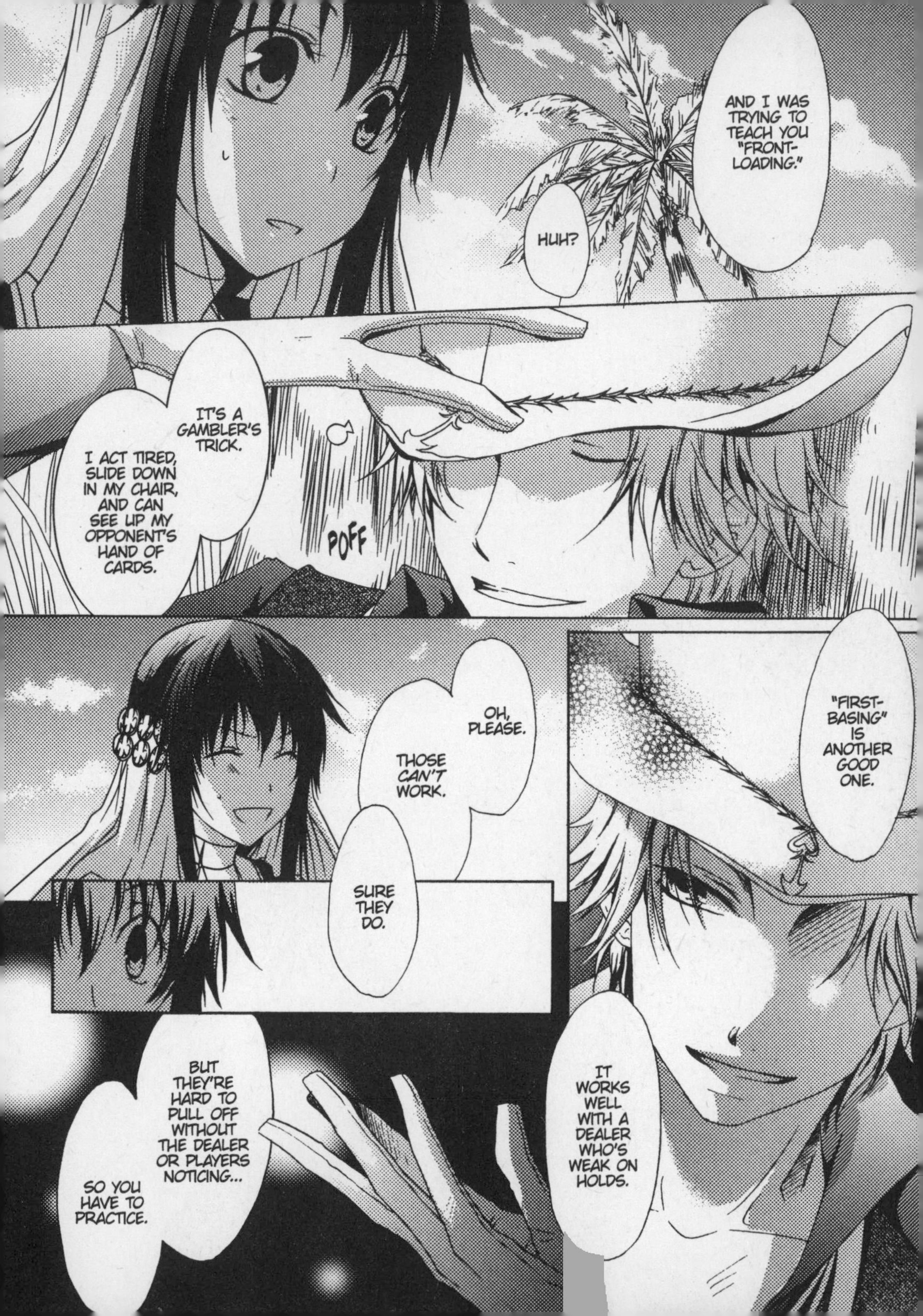
AND I WAS TRYING TO TEACH YOU "FRONT-LOADING."
HUH?
IT'S A GAMBLER'S TRICK.
I ACT TIRED, SLIDE DOWN IN MY CHAIR, AND CAN SEE UP MY OPPONENT'S HAND OF CARDS.
POFF
"FIRST-BASING" IS ANOTHER GOOD ONE.
IT WORKS WELL WITH A DEALER WHO'S WEAK ON HOLDS.
OH, PLEASE.
THOSE CAN'T WORK.
SURE THEY DO.
BUT THEY'RE HARD TO PULL OFF WITHOUT THE DEALER OR PLAYERS NOTICING...
SO YOU HAVE TO PRACTICE.

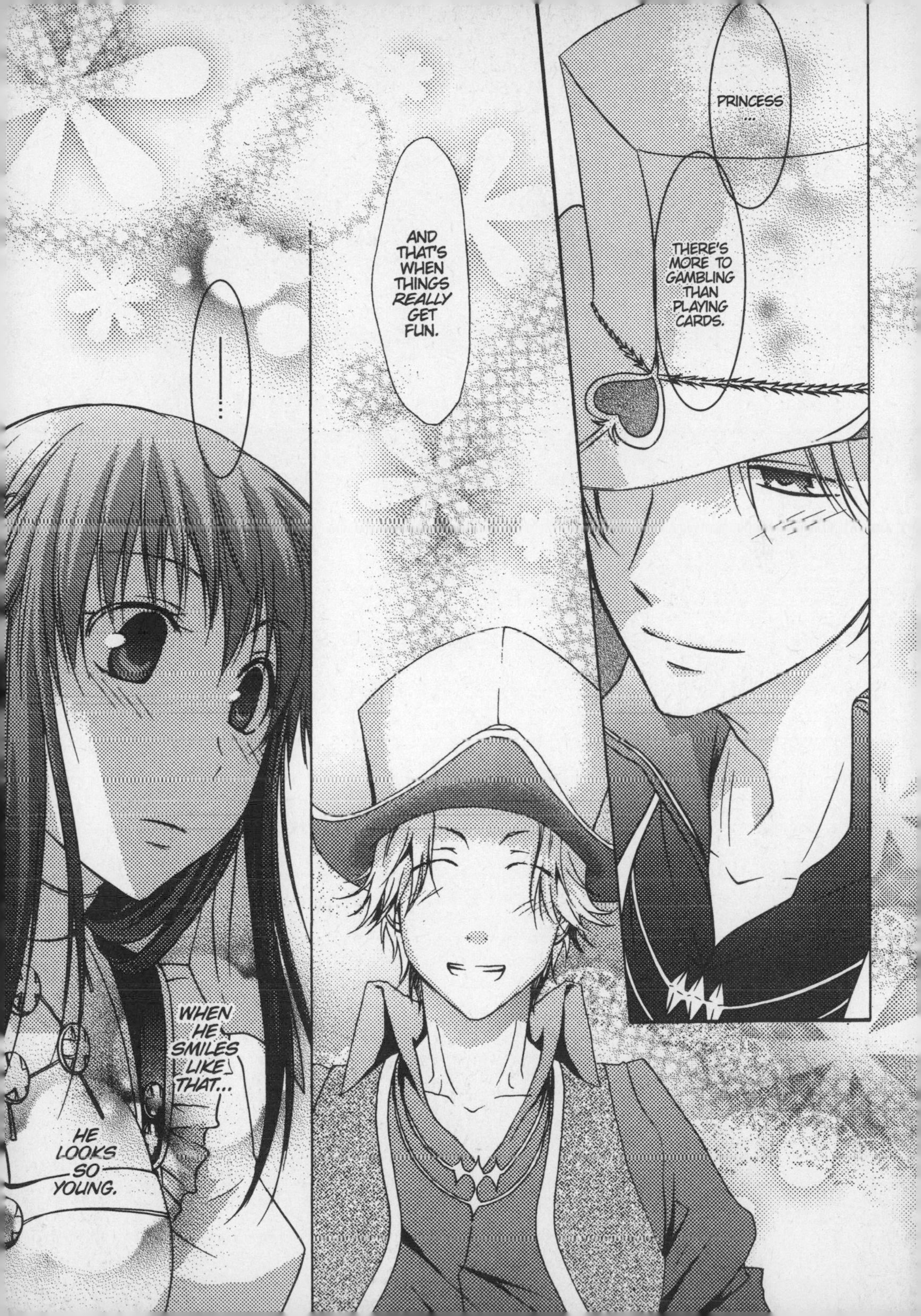
PRINCESS...
THERE'S MORE TO GAMBLING THAN PLAYING CARDS.
AND THAT'S WHEN THINGS *REALLY* GET FUN.
......
WHEN HE SMILES LIKE THAT...
HE LOOKS SO YOUNG.

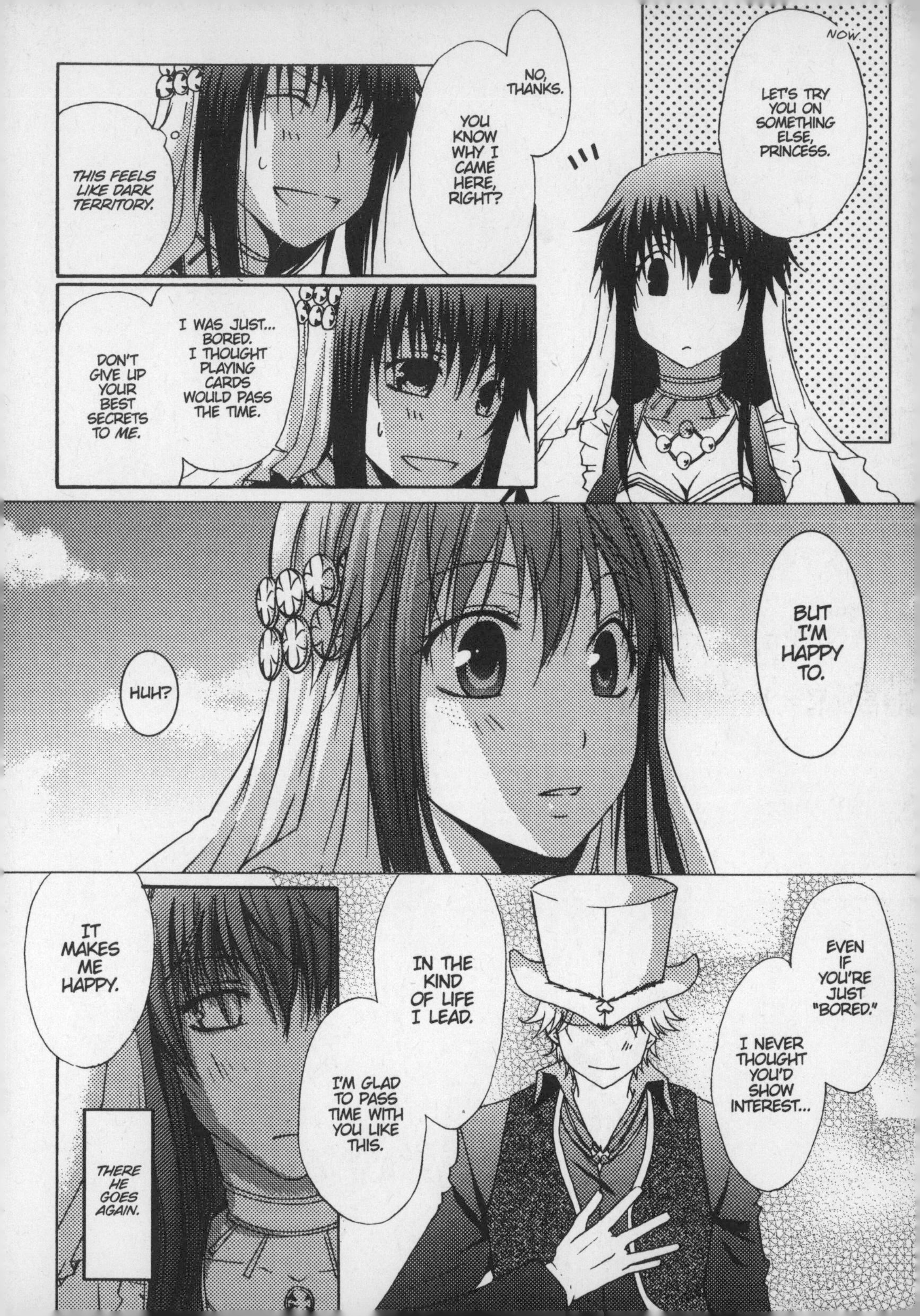
NOW.
LET'S TRY YOU ON SOMETHING ELSE, PRINCESS.
NO, THANKS.
YOU KNOW WHY I CAME HERE, RIGHT?
THIS FEELS LIKE DARK TERRITORY.
I WAS JUST... BORED. I THOUGHT PLAYING CARDS WOULD PASS THE TIME.
DON'T GIVE UP YOUR BEST SECRETS TO ME.
BUT I'M HAPPY TO.
HUH?
EVEN IF YOU'RE JUST "BORED."
I NEVER THOUGHT YOU'D SHOW INTEREST...
IN THE KIND OF LIFE I LEAD.
I'M GLAD TO PASS TIME WITH YOU LIKE THIS.
IT MAKES ME HAPPY.
THERE HE GOES AGAIN.

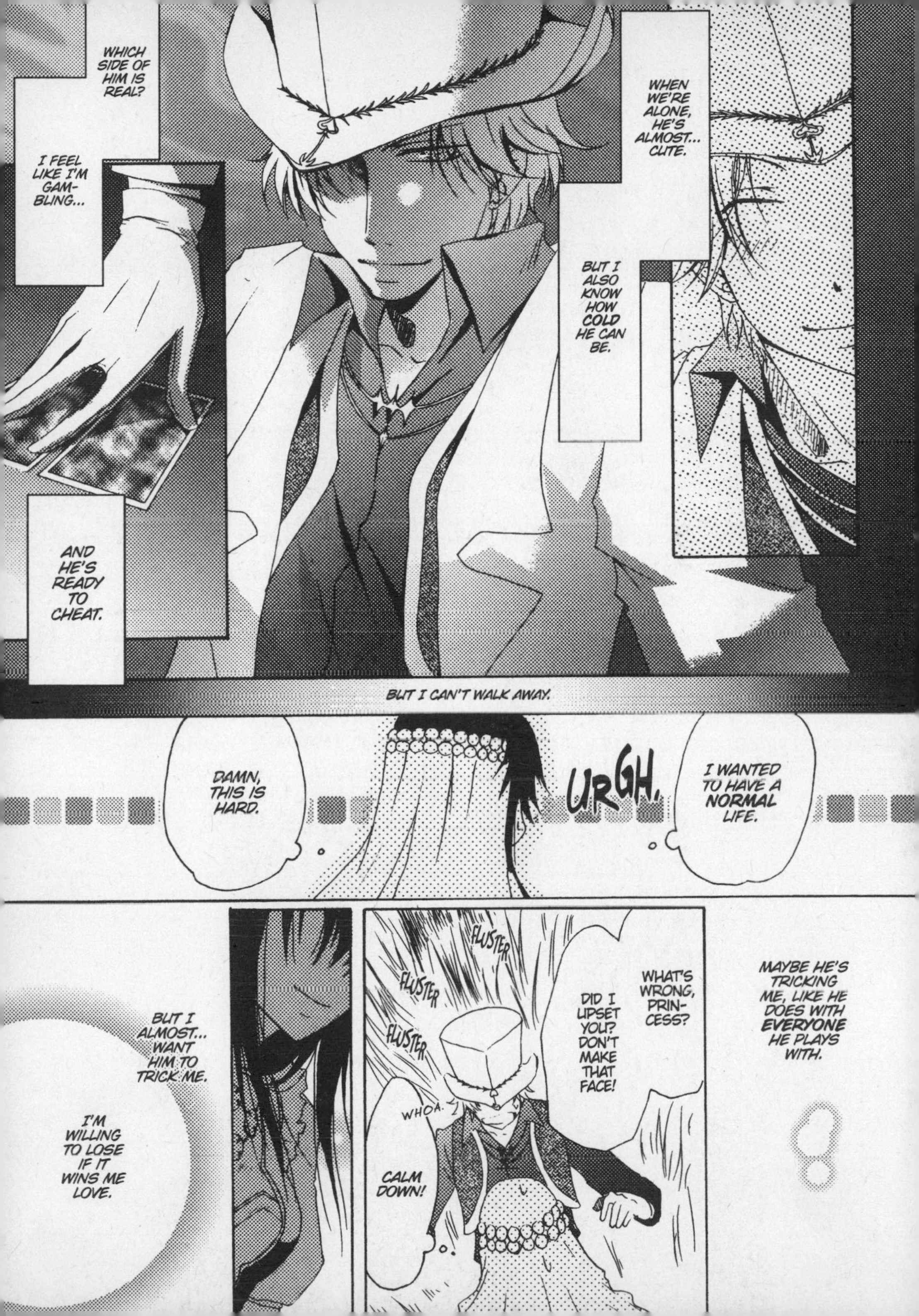
WHEN WE'RE ALONE, HE'S ALMOST... CUTE.
BUT I ALSO KNOW HOW COLD HE CAN BE.
WHICH SIDE OF HIM IS REAL?
I FEEL LIKE I'M GAM-BLING...
AND HE'S READY TO CHEAT.
BUT I CAN'T WALK AWAY.
I WANTED TO HAVE A NORMAL LIFE.
URGH.
DAMN, THIS IS HARD.
MAYBE HE'S TRICKING ME, LIKE HE DOES WITH EVERYONE HE PLAYS WITH.
WHAT'S WRONG, PRIN-CESS?
DID I UPSET YOU? DON'T MAKE THAT FACE!
FLUSTER
FLUSTER
FLUSTER
WHOA.
CALM DOWN!
BUT I ALMOST... WANT HIM TO TRICK ME.
I'M WILLING TO LOSE IF IT WINS ME LOVE.

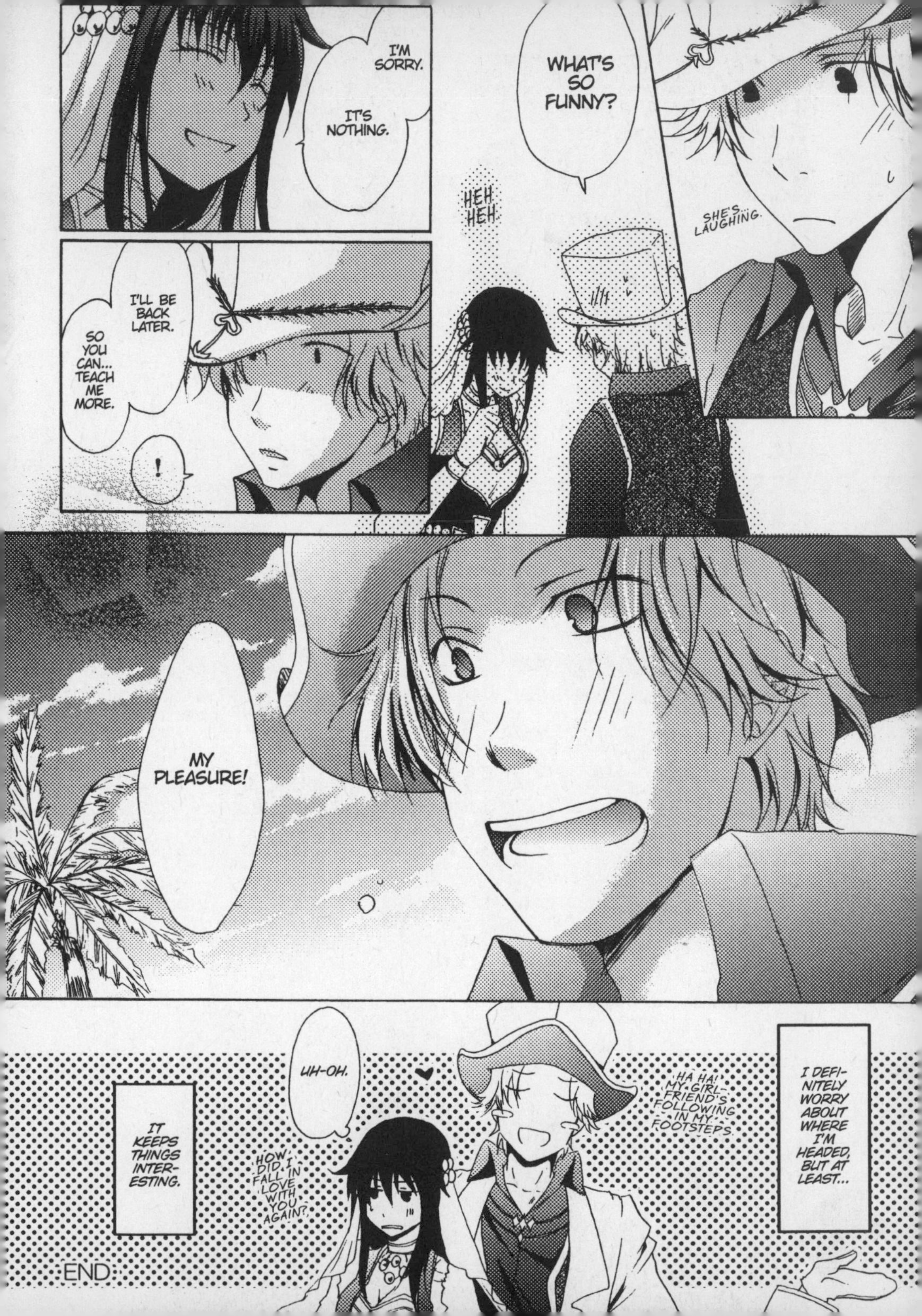
SHE'S LAUGHING.
WHAT'S SO FUNNY?
HEH HEH
I'M SORRY.
IT'S NOTHING.
I'LL BE BACK LATER.
SO YOU CAN... TEACH ME MORE.
!
MY PLEASURE!
I DEFI-NITELY WORRY ABOUT WHERE I'M HEADED, BUT AT LEAST...
HA HA! MY GIRL-FRIEND'S FOLLOWING IN MY FOOTSTEPS.
UH-OH.
HOW DID I FALL IN LOVE WITH YOU AGAIN?
IT KEEPS THINGS INTER-ESTING.
END

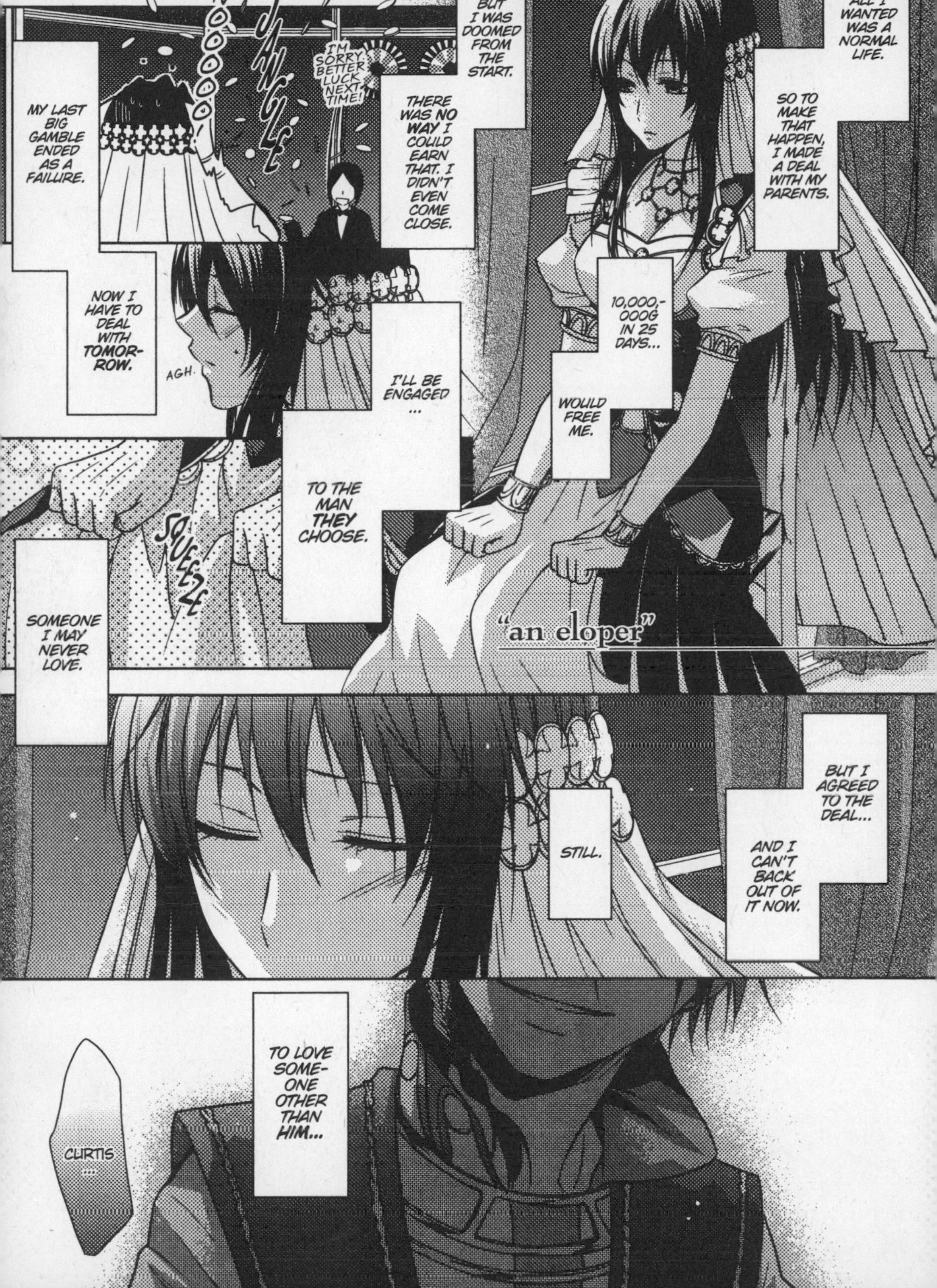
ALL I WANTED WAS A NORMAL LIFE.
SO TO MAKE THAT HAPPEN, I MADE A DEAL WITH MY PARENTS.
10,000,-000G IN 25 DAYS...
WOULD FREE ME.
BUT I WAS DOOMED FROM THE START.
THERE WAS NO WAY I COULD EARN THAT. I DIDN'T EVEN COME CLOSE.
I'M SORRY. BETTER LUCK NEXT TIME!
JANGLE
NOOOOOOO!
MY LAST BIG GAMBLE ENDED AS A FAILURE.
I'LL BE ENGAGED...
NOW I HAVE TO DEAL WITH TOMORROW.
AGH.
TO THE MAN THEY CHOOSE.
SQUEEZE
SOMEONE I MAY NEVER LOVE.
"an eloper"
BUT I AGREED TO THE DEAL...
AND I CAN'T BACK OUT OF IT NOW.
STILL.
TO LOVE SOMEONE OTHER THAN HIM...
CURTIS...

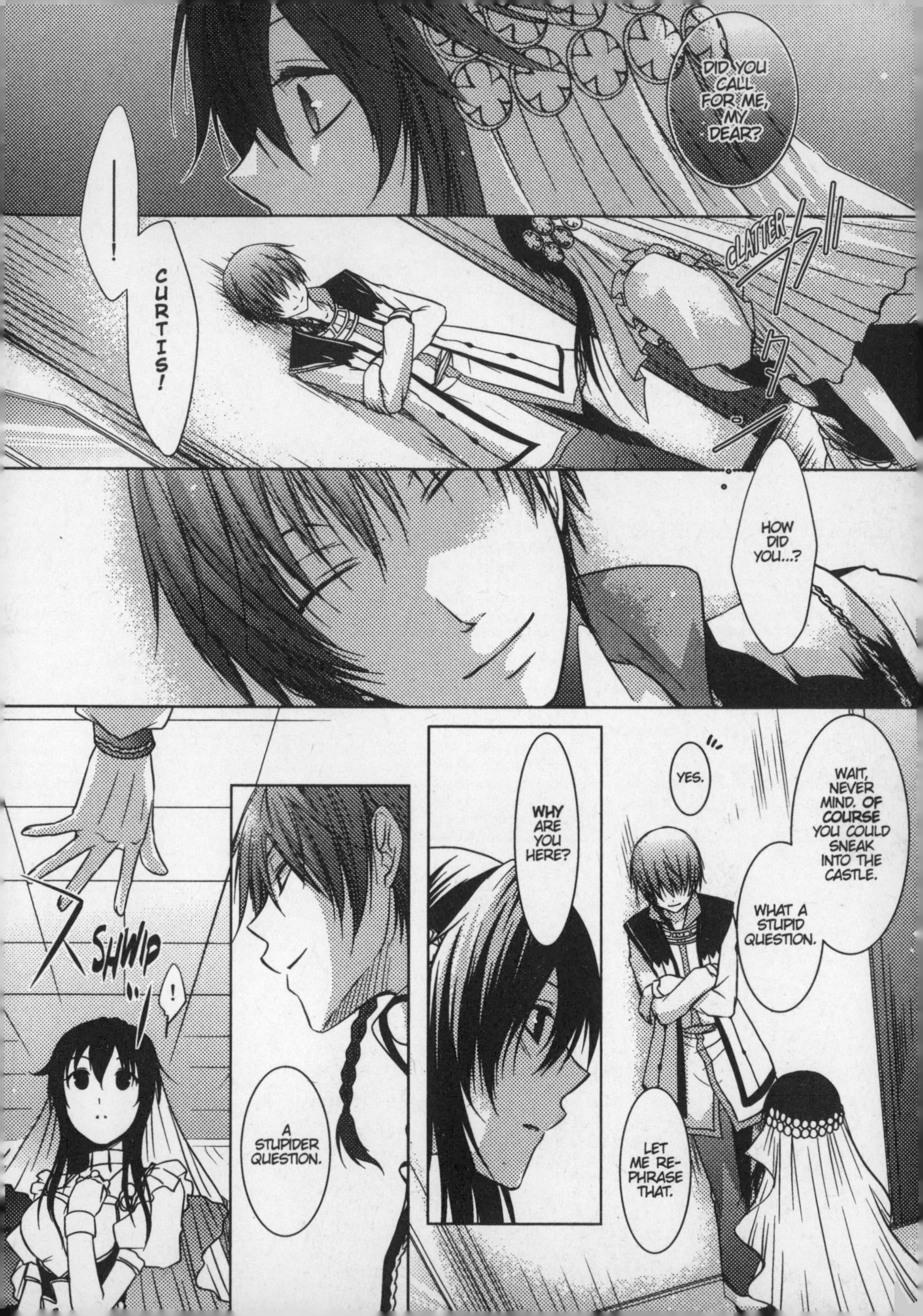
DID YOU CALL FOR ME, MY DEAR?
CLATTER
—!
CURTIS!
HOW DID YOU...?
WAIT, NEVER MIND. OF COURSE YOU COULD SNEAK INTO THE CASTLE.
YES.
WHAT A STUPID QUESTION.
LET ME RE-PHRASE THAT.
WHY ARE YOU HERE?
A STUPIDER QUESTION.
SHWIP
!

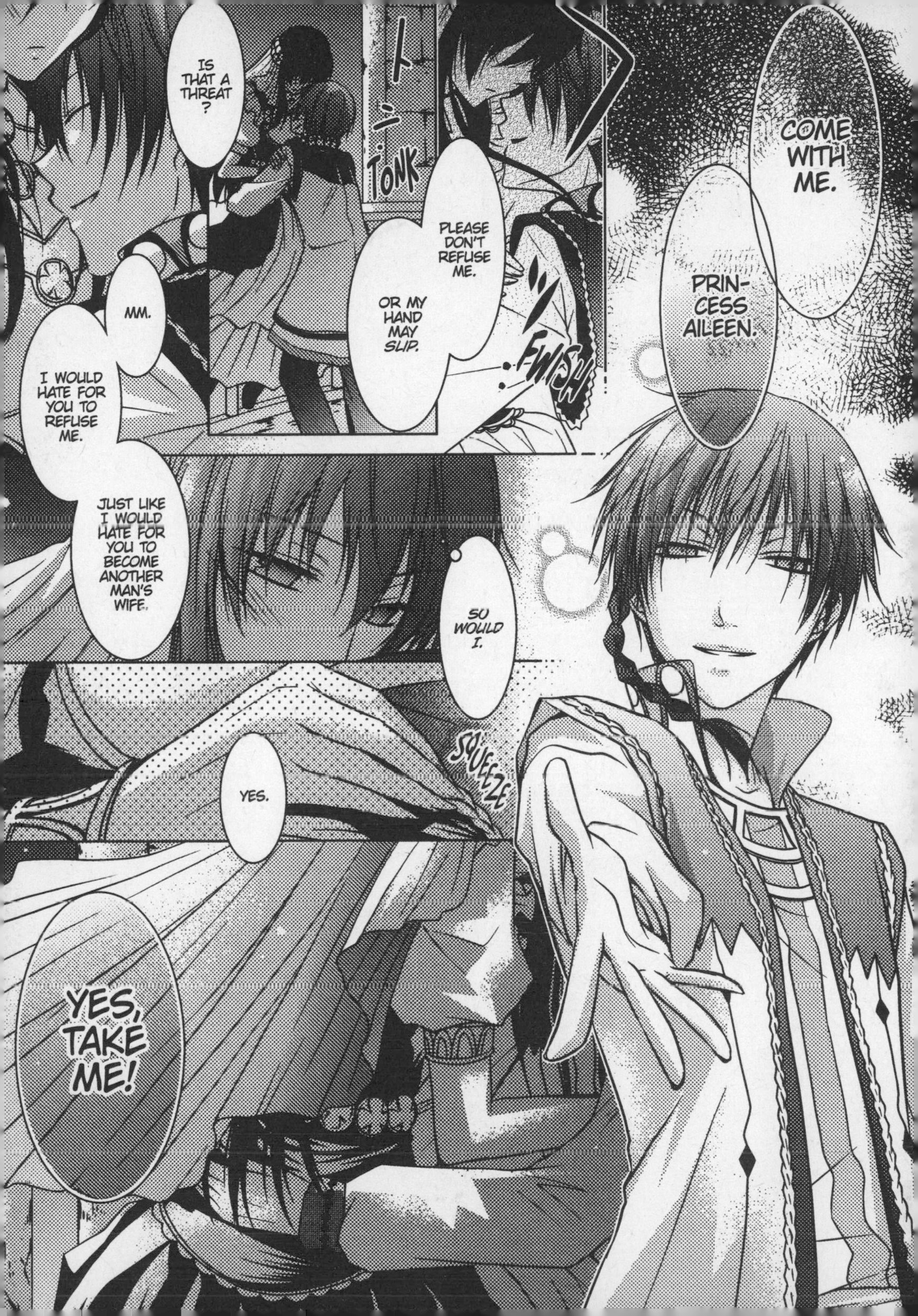
COME WITH ME.
PRIN-CESS AILEEN.
TONK
PLEASE DON'T REFUSE ME.
OR MY HAND MAY SLIP.
FWISH
IS THAT A THREAT?
MM.
I WOULD HATE FOR YOU TO REFUSE ME.
JUST LIKE I WOULD HATE FOR YOU TO BECOME ANOTHER MAN'S WIFE.
SO WOULD I.
SQUEEZE
YES.
YES, TAKE ME!

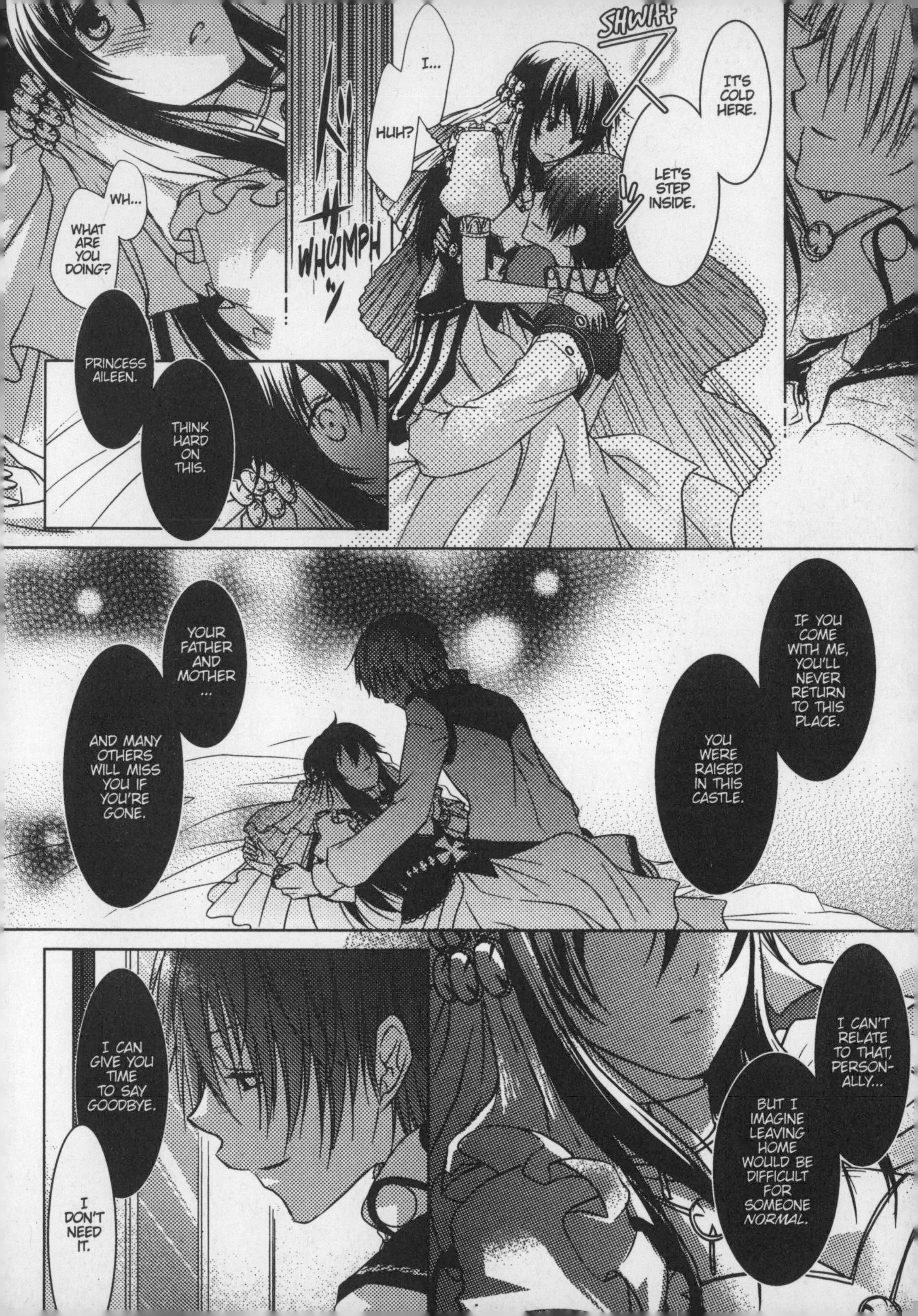
SHWIFT
IT'S COLD HERE.
LET'S STEP INSIDE.
I...
HUH?
WHUMPH
WH...
WHAT ARE YOU DOING?
PRINCESS AILEEN.
THINK HARD ON THIS.
IF YOU COME WITH ME, YOU'LL NEVER RETURN TO THIS PLACE.
YOU WERE RAISED IN THIS CASTLE.
YOUR FATHER AND MOTHER...
AND MANY OTHERS WILL MISS YOU IF YOU'RE GONE.
I CAN'T RELATE TO THAT, PERSON-ALLY...
BUT I IMAGINE LEAVING HOME WOULD BE DIFFICULT FOR SOMEONE *NORMAL*.
I CAN GIVE YOU TIME TO SAY GOODBYE.
I DON'T NEED IT.

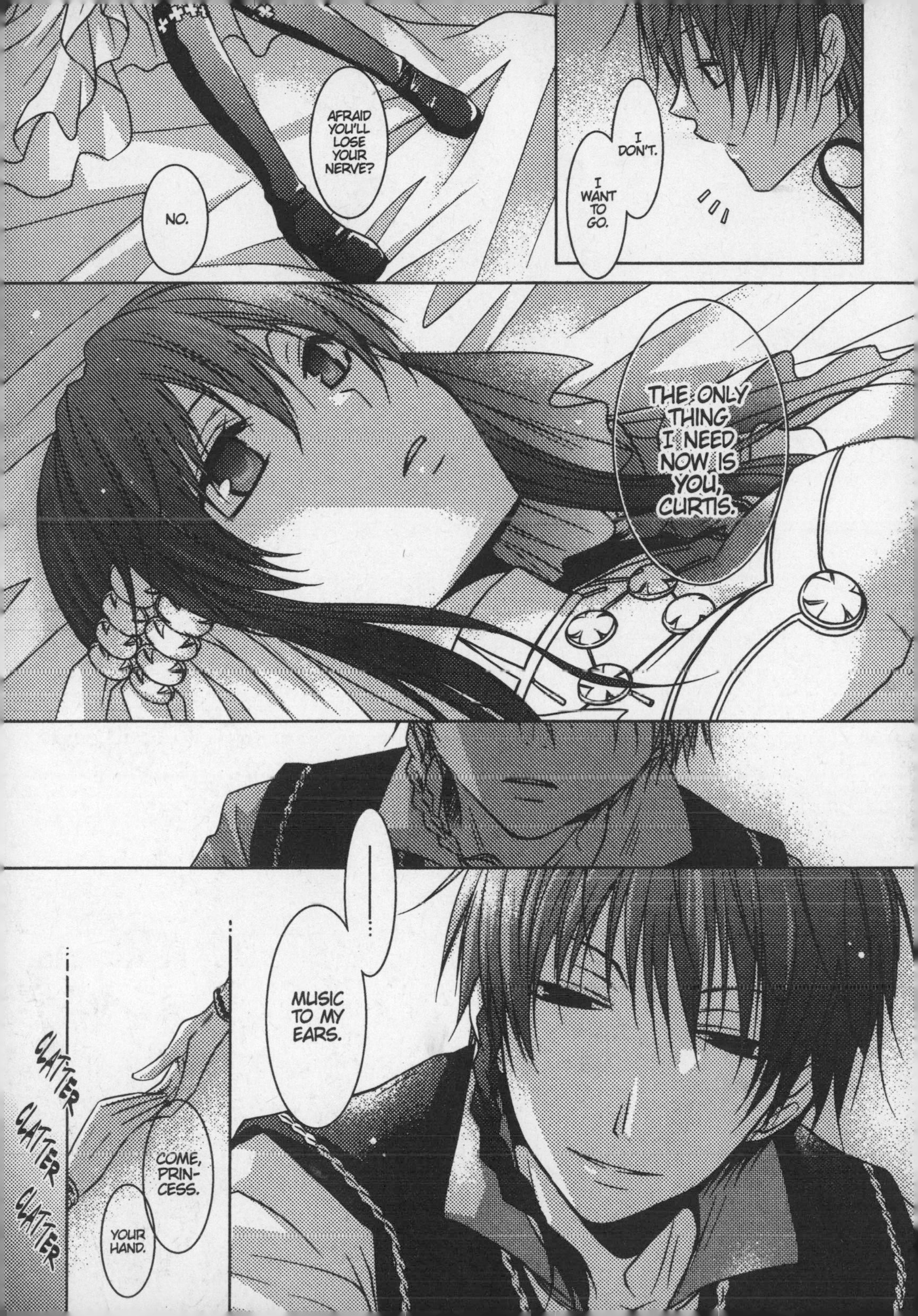
I DON'T.
I WANT TO GO.
AFRAID YOU'LL LOSE YOUR NERVE?
NO.
THE ONLY THING I NEED NOW IS YOU, CURTIS.
...
MUSIC TO MY EARS.
COME, PRIN-CESS.
YOUR HAND.
CLATTER CLATTER CLATTER

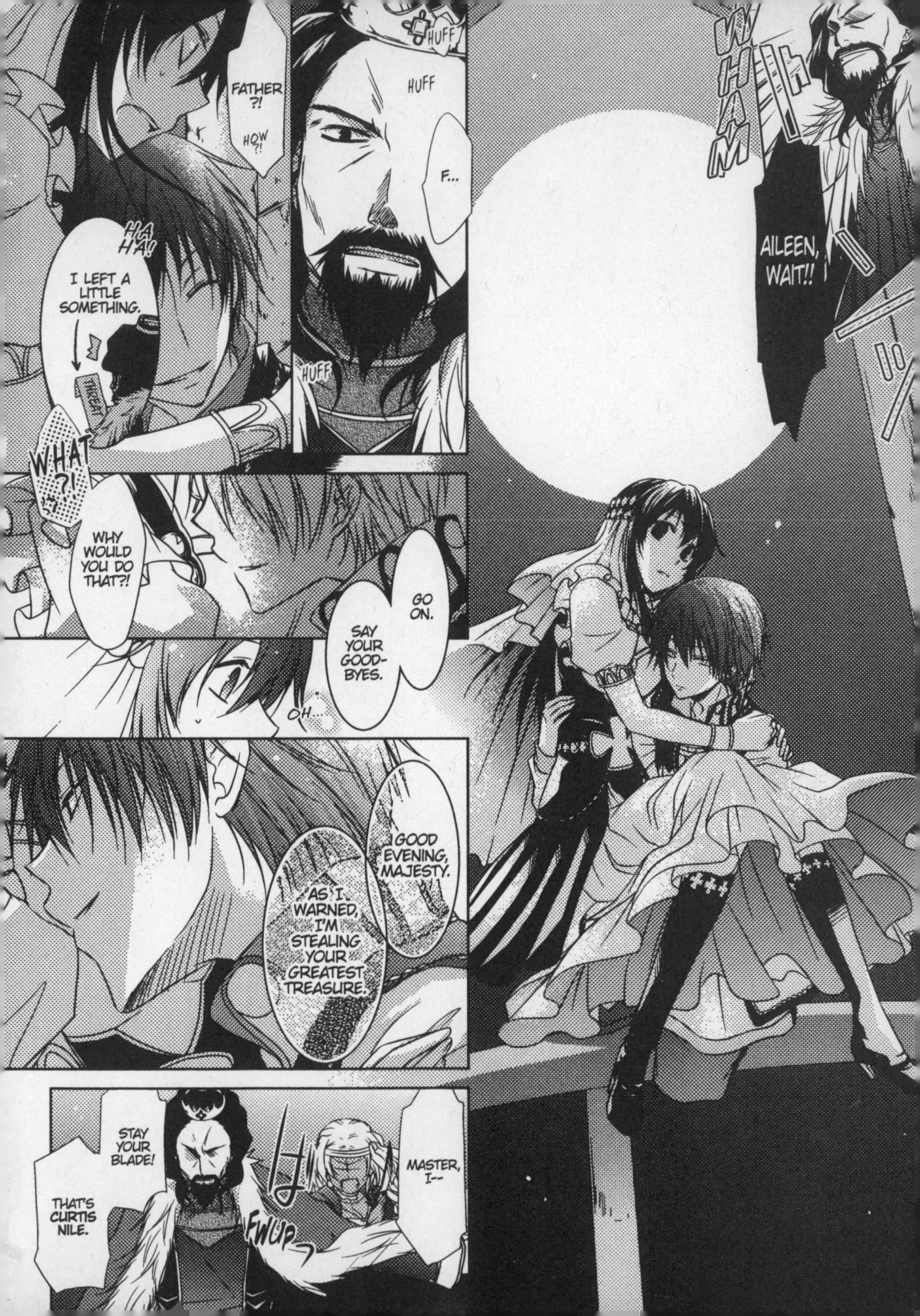
WHAM
AILEEN, WAIT!!
HUFF
HUFF
F...
HUFF
FATHER?!
HOW?!
HA HA!
I LEFT A LITTLE SOMETHING.
THREAT
WHAT?!
GO ON.
WHY WOULD YOU DO THAT?!
SAY YOUR GOOD-BYES.
OH...
GOOD EVENING, MAJESTY.
AS I WARNED, I'M STEALING YOUR GREATEST TREASURE.
MASTER, I--
FWUP
STAY YOUR BLADE!
THAT'S CURTIS NILE.

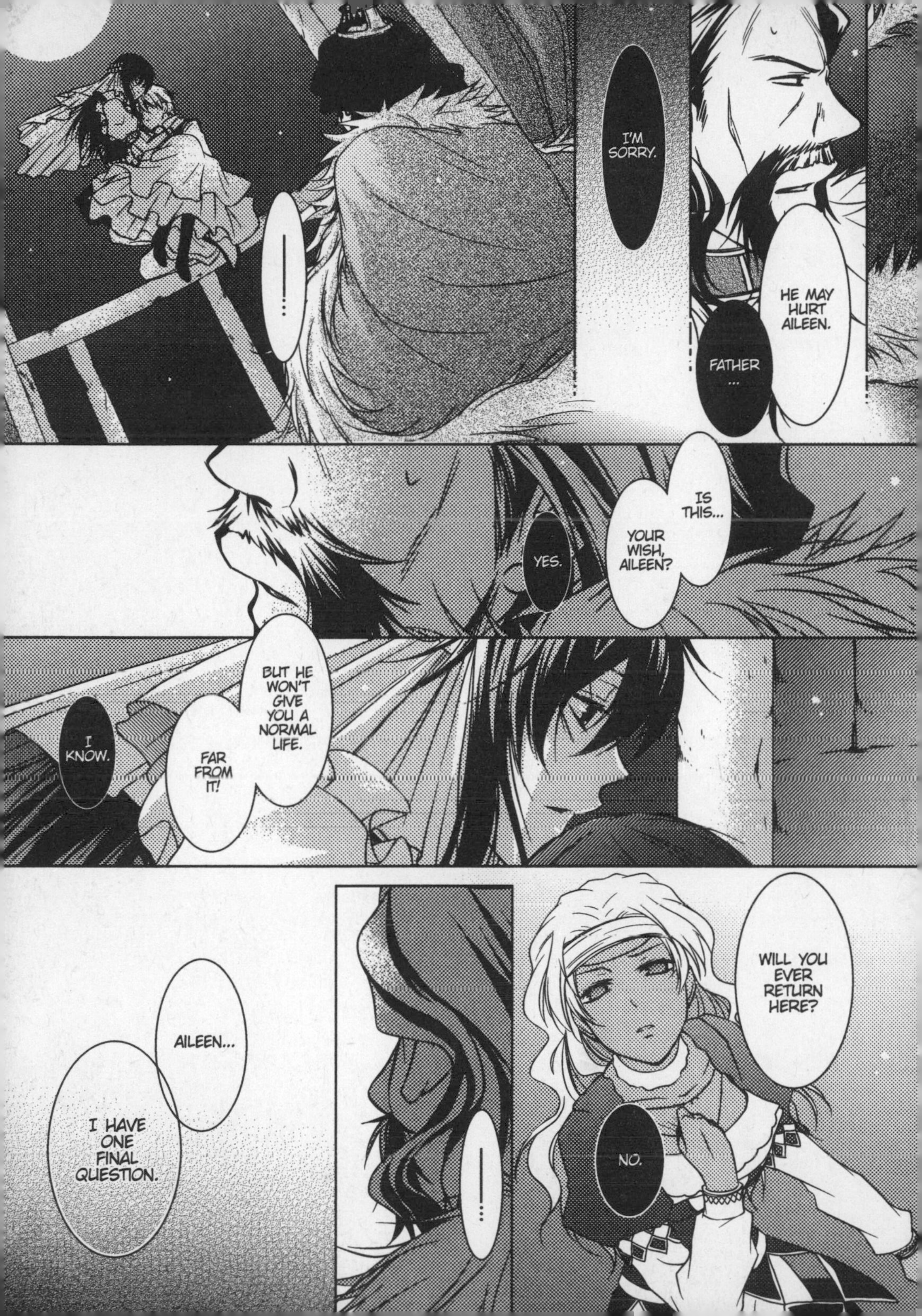
HE MAY HURT AILEEN.
FATHER...
I'M SORRY.
!...
IS THIS...
YOUR WISH, AILEEN?
YES.
BUT HE WON'T GIVE YOU A NORMAL LIFE.
FAR FROM IT!
I KNOW.
WILL YOU EVER RETURN HERE?
NO.
!...
AILEEN...
I HAVE ONE FINAL QUESTION.

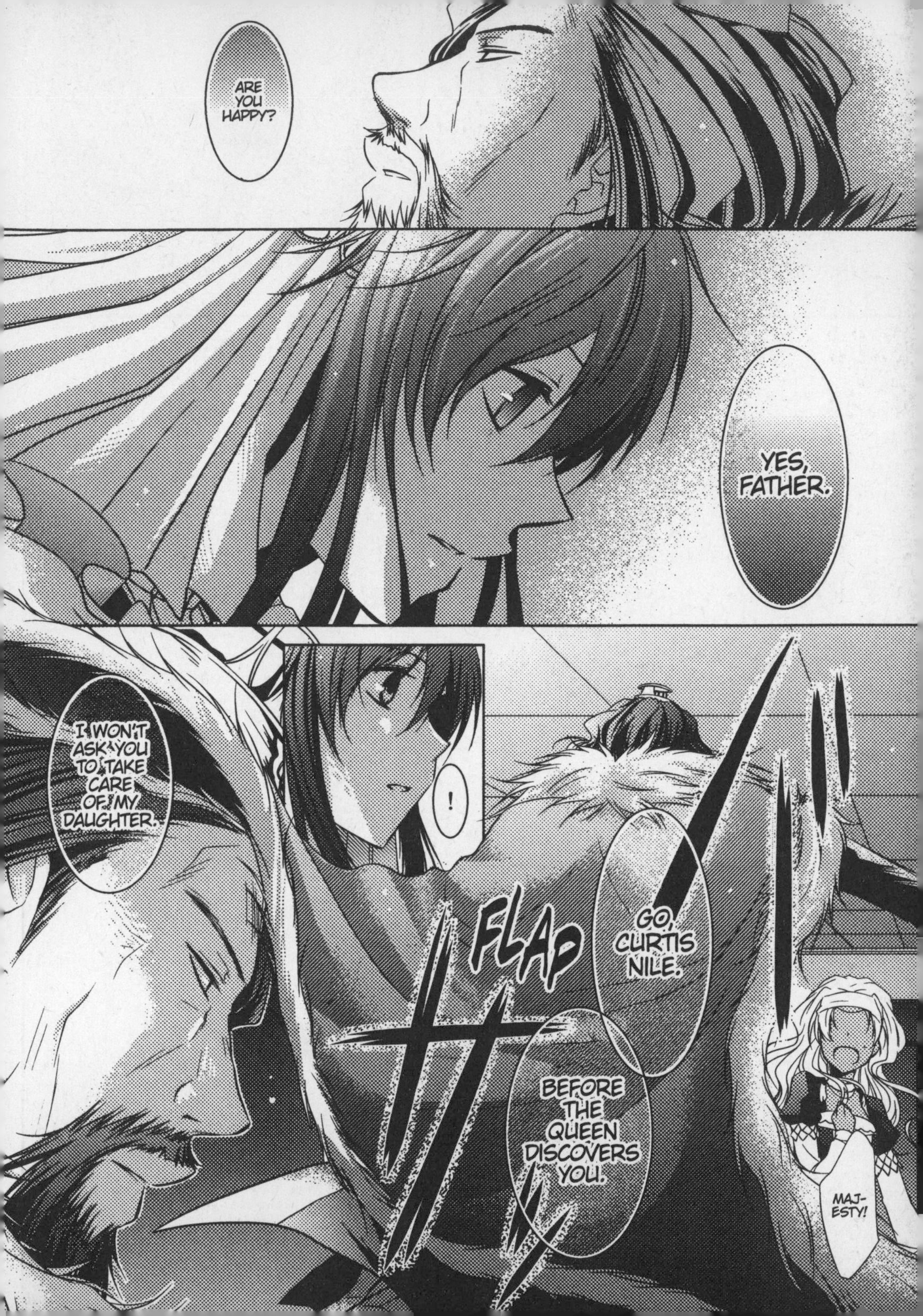

ARE YOU HAPPY?
YES, FATHER.
I WON'T ASK YOU TO TAKE CARE OF MY DAUGHTER.
!
GO, CURTIS NILE.
BEFORE THE QUEEN DISCOVERS YOU.
FLAP
MAJ-ESTY!

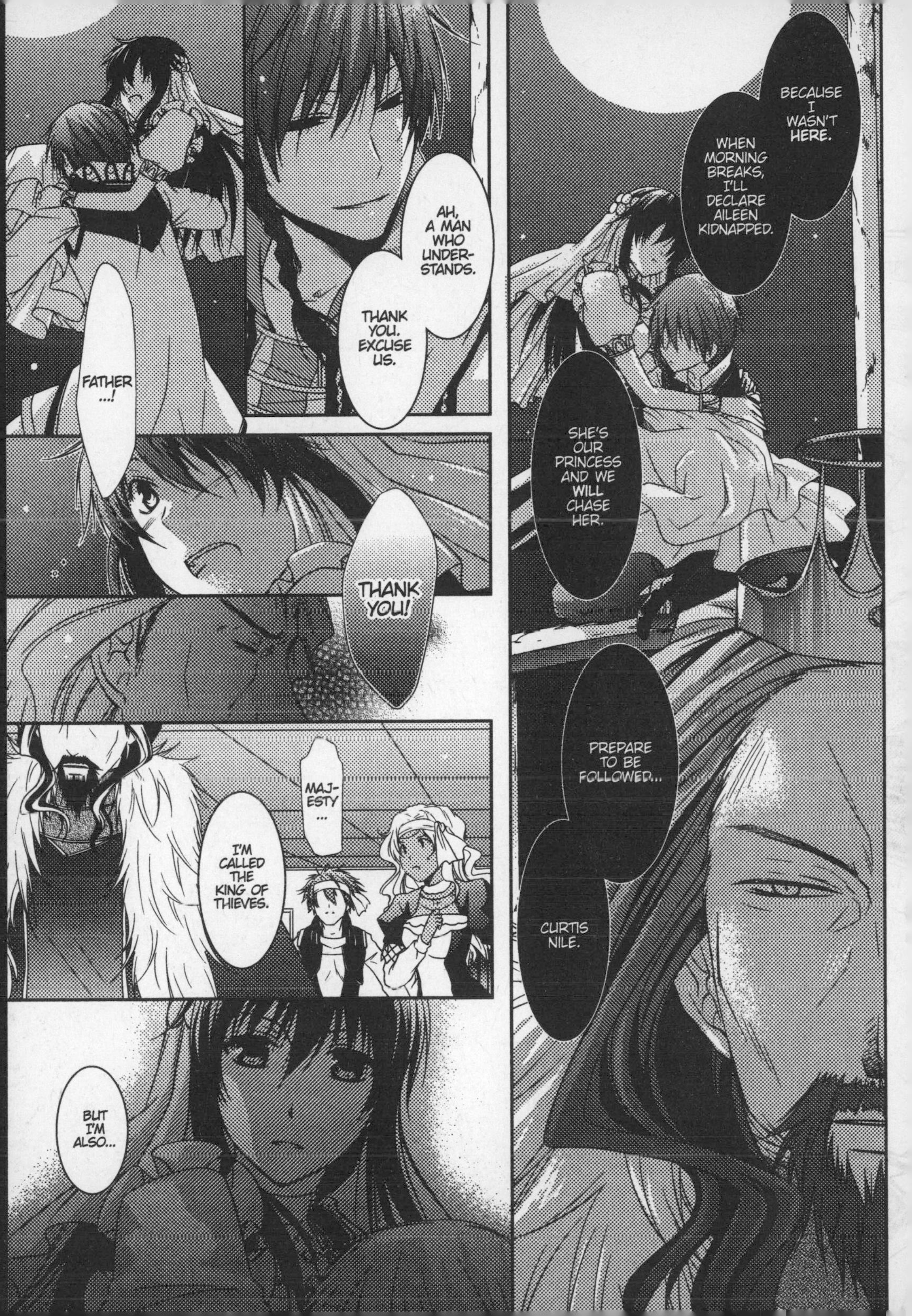
BECAUSE I WASN'T HERE.
WHEN MORNING BREAKS, I'LL DECLARE AILEEN KIDNAPPED.
SHE'S OUR PRINCESS AND WE WILL CHASE HER.
PREPARE TO BE FOLLOWED...
CURTIS NILE.
AH, A MAN WHO UNDER-STANDS.
THANK YOU. EXCUSE US.
FATHER ...!
THANK YOU!
MAJ-ESTY ...
I'M CALLED THE KING OF THIEVES.
BUT I'M ALSO...

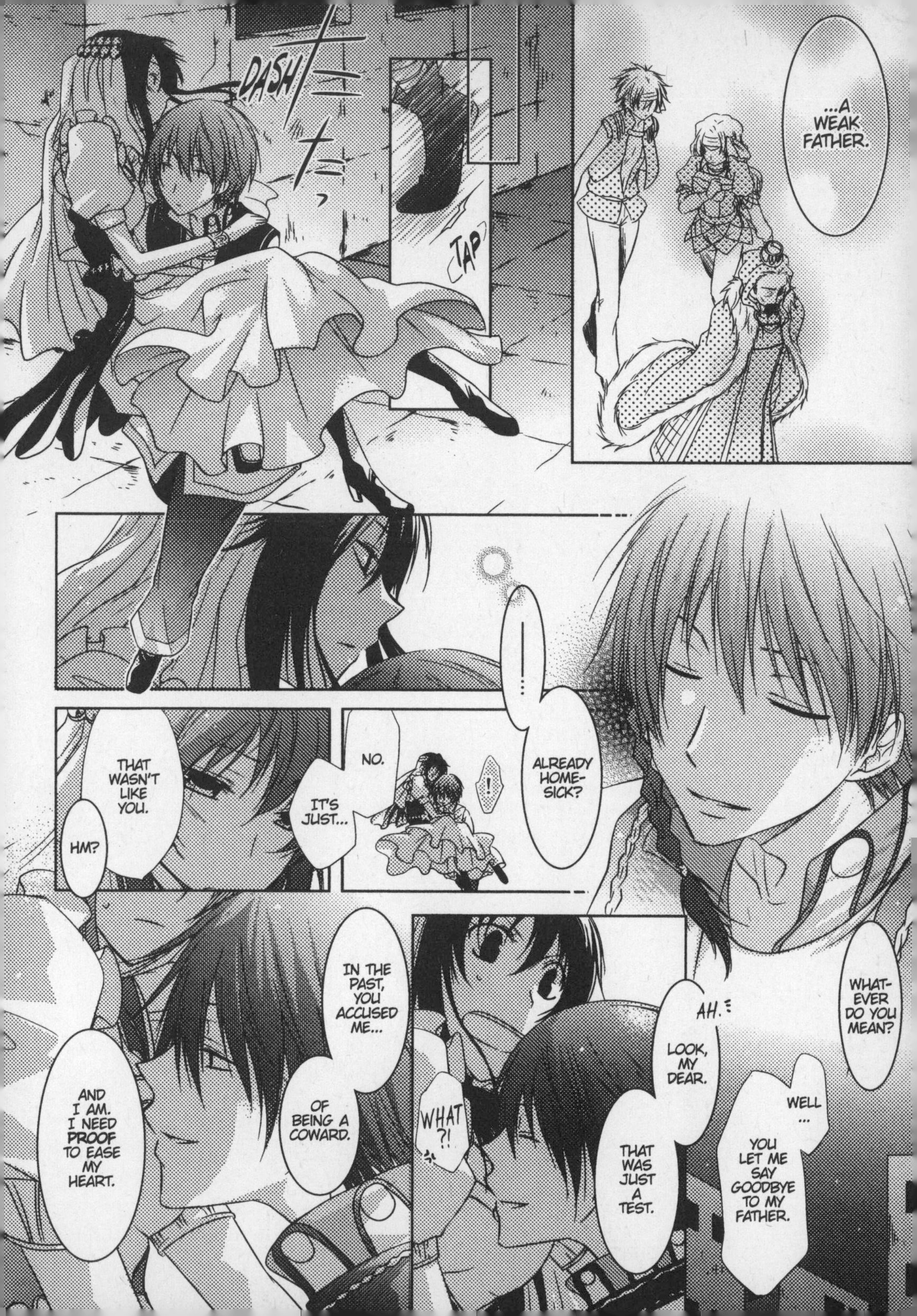
...A WEAK FATHER.
TAP
DASH
—!
...!
ALREADY HOME-SICK?
!
NO.
IT'S JUST...
THAT WASN'T LIKE YOU.
HM?
WHAT-EVER DO YOU MEAN?
WELL ...
YOU LET ME SAY GOODBYE TO MY FATHER.
AH.
LOOK, MY DEAR.
THAT WAS JUST A TEST.
WHAT?!
IN THE PAST, YOU ACCUSED ME...
OF BEING A COWARD.
AND I AM. I NEED **PROOF** TO EASE MY HEART.

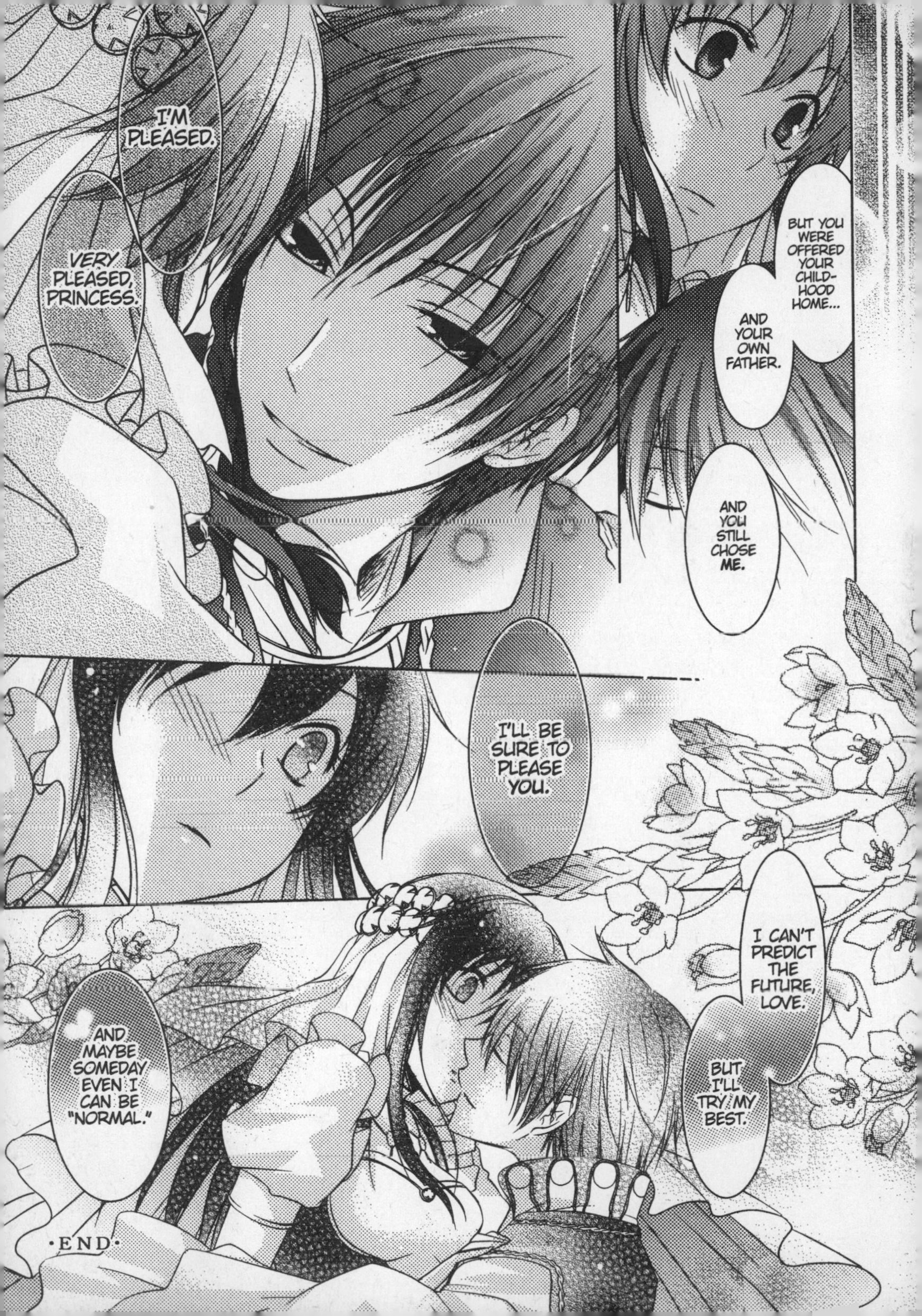
BUT YOU WERE OFFERED YOUR CHILD-HOOD HOME...
AND YOUR OWN FATHER.
AND YOU STILL CHOSE ME.
I'M PLEASED.
VERY PLEASED, PRINCESS.
I'LL BE SURE TO PLEASE YOU.
I CAN'T PREDICT THE FUTURE, LOVE.
BUT I'LL TRY MY BEST.
AND MAYBE SOMEDAY EVEN I CAN BE "NORMAL."
•END•

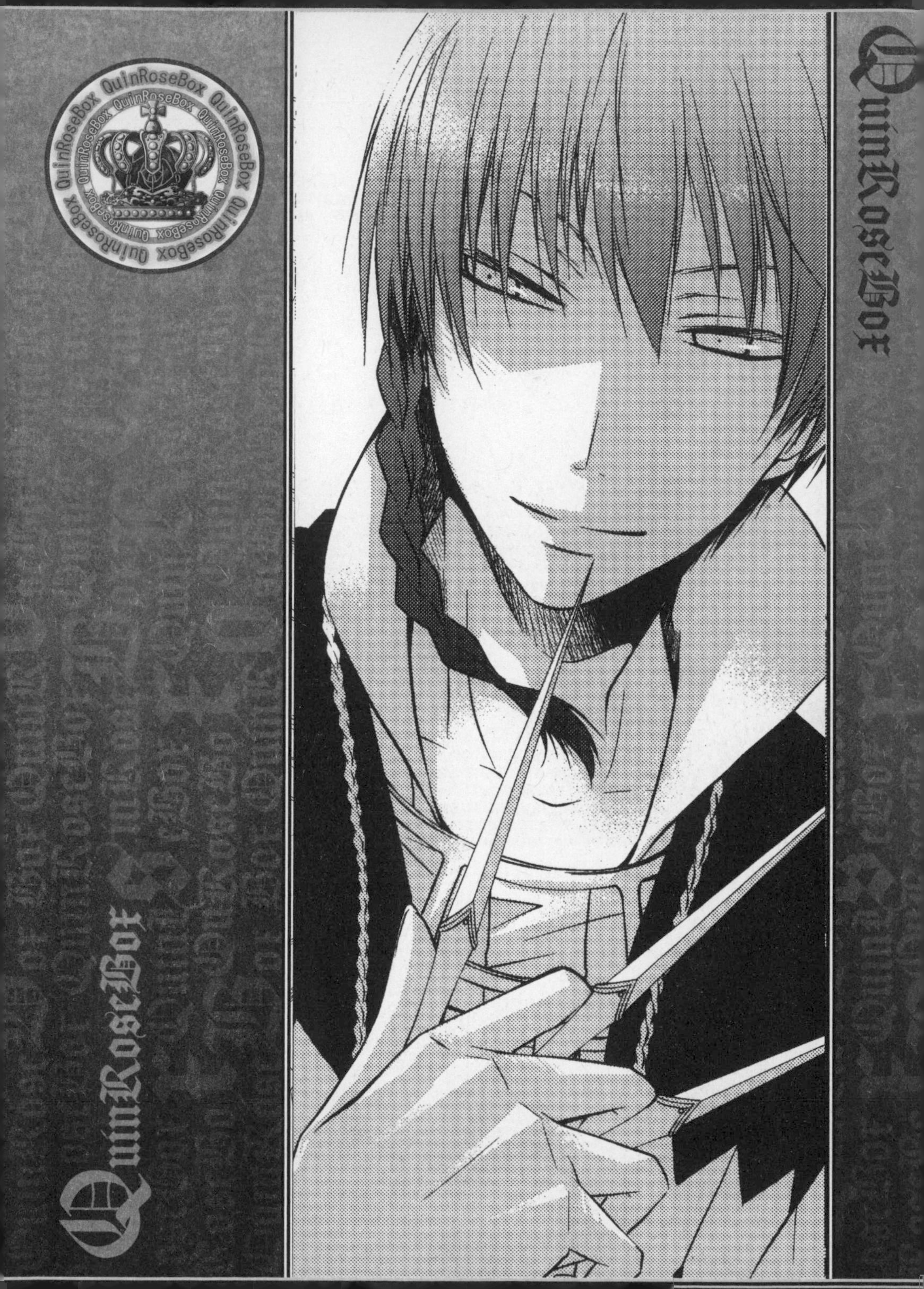
QuinRoseBox
QuinRoseBox

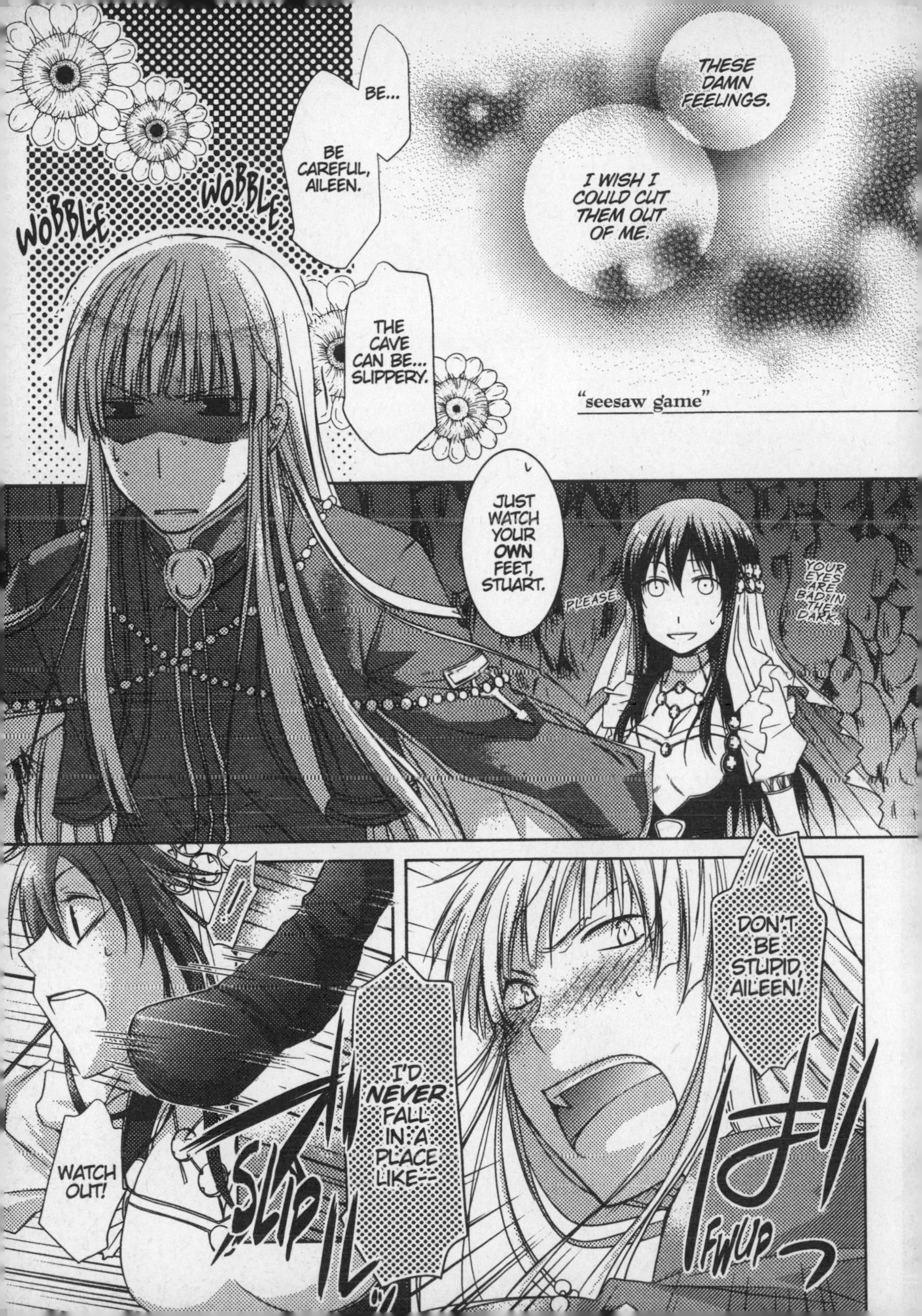
THESE DAMN FEELINGS.
I WISH I COULD CUT THEM OUT OF ME.
BE...
BE CAREFUL, AILEEN.
WOBBLE
WOBBLE
THE CAVE CAN BE... SLIPPERY.
"seesaw game"
JUST WATCH YOUR OWN FEET, STUART.
YOUR EYES ARE BAD IN THE DARK.
PLEASE.
DON'T BE STUPID, AILEEN!
I'D NEVER FALL IN A PLACE LIKE--
FWUP
SLIP
WATCH OUT!

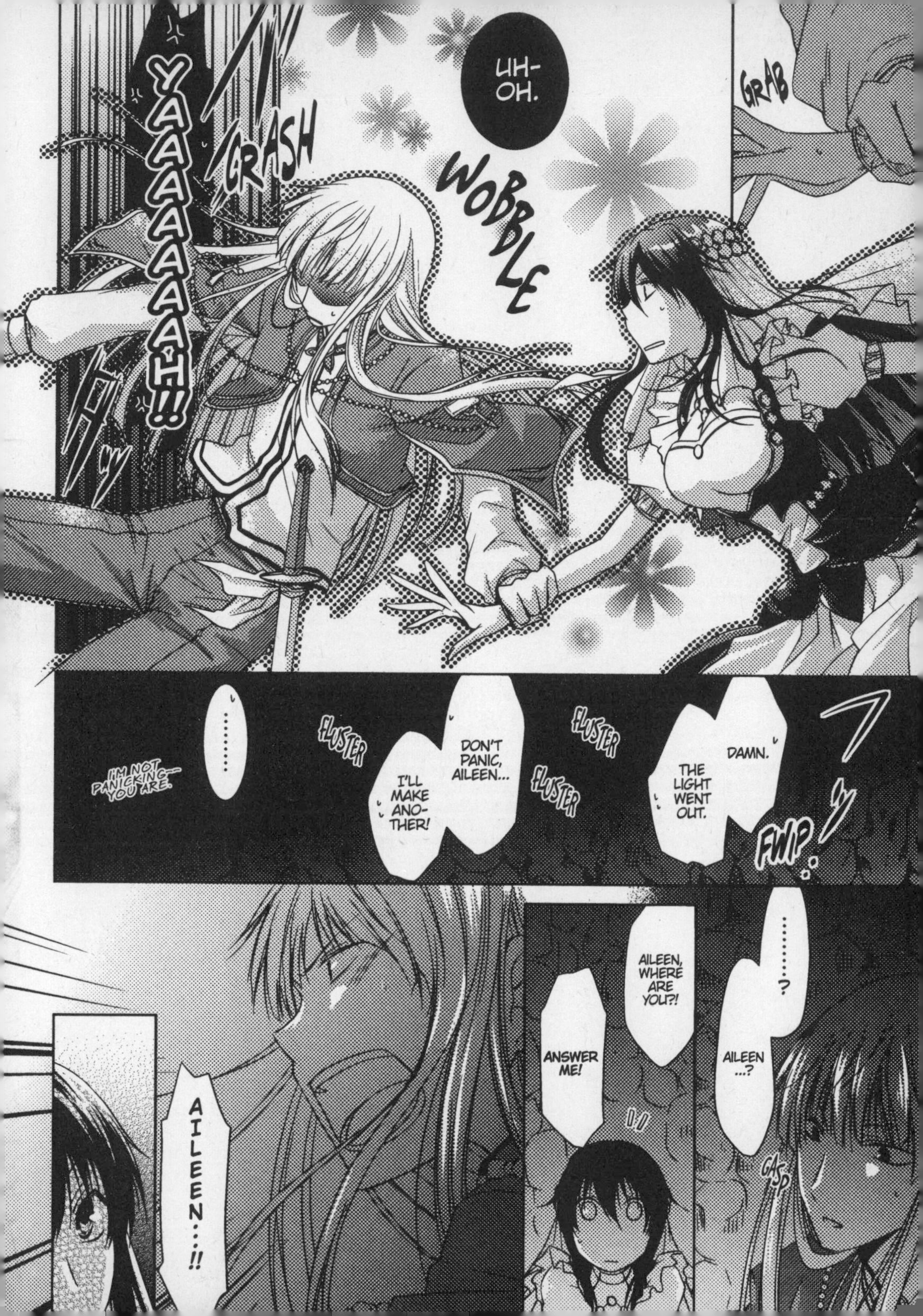
GRAB
UH-OH.
WOBBLE
CRASH
YAAAAAAAAAH!!
DAMN.
THE LIGHT WENT OUT.
FWIP
FLUSTER
FLUSTER
DON'T PANIC, AILEEN...
I'LL MAKE ANOTHER!
FLUSTER
......
I'M NOT PANICKING—YOU ARE.
......?
AILEEN...?
AILEEN, WHERE ARE YOU?!
ANSWER ME!
GASP
AILEEN...!!

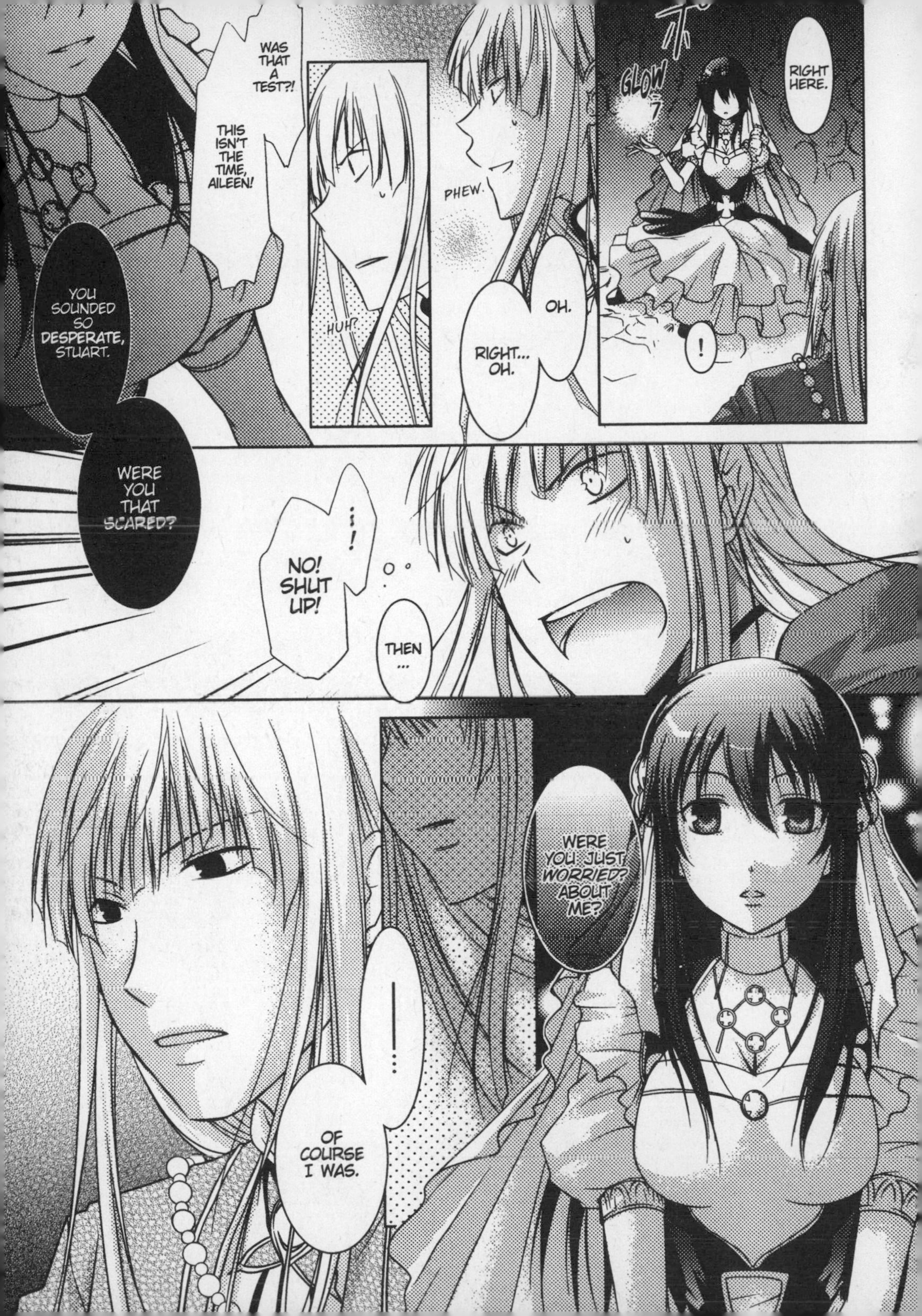
GLOW
RIGHT HERE.
!
PHEW.
OH.
RIGHT... OH.
HUH?
WAS THAT A TEST?!
THIS ISN'T THE TIME, AILEEN!
YOU SOUNDED SO DESPERATE, STUART.
WERE YOU THAT SCARED?
...!
NO! SHUT UP!
THEN ...
WERE YOU JUST WORRIED? ABOUT ME?
...!
OF COURSE I WAS.

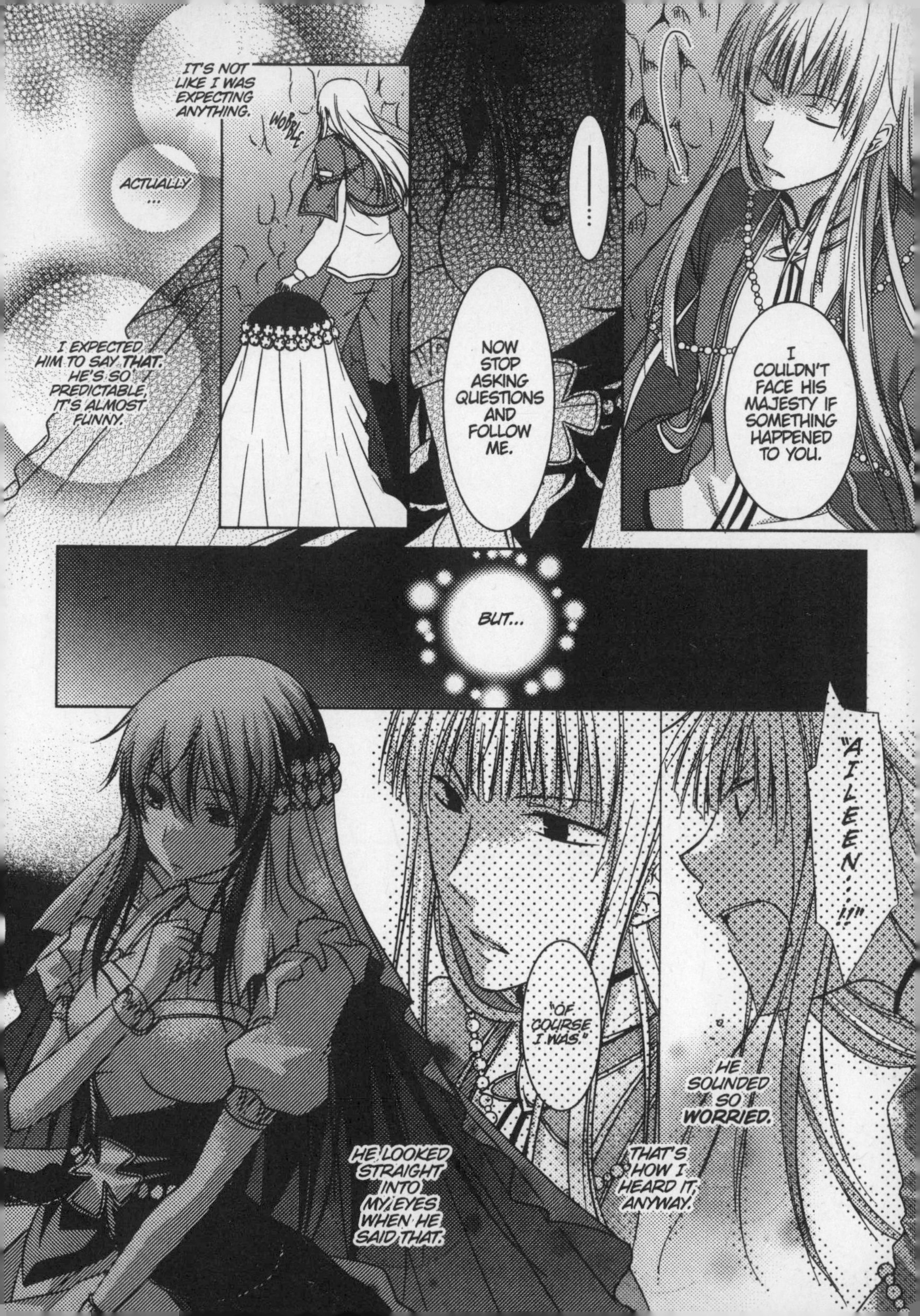
I COULDN'T FACE HIS MAJESTY IF SOMETHING HAPPENED TO YOU.
!......
NOW STOP ASKING QUESTIONS AND FOLLOW ME.
IT'S NOT LIKE I WAS EXPECTING ANYTHING.
WOBBLE
ACTUALLY ...
I EXPECTED HIM TO SAY THAT. HE'S SO PREDICTABLE, IT'S ALMOST FUNNY.
BUT...
"AILEEN...!!"
HE SOUNDED SO WORRIED.
THAT'S HOW I HEARD IT, ANYWAY.
"OF COURSE I WAS."
HE LOOKED STRAIGHT INTO MY EYES WHEN HE SAID THAT.

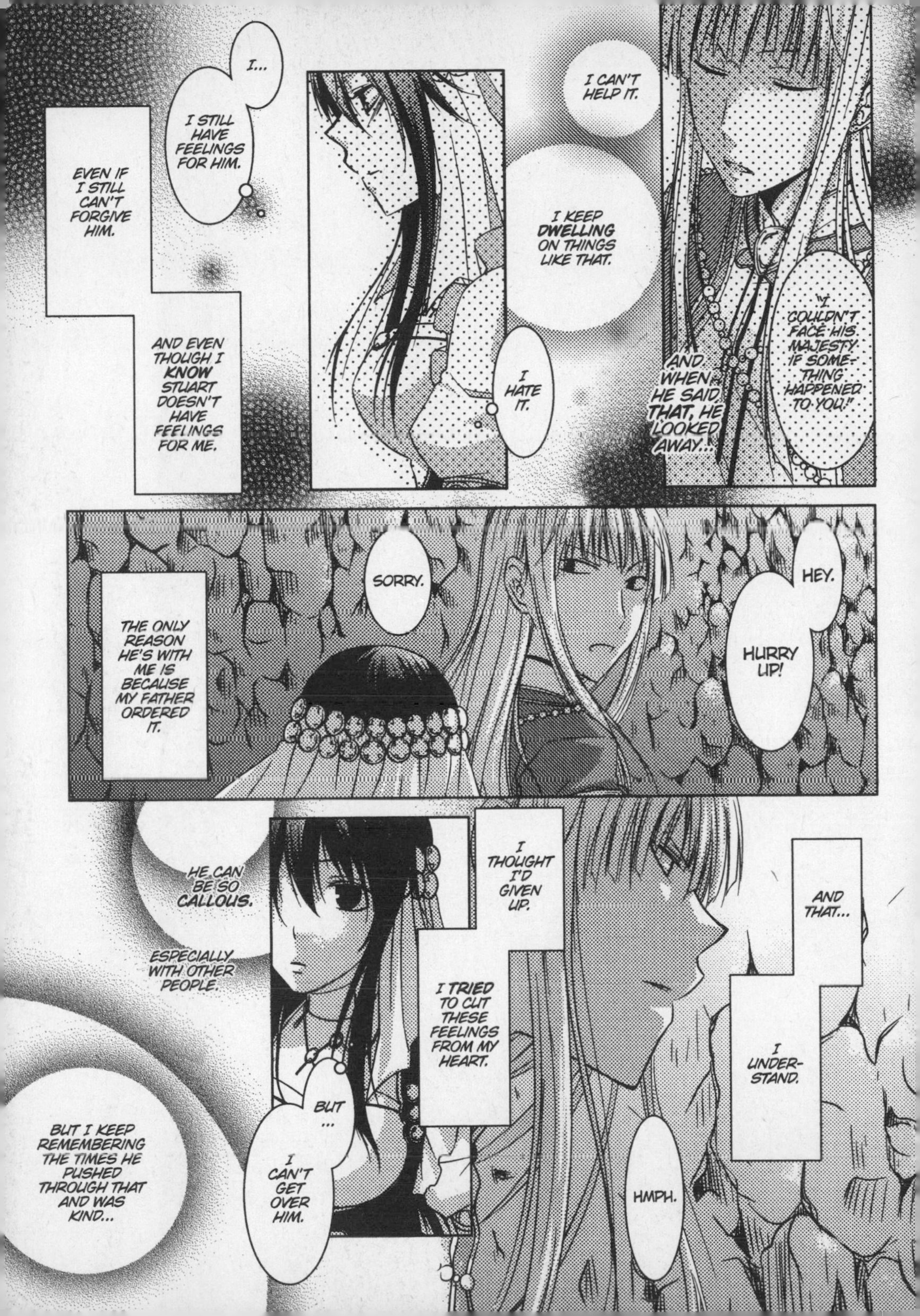
"I COULDN'T FACE HIS MAJESTY IF SOMETHING HAPPENED TO YOU!"
AND WHEN HE SAID THAT, HE LOOKED AWAY...
I CAN'T HELP IT.
I KEEP DWELLING ON THINGS LIKE THAT.
I HATE IT.
I...
I STILL HAVE FEELINGS FOR HIM.
EVEN IF I STILL CAN'T FORGIVE HIM.
AND EVEN THOUGH I KNOW STUART DOESN'T HAVE FEELINGS FOR ME.
HEY.
HURRY UP!
SORRY.
THE ONLY REASON HE'S WITH ME IS BECAUSE MY FATHER ORDERED IT.
AND THAT...
I UNDER-STAND.
HMPH.
I THOUGHT I'D GIVEN UP.
I TRIED TO CUT THESE FEELINGS FROM MY HEART.
HE CAN BE SO CALLOUS.
ESPECIALLY WITH OTHER PEOPLE.
BUT ...
I CAN'T GET OVER HIM.
BUT I KEEP REMEMBERING THE TIMES HE PUSHED THROUGH THAT AND WAS KIND...

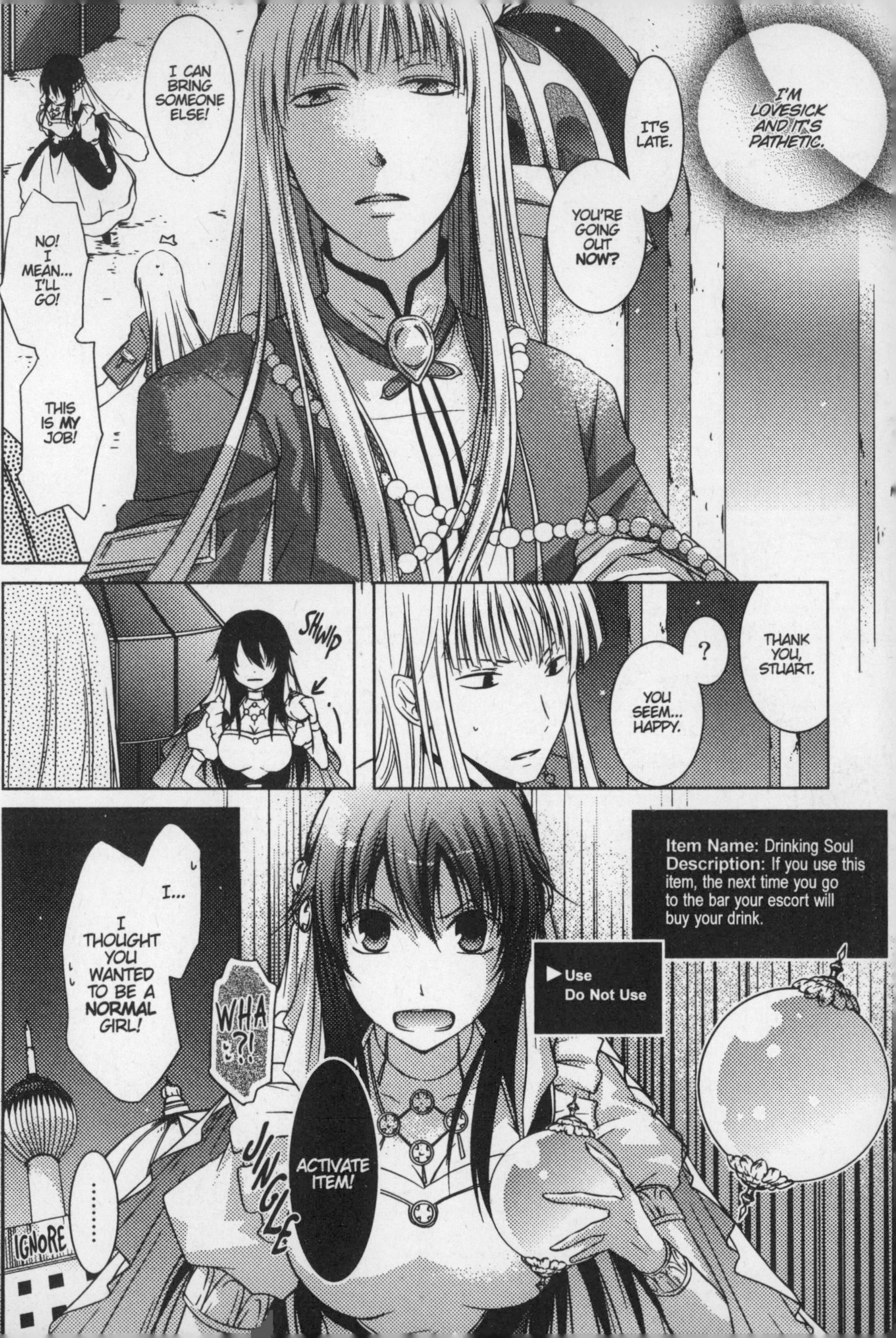
I'M LOVESICK AND IT'S PATHETIC.
IT'S LATE.
YOU'RE GOING OUT NOW?
I CAN BRING SOMEONE ELSE!
NO! I MEAN... I'LL GO!
THIS IS MY JOB!
THANK YOU, STUART.
?
YOU SEEM... HAPPY.
SHWIP
Item Name: Drinking Soul
Description: If you use this item, the next time you go to the bar your escort will buy your drink.
▶Use
Do Not Use
ACTIVATE ITEM!
JINGLE
WHA B?!
I...
I THOUGHT YOU WANTED TO BE A NORMAL GIRL!
......
IGNORE

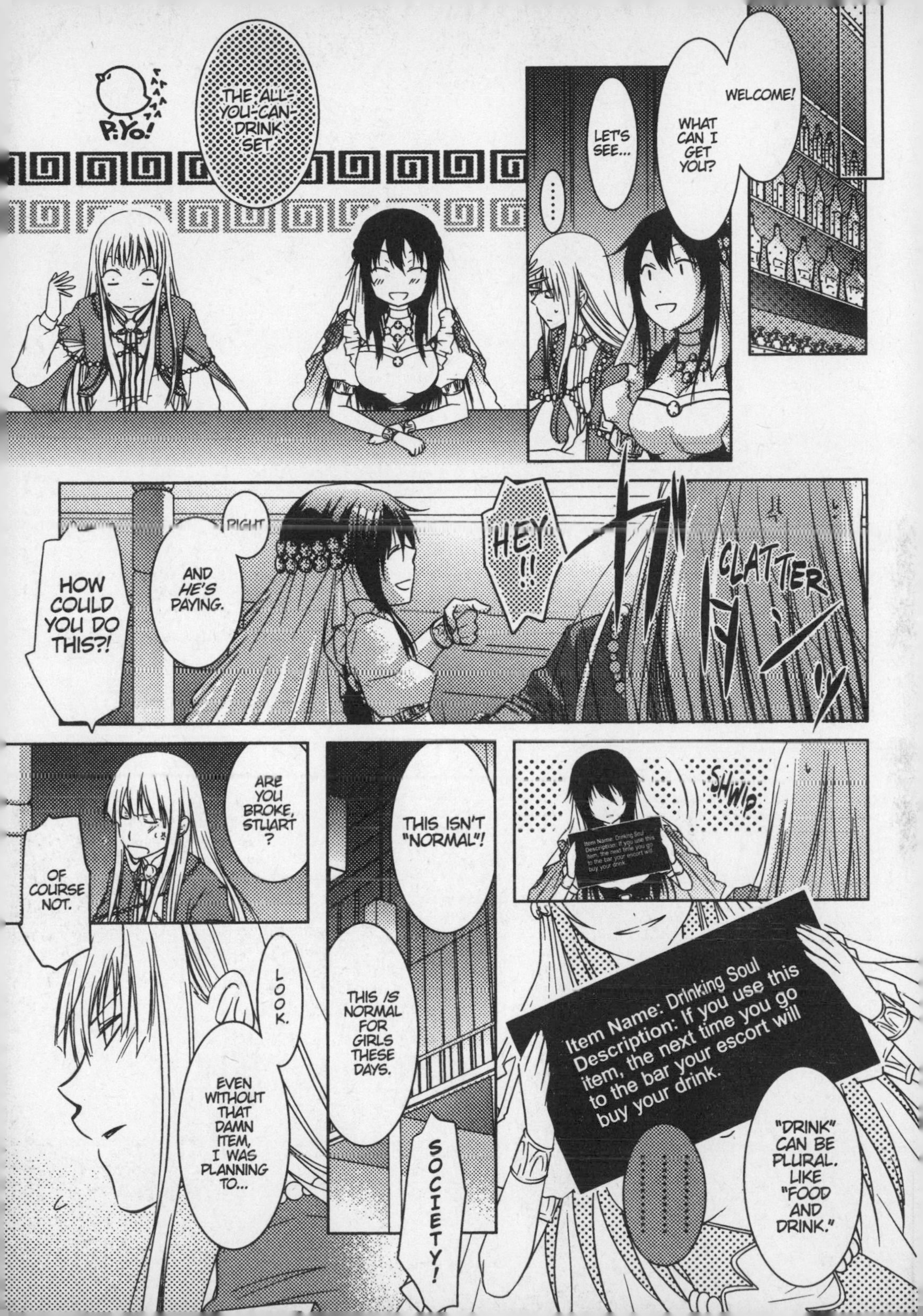
WELCOME!
WHAT CAN I GET YOU?
LET'S SEE...
......
THE ALL-YOU-CAN-DRINK SET.
PiYo!
HEY!!
CLATTER
RIGHT
AND HE'S PAYING.
HOW COULD YOU DO THIS?!
SHWIP
Item Name: Drinking Soul Description: If you use this item, the next time you go to the bar your escort will buy your drink.
THIS ISN'T "NORMAL"!
ARE YOU BROKE, STUART?
OF COURSE NOT.
Item Name: Drinking Soul
Description: If you use this item, the next time you go to the bar your escort will buy your drink.
"DRINK" CAN BE PLURAL. LIKE "FOOD AND DRINK."
......
THIS IS NORMAL FOR GIRLS THESE DAYS.
SOCIETY!
LOOK.
EVEN WITHOUT THAT DAMN ITEM, I WAS PLANNING TO...

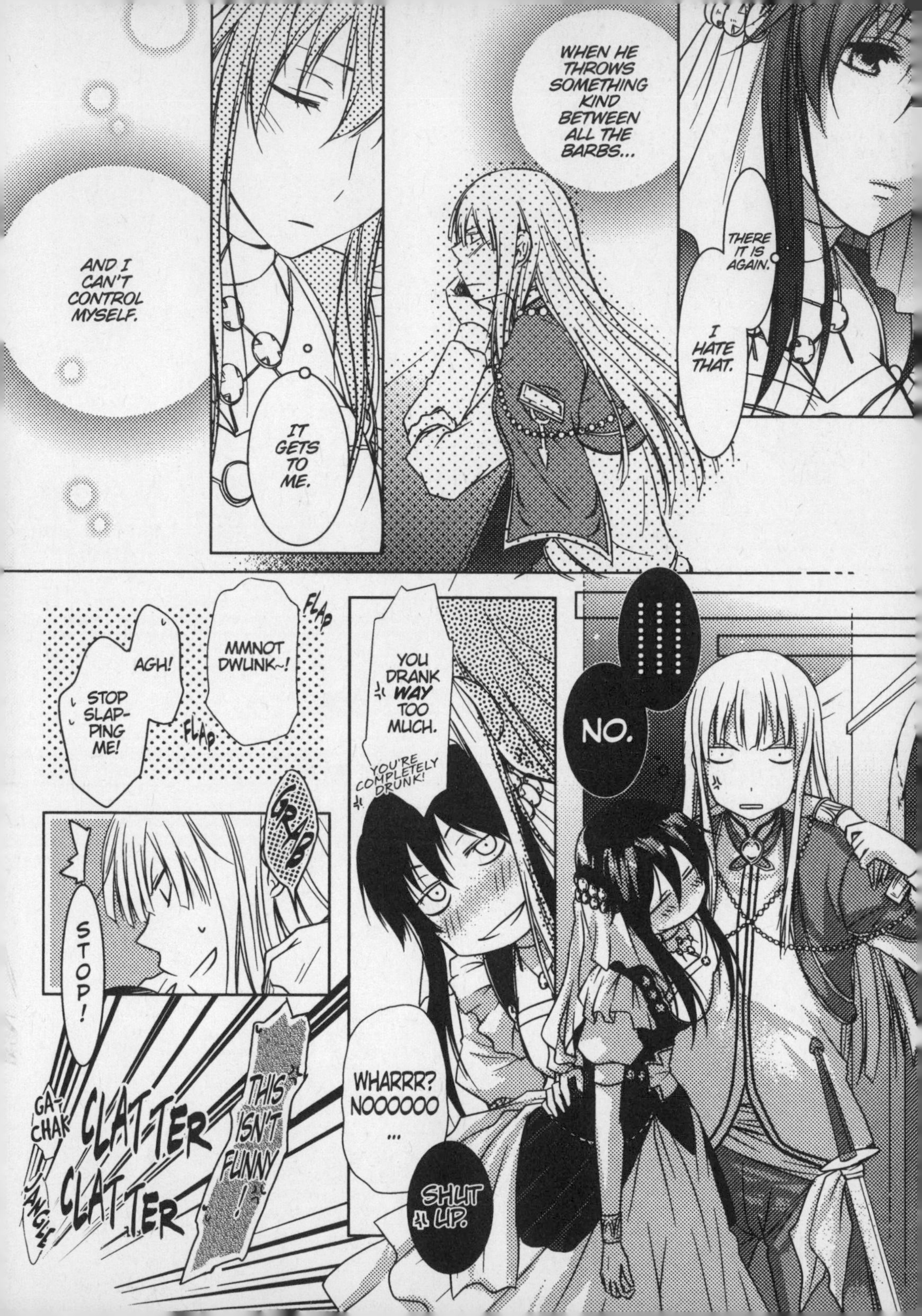
THERE IT IS AGAIN.
I HATE THAT.
WHEN HE THROWS SOMETHING KIND BETWEEN ALL THE BARBS...
IT GETS TO ME.
AND I CAN'T CONTROL MYSELF.
......
NO.
SHUT UP.
YOU DRANK WAY TOO MUCH.
YOU'RE COMPLETELY DRUNK!
WHARRR? NOOOOOO ...
MMNOT DWUNK~!
FLAP
FLAP
AGH!
STOP SLAPPING ME!
GRAB
STOP!
THIS ISN'T FUNNY!
GA-CHAK
CLATTER
CLATTER
DANGLE

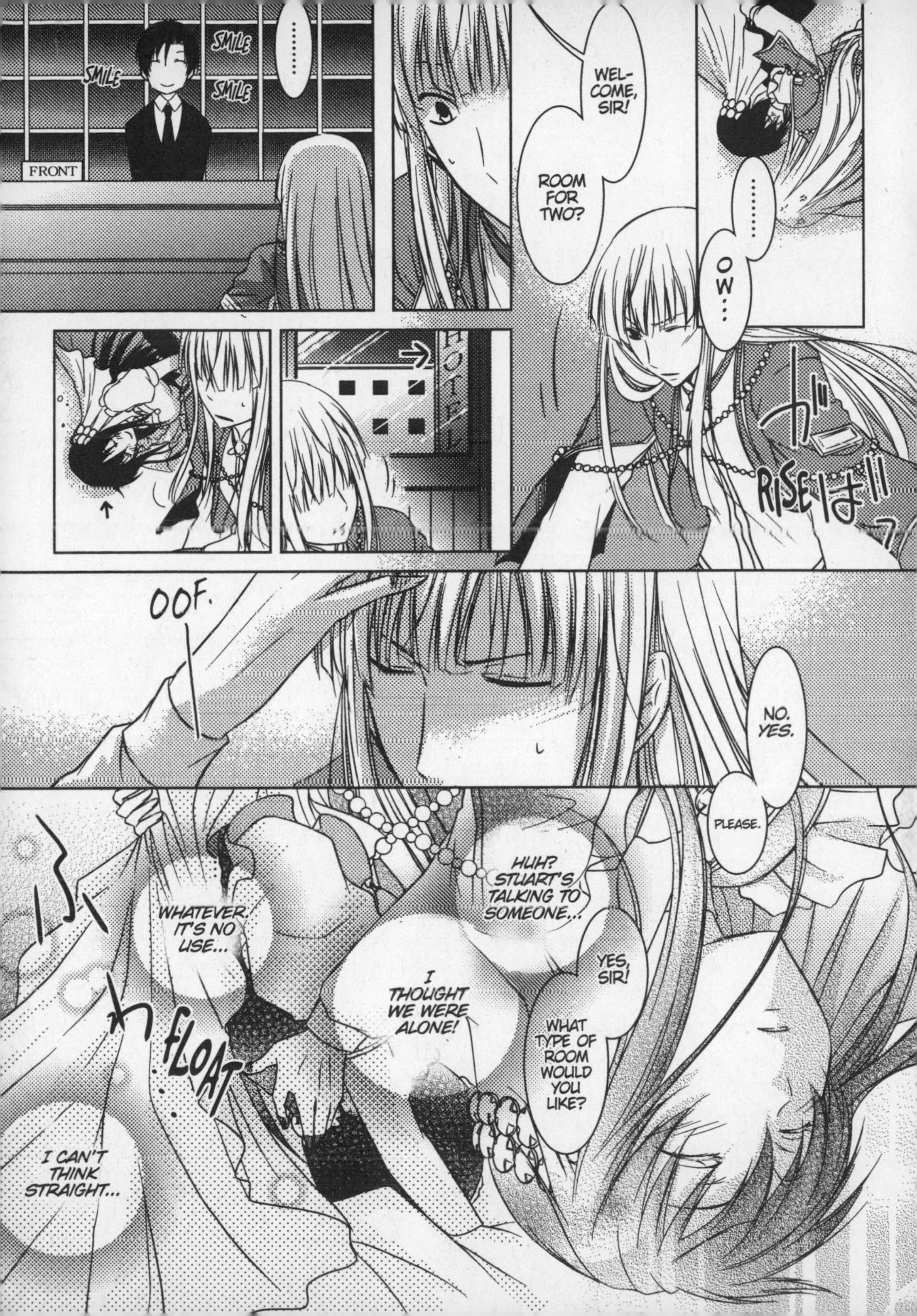
......
OW...
ガー
RISE
WEL-COME, SIR!
ROOM FOR TWO?
......
SMILE
SMILE
SMILE
FRONT
HOTEL
NO. YES.
OOF.
PLEASE.
YES, SIR!
WHAT TYPE OF ROOM WOULD YOU LIKE?
HUH? STUART'S TALKING TO SOMEONE...
I THOUGHT WE WERE ALONE!
WHATEVER. IT'S NO USE...
ふわ
FLOAT
I CAN'T THINK STRAIGHT...

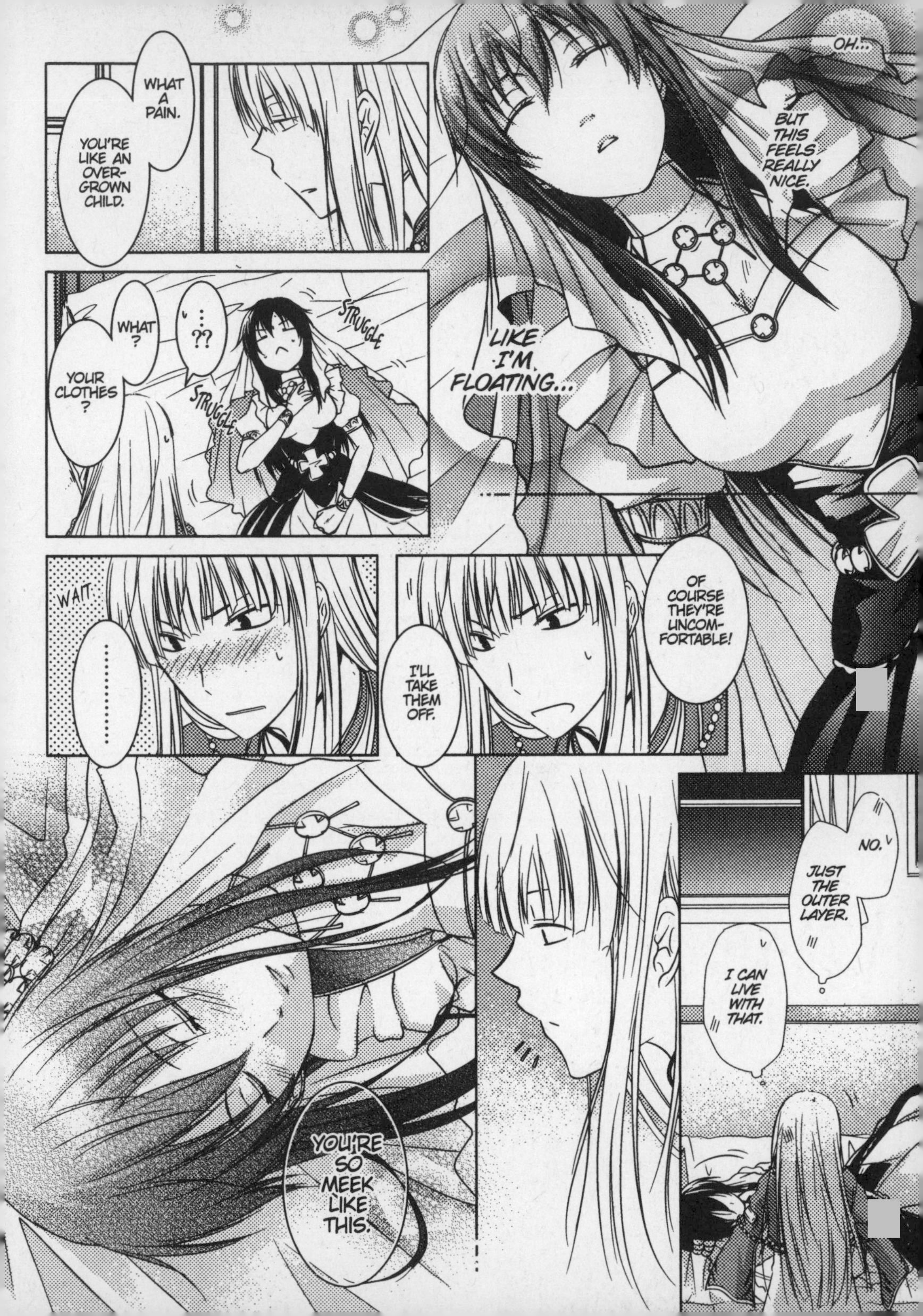
OH...
BUT THIS FEELS REALLY NICE.
LIKE I'M FLOATING...
WHAT A PAIN.
YOU'RE LIKE AN OVER-GROWN CHILD.
STRUGGLE
...??
WHAT?
YOUR CLOTHES?
STRUGGLE
OF COURSE THEY'RE UNCOM-FORTABLE!
I'LL TAKE THEM OFF.
WAIT
......
NO.
JUST THE OUTER LAYER.
I CAN LIVE WITH THAT.
YOU'RE SO MEEK LIKE THIS.

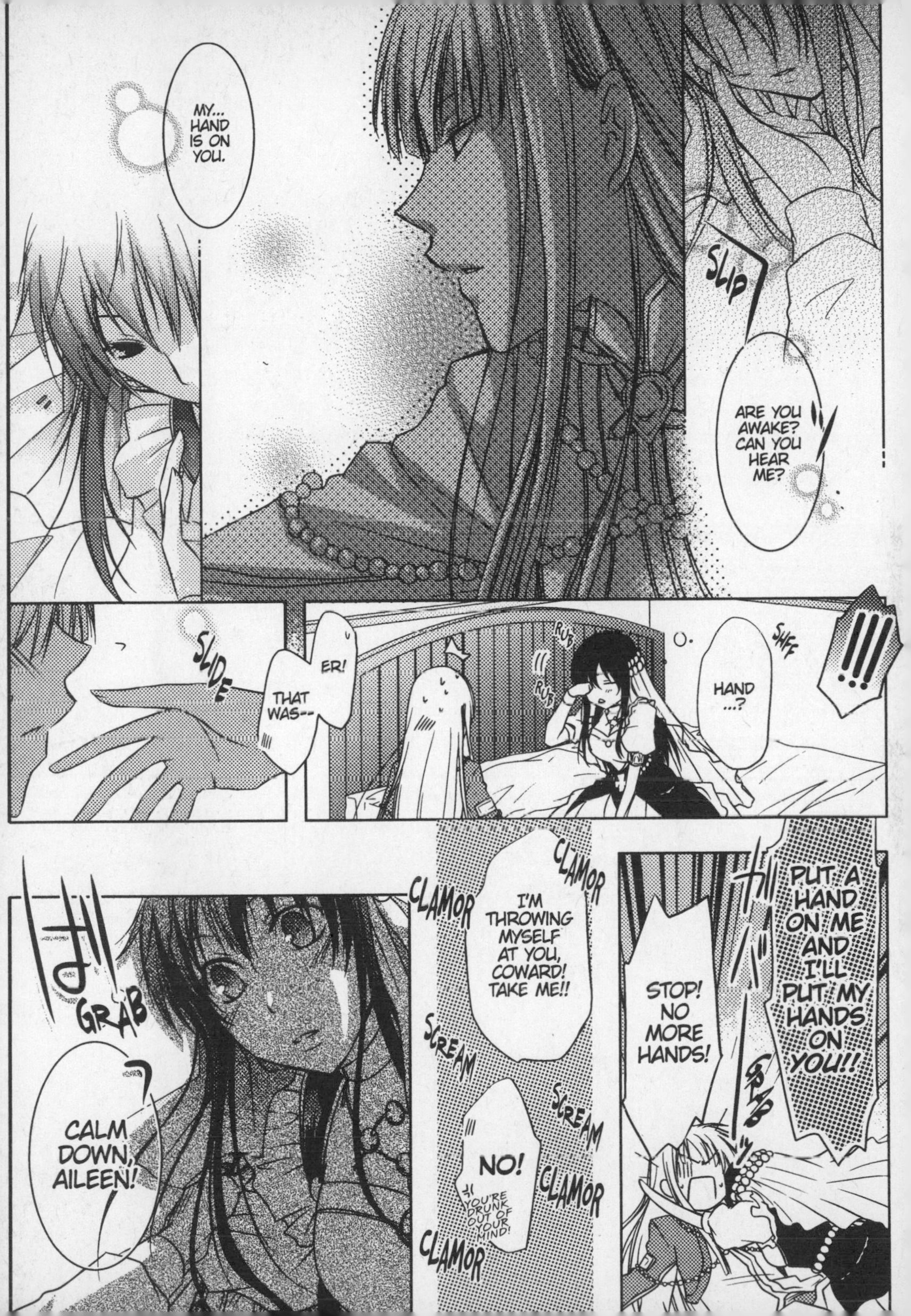
SLIP
ARE YOU AWAKE? CAN YOU HEAR ME?
MY... HAND IS ON YOU.
!!!
SHFF
HAND ...?
O.
RUB
RUB
ER! THAT WAS--
SLIDE
PUT A HAND ON ME AND I'LL PUT MY HANDS ON YOU!!
GRAB
STOP! NO MORE HANDS!
CLAMOR
I'M THROWING MYSELF AT YOU, COWARD! TAKE ME!!
CLAMOR
SCREAM
SCREAM
NO!
YOU'RE DRUNK OUT OF YOUR MIND!
CLAMOR
CLAMOR
GRAB
CALM DOWN, AILEEN!

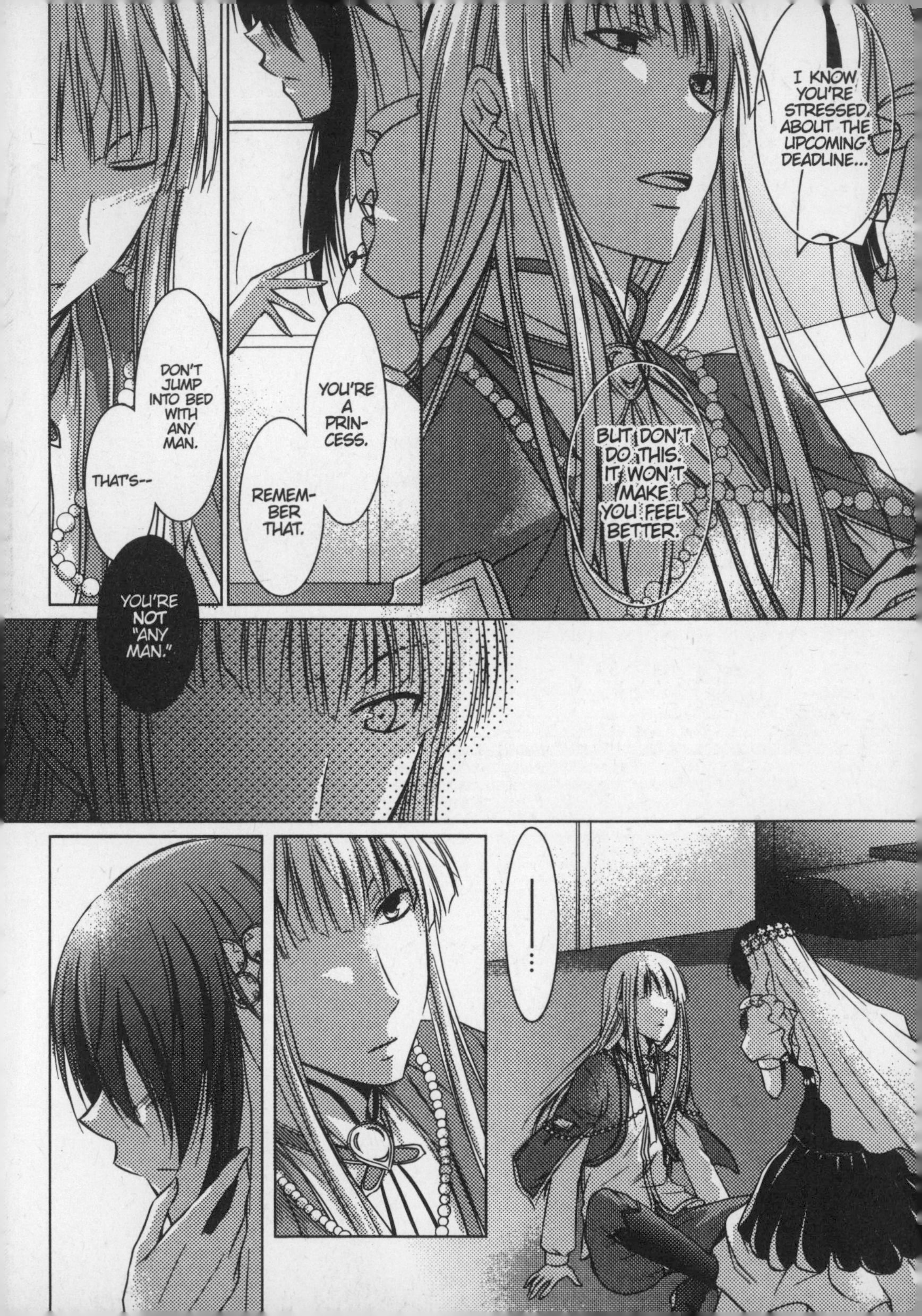

I KNOW YOU'RE STRESSED ABOUT THE UPCOMING DEADLINE...
BUT DON'T DO THIS. IT WON'T MAKE YOU FEEL BETTER.
YOU'RE A PRINCESS.
REMEMBER THAT.
DON'T JUMP INTO BED WITH ANY MAN.
THAT'S--
YOU'RE NOT "ANY MAN."
—...

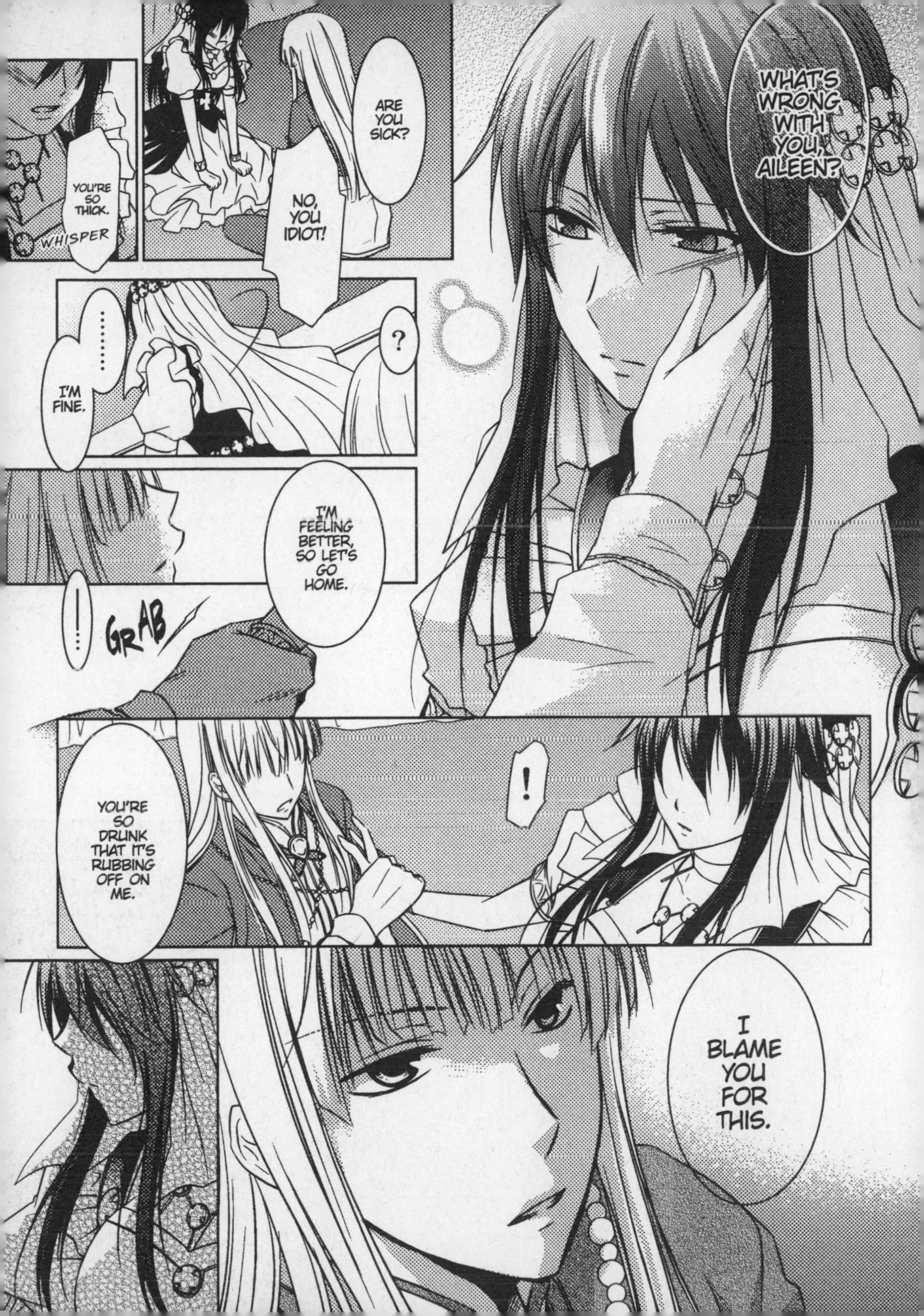
WHAT'S WRONG WITH YOU, AILEEN?
ARE YOU SICK?
NO, YOU IDIOT!
YOU'RE SO THICK.
WHISPER
?
......
I'M FINE.
I'M FEELING BETTER, SO LET'S GO HOME.
!...
GRAB
!
YOU'RE SO DRUNK THAT IT'S RUBBING OFF ON ME.
I BLAME YOU FOR THIS.

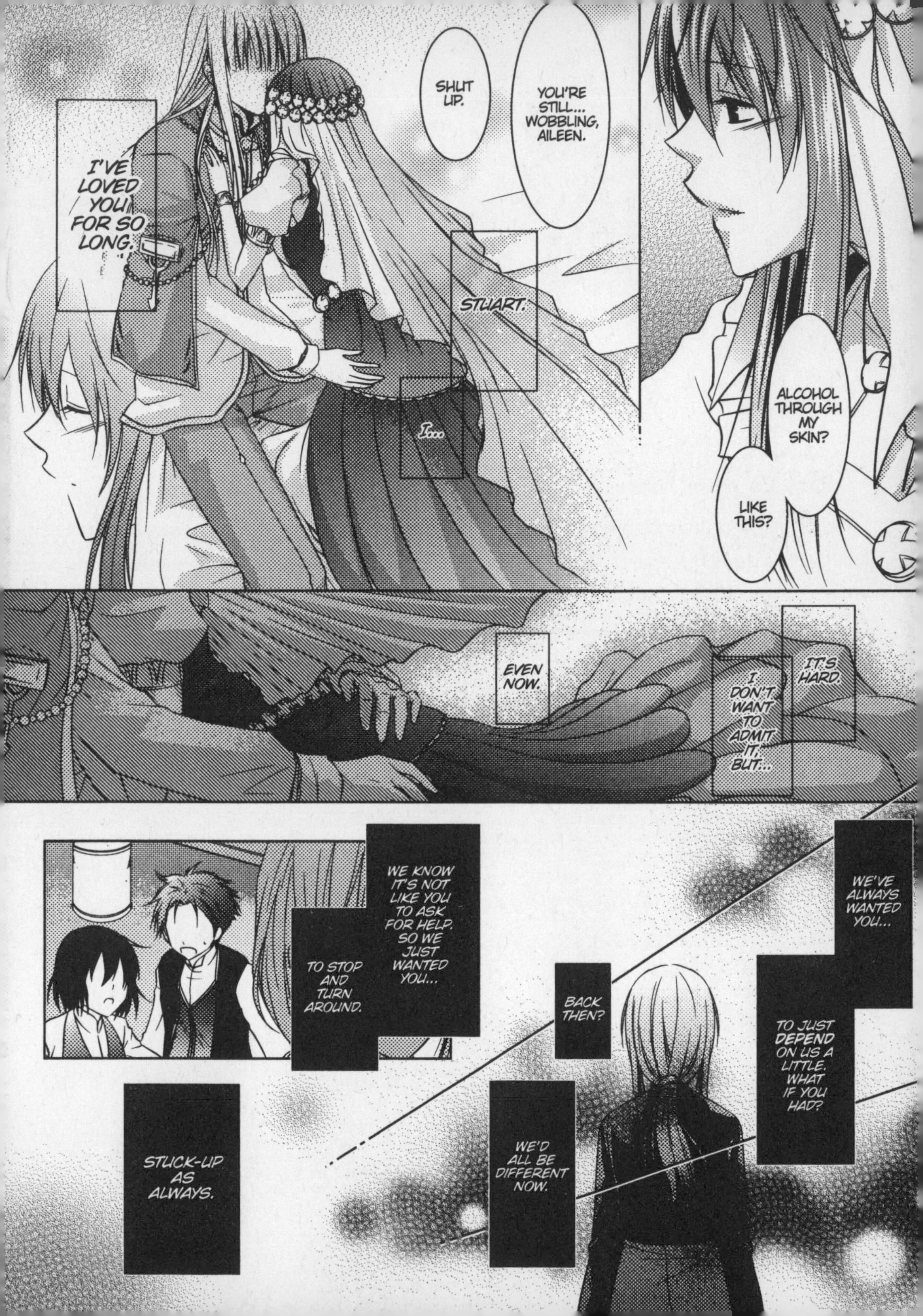
ALCOHOL THROUGH MY SKIN?
LIKE THIS?
YOU'RE STILL... WOBBLING, AILEEN.
SHUT UP.
STUART.
I'VE LOVED YOU FOR SO LONG.
IT'S HARD.
I DON'T WANT TO ADMIT IT, BUT...
EVEN NOW.
WE'VE ALWAYS WANTED YOU...
TO JUST DEPEND ON US A LITTLE. WHAT IF YOU HAD?
BACK THEN?
WE'D ALL BE DIFFERENT NOW.
WE KNOW IT'S NOT LIKE YOU TO ASK FOR HELP. SO WE JUST WANTED YOU...
TO STOP AND TURN AROUND.
STUCK-UP AS ALWAYS.

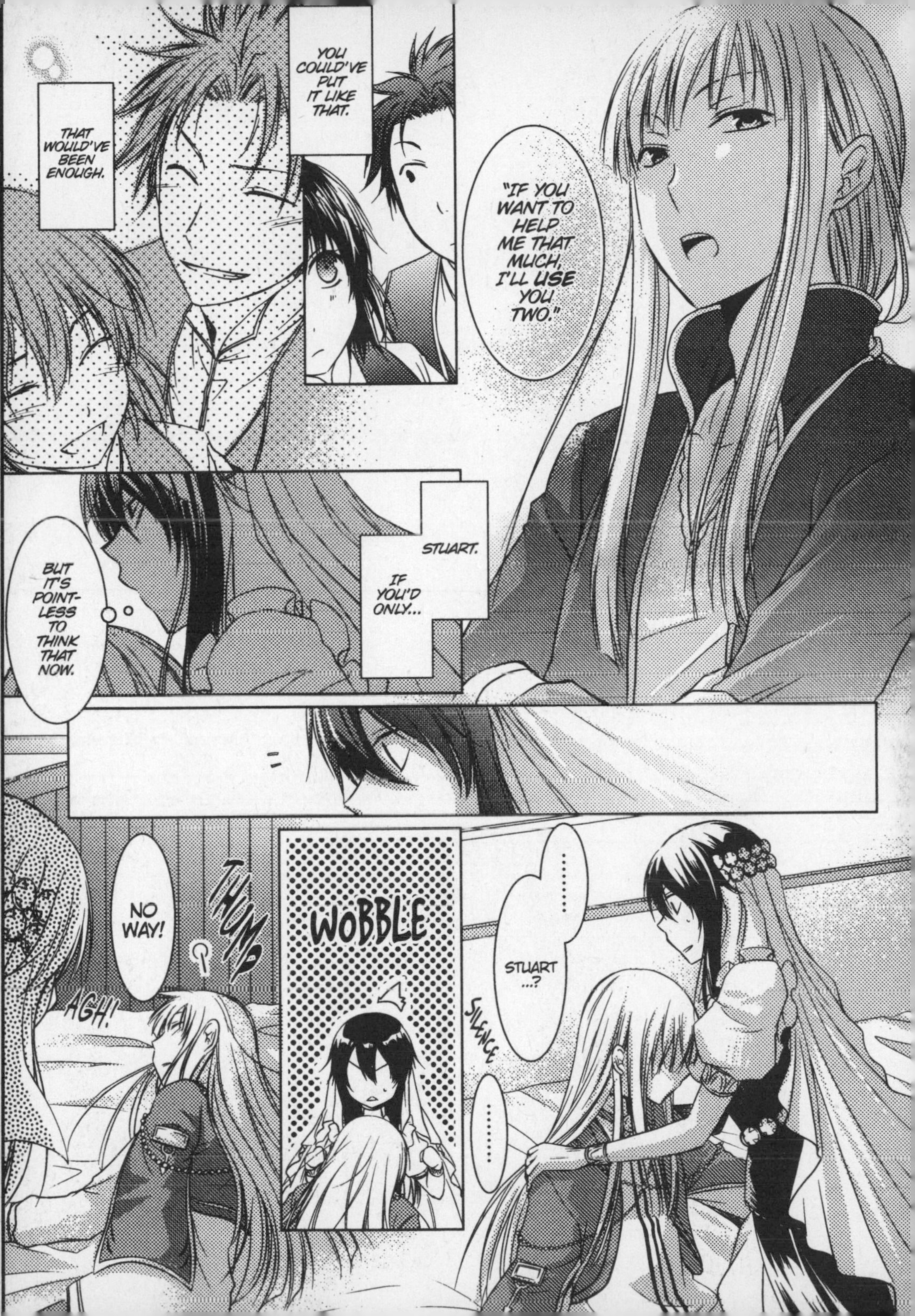
"IF YOU WANT TO HELP ME THAT MUCH, I'LL USE YOU TWO."
YOU COULD'VE PUT IT LIKE THAT.
THAT WOULD'VE BEEN ENOUGH.
STUART.
IF YOU'D ONLY...
BUT IT'S POINTLESS TO THINK THAT NOW.
......
STUART ...?
SILENCE
......
WOBBLE
THUMP
NO WAY!
AGH!

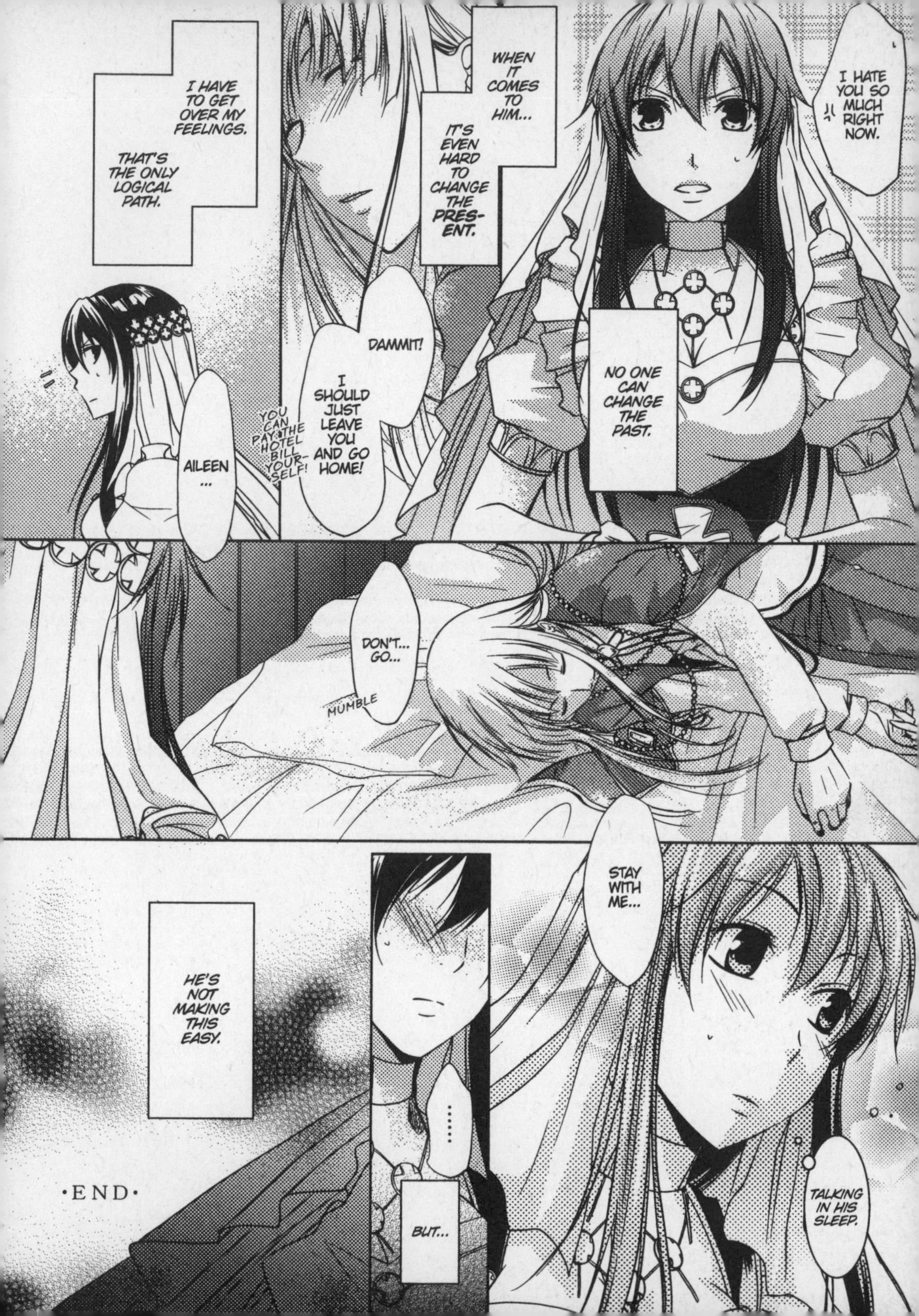
I HATE YOU SO MUCH RIGHT NOW.
NO ONE CAN CHANGE THE PAST.
WHEN IT COMES TO HIM...
IT'S EVEN HARD TO CHANGE THE PRESENT.
DAMMIT!
I SHOULD JUST LEAVE YOU AND GO HOME!
YOU CAN PAY THE HOTEL BILL YOURSELF!
I HAVE TO GET OVER MY FEELINGS.
THAT'S THE ONLY LOGICAL PATH.
AILEEN...
DON'T... GO...
MUMBLE
STAY WITH ME...
TALKING IN HIS SLEEP.
......
BUT...
HE'S NOT MAKING THIS EASY.
•END•

Alice in the Country of Hearts

ハートの国の アリス

～Wonderful Wonder World～

- STORY -

This is a love adventure game. It is based on *Alice in Wonderland*, but evolves into a completely different story.

The main character is far from a romantic. In fact, she's especially sick of love relationships.

She's pulled (against her will) into the dangerous Country of Hearts, which is not as peaceful as the name makes it sound. The Hatters are a mafia family, and even the employees of the Amusement Park carry weapons.

The leaders of the three domains are constantly trying to kill each other. Many of the skirmishes are the result of territory grabs by three major powers trying to control more land: the Hatter, the Queen of Hearts, and Gowland.

After drinking some strange medicine (again, against her will), the main character is unable to return to her world. She quickly decides that she's trapped in a dream and allows herself to enjoy(?) the extraordinary experience she's been thrown into.

What territory will she stay with and who will she interact with to get herself home?
And will this girl, so jaded about love, fall into a relationship she doesn't expect?

Alice in Country of Hearts
Character Information

Elliot March
VA: Tsuguo Mogami

The No. 2 of the Hatter Family and Blood's right-hand man, Elliot is an ex-criminal and an escaped convict. Very short-tempered, he used to be a "very bad guy" who shot before asking questions. After partnering up with Blood, he rounded out and changed to a "slightly bad guy" who thinks for about three seconds before shooting. In his mind, this is a vast improvement.

Blood Dupre
VA: Katsuyuki Konishi

The dangerous leader of the crime syndicate known as the Hatter Family. Since he enjoys plotting more than working directly, he controls everything from the shadows. He's incredibly smart, but due to his temperamental moods and his desire to keep things "interesting," he often digs his own grave in his secret plans.

Alice Liddell
VA: Rie Kugimiya

She grew up to be a responsible young woman after losing her mother early, but Alice still carries a complex toward her older sister. She respects her older sister very much, but is frustrated about always being compared to her. Since her first love fell for her older sister, she has no confidence in herself when it comes to romance.

Vivaldi
VA: Yuuko Kaida

Ruthless and cruel, the Queen of Hearts is an arrogant beauty with a wild temper. She's enemies with the Hatter and Gowland. Impatient at heart, Vivaldi takes her fury out on everyone around her including her subordinates, whom she considers pawns. Anyone **not** working for her doesn't even register as existing.

Tweedle Dum
VA: Jun Fukuyama

The second "Bloody Twin" and a dead ringer for his brother—in both appearance and personality. As they often change places, it's uncertain which one is the older twin.

Tweedle Dee
VA: Jun Fukuyama

Gatekeeper of the Hatter territory, and one of the dark, sneaky twins. They sometimes show an innocent side, but they usually have a malicious agenda. Also known as the "Bloody Twins" due to their unsavory activities.

Ace
VA: Daisuke Hirakawa

The knight of Hearts and the ex-subordinate of Vivaldi. He's left the castle and is currently wandering. He's a very unlucky and unfortunate man, yet remains strangely positive, thus he tends to plow forward and make mistakes that only worsen his situation. He's one of the few friends of the clockmaker, Julius.

Julius Monrey
VA: Takehito Koyasu

The clockmaker, a gloomy machine expert who easily falls into depression. He lives in the Clock Tower and doesn't get out much. He always thinks of everything in the most negative way and tends to distrust people, but he gets along with Ace. He had some part in the imprisonment of the March Hare, Elliot, and is thus the target of Elliot's hatred.

Peter White
VA: Kouki Miyata

Don't be fooled by the cute ears—Peter is the dangerous guide who dragged Alice to Wonderland in the first place. He claims to always be worried about the time, despite having a strange grasp on it. Rumors say his heart is as black as his hair is white.

Nightmare
VA: Tomokazu Sugita

A sickly nightmare. He appears in Alice's dream, sometimes to guide her— and other times, to **misguide** her.

Mary Gowland
VA: Kenyuu Horiuchi

The owner of the Amusement Park. He hides his hated first name, Mary, but pretty much everyone already knows it. His full name is a play on words that sounds like "Merry Go Round" when said quickly. If his musical talent was given a numerical value, it would be closer to negatives than zero.

Boris Airay
VA: Noriaki Sugiyama

A riddle-loving cat with his signature smirk. He sometimes gives hints to his riddles, but the hints usually just cause more confusion. He also has a tendency to pose questions and never answer them.

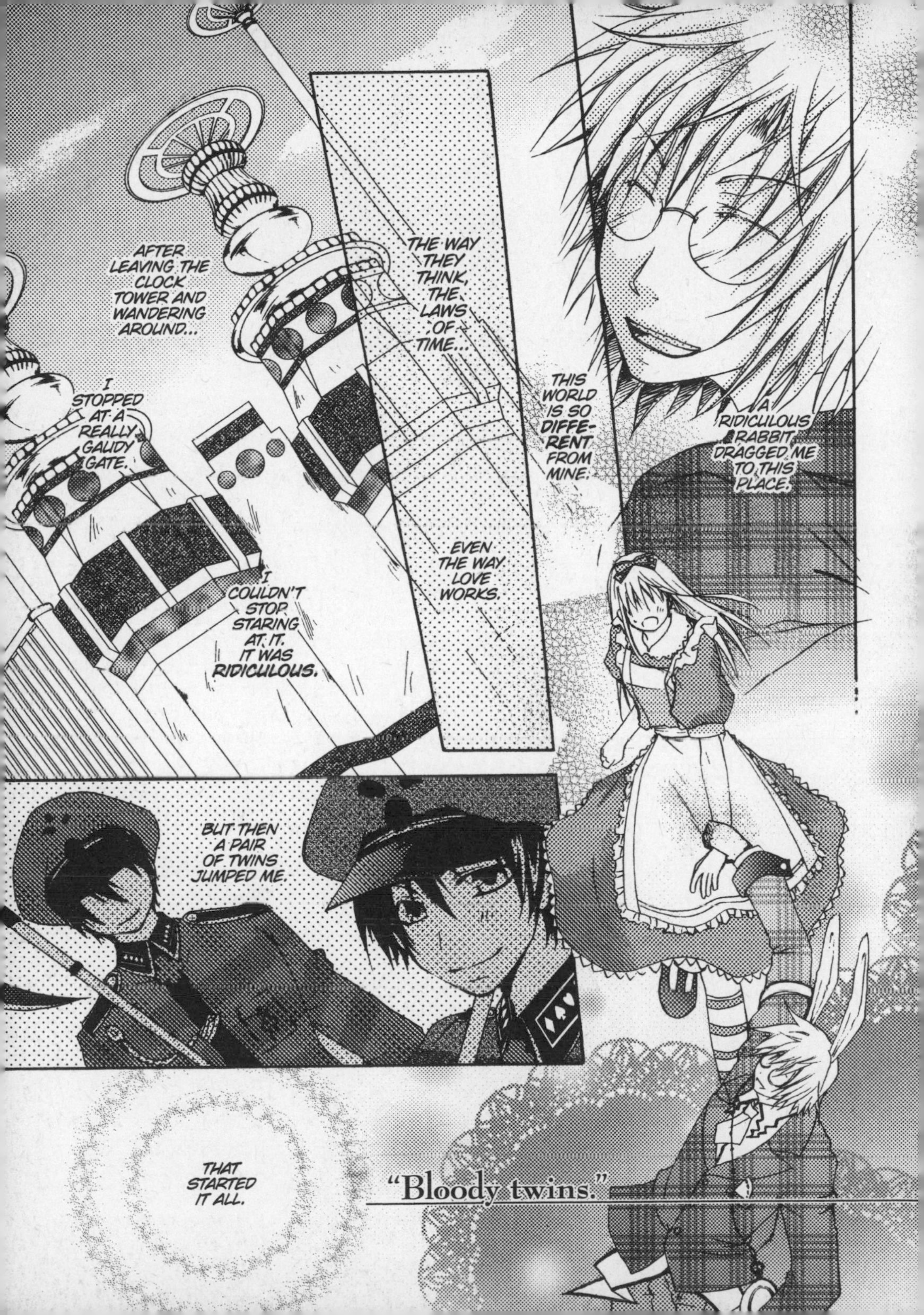
A RIDICULOUS RABBIT DRAGGED ME TO THIS PLACE.
THIS WORLD IS SO DIFFERENT FROM MINE.
THE WAY THEY THINK, THE LAWS OF TIME...
EVEN THE WAY LOVE WORKS.
AFTER LEAVING THE CLOCK TOWER AND WANDERING AROUND...
I STOPPED AT A REALLY GAUDY GATE.
I COULDN'T STOP STARING AT IT. IT WAS RIDICULOUS.
BUT THEN A PAIR OF TWINS JUMPED ME.
"Bloody twins."
THAT STARTED IT ALL.

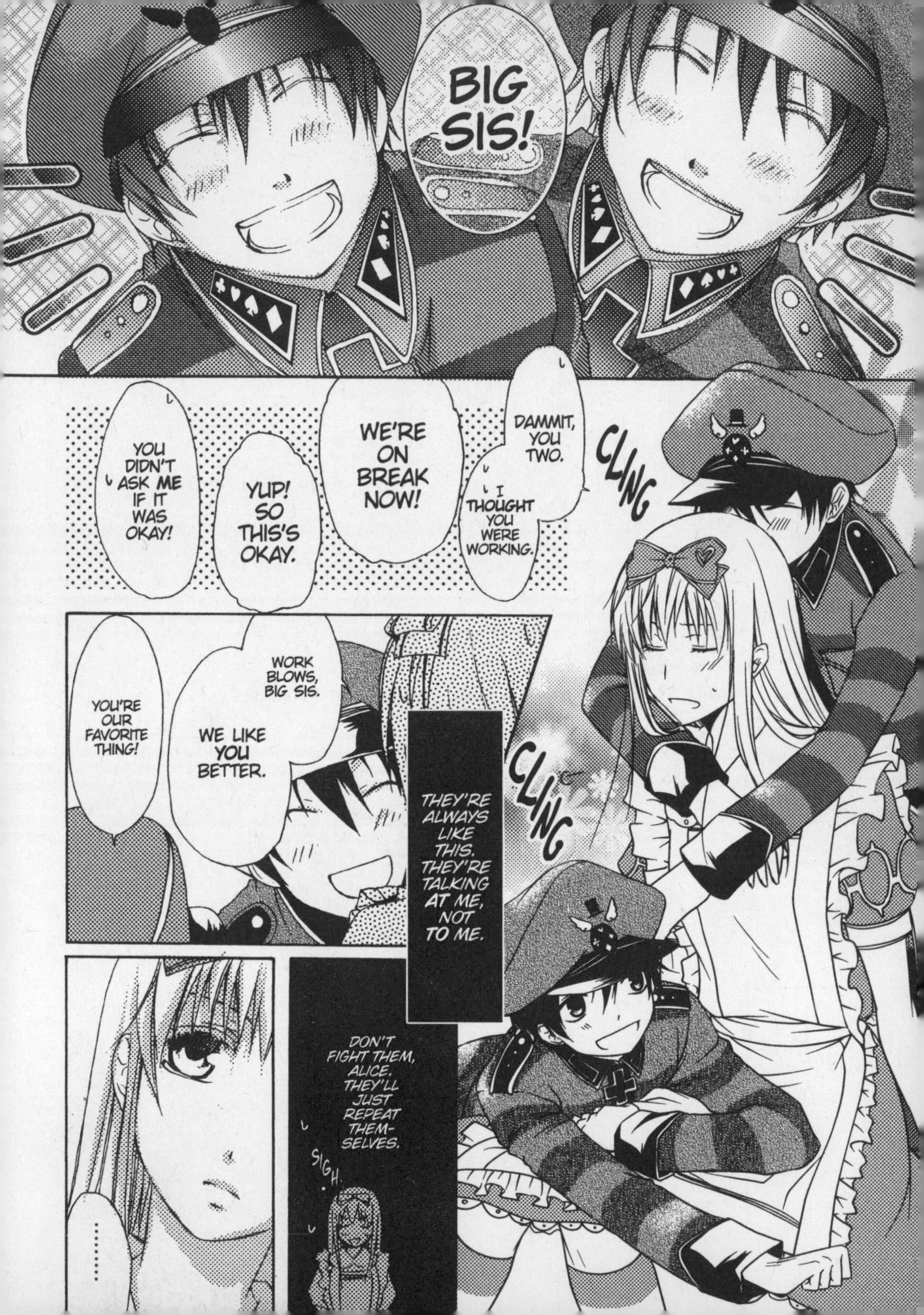
BIG SIS!
DAMMIT, YOU TWO.
I THOUGHT YOU WERE WORKING.
WE'RE ON BREAK NOW!
YUP! SO THIS'S OKAY.
YOU DIDN'T ASK ME IF IT WAS OKAY!
CLING
CLING
CLING
THEY'RE ALWAYS LIKE THIS. THEY'RE TALKING AT ME, NOT TO ME.
WORK BLOWS, BIG SIS.
WE LIKE YOU BETTER.
YOU'RE OUR FAVORITE THING!
DON'T FIGHT THEM, ALICE. THEY'LL JUST REPEAT THEM-SELVES.
SIGH.
......

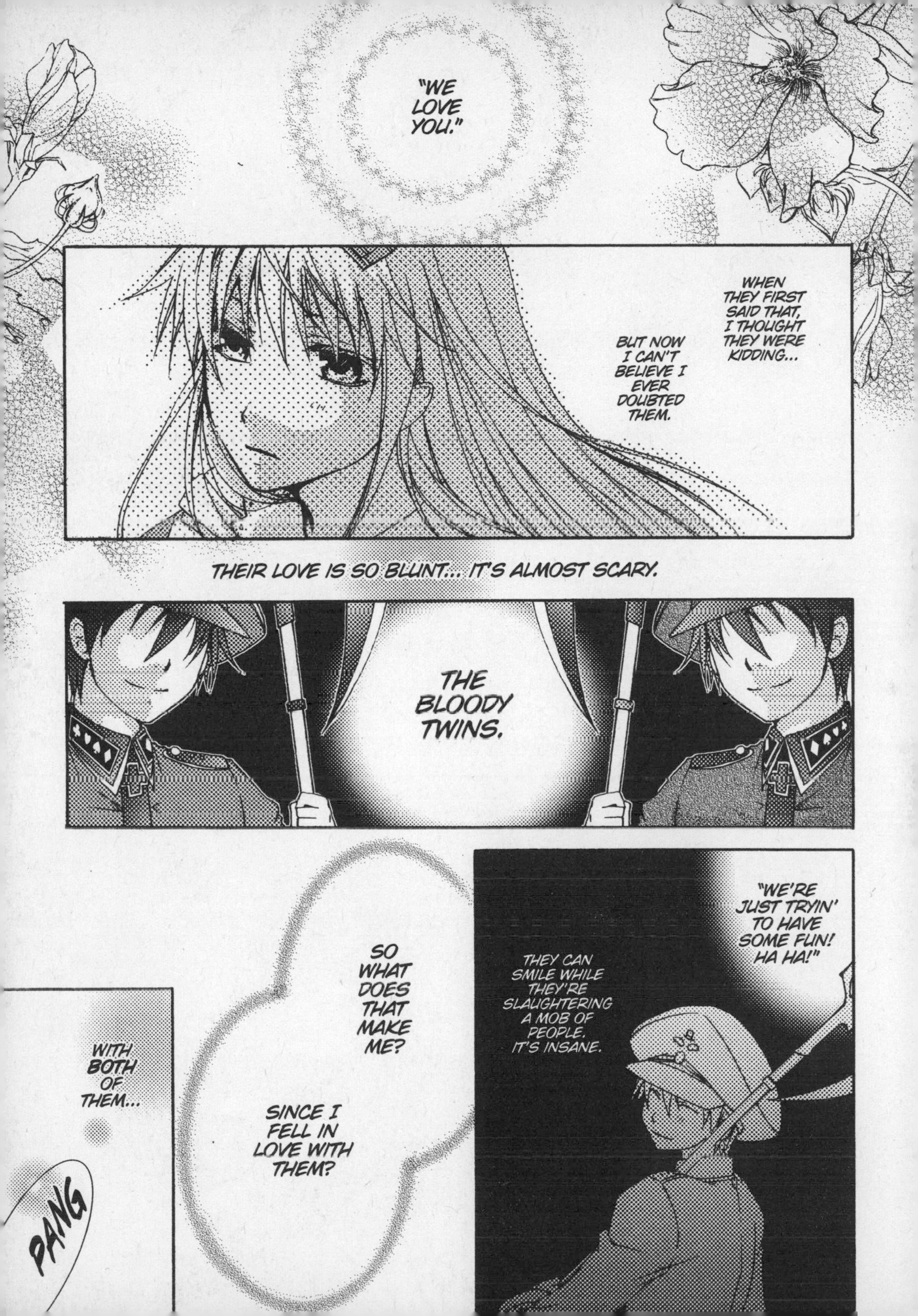
"WE LOVE YOU."
WHEN THEY FIRST SAID THAT, I THOUGHT THEY WERE KIDDING...
BUT NOW I CAN'T BELIEVE I EVER DOUBTED THEM.
THEIR LOVE IS SO BLUNT... IT'S ALMOST SCARY.
THE BLOODY TWINS.
"WE'RE JUST TRYIN' TO HAVE SOME FUN! HA HA!"
THEY CAN SMILE WHILE THEY'RE SLAUGHTERING A MOB OF PEOPLE. IT'S INSANE.
SO WHAT DOES THAT MAKE ME?
SINCE I FELL IN LOVE WITH THEM?
WITH BOTH OF THEM...
PANG

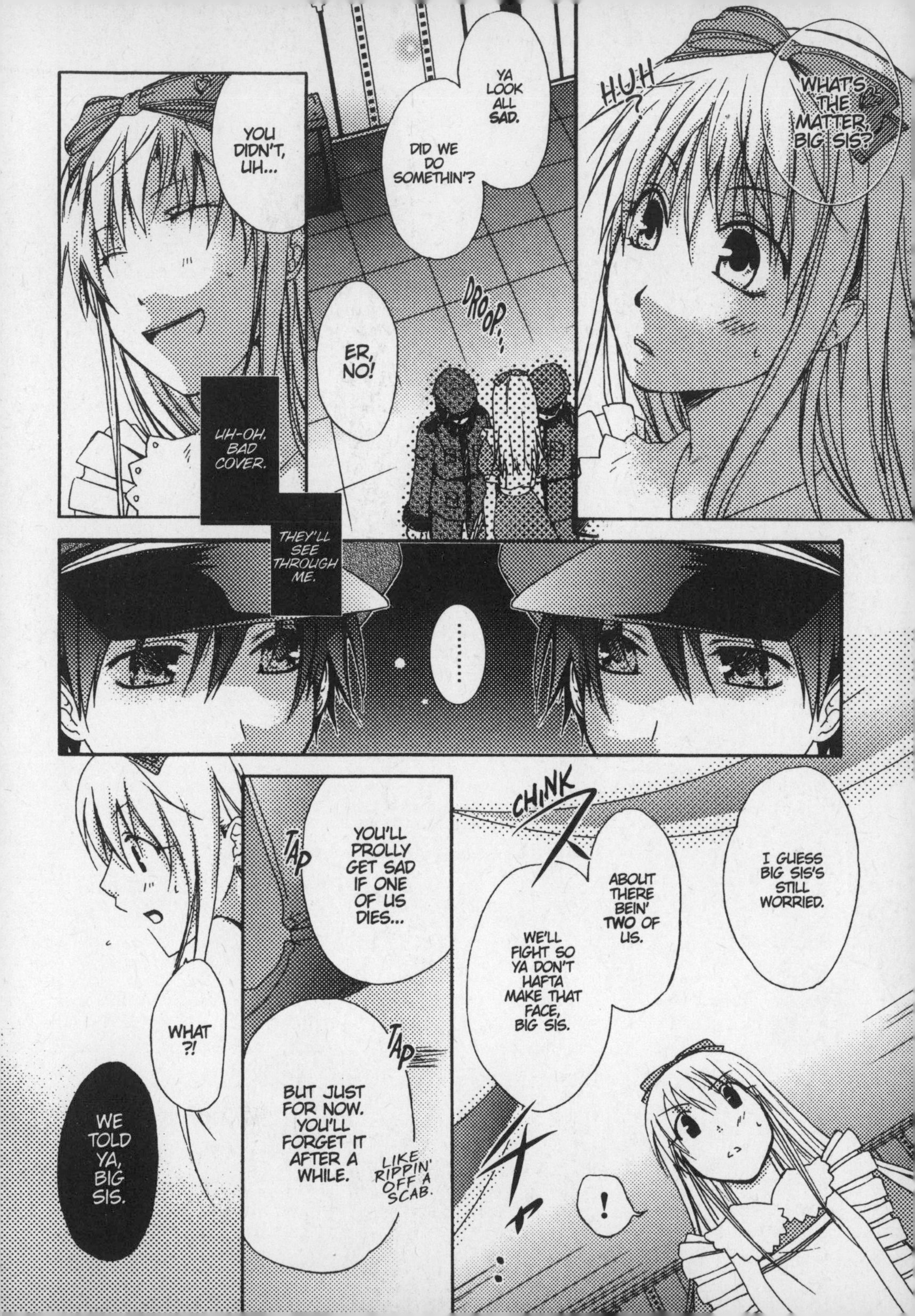
HUH?
WHAT'S THE MATTER, BIG SIS?
YA LOOK ALL SAD.
DID WE DO SOMETHIN'?
DROOP...
ER, NO!
YOU DIDN'T, UH...
UH-OH. BAD COVER.
THEY'LL SEE THROUGH ME.
......
CHINK
I GUESS BIG SIS'S STILL WORRIED.
ABOUT THERE BEIN' TWO OF US.
WE'LL FIGHT SO YA DON'T HAFTA MAKE THAT FACE, BIG SIS.
!
TAP
YOU'LL PROLLY GET SAD IF ONE OF US DIES...
TAP
BUT JUST FOR NOW. YOU'LL FORGET IT AFTER A WHILE.
LIKE RIPPIN' OFF A SCAB.
WHAT?!
WE TOLD YA, BIG SIS.

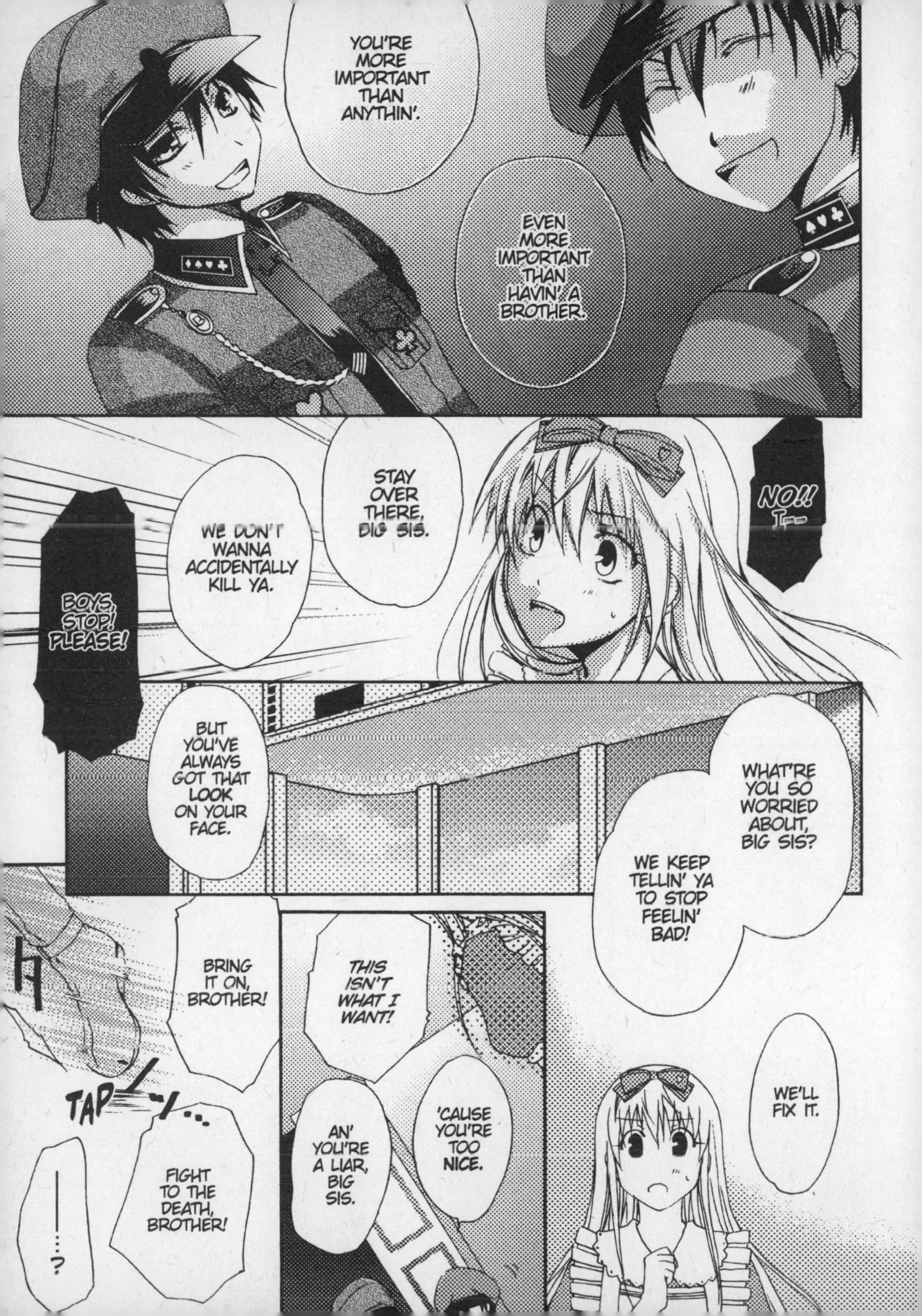
YOU'RE MORE IMPORTANT THAN ANYTHIN'.
EVEN MORE IMPORTANT THAN HAVIN' A BROTHER.
NO!! I--
STAY OVER THERE, BIG SIS.
WE DON'T WANNA ACCIDENTALLY KILL YA.
BOYS, STOP! PLEASE!
WHAT'RE YOU SO WORRIED ABOUT, BIG SIS?
WE KEEP TELLIN' YA TO STOP FEELIN' BAD!
BUT YOU'VE ALWAYS GOT THAT LOOK ON YOUR FACE.
WE'LL FIX IT.
THIS ISN'T WHAT I WANT!
'CAUSE YOU'RE TOO NICE.
AN' YOU'RE A LIAR, BIG SIS.
BRING IT ON, BROTHER!
TAP
FIGHT TO THE DEATH, BROTHER!
......?

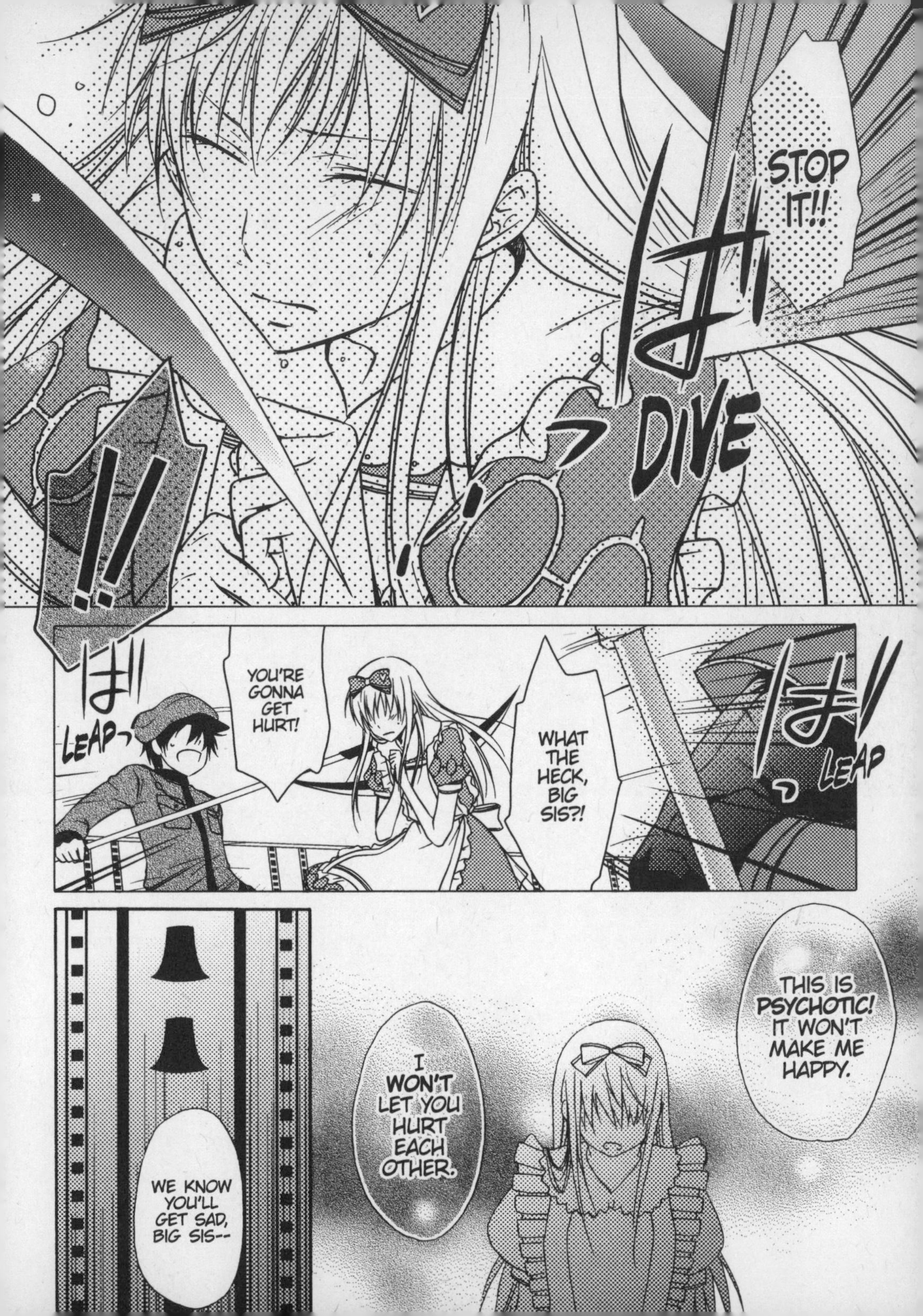
STOP IT!!
DIVE
!!
はっ
LEAP
WHAT THE HECK, BIG SIS?!
YOU'RE GONNA GET HURT!
ばっ
LEAP
THIS IS PSYCHOTIC! IT WON'T MAKE ME HAPPY.
I WON'T LET YOU HURT EACH OTHER.
WE KNOW YOU'LL GET SAD, BIG SIS--

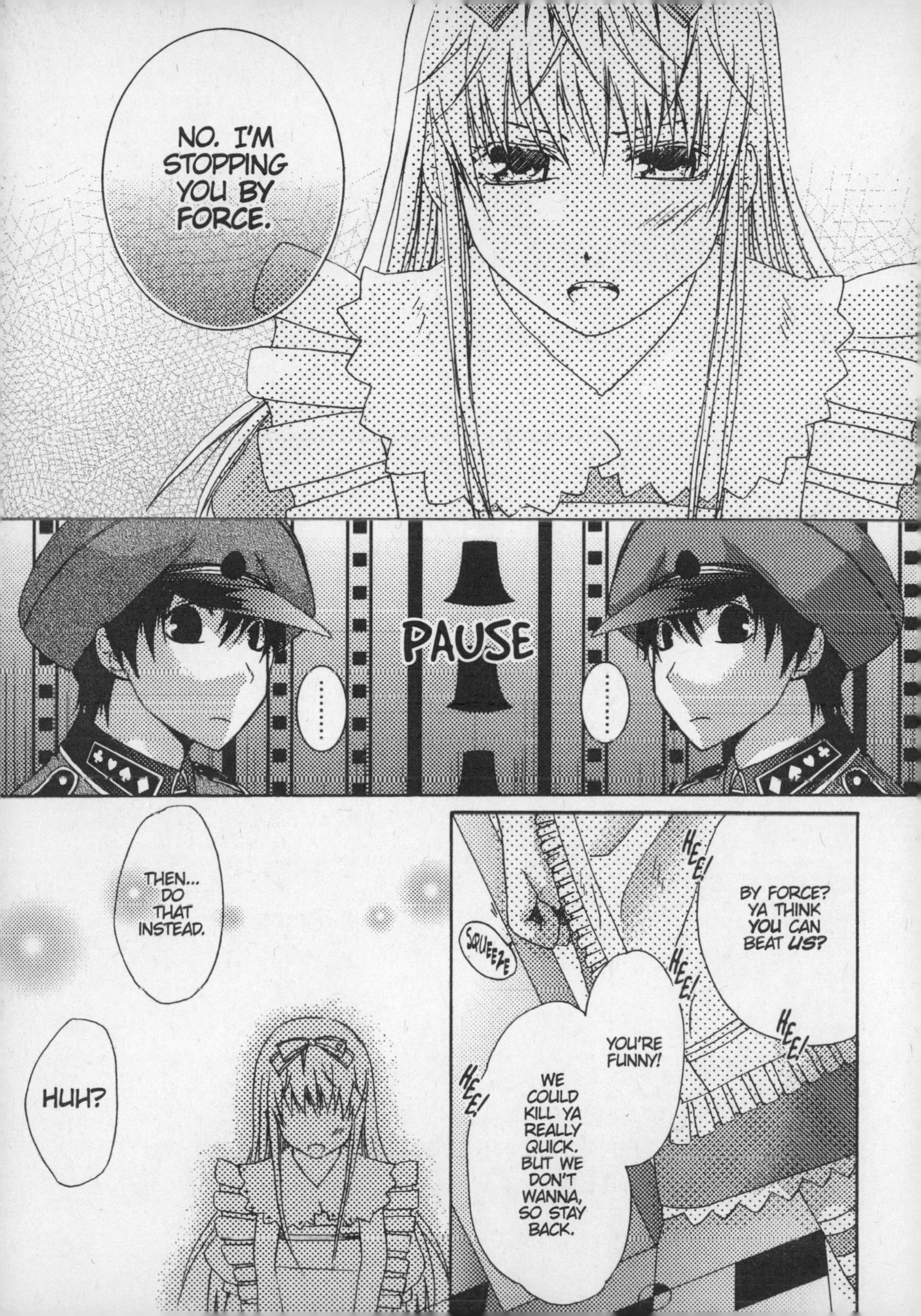
NO. I'M STOPPING YOU BY FORCE.
......
PAUSE
......
HEE!
BY FORCE? YA THINK YOU CAN BEAT US?
SQUEEZE
HEE!
HEE!
YOU'RE FUNNY!
HEE!
WE COULD KILL YA REALLY QUICK. BUT WE DON'T WANNA, SO STAY BACK.
THEN... DO THAT INSTEAD.
HUH?

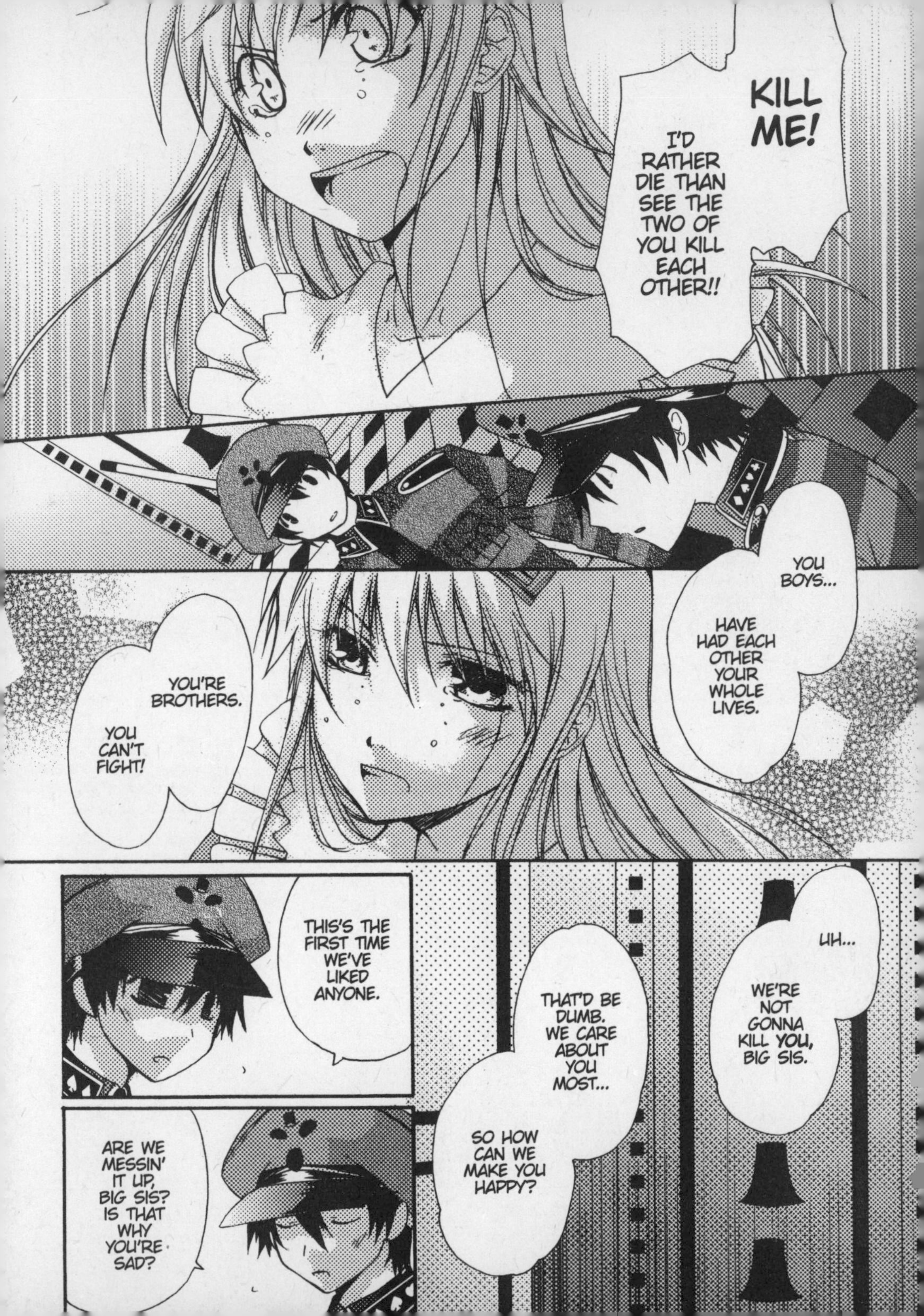
KILL ME!
I'D RATHER DIE THAN SEE THE TWO OF YOU KILL EACH OTHER!!
YOU BOYS...
HAVE HAD EACH OTHER YOUR WHOLE LIVES.
YOU'RE BROTHERS.
YOU CAN'T FIGHT!
UH...
WE'RE NOT GONNA KILL YOU, BIG SIS.
THAT'D BE DUMB. WE CARE ABOUT YOU MOST...
SO HOW CAN WE MAKE YOU HAPPY?
THIS'S THE FIRST TIME WE'VE LIKED ANYONE.
ARE WE MESSIN' IT UP, BIG SIS? IS THAT WHY YOU'RE SAD?

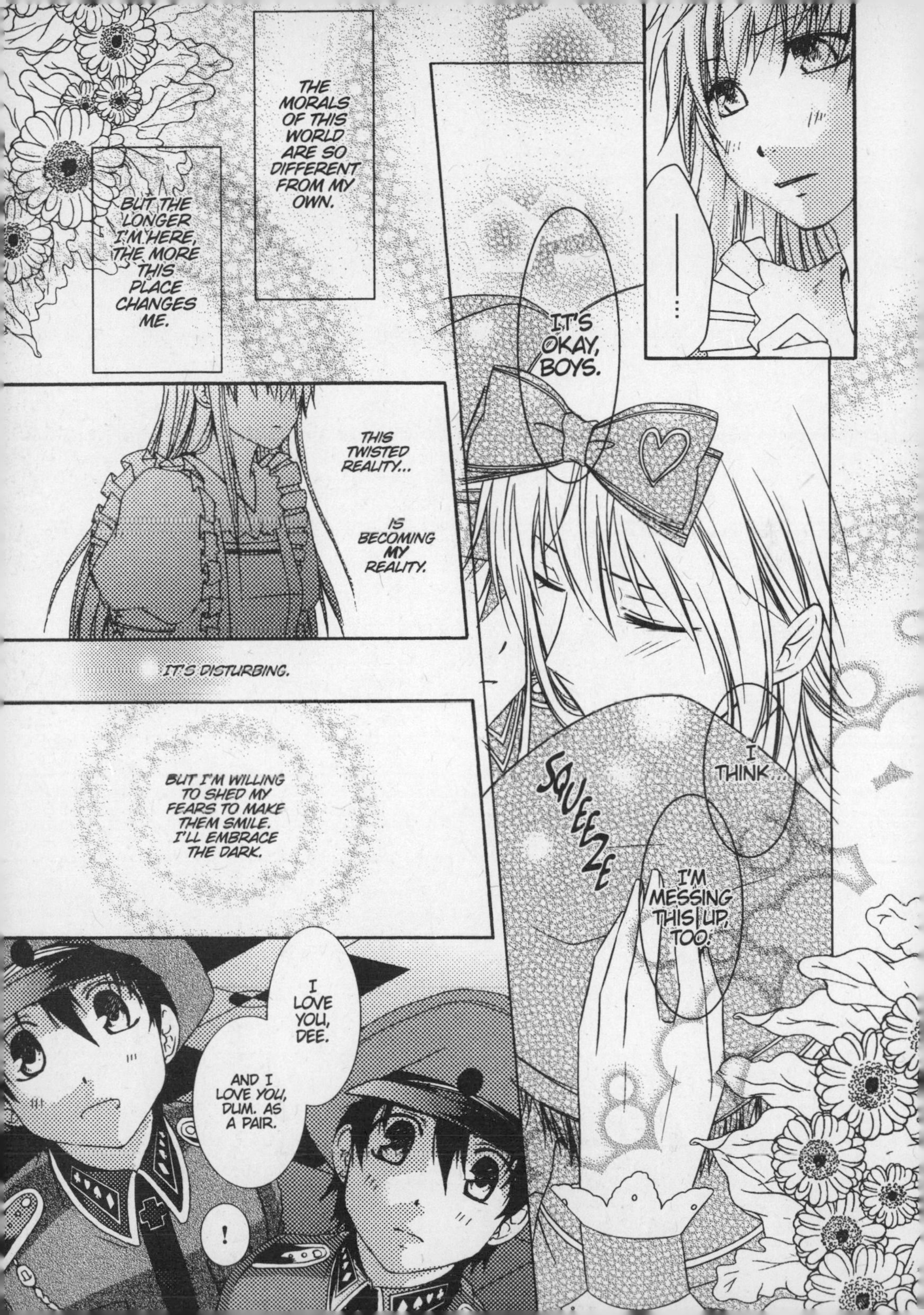
......
IT'S OKAY, BOYS.
I THINK...
SQUEEZE
I'M MESSING THIS UP, TOO.
THE MORALS OF THIS WORLD ARE SO DIFFERENT FROM MY OWN.
BUT THE LONGER I'M HERE, THE MORE THIS PLACE CHANGES ME.
THIS TWISTED REALITY...
IS BECOMING MY REALITY.
IT'S DISTURBING.
BUT I'M WILLING TO SHED MY FEARS TO MAKE THEM SMILE. I'LL EMBRACE THE DARK.
I LOVE YOU, DEE.
AND I LOVE YOU, DUM. AS A PAIR.
!

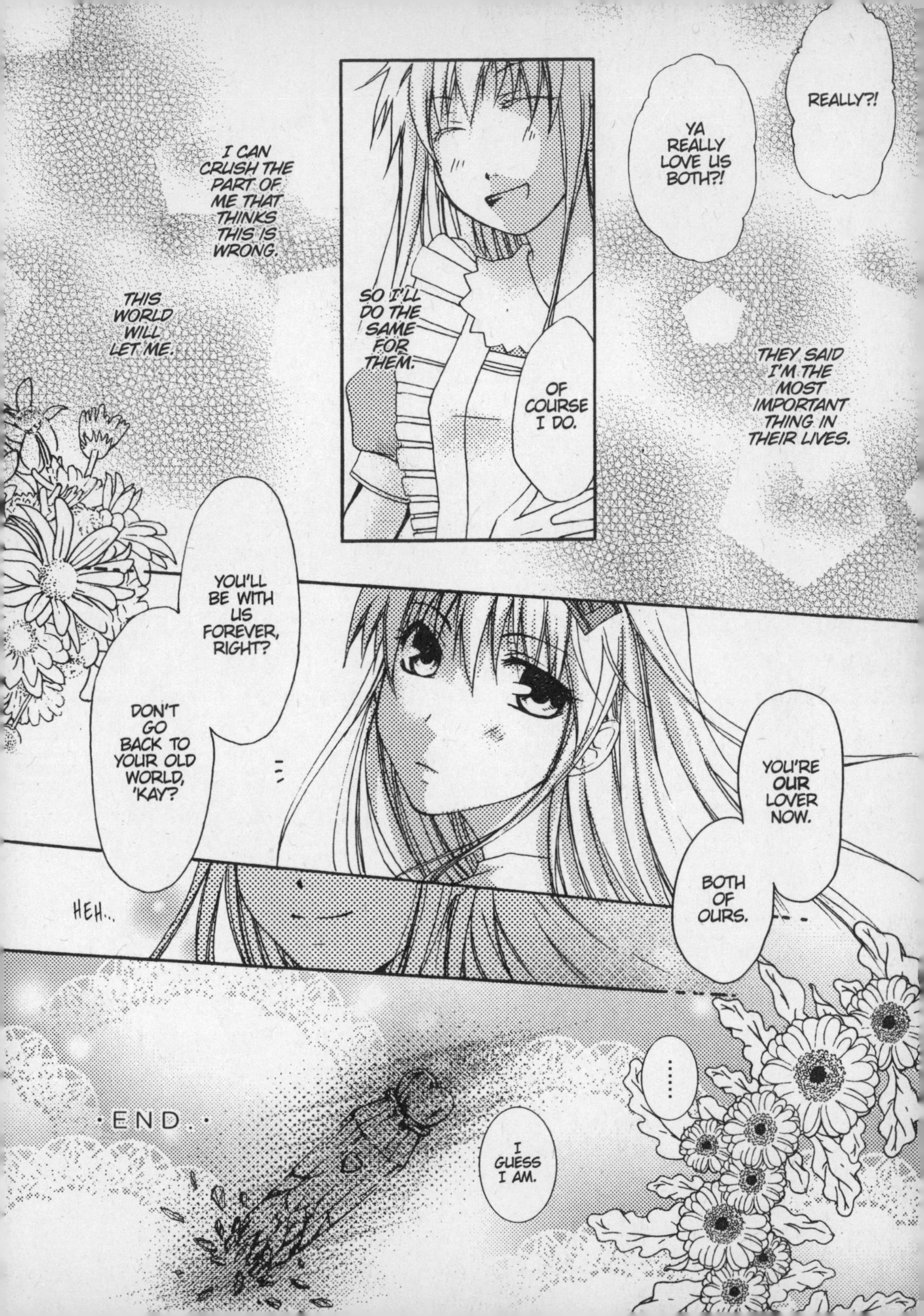
REALLY?!
YA REALLY LOVE US BOTH?!
THEY SAID I'M THE MOST IMPORTANT THING IN THEIR LIVES.
OF COURSE I DO.
SO I'LL DO THE SAME FOR THEM.
I CAN CRUSH THE PART OF ME THAT THINKS THIS IS WRONG.
THIS WORLD WILL LET ME.
YOU'RE OUR LOVER NOW.
BOTH OF OURS.
YOU'LL BE WITH US FOREVER, RIGHT?
DON'T GO BACK TO YOUR OLD WORLD, 'KAY?
HEH...
......
I GUESS I AM.
•END.•

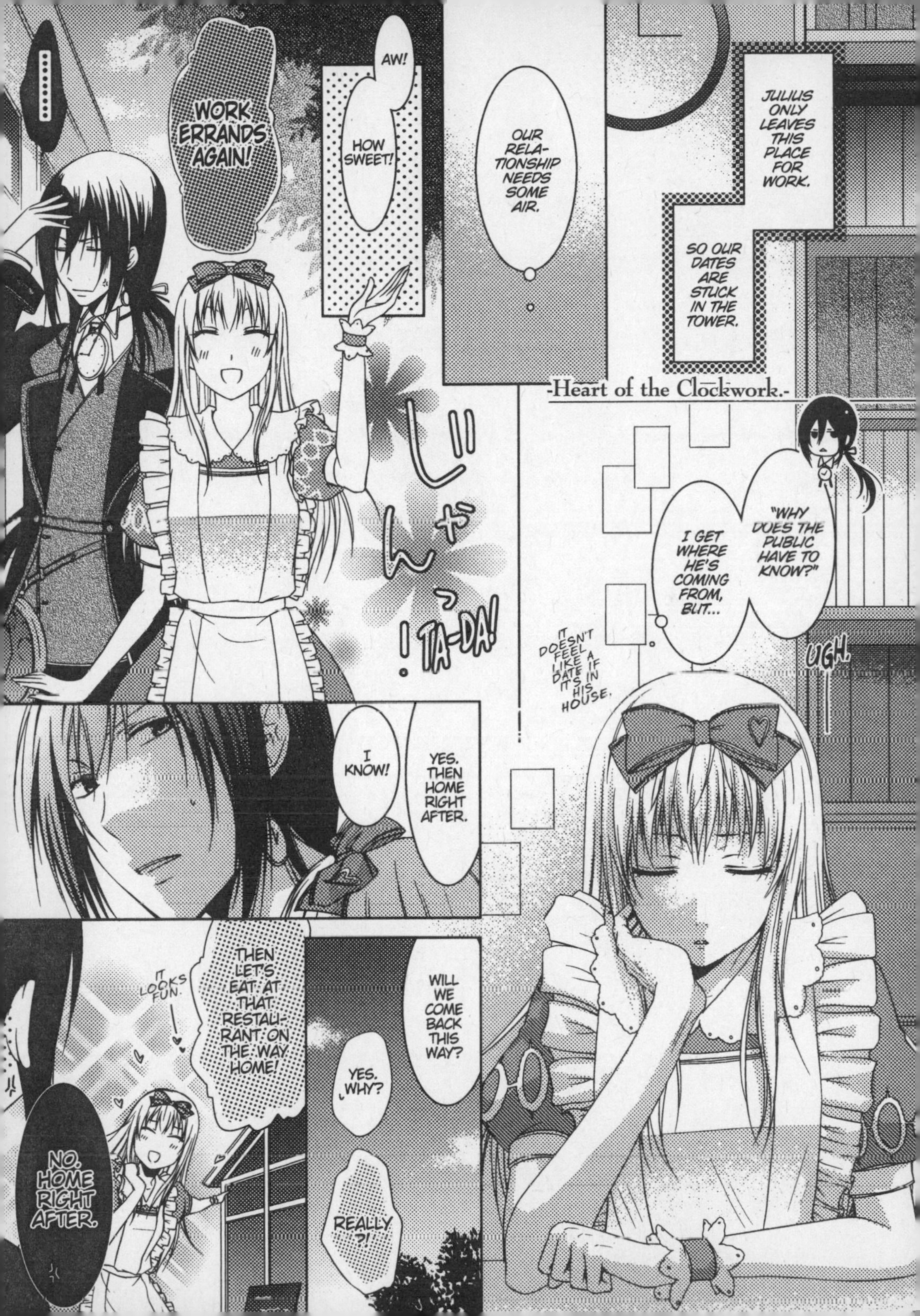
JULIUS ONLY LEAVES THIS PLACE FOR WORK.
SO OUR DATES ARE STUCK IN THE TOWER.
OUR RELATIONSHIP NEEDS SOME AIR.
-Heart of the Clockwork.-
"WHY DOES THE PUBLIC HAVE TO KNOW?"
I GET WHERE HE'S COMING FROM, BUT...
UGH.
IT DOESN'T FEEL LIKE A DATE IF IT'S IN HIS HOUSE.
AW!
HOW SWEET!
じゃんっ!
TA-DA!
WORK ERRANDS AGAIN!
......
YES. THEN HOME RIGHT AFTER.
I KNOW!
WILL WE COME BACK THIS WAY?
YES. WHY?
REALLY?!
THEN LET'S EAT AT THAT RESTAURANT ON THE WAY HOME!
IT LOOKS FUN.
NO. HOME RIGHT AFTER.

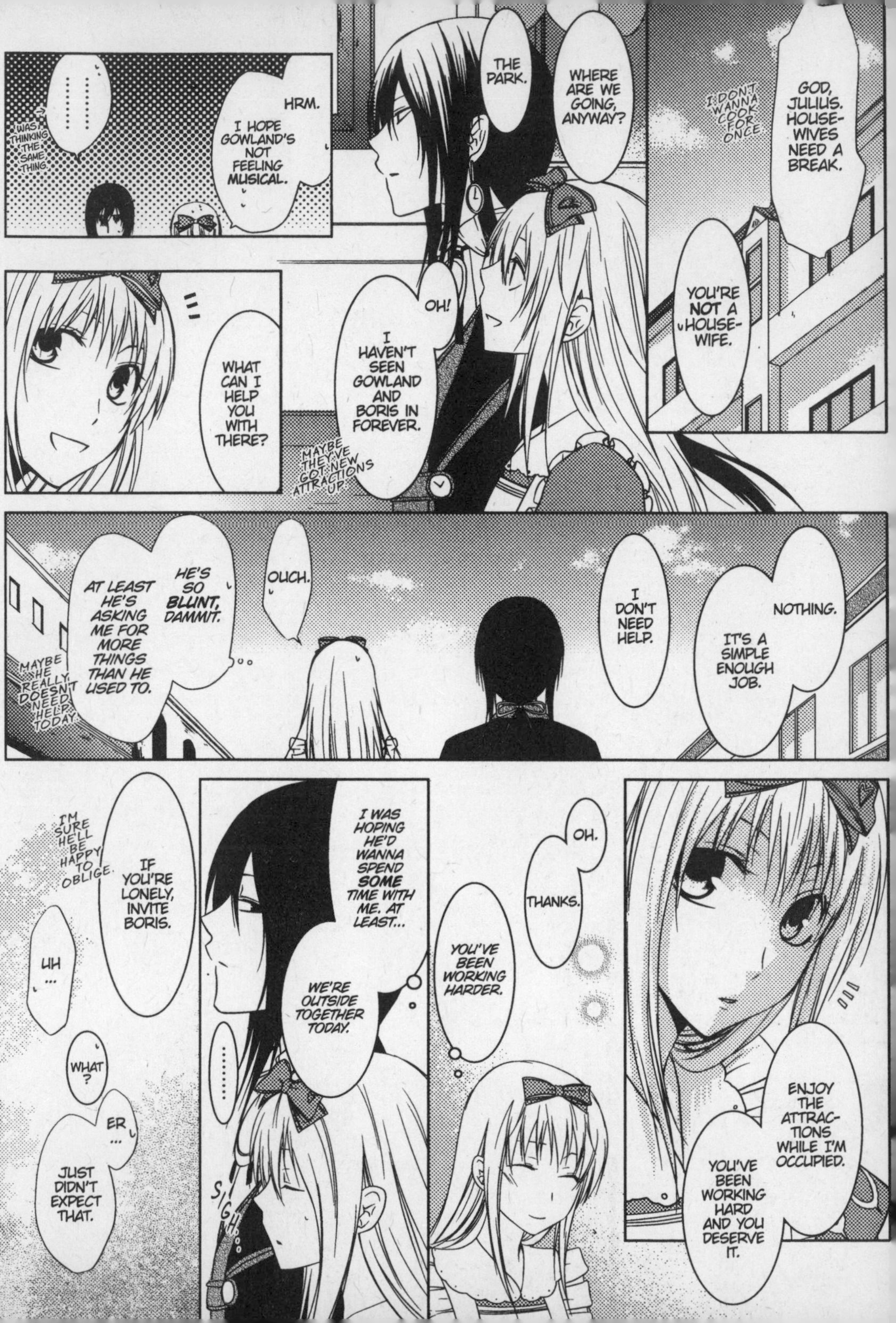
GOD, JULIUS. HOUSE-WIVES NEED A BREAK.
I DON'T WANNA COOK FOR ONCE.
YOU'RE NOT A HOUSE-WIFE.
WHERE ARE WE GOING, ANYWAY?
THE PARK.
HRM.
I HOPE GOWLAND'S NOT FEELING MUSICAL.
......
→WAS THINKING THE SAME THING.
OH!
I HAVEN'T SEEN GOWLAND AND BORIS IN FOREVER.
MAYBE THEY'VE GOT NEW ATTRACTIONS UP.
WHAT CAN I HELP YOU WITH THERE?
NOTHING.
IT'S A SIMPLE ENOUGH JOB.
I DON'T NEED HELP.
OUCH.
HE'S SO BLUNT, DAMMIT.
AT LEAST HE'S ASKING ME FOR MORE THINGS THAN HE USED TO.
MAYBE HE REALLY DOESN'T NEED HELP TODAY.
ENJOY THE ATTRAC-TIONS WHILE I'M OCCUPIED.
YOU'VE BEEN WORKING HARD AND YOU DESERVE IT.
OH.
THANKS.
YOU'VE BEEN WORKING HARDER.
I WAS HOPING HE'D WANNA SPEND SOME TIME WITH ME. AT LEAST...
WE'RE OUTSIDE TOGETHER TODAY.
......
SIGH
IF YOU'RE LONELY, INVITE BORIS.
I'M SURE HE'LL BE HAPPY TO OBLIGE.
UH ...
WHAT ?
ER ...
JUST DIDN'T EXPECT THAT.

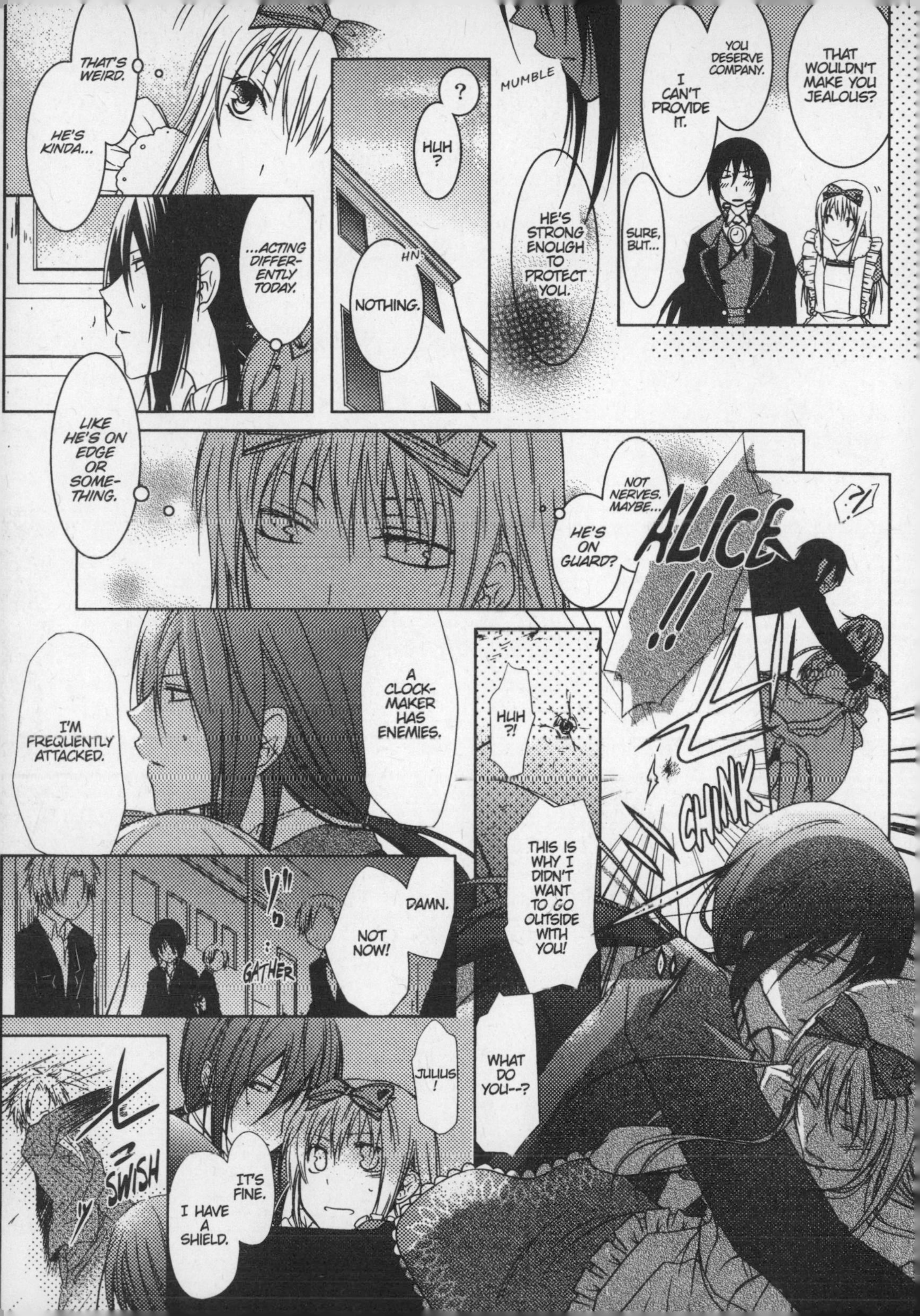
THAT WOULDN'T MAKE YOU JEALOUS?
YOU DESERVE COMPANY.
I CAN'T PROVIDE IT.
SURE, BUT...
MUMBLE
HE'S STRONG ENOUGH TO PROTECT YOU.
?
HUH?
HN
NOTHING.
THAT'S WEIRD.
HE'S KINDA...
...ACTING DIFFERENTLY TODAY.
LIKE HE'S ON EDGE OR SOMETHING.
NOT NERVES. MAYBE...
HE'S ON GUARD?
?!
ALICE!!
HUH?!
CHINK
A CLOCKMAKER HAS ENEMIES.
I'M FREQUENTLY ATTACKED.
THIS IS WHY I DIDN'T WANT TO GO OUTSIDE WITH YOU!
DAMN.
NOT NOW!
GATHER
WHAT DO YOU--?
JULIUS!
IT'S FINE.
I HAVE A SHIELD.
SWISH

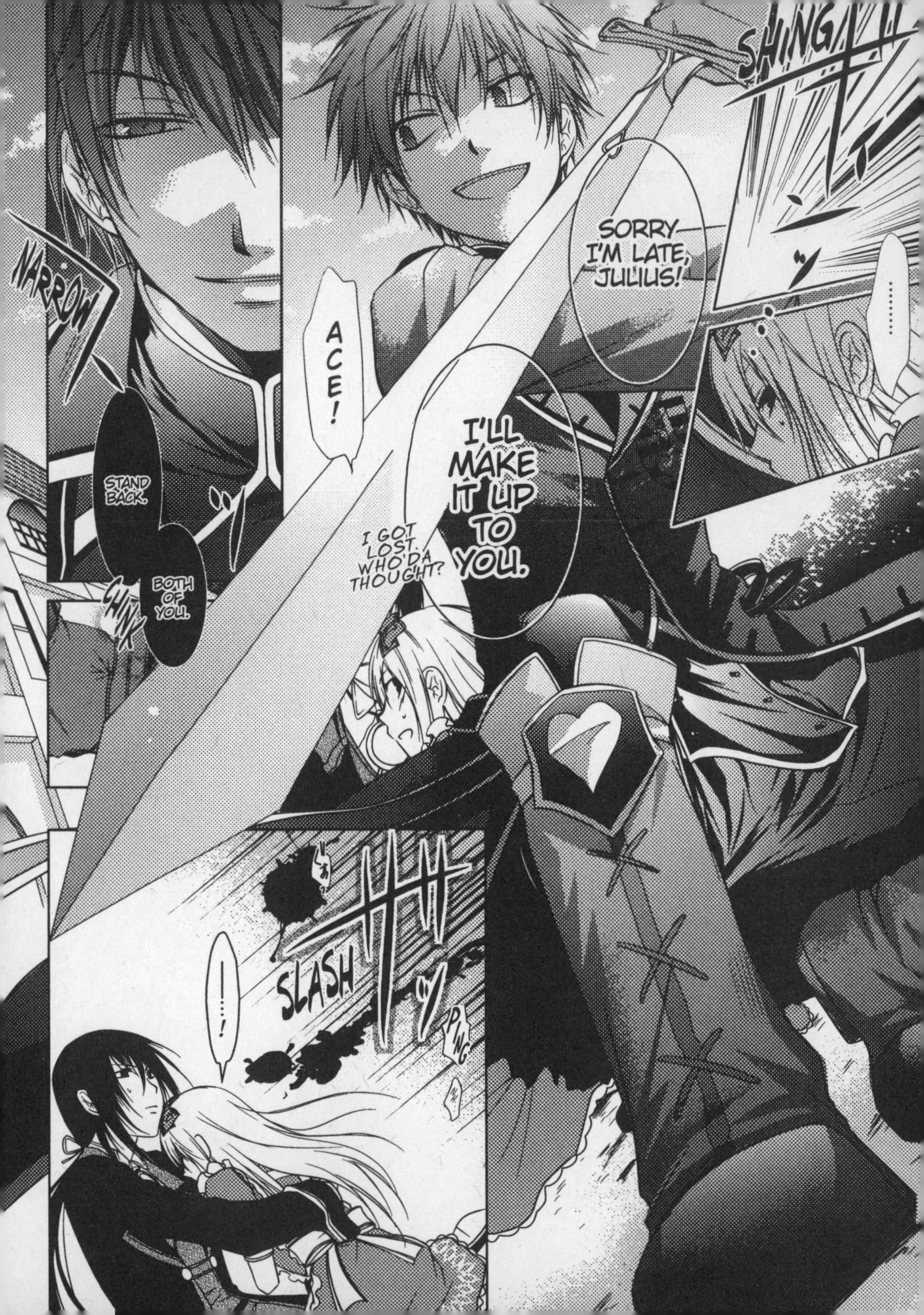
SHING
......
SORRY I'M LATE, JULIUS!
ACE!
I'LL MAKE IT UP TO YOU.
I GOT LOST. WHO'DA THOUGHT?
NARROW
STAND BACK.
BOTH OF YOU.
CHINK
SLASH
PING
...!

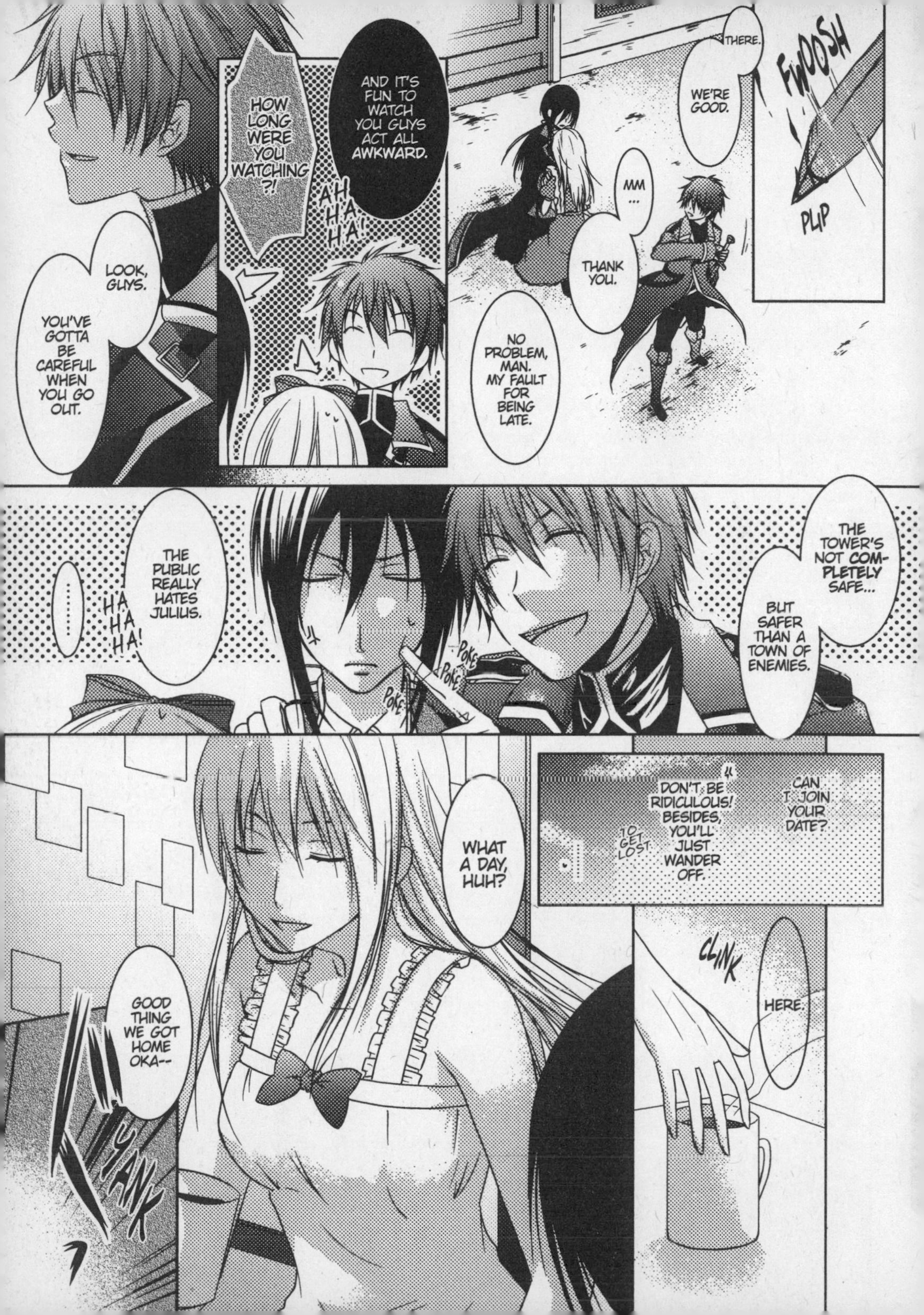
FWOOSH
PLIP
THERE.
WE'RE GOOD.
MM...
THANK YOU.
NO PROBLEM, MAN. MY FAULT FOR BEING LATE.
AND IT'S FUN TO WATCH YOU GUYS ACT ALL AWKWARD.
HOW LONG WERE YOU WATCHING?!
AH HA HA!
LOOK, GUYS.
YOU'VE GOTTA BE CAREFUL WHEN YOU GO OUT.
THE TOWER'S NOT COMPLETELY SAFE...
BUT SAFER THAN A TOWN OF ENEMIES.
POKE POKE POKE
THE PUBLIC REALLY HATES JULIUS.
HA HA HA!
......
CAN I JOIN YOUR DATE?
DON'T BE RIDICULOUS! BESIDES, YOU'LL JUST WANDER OFF.
TO GET LOST.
...
CLINK
HERE.
WHAT A DAY, HUH?
GOOD THING WE GOT HOME OKA--
YANK

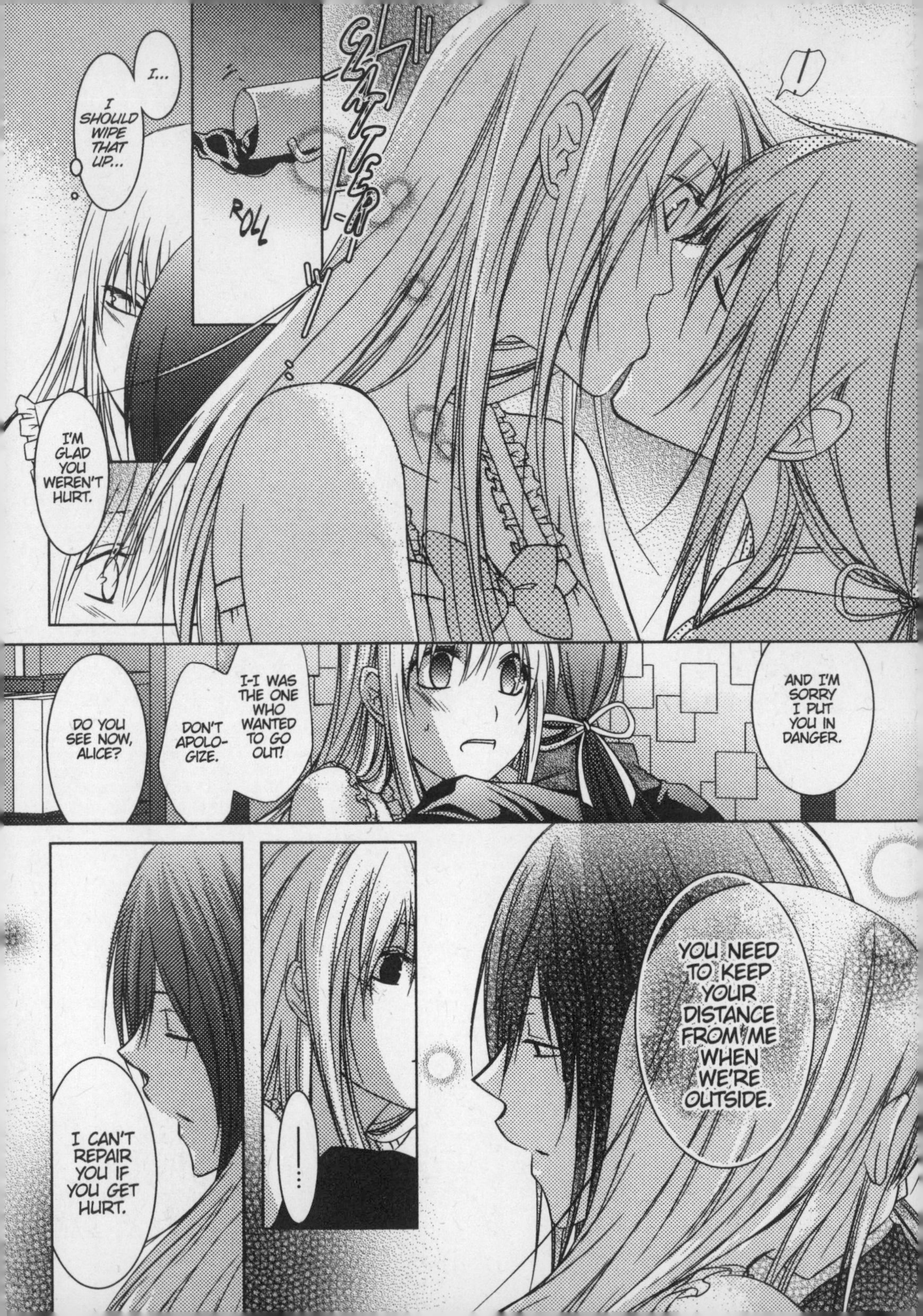
!
CLATTER
ROLL
I...
I SHOULD WIPE THAT UP...
I'M GLAD YOU WEREN'T HURT.
AND I'M SORRY I PUT YOU IN DANGER.
I-I WAS THE ONE WHO WANTED TO GO OUT!
DON'T APOLOGIZE.
DO YOU SEE NOW, ALICE?
YOU NEED TO KEEP YOUR DISTANCE FROM ME WHEN WE'RE OUTSIDE.
!...
I CAN'T REPAIR YOU IF YOU GET HURT.

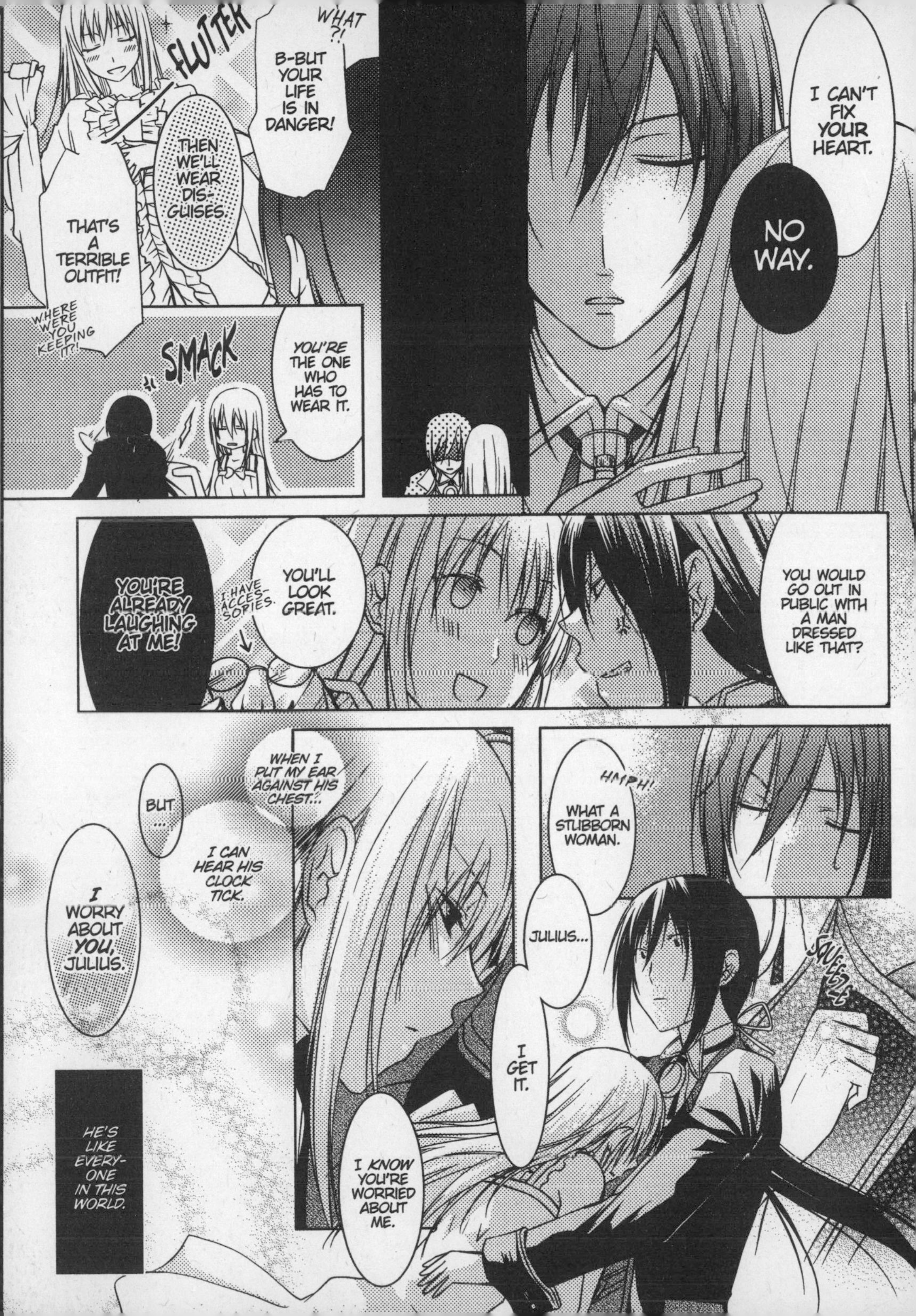
I CAN'T FIX YOUR HEART.
NO WAY.
WHAT?!
B-BUT YOUR LIFE IS IN DANGER!
FLUTTER
THEN WE'LL WEAR DISGUISES.
THAT'S A TERRIBLE OUTFIT!
WHERE WERE YOU KEEPING IT?!
YOU'RE THE ONE WHO HAS TO WEAR IT.
SMACK
YOU WOULD GO OUT IN PUBLIC WITH A MAN DRESSED LIKE THAT?
YOU'LL LOOK GREAT.
I HAVE ACCESSORIES.
YOU'RE ALREADY LAUGHING AT ME!
HMPH!
WHAT A STUBBORN WOMAN.
JULIUS...
SQUEEZE
I GET IT.
I KNOW YOU'RE WORRIED ABOUT ME.
WHEN I PUT MY EAR AGAINST HIS CHEST...
BUT...
I CAN HEAR HIS CLOCK TICK.
I WORRY ABOUT YOU, JULIUS.
HE'S LIKE EVERYONE IN THIS WORLD.

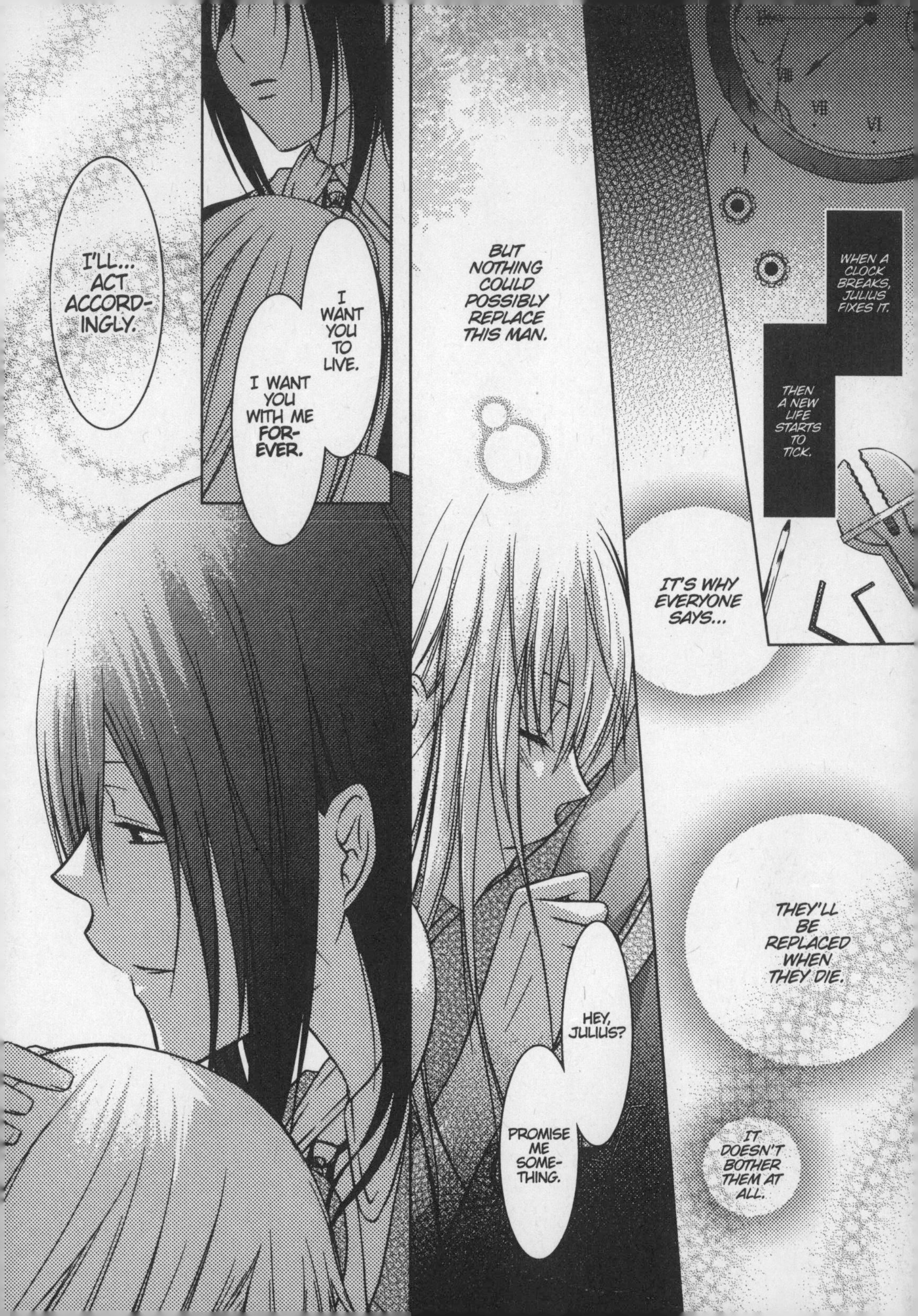
WHEN A CLOCK BREAKS, JULIUS FIXES IT.
THEN A NEW LIFE STARTS TO TICK.
IT'S WHY EVERYONE SAYS...
THEY'LL BE REPLACED WHEN THEY DIE.
IT DOESN'T BOTHER THEM AT ALL.
BUT NOTHING COULD POSSIBLY REPLACE THIS MAN.
HEY, JULIUS?
PROMISE ME SOMETHING.
I WANT YOU TO LIVE.
I WANT YOU WITH ME FOREVER.
I'LL... ACT ACCORDINGLY.

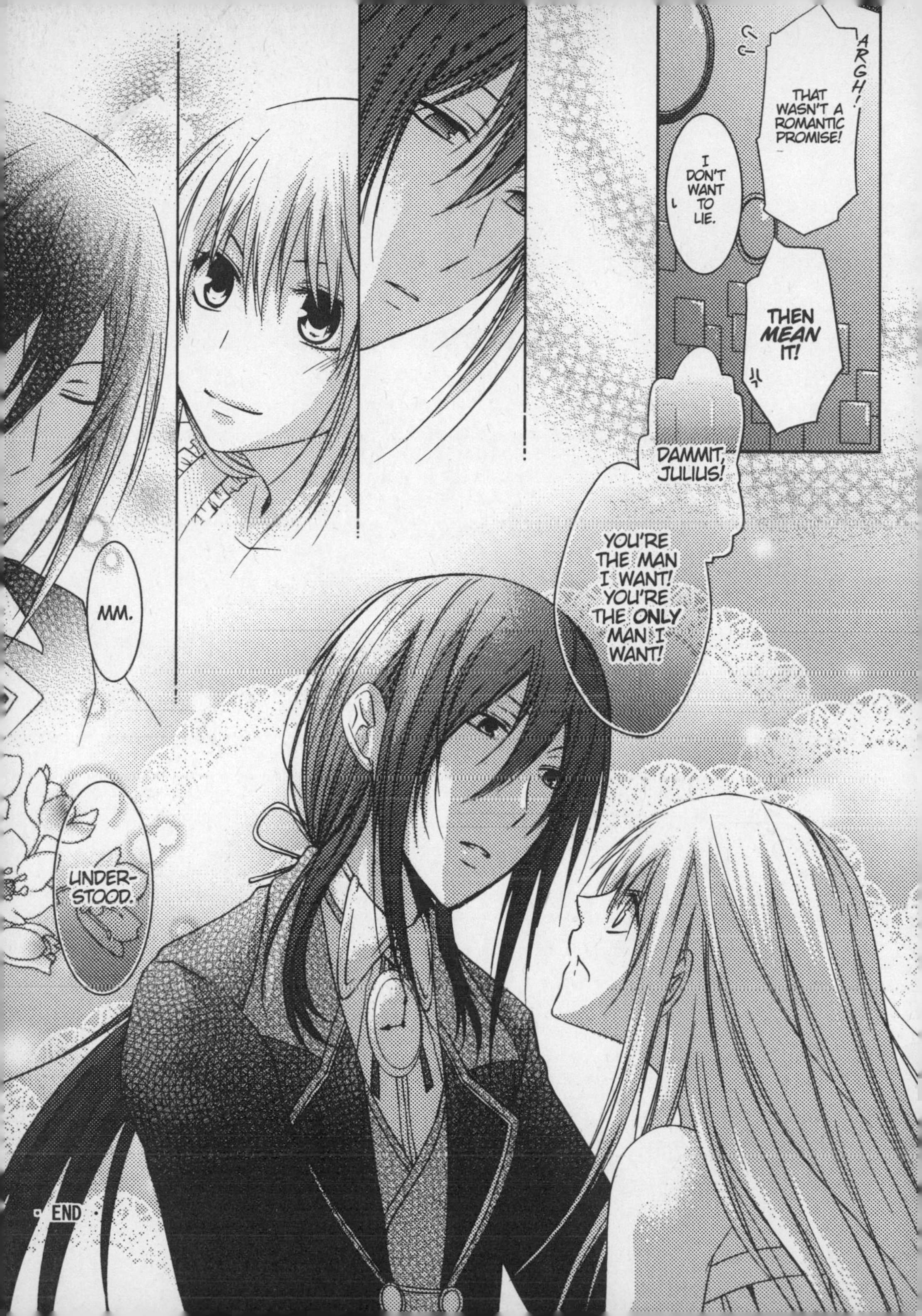
ARGH!
THAT WASN'T A ROMANTIC PROMISE!
I DON'T WANT TO LIE.
THEN MEAN IT!
DAMMIT, JULIUS!
YOU'RE THE MAN I WANT! YOU'RE THE ONLY MAN I WANT!
MM.
UNDER-STOOD.
END

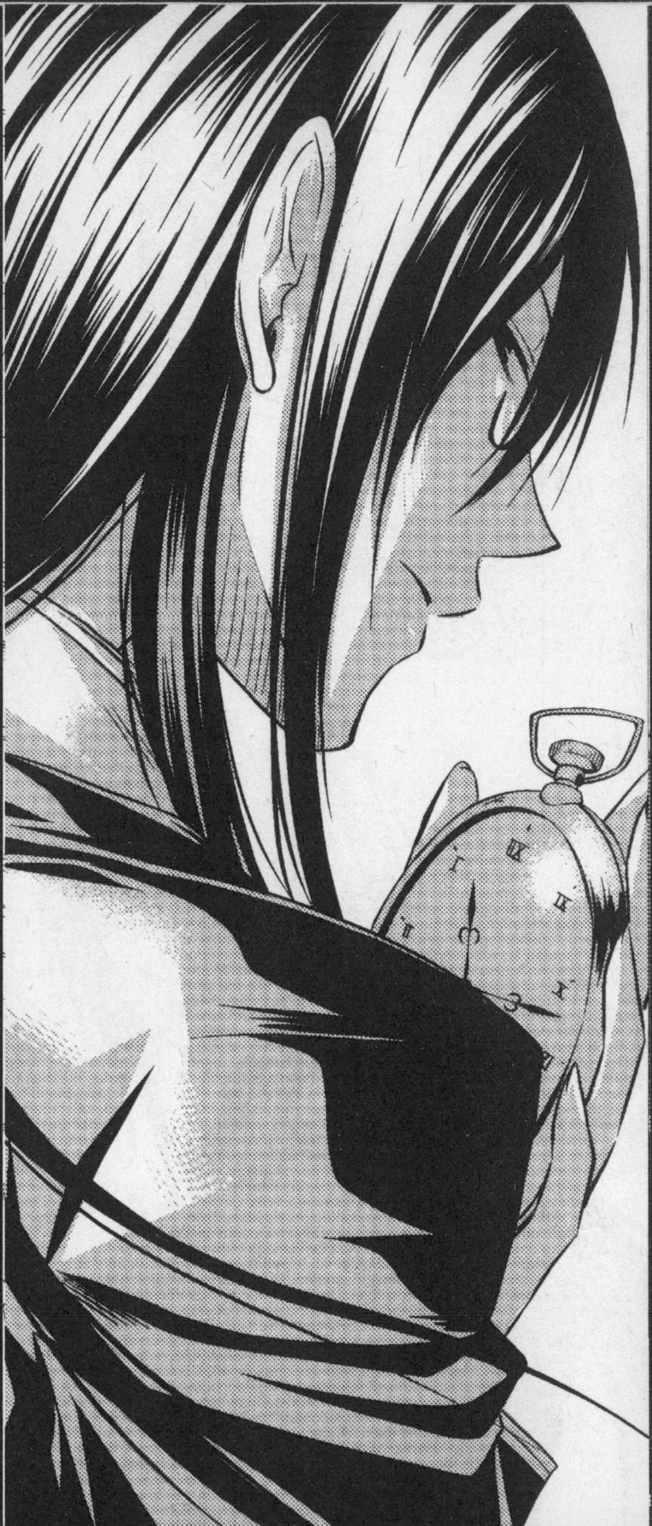

QuinRoseBox

QuinRoseBox

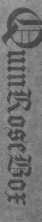

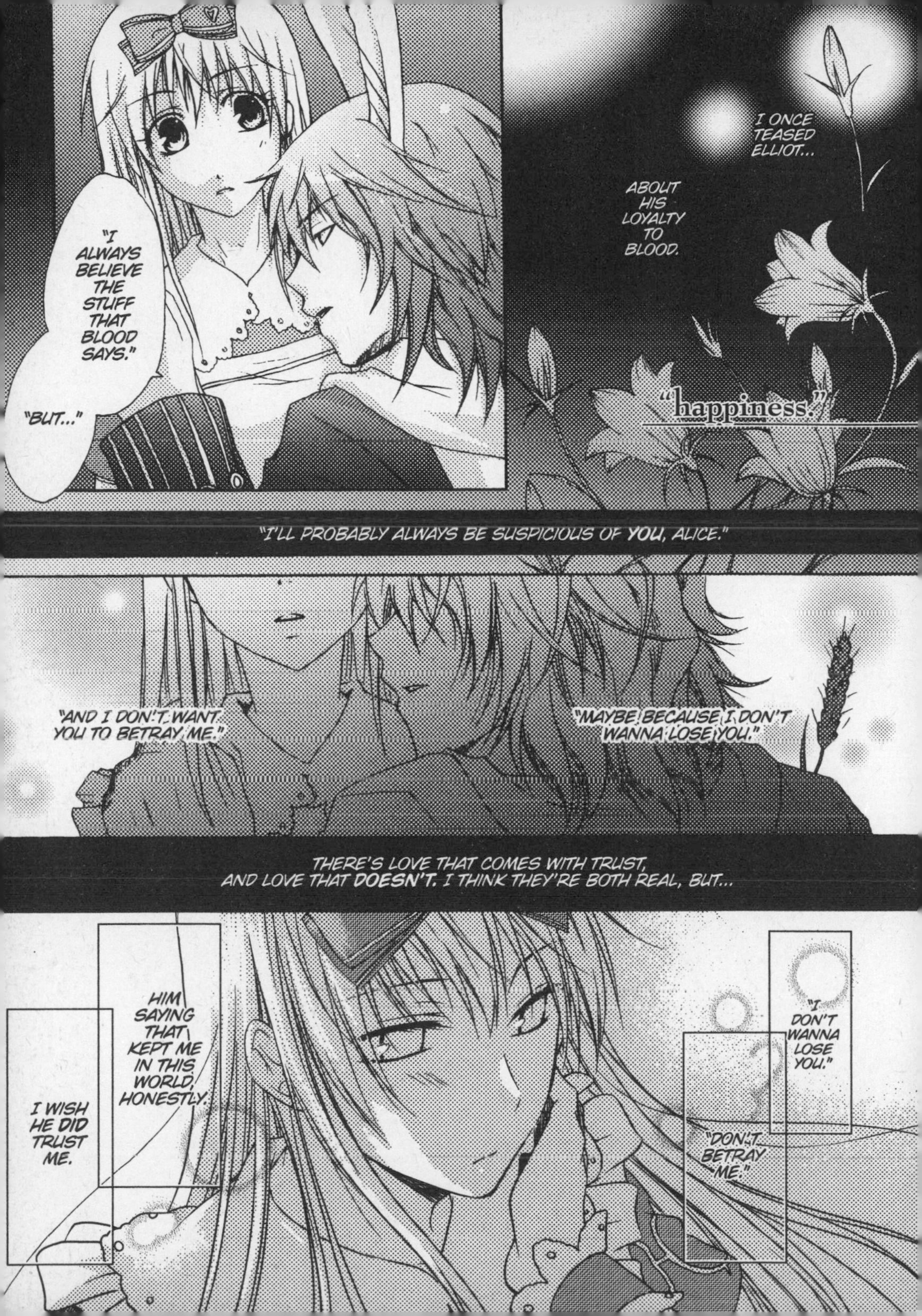
I ONCE TEASED ELLIOT...
ABOUT HIS LOYALTY TO BLOOD.
"happiness."
"I ALWAYS BELIEVE THE STUFF THAT BLOOD SAYS."
"BUT..."
"I'LL PROBABLY ALWAYS BE SUSPICIOUS OF YOU, ALICE."
"MAYBE BECAUSE I DON'T WANNA LOSE YOU."
"AND I DON'T WANT YOU TO BETRAY ME."
THERE'S LOVE THAT COMES WITH TRUST, AND LOVE THAT DOESN'T. I THINK THEY'RE BOTH REAL, BUT...
"I DON'T WANNA LOSE YOU."
"DON'T BETRAY ME."
HIM SAYING THAT KEPT ME IN THIS WORLD, HONESTLY.
I WISH HE DID TRUST ME.

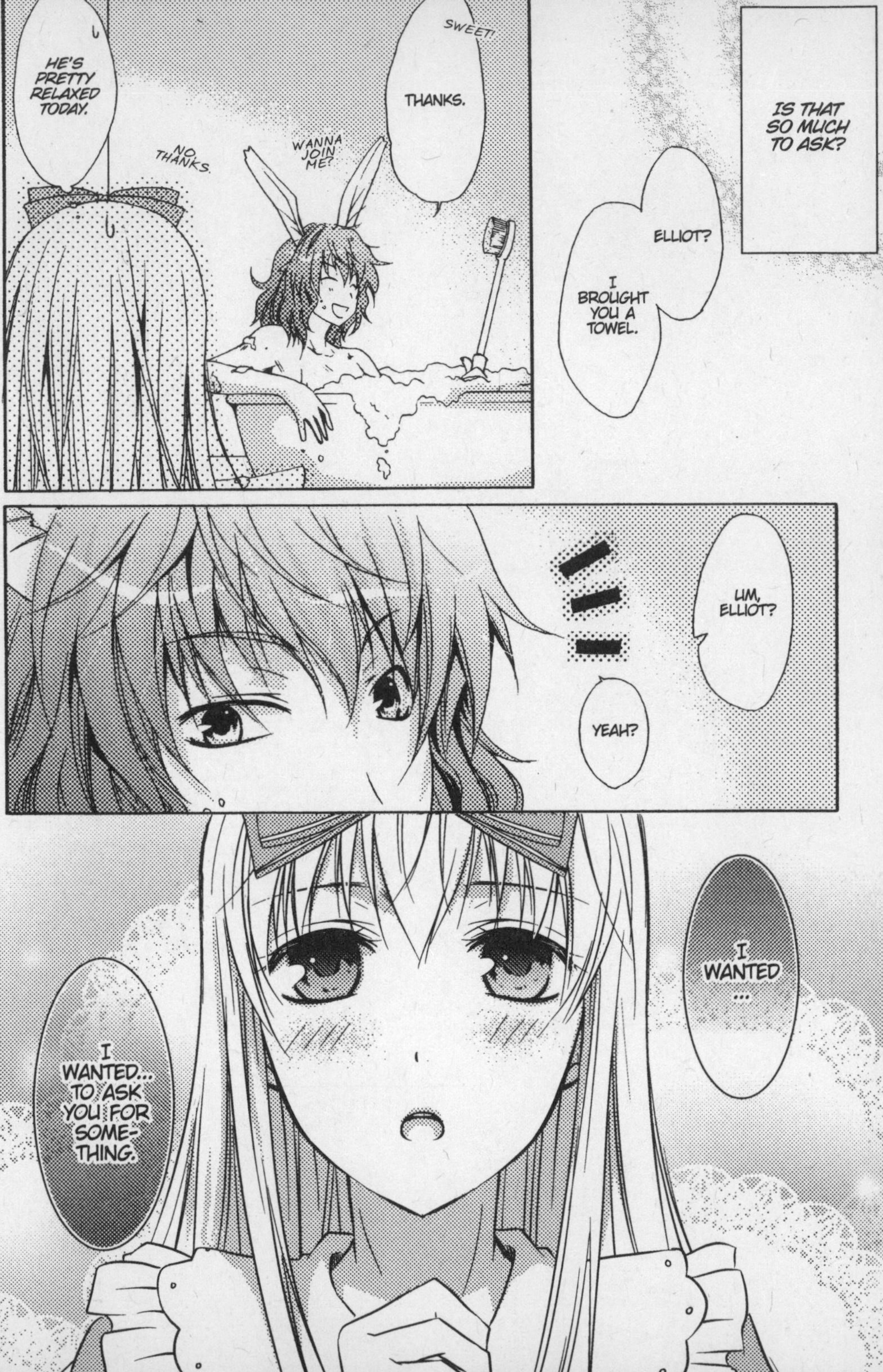
IS THAT SO MUCH TO ASK?
ELLIOT?
I BROUGHT YOU A TOWEL.
SWEET!
THANKS.
WANNA JOIN ME?
NO THANKS.
HE'S PRETTY RELAXED TODAY.
UM, ELLIOT?
YEAH?
I WANTED...
I WANTED... TO ASK YOU FOR SOME-THING.

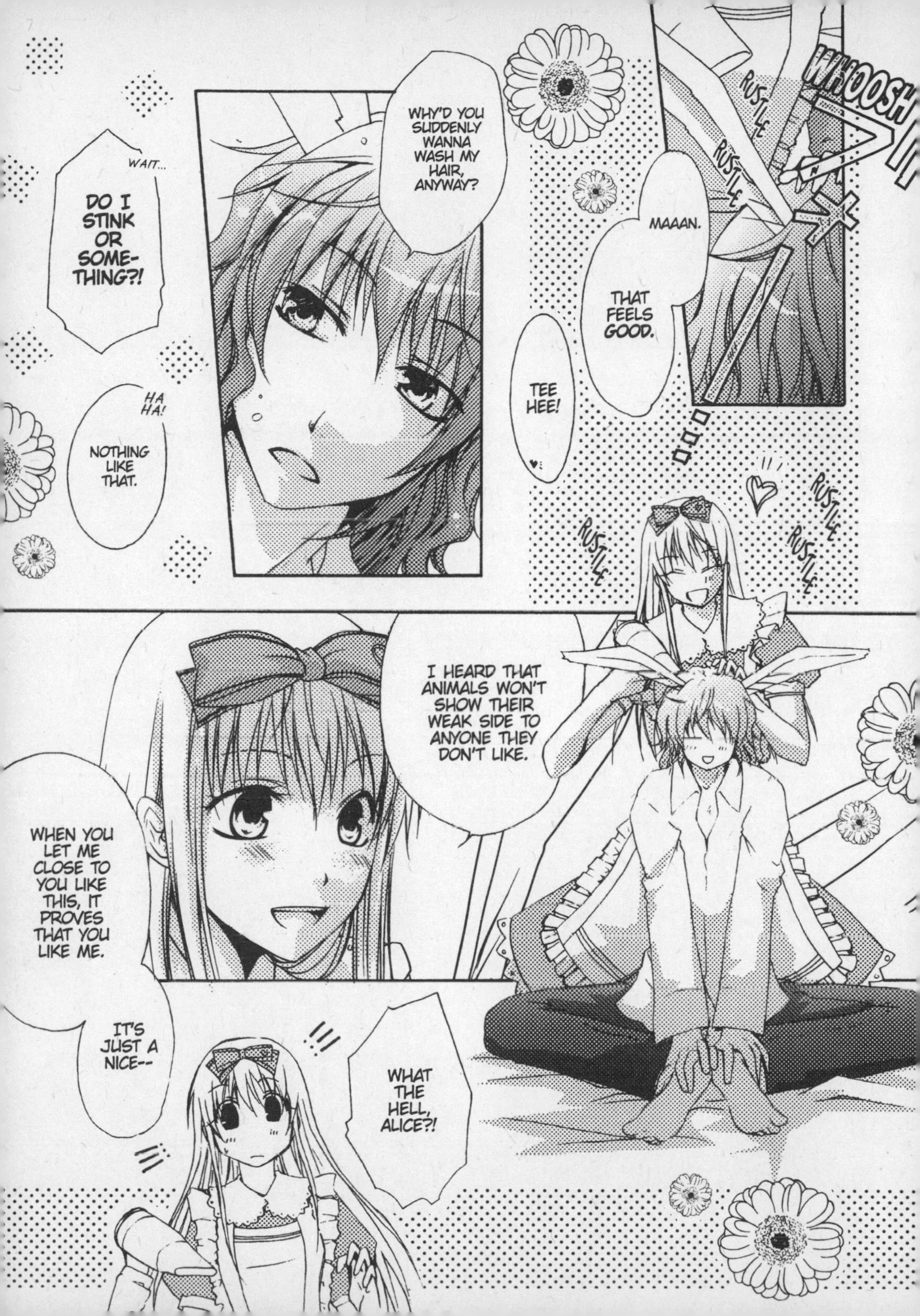
WHOOSH
RUSTLE
RUSTLE
MAAAN.
THAT FEELS GOOD.
TEE HEE!
RUSTLE
RUSTLE
RUSTLE
WHY'D YOU SUDDENLY WANNA WASH MY HAIR, ANYWAY?
WAIT...
DO I STINK OR SOME-THING?!
HA HA!
NOTHING LIKE THAT.
I HEARD THAT ANIMALS WON'T SHOW THEIR WEAK SIDE TO ANYONE THEY DON'T LIKE.
WHEN YOU LET ME CLOSE TO YOU LIKE THIS, IT PROVES THAT YOU LIKE ME.
IT'S JUST A NICE--
WHAT THE HELL, ALICE?!

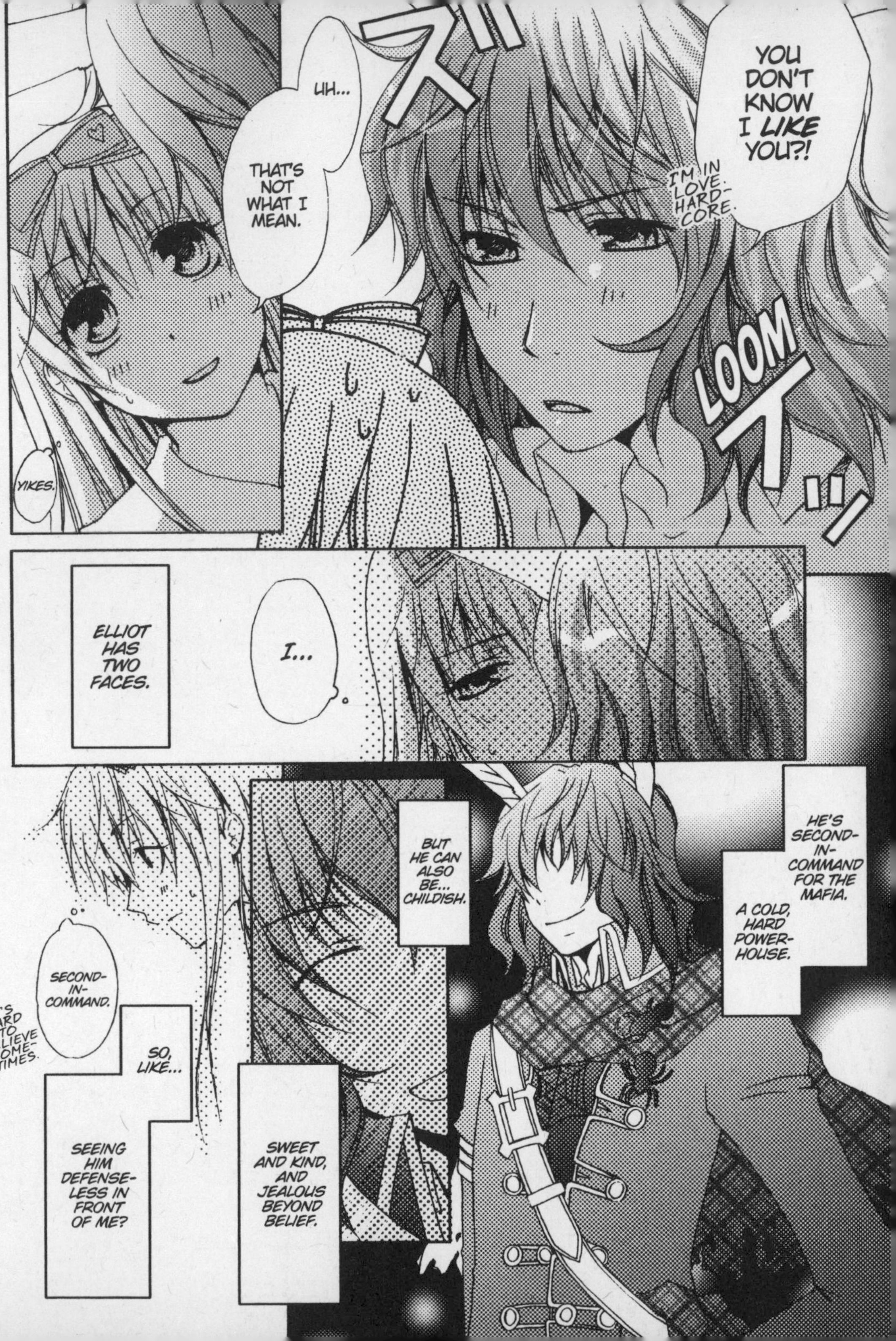
YOU DON'T KNOW I LIKE YOU?!
I'M IN LOVE. HARD-CORE.
LOOM
UH...
THAT'S NOT WHAT I MEAN.
YIKES.
I...
ELLIOT HAS TWO FACES.
HE'S SECOND-IN-COMMAND FOR THE MAFIA.
A COLD, HARD POWER-HOUSE.
BUT HE CAN ALSO BE... CHILDISH.
SWEET AND KIND, AND JEALOUS BEYOND BELIEF.
SECOND-IN-COMMAND.
IT'S HARD TO BELIEVE SOMETIMES.
SO, LIKE...
SEEING HIM DEFENSELESS IN FRONT OF ME?

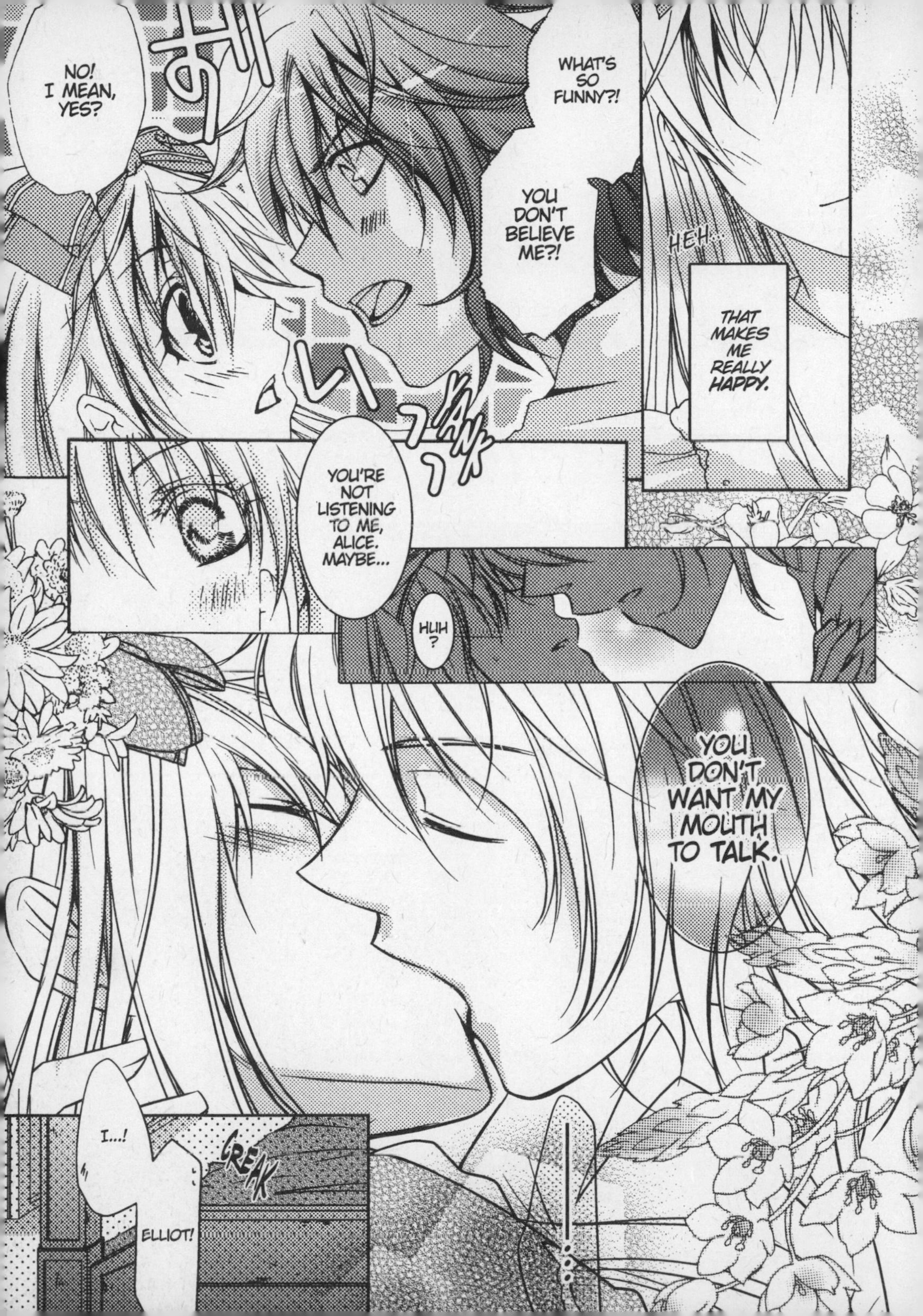
HEH...
THAT MAKES ME REALLY HAPPY.
WHAT'S SO FUNNY?!
YOU DON'T BELIEVE ME?!
NO! I MEAN, YES?
YANK
YOU'RE NOT LISTENING TO ME, ALICE. MAYBE...
HUH?
YOU DON'T WANT MY MOUTH TO TALK.
......!
I...!
CREAK
ELLIOT!

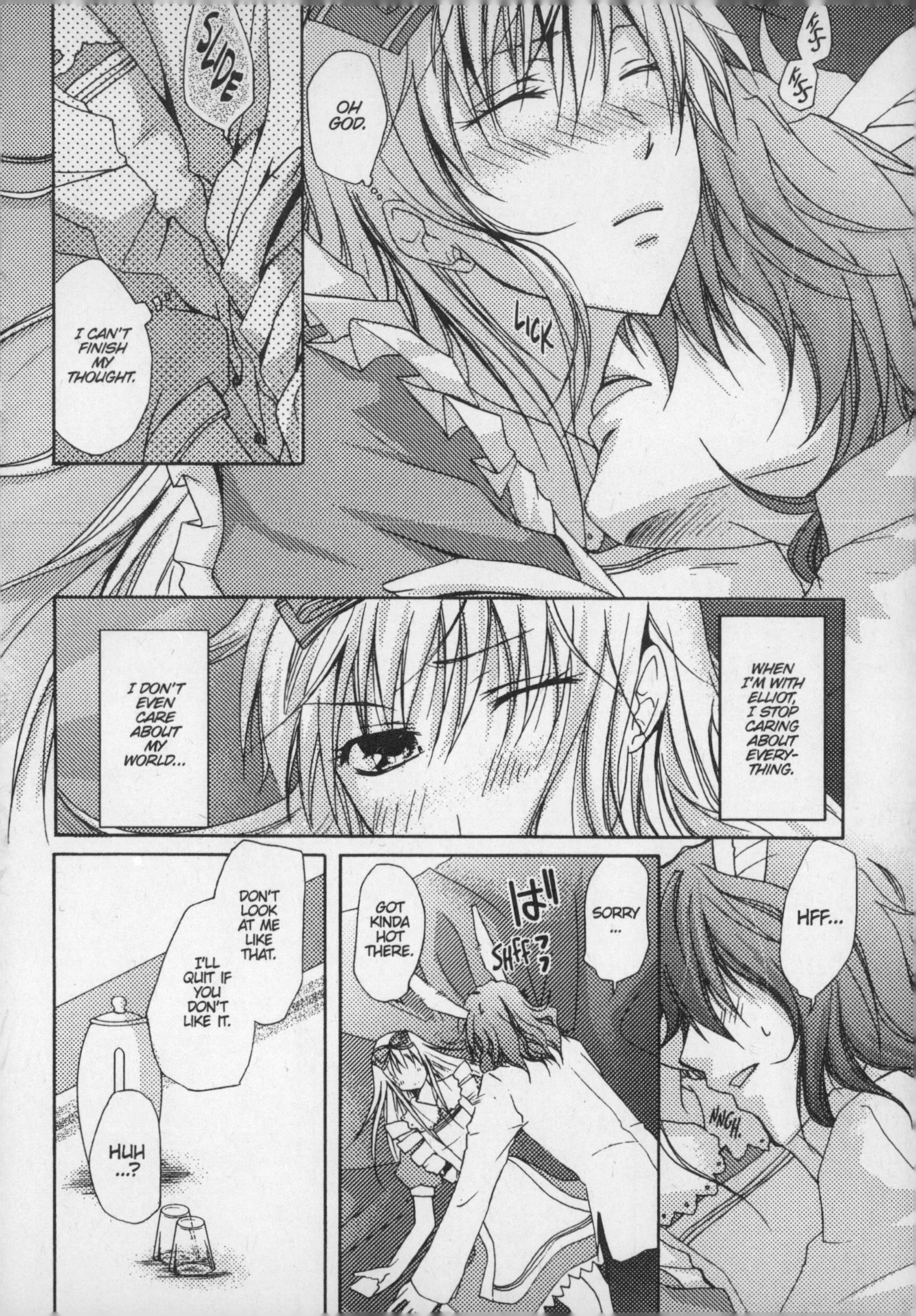
KISS
KISS
OH GOD.
LICK
SLIDE
I CAN'T FINISH MY THOUGHT.
WHEN I'M WITH ELLIOT, I STOP CARING ABOUT EVERY-THING.
I DON'T EVEN CARE ABOUT MY WORLD...
HFF...
SORRY...
ぱ
SHFF
GOT KINDA HOT THERE.
NNGH.
DON'T LOOK AT ME LIKE THAT.
I'LL QUIT IF YOU DON'T LIKE IT.
HUH...?

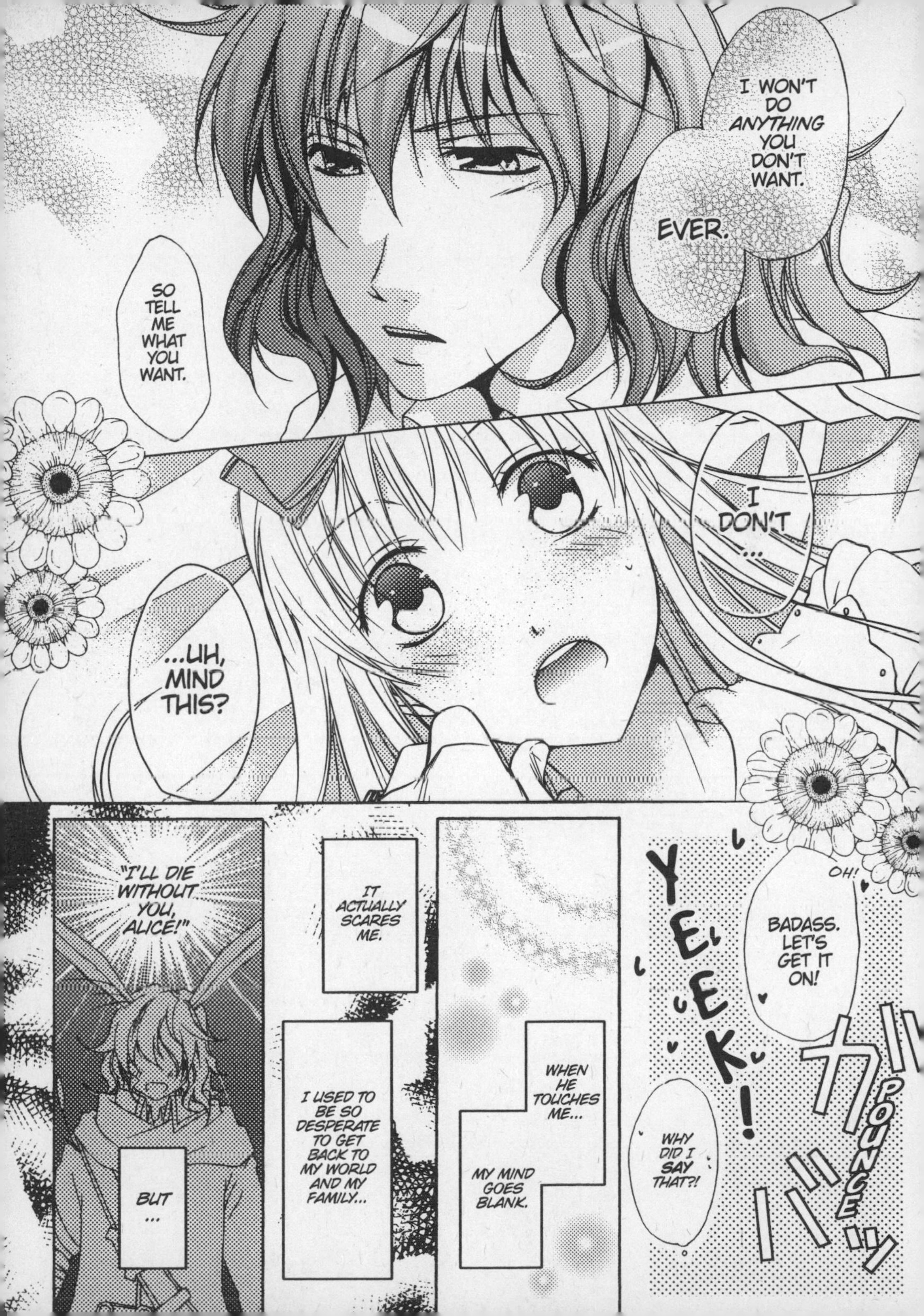
I WON'T DO ANYTHING YOU DON'T WANT.
EVER.
SO TELL ME WHAT YOU WANT.
I DON'T ...
...UH, MIND THIS?
OH!
BADASS. LET'S GET IT ON!
YEEK!
POUNCE
WHY DID I SAY THAT?!
WHEN HE TOUCHES ME...
MY MIND GOES BLANK.
IT ACTUALLY SCARES ME.
I USED TO BE SO DESPERATE TO GET BACK TO MY WORLD AND MY FAMILY...
"I'LL DIE WITHOUT YOU, ALICE!"
BUT ...

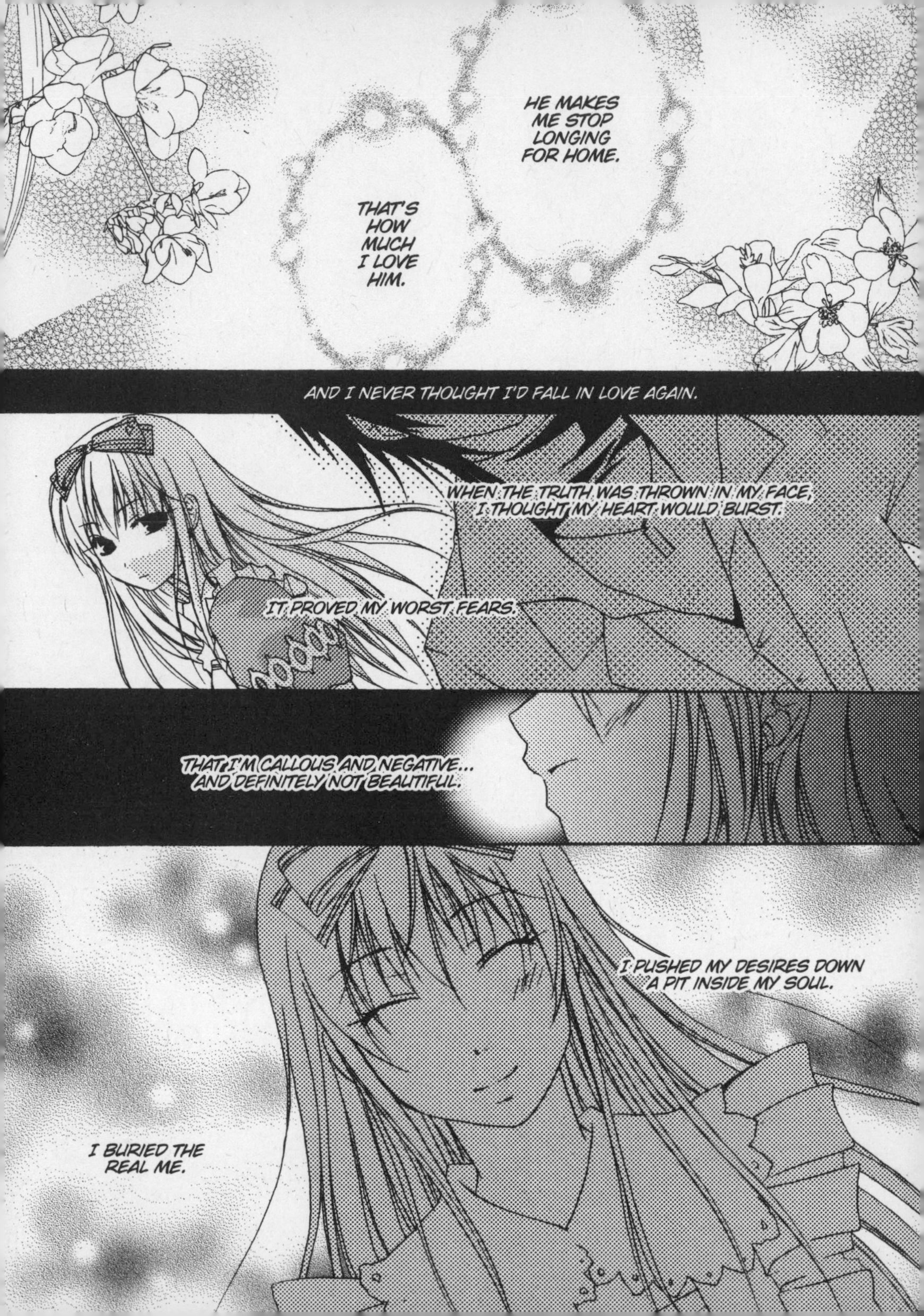
HE MAKES ME STOP LONGING FOR HOME.
THAT'S HOW MUCH I LOVE HIM.
AND I NEVER THOUGHT I'D FALL IN LOVE AGAIN.
WHEN THE TRUTH WAS THROWN IN MY FACE, I THOUGHT MY HEART WOULD BURST.
IT PROVED MY WORST FEARS.
THAT I'M CALLOUS AND NEGATIVE... AND DEFINITELY NOT BEAUTIFUL.
I PUSHED MY DESIRES DOWN A PIT INSIDE MY SOUL.
I BURIED THE REAL ME.

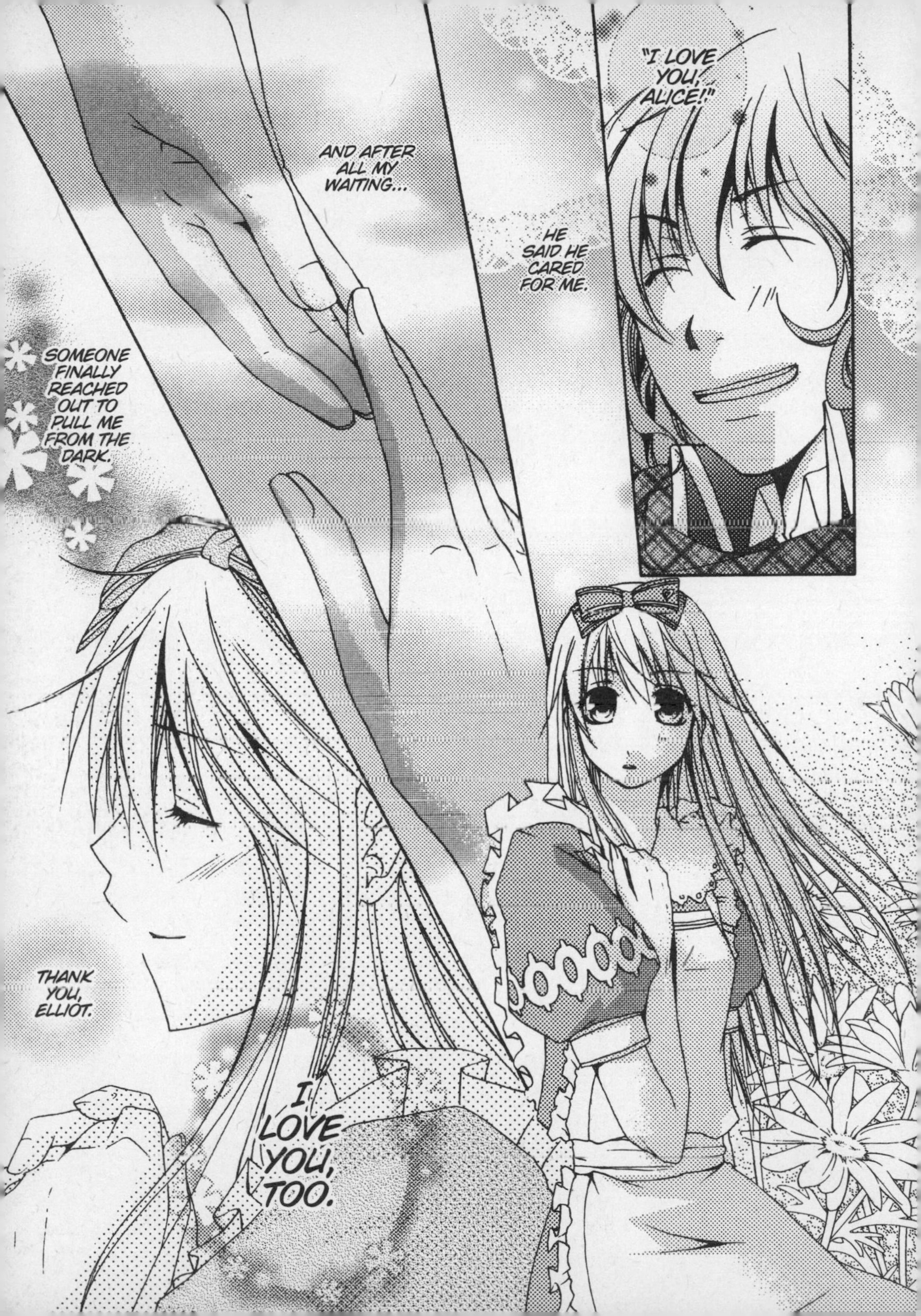
"I LOVE YOU, ALICE!"
HE SAID HE CARED FOR ME.
AND AFTER ALL MY WAITING...
SOMEONE FINALLY REACHED OUT TO PULL ME FROM THE DARK.
THANK YOU, ELLIOT.
I LOVE YOU, TOO.

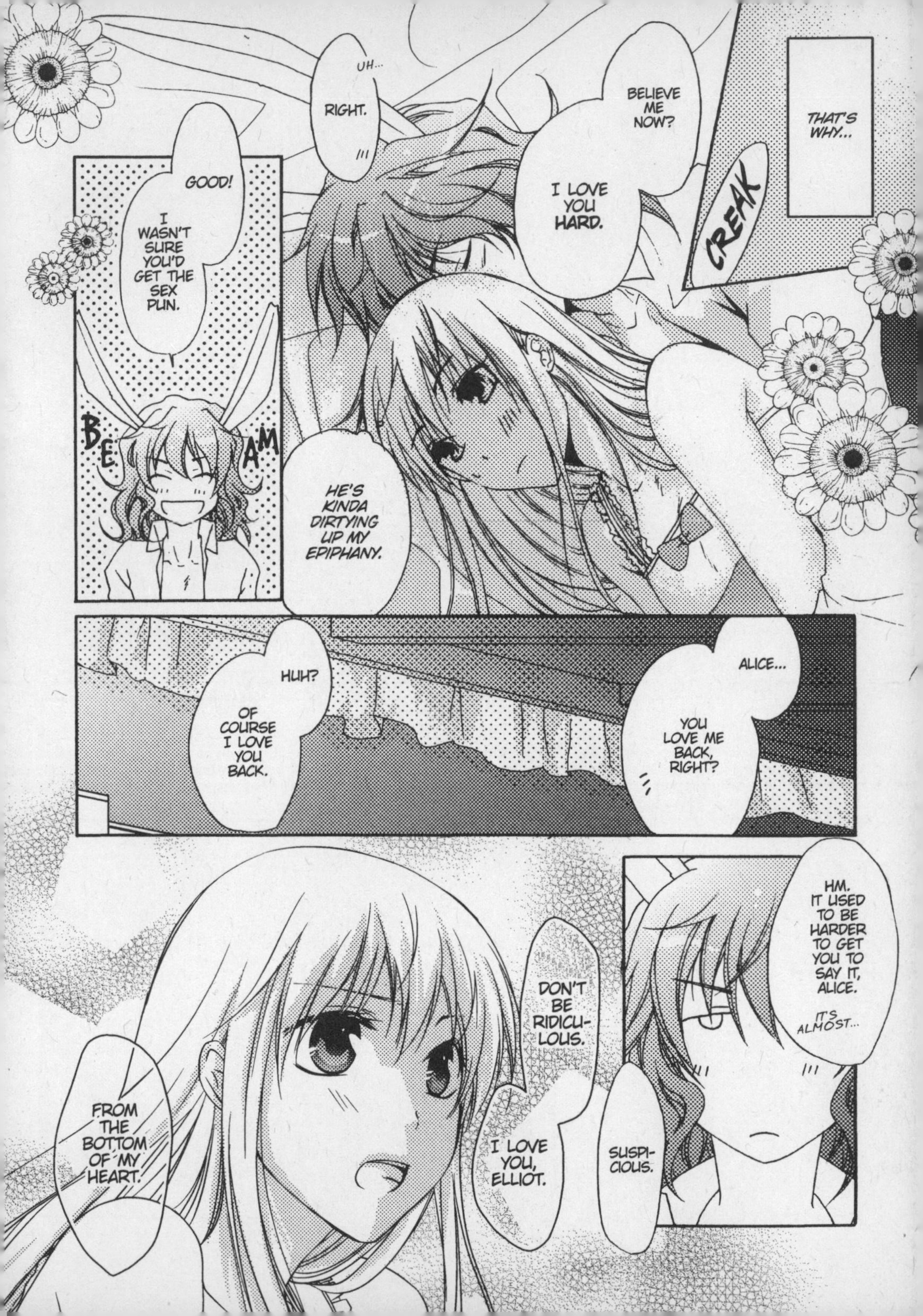
THAT'S WHY...
CREAK
BELIEVE ME NOW?
I LOVE YOU HARD.
UH... RIGHT.
GOOD!
I WASN'T SURE YOU'D GET THE SEX PUN.
BEAM
HE'S KINDA DIRTYING UP MY EPIPHANY.
ALICE...
YOU LOVE ME BACK, RIGHT?
HUH?
OF COURSE I LOVE YOU BACK.
HM. IT USED TO BE HARDER TO GET YOU TO SAY IT, ALICE.
IT'S ALMOST...
SUSPICIOUS.
DON'T BE RIDICULOUS.
I LOVE YOU, ELLIOT.
FROM THE BOTTOM OF MY HEART.

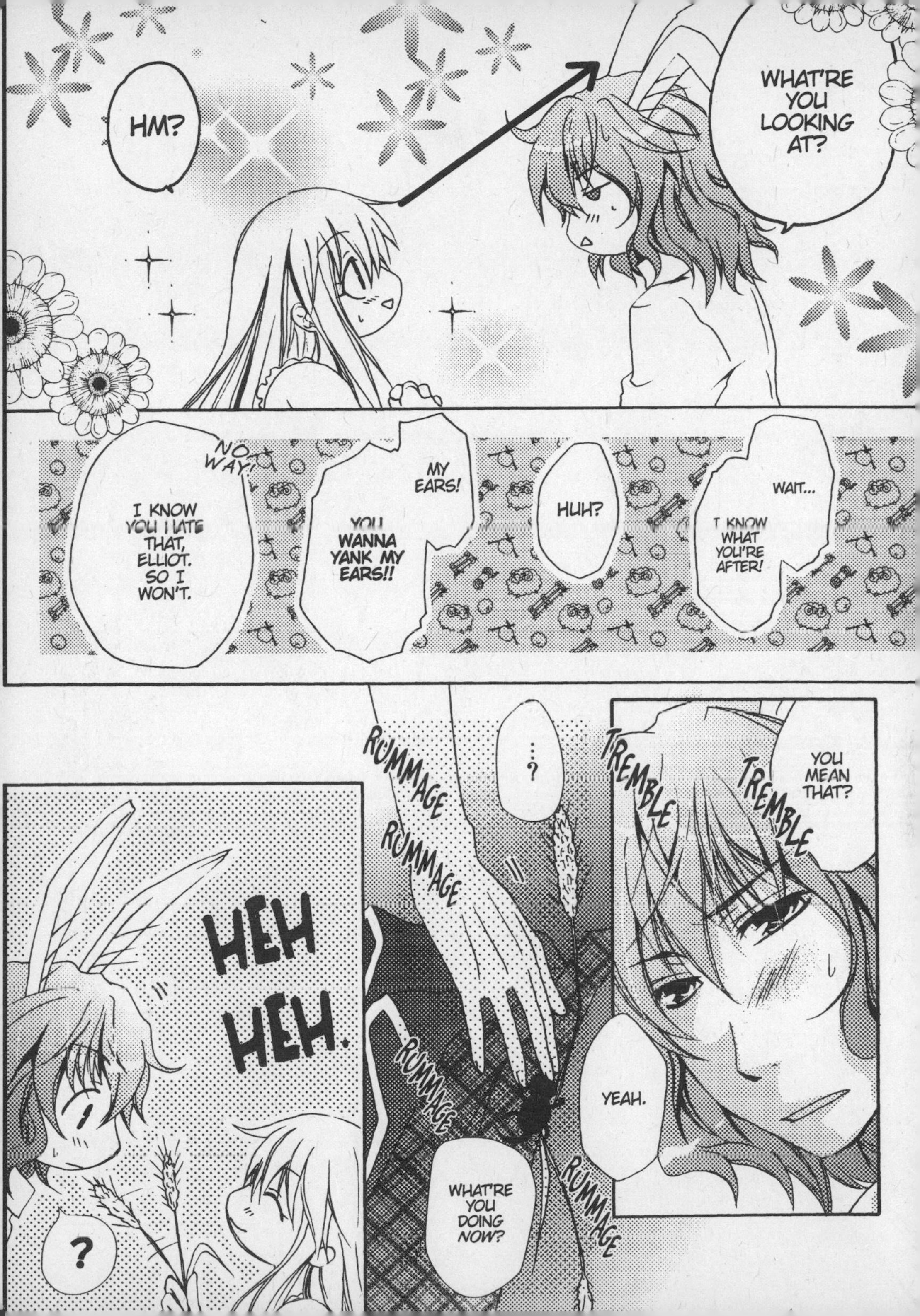
WHAT'RE YOU LOOKING AT?
HM?
WAIT...
I KNOW WHAT YOU'RE AFTER!
HUH?
MY EARS!
YOU WANNA YANK MY EARS!!
NO WAY!
I KNOW YOU HATE THAT, ELLIOT. SO I WON'T.
YOU MEAN THAT?
TREMBLE
TREMBLE
YEAH.
...?
RUMMAGE
RUMMAGE
RUMMAGE
RUMMAGE
WHAT'RE YOU DOING NOW?
HEH HEH.
?

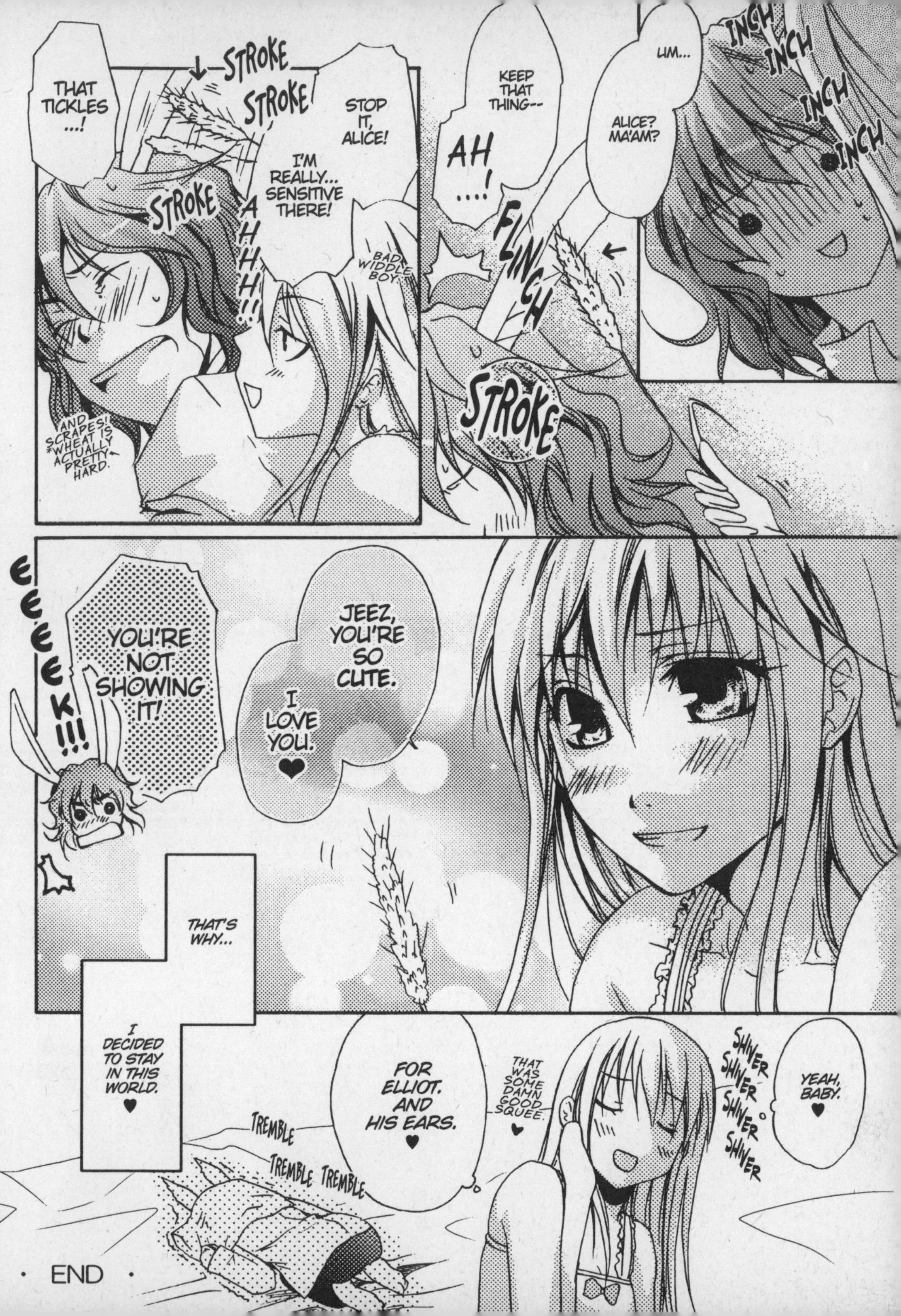
UM...
ALICE? MA'AM?
INCH INCH INCH INCH
KEEP THAT THING--
AH...!
FLINCH
STROKE
STROKE STROKE
THAT TICKLES...!
STOP IT, ALICE!
I'M REALLY... SENSITIVE THERE!
STROKE
AHHHH!!
BAD WIDDLE BOY.
AND SCRAPES! *WHEAT IS ACTUALLY PRETTY HARD.
JEEZ, YOU'RE SO CUTE.
I LOVE YOU. ♥
YOU'RE NOT SHOWING IT!
EEEEEK!!!
THAT'S WHY...
I DECIDED TO STAY IN THIS WORLD. ♥
YEAH, BABY. ♥
SHIVER SHIVER SHIVER SHIVER SHIVER
THAT WAS SOME DAMN GOOD SQUEE. ♥
FOR ELLIOT. AND HIS EARS. ♥
TREMBLE TREMBLE TREMBLE
• END •

Alice in the Country of Clover
クローバーの国の
アリス
~ Wonderful Wonder World ~

- STORY -

In *Alice in the Country of Clover*, the game starts with Alice having not fallen in love, but still deciding to stay in Wonderland.

She's acquainted with all the characters from the previous game, *Alice in the Country of Hearts*.

Since love would now start from a place of friendship rather than passion with a new stranger, she can experience a different type of romance from that in the previous game. Her dynamic with the characters is different through this friendship—characters can't always be forceful with her, and in many ways it's more comfortable to grow intimate. The relationships *between* the Ones With Duties have also become more of a factor.

In this game, the story focuses on the mafia. Alice attends the suited meetings (forcefully) and gets involved in various gunfights (forcefully), among other things.

Land fluctuations, sea creatures in the forest, and whispering doors—it's a game more fantastic and more eerie than the first.

Will our everywoman Alice be able to have a romantic relationship in a world devoid of common sense?

Alice in the Country of Clover
Character Information

Elliot March
VA: Tsuguo Mogami

Blood's right-hand man has a criminal past... and a temperamental present. But he's not as bad as he used to be, so that's something. Joining Blood has been good(?) for him.

Blood Dupre
VA: Katsuyuki Konishi

The head of the mafia Hatter Family, Blood is a cunning yet moody puppet-master. Alice now has the pleasure of having him for a landlord.

Alice Liddell
VA: Rie Kugimiya

A normal girl with a bit of a chip on her shoulder. Deciding to stay in the Wonderland she was carried to, she's adapted to her strange new lifestyle.

Vivaldi
VA: Yuuko Kaida

The beautiful Queen of Hearts has an unrivaled temper—which is really saying something in Wonderland. Although a picture-perfect Mad Queen, she cares for Alice as if Alice were her little sister...or a very interesting plaything.

Tweedle Dum
VA: Jun Fukuyama

The second "Bloody Twin" is equally cute and equally scary. In *Clover*, Dum can also turn into an adult.

Tweedle Dee
VA: Jun Fukuyama

One of the "Bloody Twin" gatekeepers of the Hatter territory, Dee can be cute when he's not being terrifying. In *Clover*, he sometimes turns into an adult.

Boris Airay
VA: Noriaki Sugiyama

This riddle-loving cat has a signature smirk—and in *Clover*, a new toy. One of his favorite pastimes is giving the Sleepy Mouse a hard time.

Ace
VA: Daisuke Hirakawa

The unlucky knight of Hearts was a former subordinate of Vivaldi and is perpetually lost. Even though he's depressed to be separated from his friend and boss Julius, he stays positive and tries to overcome it with a smile. He seems like a classic nice guy... or is he?

Peter White
VA: Kouki Miyata

The Prime Minister of Heart Castle—who has rabbit ears growing out of his head—invited (kidnapped) Alice to Wonderland. He loves Alice and hates everything else. His cruel, irrational actions are disturbing, but he acts like a completely different person (rabbit?) when in the throes of his love for Alice.

Gray Ringmarc
VA: Kazuya Nakai

Nightmare's subordinate in *Clover*. He used to have strong social ambition and considered assassinating Nightmare... but since Nightmare was such a useless boss, Gray couldn't help but feel sorry for him and ended up a dedicated assistant. He's a sound thinker with a strong work ethic. He's also highly skilled with his blades, rivaling even Ace.

Nightmare Gottschalk
VA: Tomokazu Sugita

A sickly nightmare who hates the hospital and needles. He has the power to read people's thoughts and enter dreams. Even though he likes to shut himself away in dreams, Gray drags him out to sulk from time to time. He technically holds a high position and has many subordinates, but since he can't even take care of his own health, he leaves most things to Gray.

Pierce Villiers
VA: Souichirou Hoshi

New to *Clover*, Pierce is an insomniac mouse who drinks too much coffee. He loves Nightmare (who can help him sleep) and hates Boris (who terrifies him). He dislikes Blood and Vivaldi for discarding coffee in favor of tea. He likes Elliot and Peter well enough, since rabbits aren't natural predators of mice.

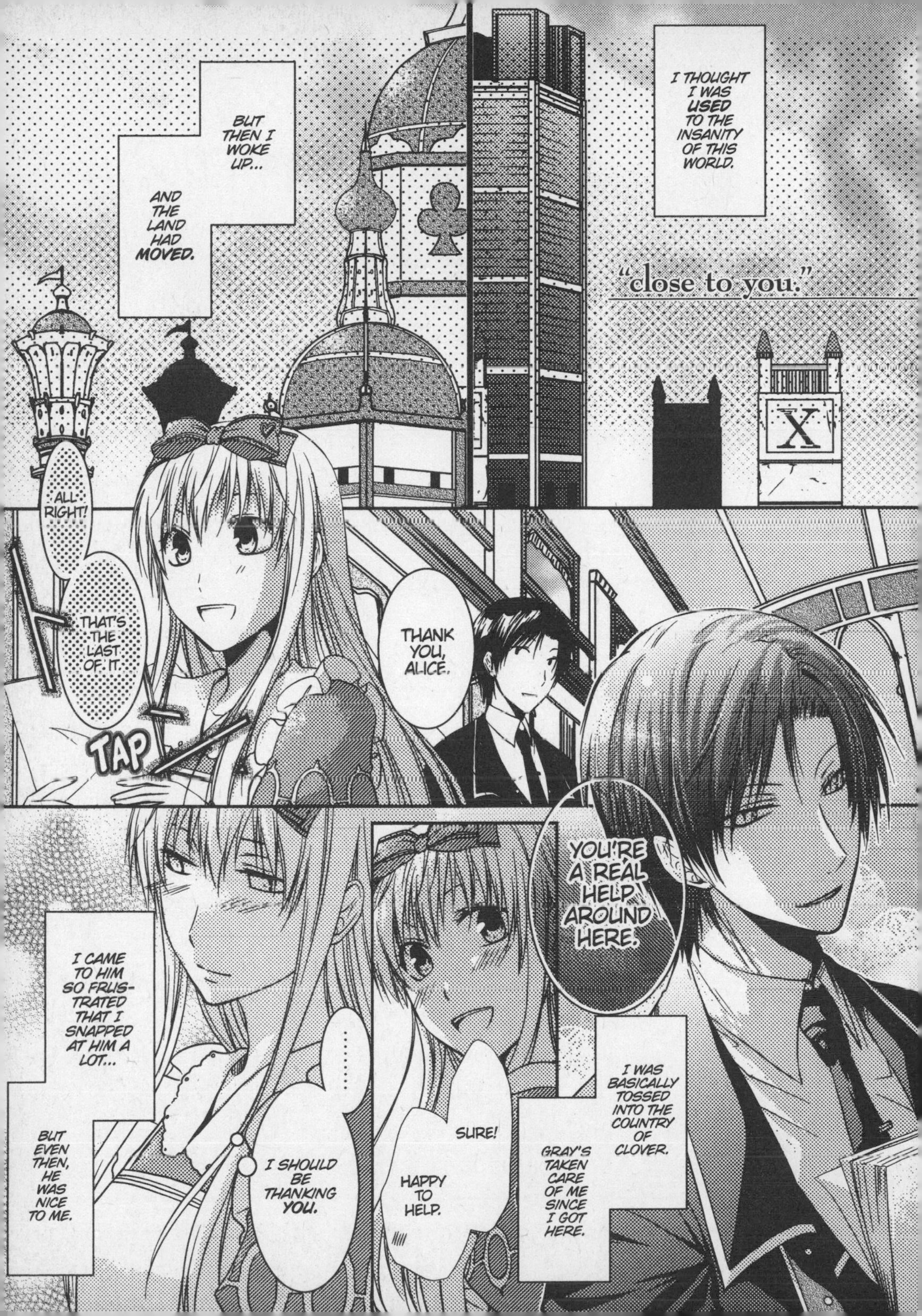
I THOUGHT I WAS USED TO THE INSANITY OF THIS WORLD.
"close to you."
BUT THEN I WOKE UP...
AND THE LAND HAD MOVED.
ALL RIGHT!
THAT'S THE LAST OF IT.
TAP
THANK YOU, ALICE.
YOU'RE A REAL HELP AROUND HERE.
I WAS BASICALLY TOSSED INTO THE COUNTRY OF CLOVER.
GRAY'S TAKEN CARE OF ME SINCE I GOT HERE.
SURE!
HAPPY TO HELP.
I CAME TO HIM SO FRUS-TRATED THAT I SNAPPED AT HIM A LOT...
......
BUT EVEN THEN, HE WAS NICE TO ME.
I SHOULD BE THANKING YOU.

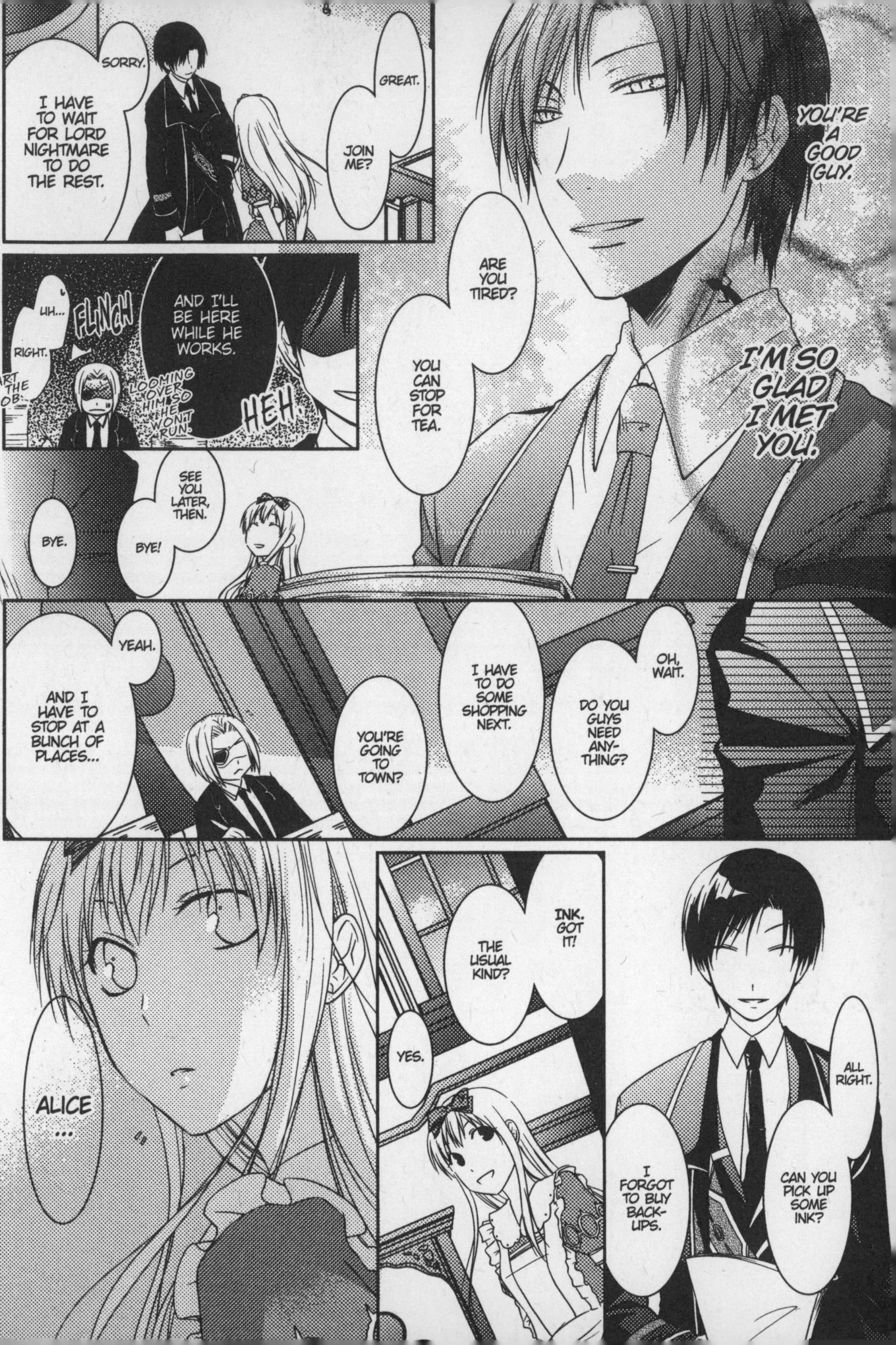
YOU'RE A GOOD GUY.
ARE YOU TIRED?
YOU CAN STOP FOR TEA.
I'M SO GLAD I MET YOU.
GREAT.
JOIN ME?
SORRY.
I HAVE TO WAIT FOR LORD NIGHTMARE TO DO THE REST.
AND I'LL BE HERE WHILE HE WORKS.
HEH.
LOOMING OVER HIM SO HE WON'T RUN.
FLINCH
UH...
RIGHT.
PART OF THE JOB.
SEE YOU LATER, THEN.
BYE!
BYE.
OH, WAIT.
DO YOU GUYS NEED ANY-THING?
I HAVE TO DO SOME SHOPPING NEXT.
YOU'RE GOING TO TOWN?
YEAH.
AND I HAVE TO STOP AT A BUNCH OF PLACES...
ALL RIGHT.
CAN YOU PICK UP SOME INK?
I FORGOT TO BUY BACK-UPS.
INK. GOT IT!
THE USUAL KIND?
YES.
ALICE ...

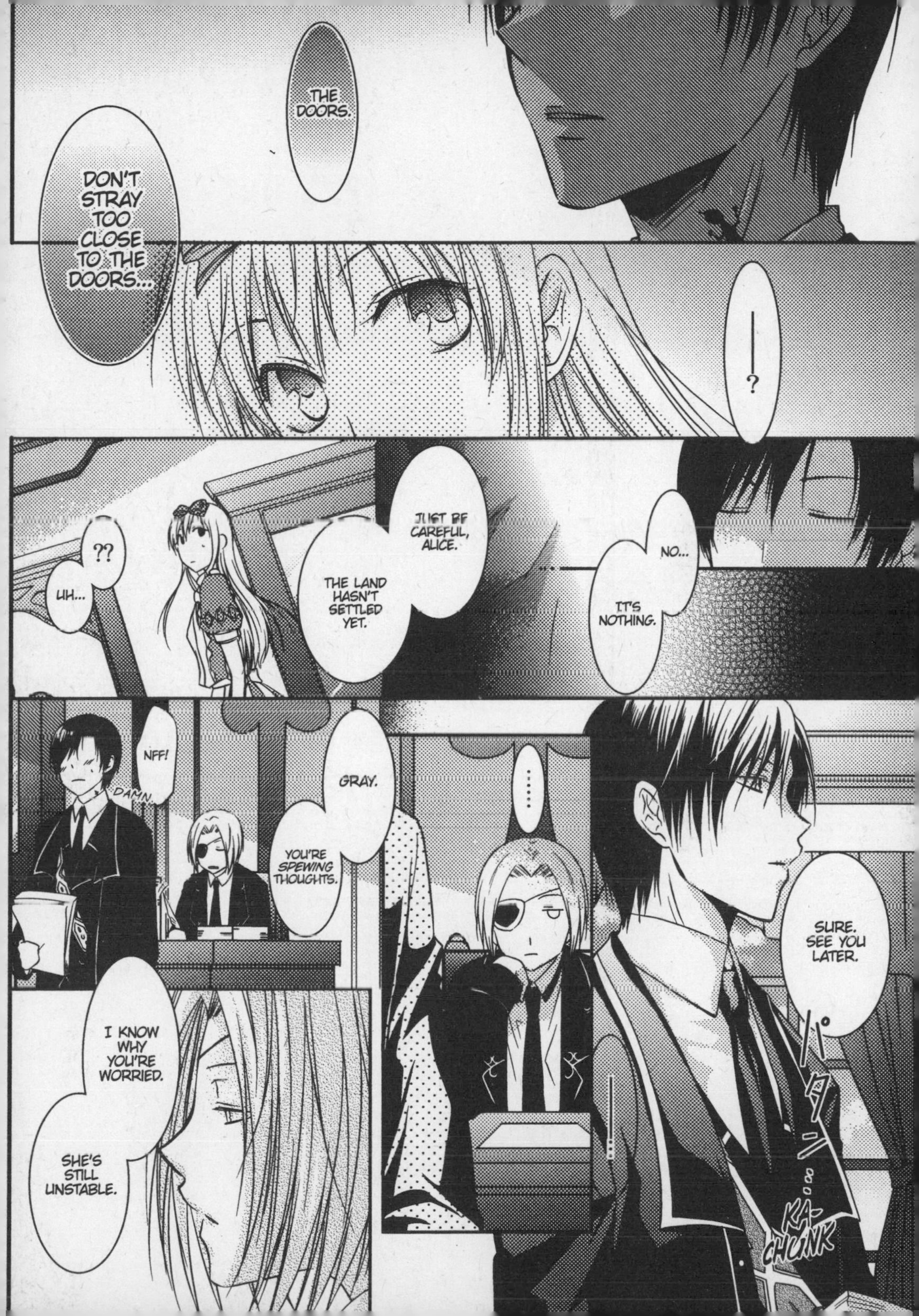
THE DOORS.
DON'T STRAY TOO CLOSE TO THE DOORS...
—?
NO...
IT'S NOTHING.
JUST BE CAREFUL, ALICE.
THE LAND HASN'T SETTLED YET.
??
UH...
SURE. SEE YOU LATER.
KA-CHUNK
—...
......
GRAY.
YOU'RE SPEWING THOUGHTS.
NFF!
DAMN.
I KNOW WHY YOU'RE WORRIED.
SHE'S STILL UNSTABLE.

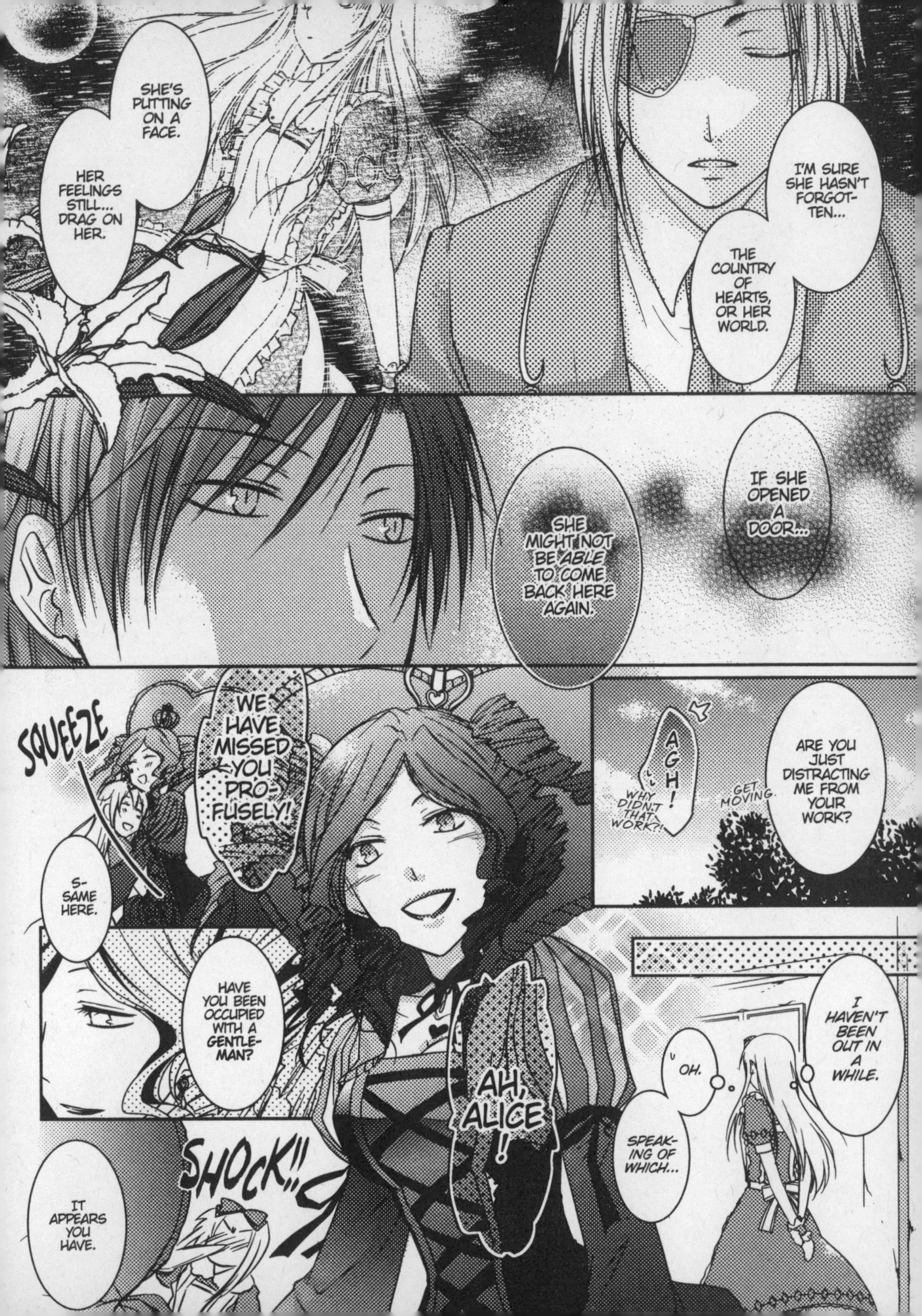
I'M SURE SHE HASN'T FORGOT-TEN...
THE COUNTRY OF HEARTS, OR HER WORLD.
SHE'S PUTTING ON A FACE.
HER FEELINGS STILL... DRAG ON HER.
IF SHE OPENED A DOOR...
SHE MIGHT NOT BE ABLE TO COME BACK HERE AGAIN.
ARE YOU JUST DISTRACTING ME FROM YOUR WORK?
GET MOVING.
AGH!
WHY DIDN'T THAT WORK?!
WE HAVE MISSED YOU PRO-FUSELY!
SQUEEZE
S-SAME HERE.
I HAVEN'T BEEN OUT IN A WHILE.
OH.
SPEAKING OF WHICH...
AH, ALICE!
HAVE YOU BEEN OCCUPIED WITH A GENTLE-MAN?
SHOCK!!
IT APPEARS YOU HAVE.

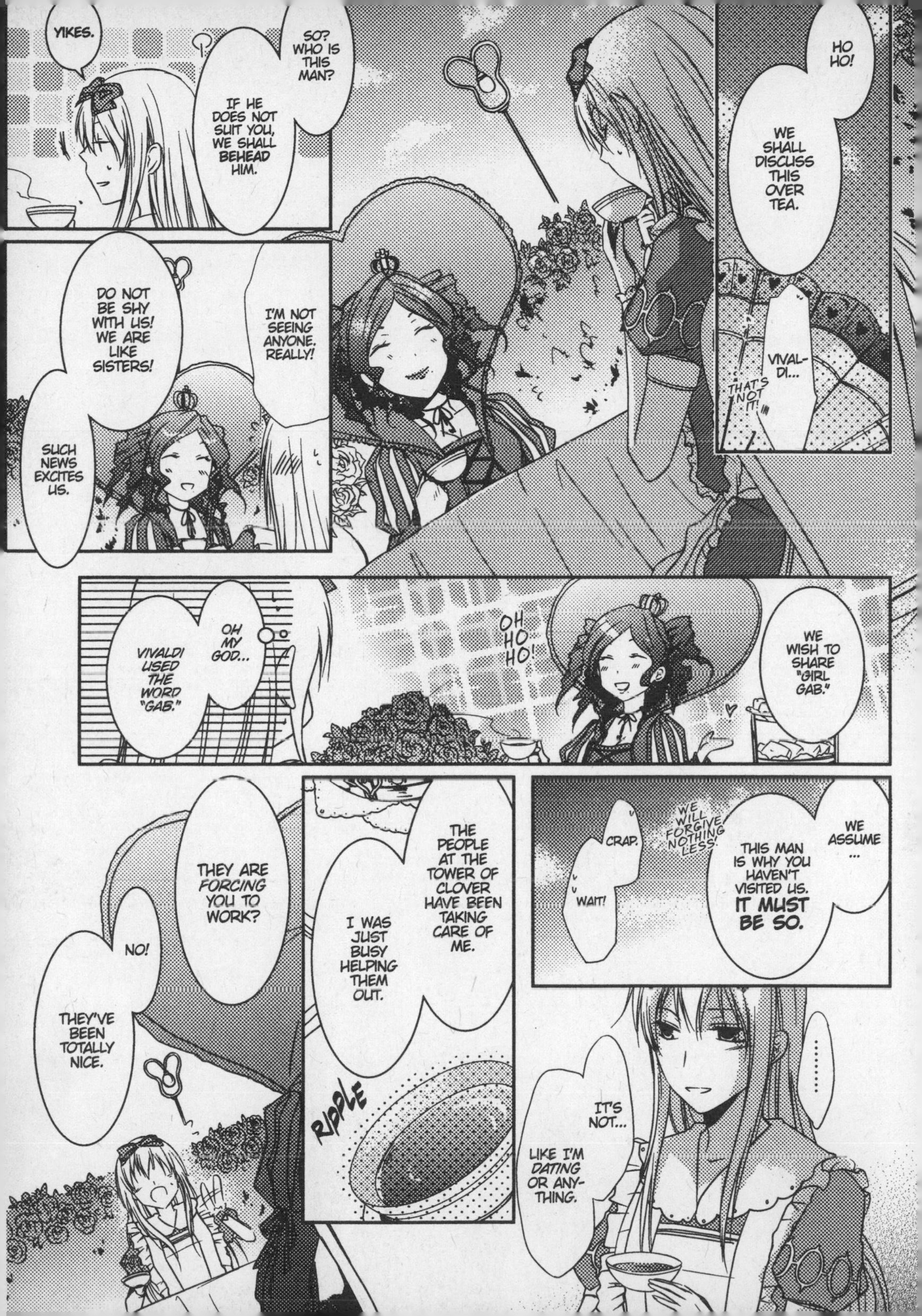
HO HO!
WE SHALL DISCUSS THIS OVER TEA.
VIVALDI...
THAT'S NOT IT!
SO? WHO IS THIS MAN?
IF HE DOES NOT SUIT YOU, WE SHALL BEHEAD HIM.
YIKES.
I'M NOT SEEING ANYONE. REALLY!
DO NOT BE SHY WITH US! WE ARE LIKE SISTERS!
SUCH NEWS EXCITES US.
WE WISH TO SHARE "GIRL GAB."
OH HO HO!
OH MY GOD...
VIVALDI USED THE WORD "GAB."
WE ASSUME...
THIS MAN IS WHY YOU HAVEN'T VISITED US. **IT MUST BE SO.**
WE WILL FORGIVE NOTHING LESS.
CRAP.
WAIT!
......
IT'S NOT...
LIKE I'M *DATING* OR ANYTHING.
THE PEOPLE AT THE TOWER OF CLOVER HAVE BEEN TAKING CARE OF ME.
I WAS JUST BUSY HELPING THEM OUT.
RIPPLE
THEY ARE *FORCING* YOU TO WORK?
NO!
THEY'VE BEEN TOTALLY NICE.

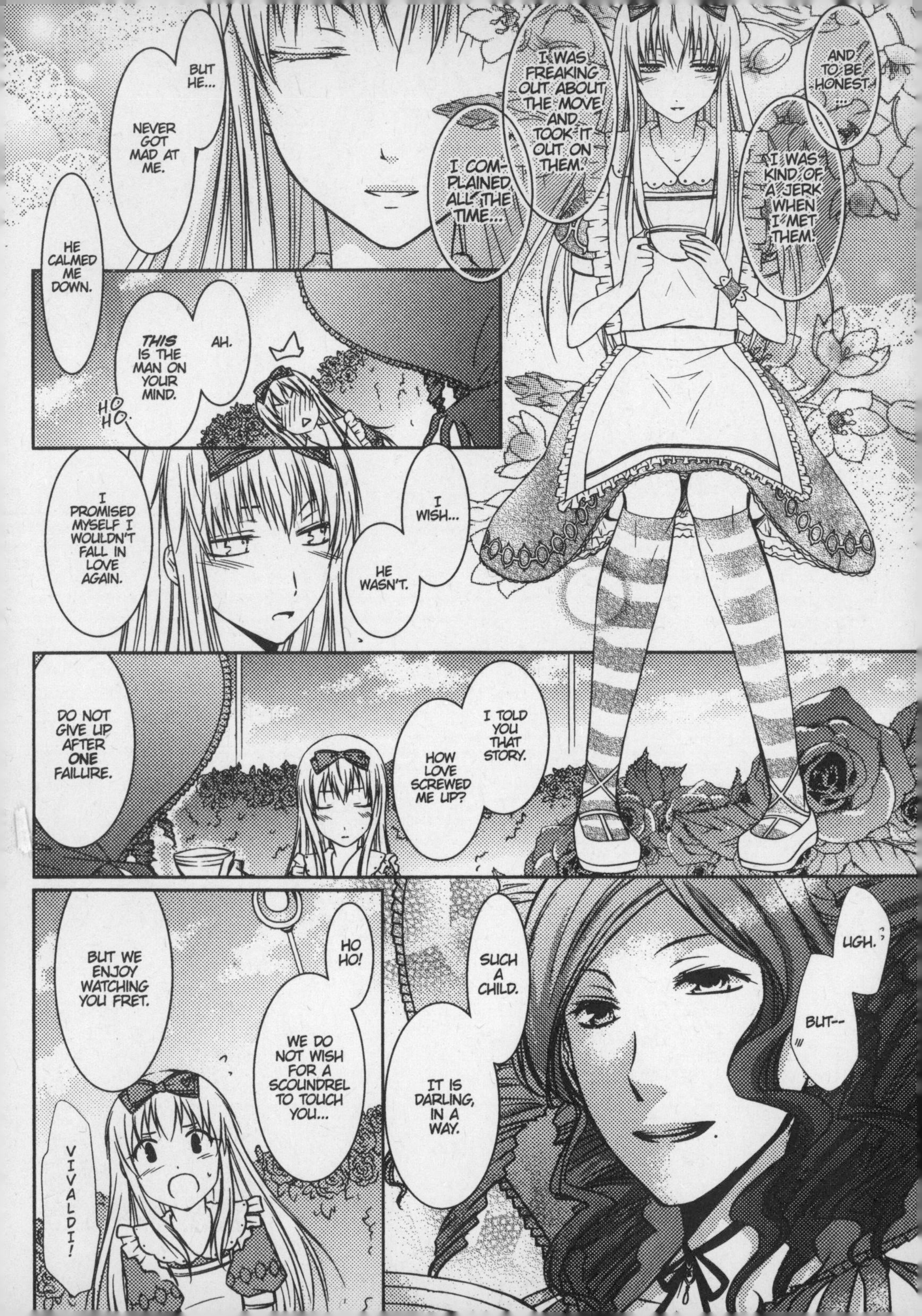
AND TO BE HONEST...
I WAS KIND OF A JERK WHEN I MET THEM.
I WAS FREAKING OUT ABOUT THE MOVE AND TOOK IT OUT ON THEM.
I COMPLAINED ALL THE TIME...
BUT HE...
NEVER GOT MAD AT ME.
HE CALMED ME DOWN.
AH.
THIS IS THE MAN ON YOUR MIND.
HO HO.
I WISH...
HE WASN'T.
I PROMISED MYSELF I WOULDN'T FALL IN LOVE AGAIN.
I TOLD YOU THAT STORY.
HOW LOVE SCREWED ME UP?
DO NOT GIVE UP AFTER ONE FAILURE.
UGH.
BUT--
SUCH A CHILD.
IT IS DARLING, IN A WAY.
HO HO!
WE DO NOT WISH FOR A SCOUNDREL TO TOUCH YOU...
BUT WE ENJOY WATCHING YOU FRET.
VIVALDI!

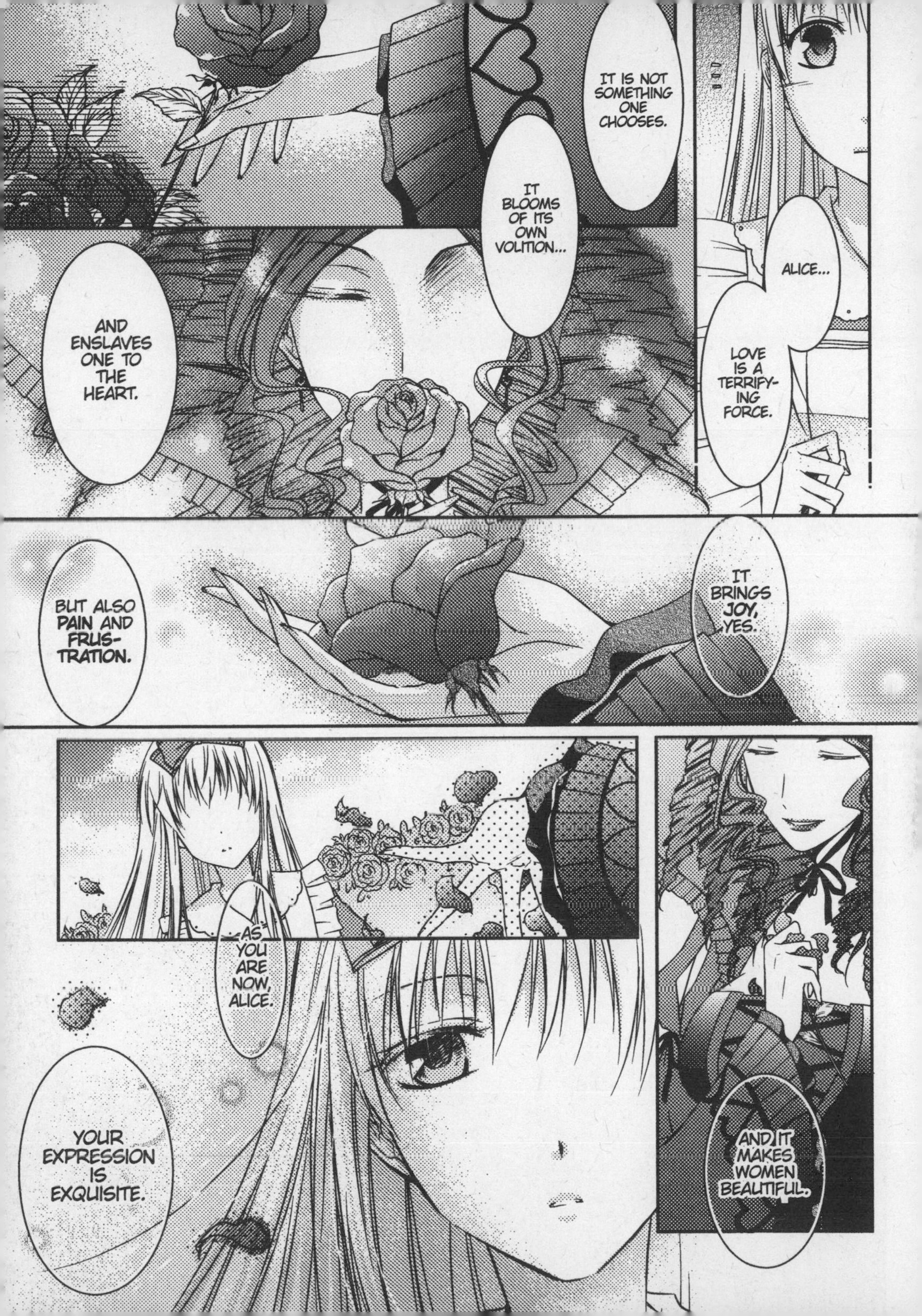
ALICE...
LOVE IS A TERRIFYING FORCE.
IT IS NOT SOMETHING ONE CHOOSES.
IT BLOOMS OF ITS OWN VOLITION...
AND ENSLAVES ONE TO THE HEART.
IT BRINGS JOY, YES.
BUT ALSO PAIN AND FRUSTRATION.
AND IT MAKES WOMEN BEAUTIFUL.
AS YOU ARE NOW, ALICE.
YOUR EXPRESSION IS EXQUISITE.

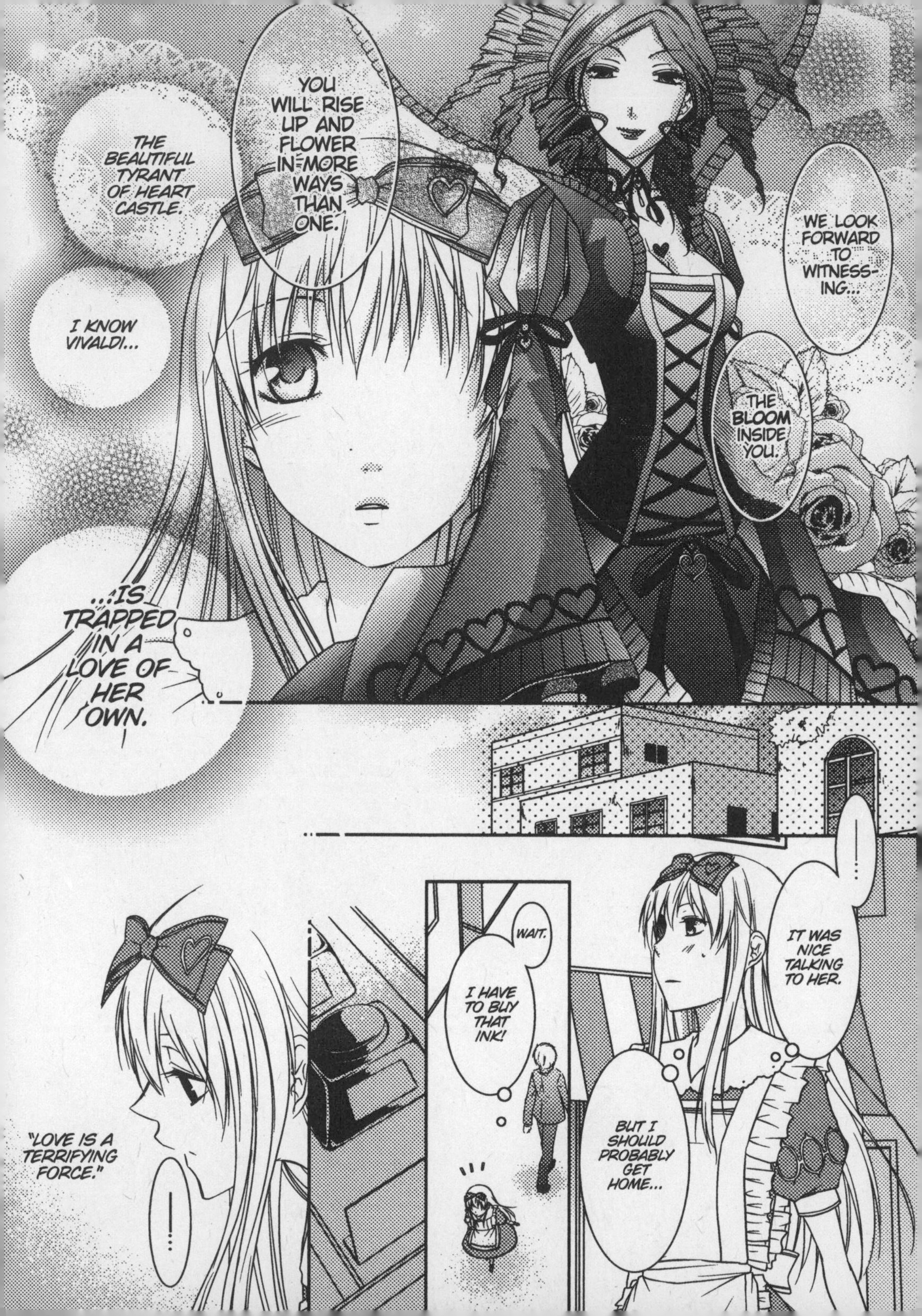
YOU WILL RISE UP AND FLOWER IN MORE WAYS THAN ONE.
WE LOOK FORWARD TO WITNESSING...
THE BLOOM INSIDE YOU.
THE BEAUTIFUL TYRANT OF HEART CASTLE.
I KNOW VIVALDI...
...IS TRAPPED IN A LOVE OF HER OWN.
!
IT WAS NICE TALKING TO HER.
BUT I SHOULD PROBABLY GET HOME...
WAIT.
I HAVE TO BUY THAT INK!
!
"LOVE IS A TERRIFYING FORCE."

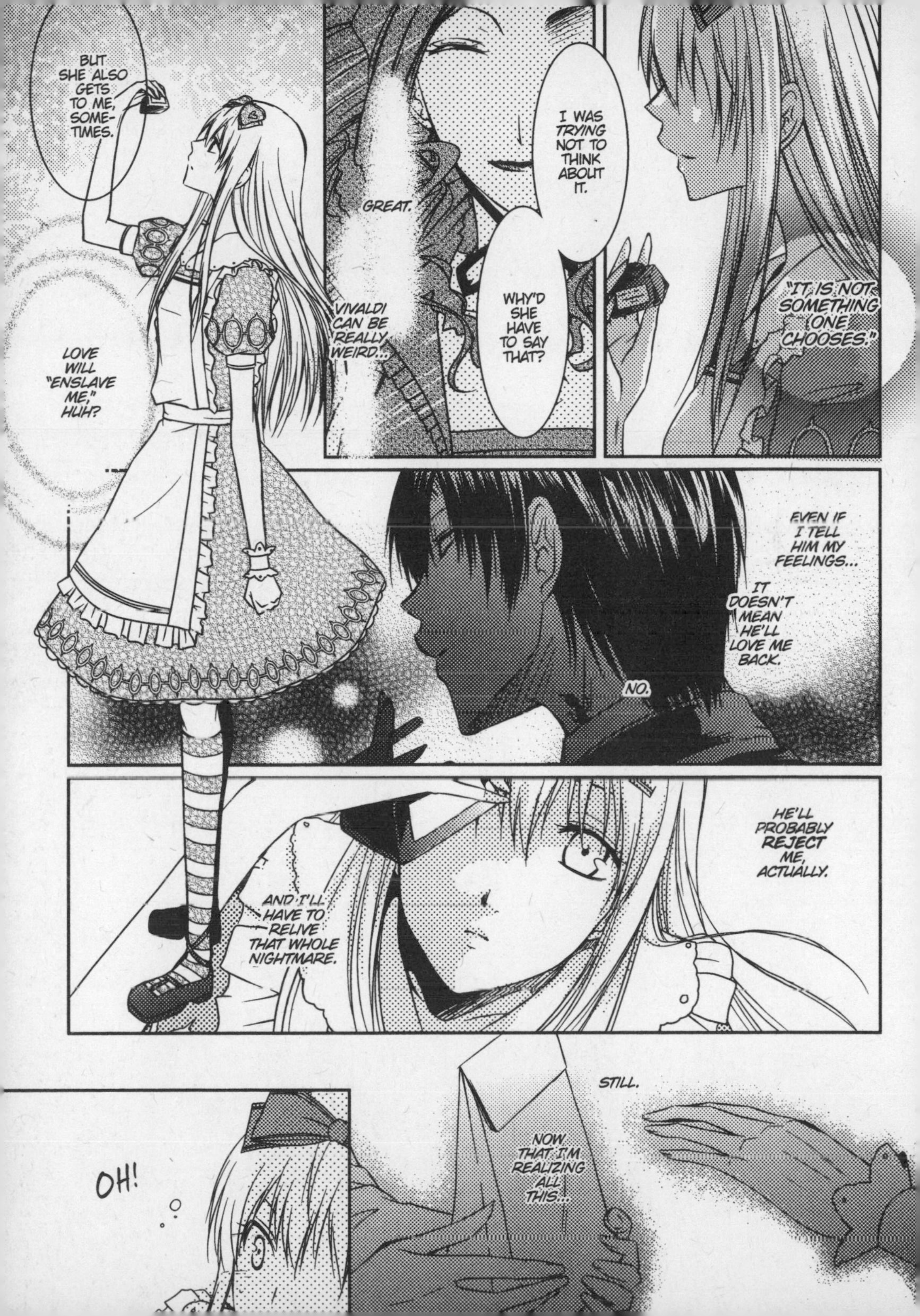

"IT IS NOT SOMETHING ONE CHOOSES."
I WAS TRYING NOT TO THINK ABOUT IT.
WHY'D SHE HAVE TO SAY THAT?
GREAT.
VIVALDI CAN BE REALLY WEIRD...
BUT SHE ALSO GETS TO ME, SOME-TIMES.
LOVE WILL "ENSLAVE ME," HUH?
EVEN IF I TELL HIM MY FEELINGS...
IT DOESN'T MEAN HE'LL LOVE ME BACK.
NO.
HE'LL PROBABLY REJECT ME, ACTUALLY.
AND I'LL HAVE TO RELIVE THAT WHOLE NIGHTMARE.
STILL.
NOW THAT I'M REALIZING ALL THIS...
OH!

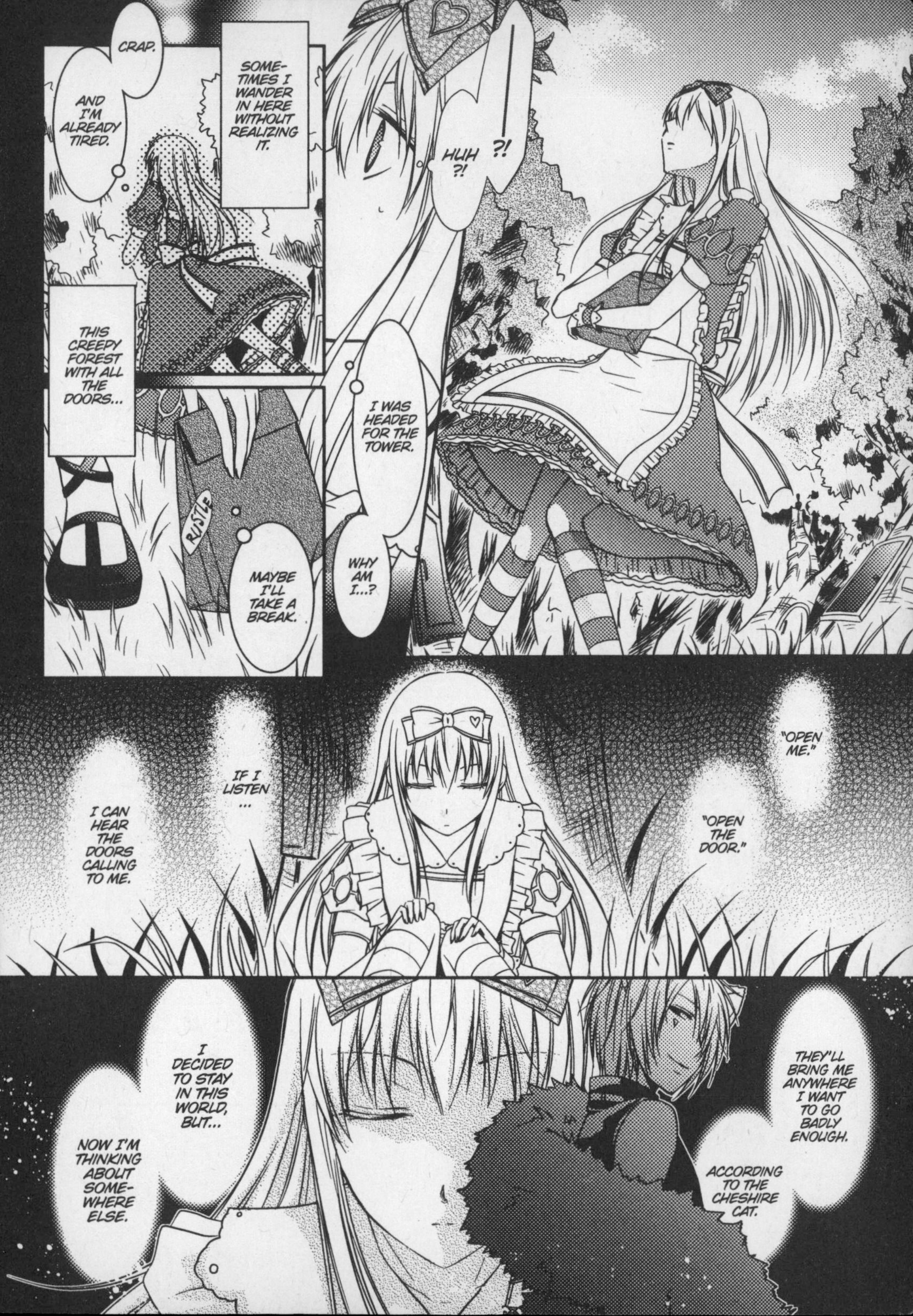
!
?!
HUH ?!
I WAS HEADED FOR THE TOWER.
WHY AM I...?
SOME-TIMES I WANDER IN HERE WITHOUT REALIZING IT.
CRAP.
AND I'M ALREADY TIRED.
THIS CREEPY FOREST WITH ALL THE DOORS...
RUSTLE
MAYBE I'LL TAKE A BREAK.
"OPEN ME."
"OPEN THE DOOR."
IF I LISTEN ...
I CAN HEAR THE DOORS CALLING TO ME.
THEY'LL BRING ME ANYWHERE I WANT TO GO BADLY ENOUGH.
ACCORDING TO THE CHESHIRE CAT.
I DECIDED TO STAY IN THIS WORLD, BUT...
NOW I'M THINKING ABOUT SOME-WHERE ELSE.

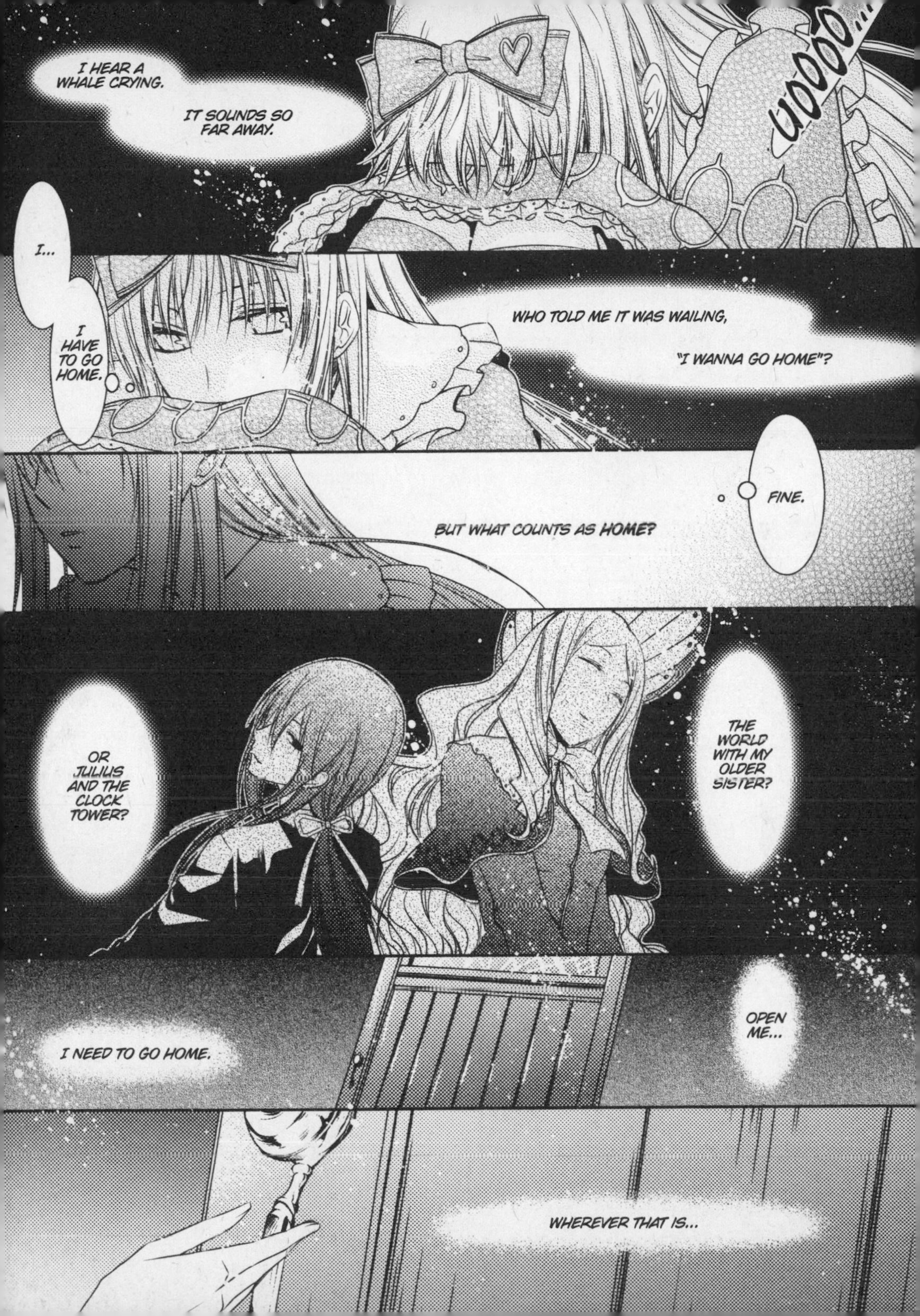
UOOO...
I HEAR A WHALE CRYING.
IT SOUNDS SO FAR AWAY.
WHO TOLD ME IT WAS WAILING,
"I WANNA GO HOME"?
I...
I HAVE TO GO HOME.
FINE.
BUT WHAT COUNTS AS HOME?
THE WORLD WITH MY OLDER SISTER?
OR JULIUS AND THE CLOCK TOWER?
OPEN ME...
I NEED TO GO HOME.
WHEREVER THAT IS...

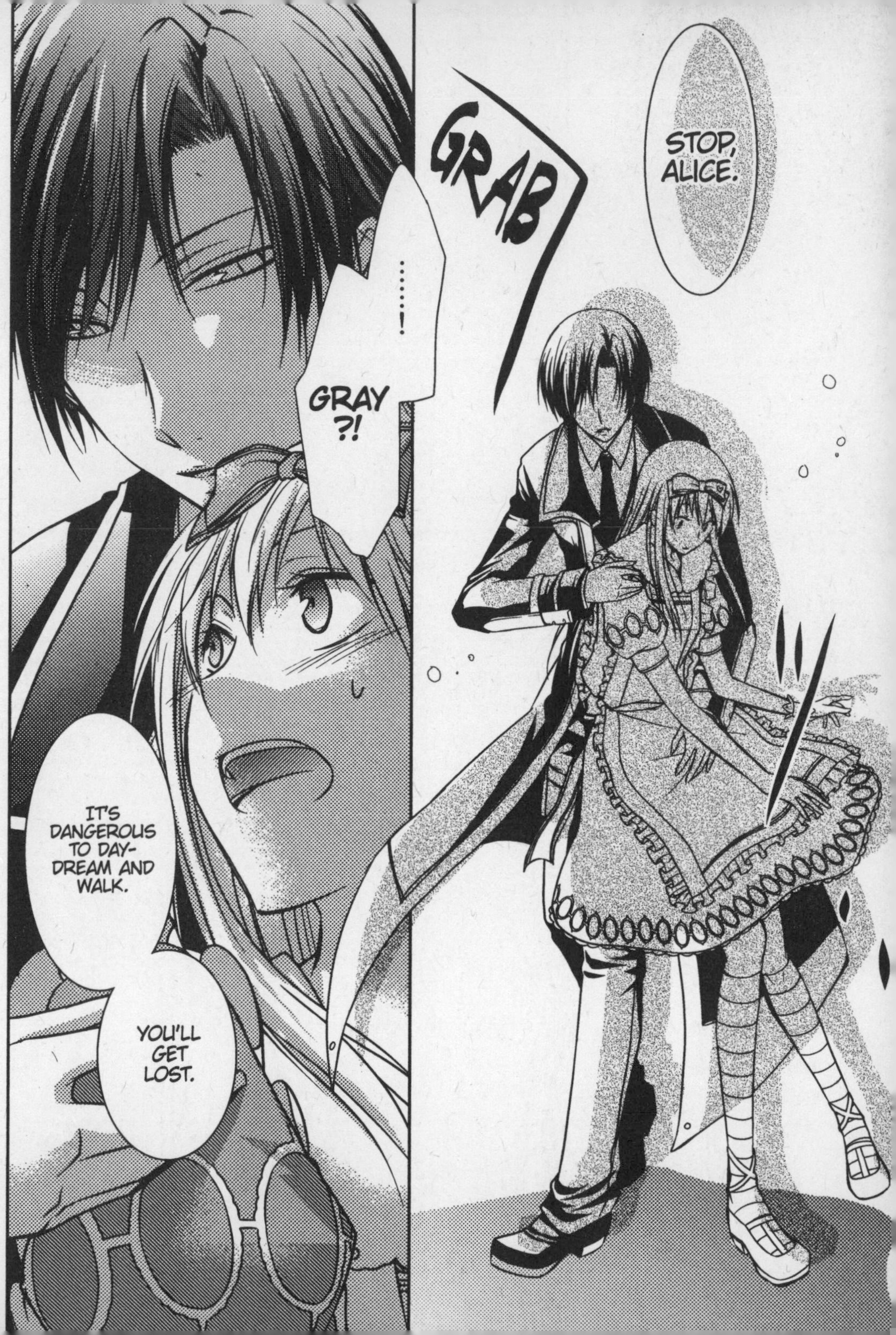
STOP, ALICE.
GRAB
......!
GRAY ?!
IT'S DANGEROUS TO DAY-DREAM AND WALK.
YOU'LL GET LOST.

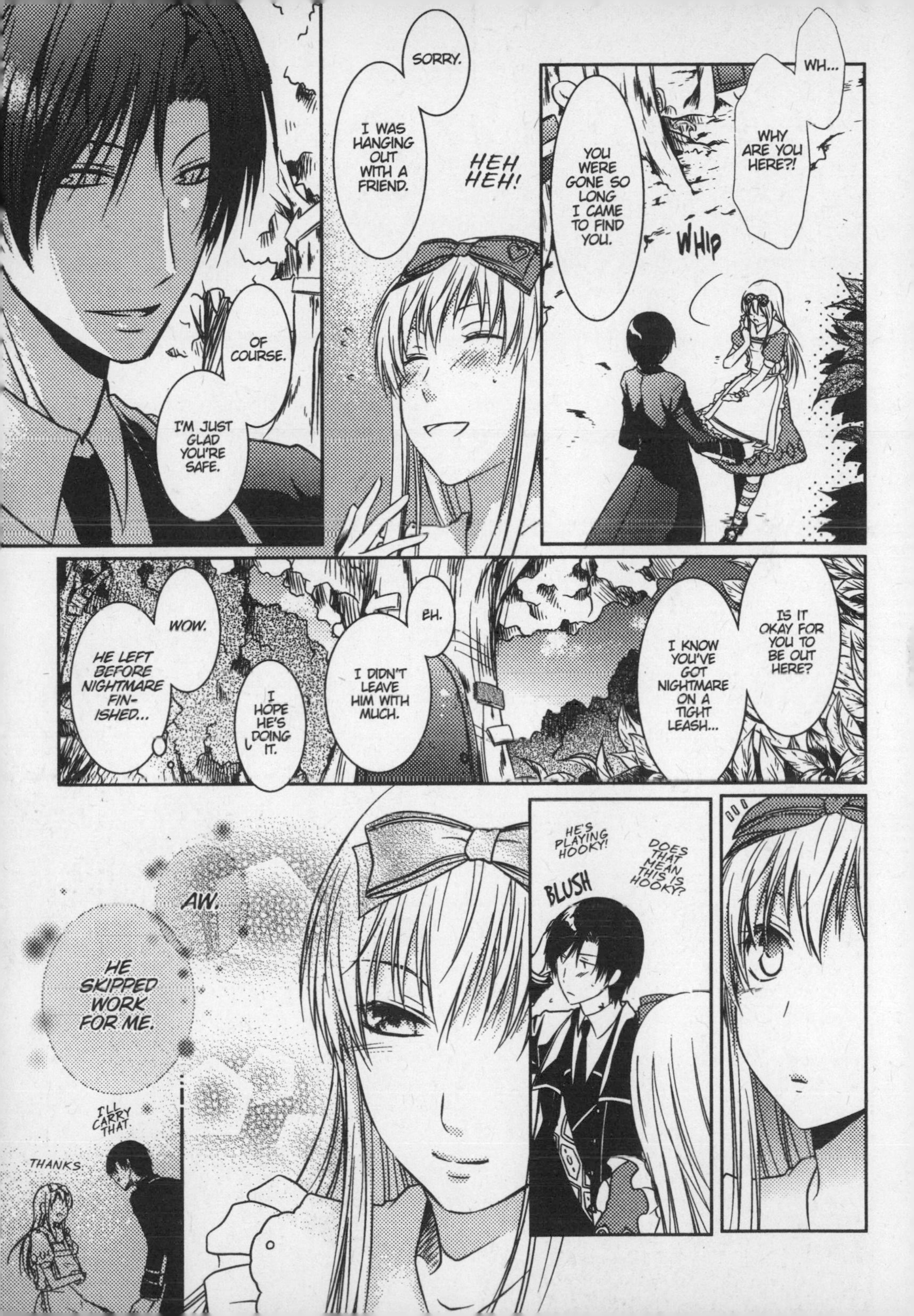
WH...
WHY ARE YOU HERE?!
WHIP
YOU WERE GONE SO LONG I CAME TO FIND YOU.
SORRY.
I WAS HANGING OUT WITH A FRIEND.
HEH HEH!
OF COURSE.
I'M JUST GLAD YOU'RE SAFE.
IS IT OKAY FOR YOU TO BE OUT HERE?
I KNOW YOU'VE GOT NIGHTMARE ON A TIGHT LEASH...
EH.
I DIDN'T LEAVE HIM WITH MUCH.
I HOPE HE'S DOING IT.
WOW.
HE LEFT BEFORE NIGHTMARE FIN-ISHED...
DOES THAT MEAN THIS IS HOOKY?
HE'S PLAYING HOOKY!
BLUSH
AW.
HE SKIPPED WORK FOR ME.
I'LL CARRY THAT.
THANKS.

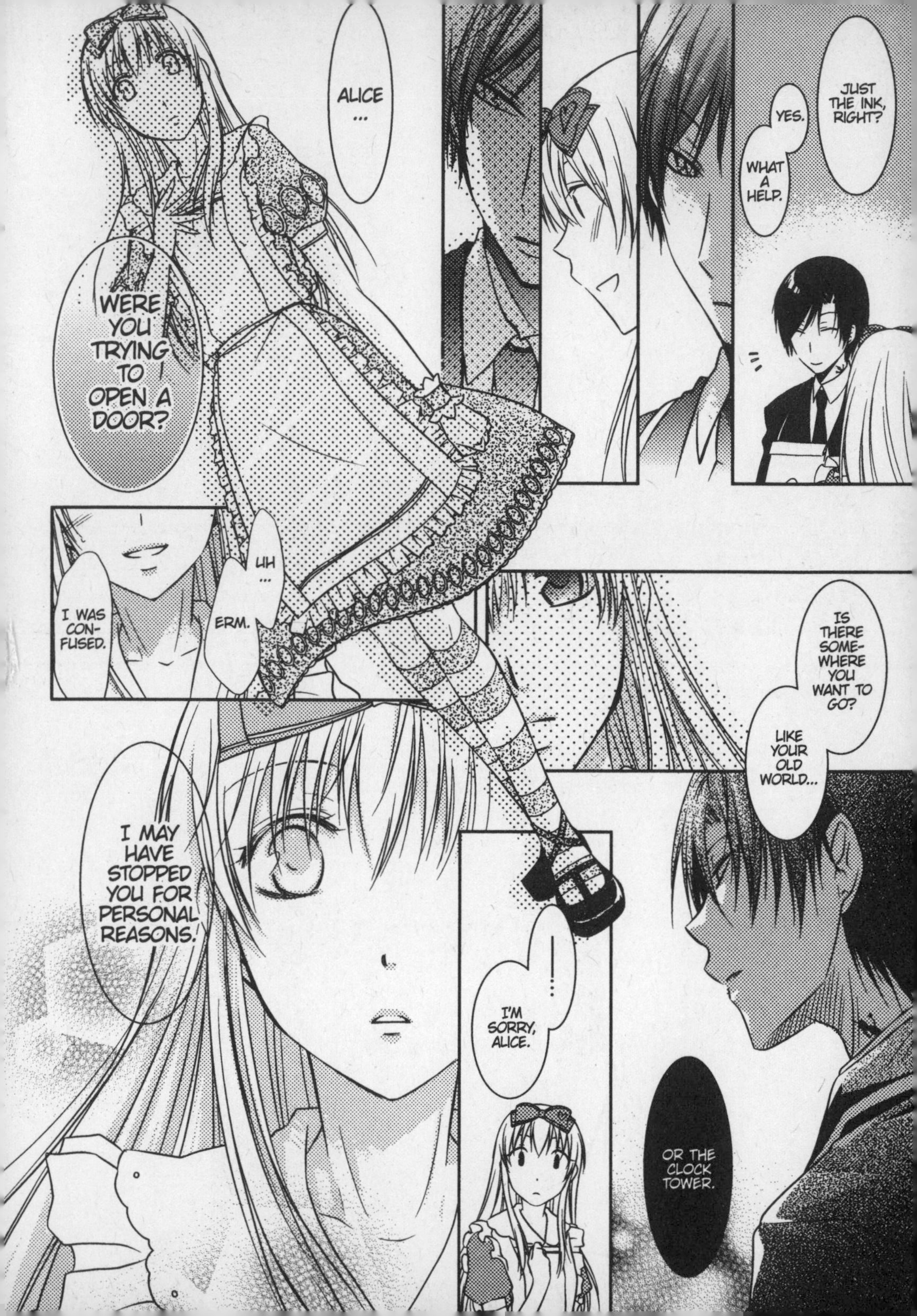
JUST THE INK, RIGHT?
YES.
WHAT A HELP.
ALICE ...
WERE YOU TRYING TO OPEN A DOOR?
IS THERE SOMEWHERE YOU WANT TO GO?
LIKE YOUR OLD WORLD...
UH ...
ERM.
I WAS CONFUSED.
OR THE CLOCK TOWER.
...!
I'M SORRY, ALICE.
I MAY HAVE STOPPED YOU FOR PERSONAL REASONS.

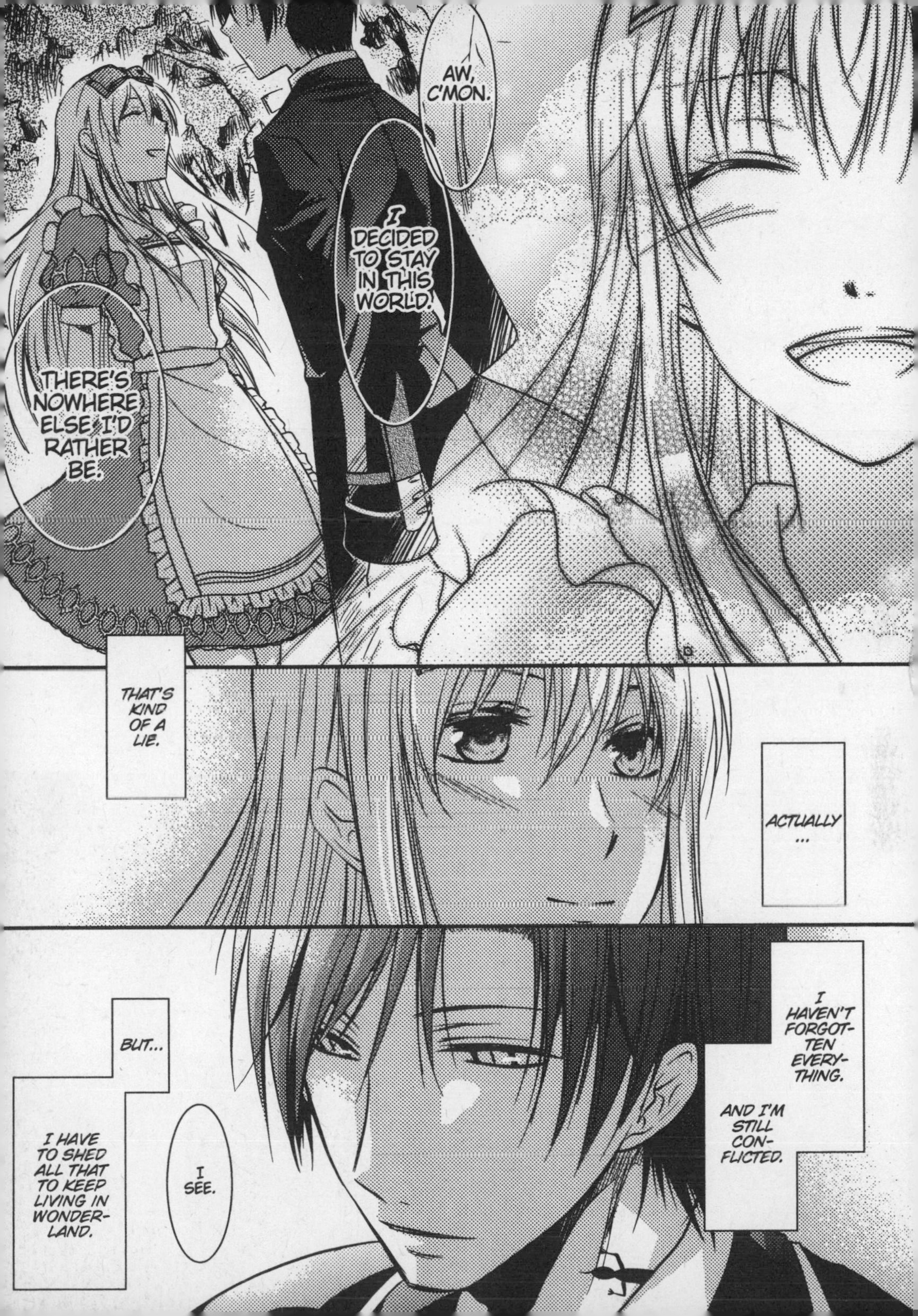
AW, C'MON.
I DECIDED TO STAY IN THIS WORLD.
THERE'S NOWHERE ELSE I'D RATHER BE.
ACTUALLY...
THAT'S KIND OF A LIE.
I HAVEN'T FORGOT-TEN EVERY-THING.
AND I'M STILL CON-FLICTED.
I SEE.
BUT...
I HAVE TO SHED ALL THAT TO KEEP LIVING IN WONDER-LAND.

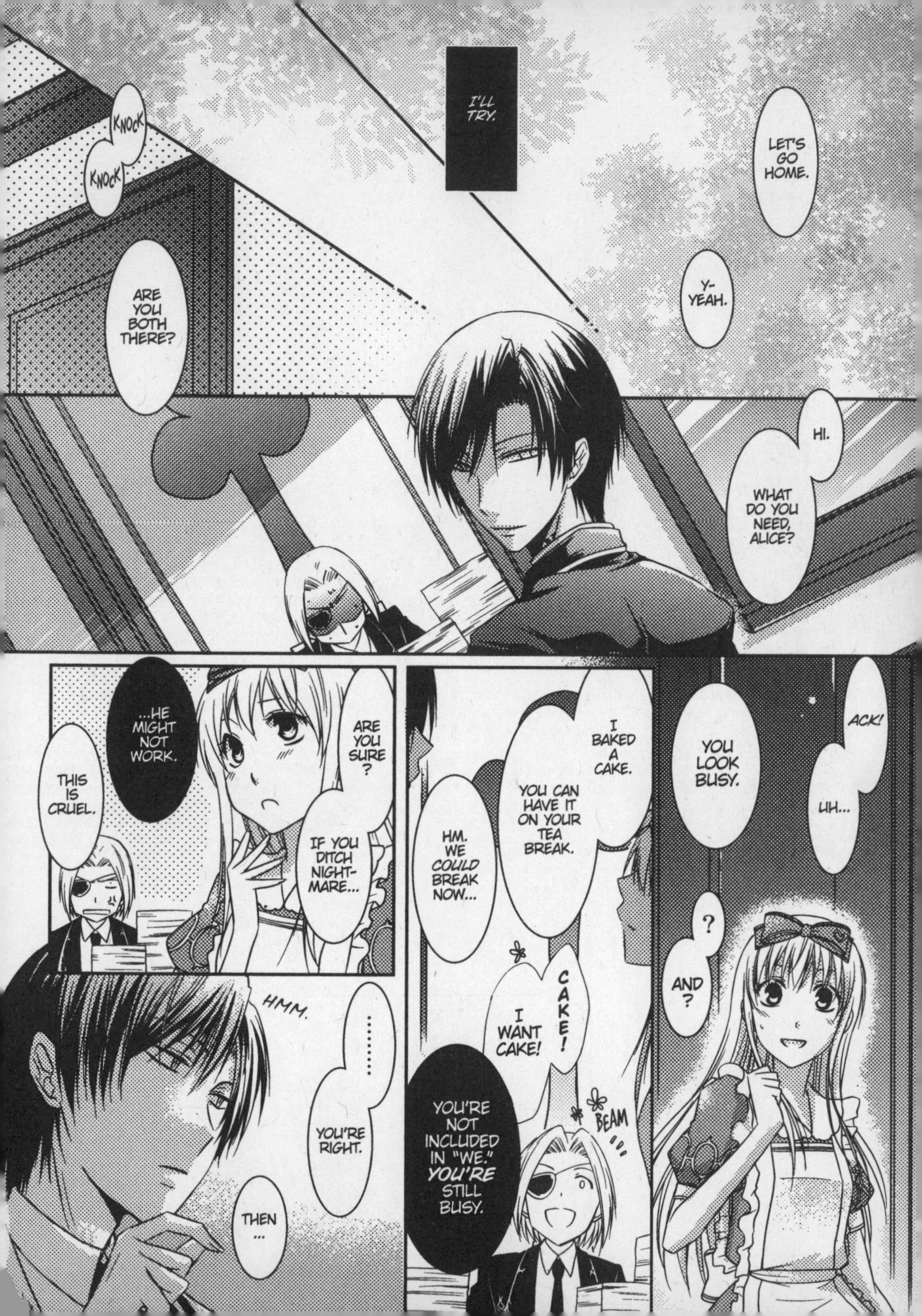

LET'S GO HOME.
Y-YEAH.
I'LL TRY.
KNOCK
KNOCK
ARE YOU BOTH THERE?
HI.
WHAT DO YOU NEED, ALICE?
ACK!
UH...
YOU LOOK BUSY.
?
AND ?
I BAKED A CAKE.
YOU CAN HAVE IT ON YOUR TEA BREAK.
HM. WE *COULD* BREAK NOW...
CAKE!
I WANT CAKE!
BEAM
YOU'RE NOT INCLUDED IN "WE." *YOU'RE* STILL BUSY.
ARE YOU SURE ?
...HE MIGHT NOT WORK.
IF YOU DITCH NIGHT-MARE...
THIS IS CRUEL.
HMM.
......
YOU'RE RIGHT.
THEN ...

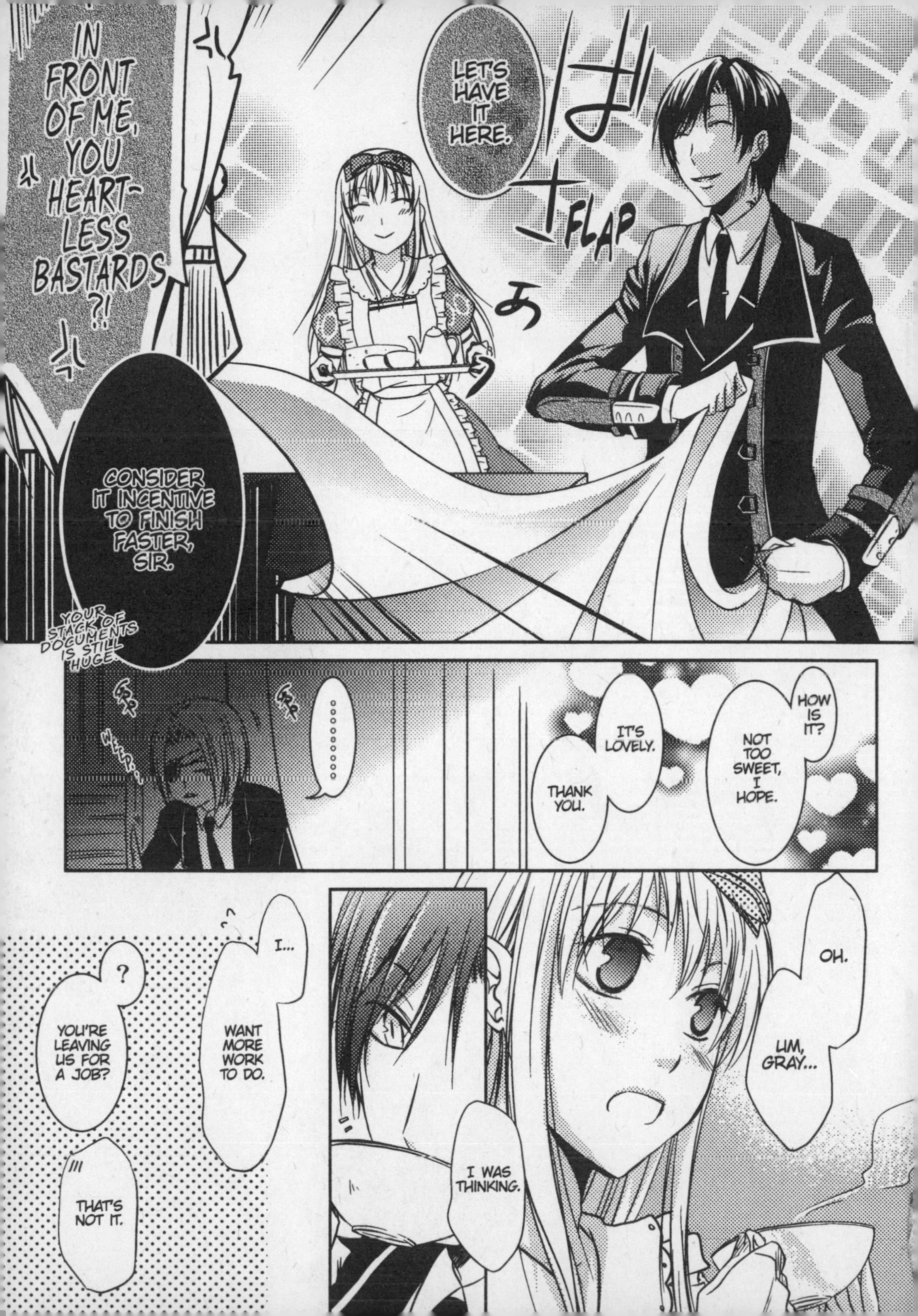
LET'S HAVE IT HERE.
FLAP
IN FRONT OF ME, YOU HEARTLESS BASTARDS?!
CONSIDER IT INCENTIVE TO FINISH FASTER, SIR.
YOUR STACK OF DOCUMENTS IS STILL HUGE.
HOW IS IT?
NOT TOO SWEET, I HOPE.
IT'S LOVELY.
THANK YOU.
....
GRR
GRR
OH.
UM, GRAY...
I WAS THINKING.
I...
WANT MORE WORK TO DO.
?
YOU'RE LEAVING US FOR A JOB?
THAT'S NOT IT.

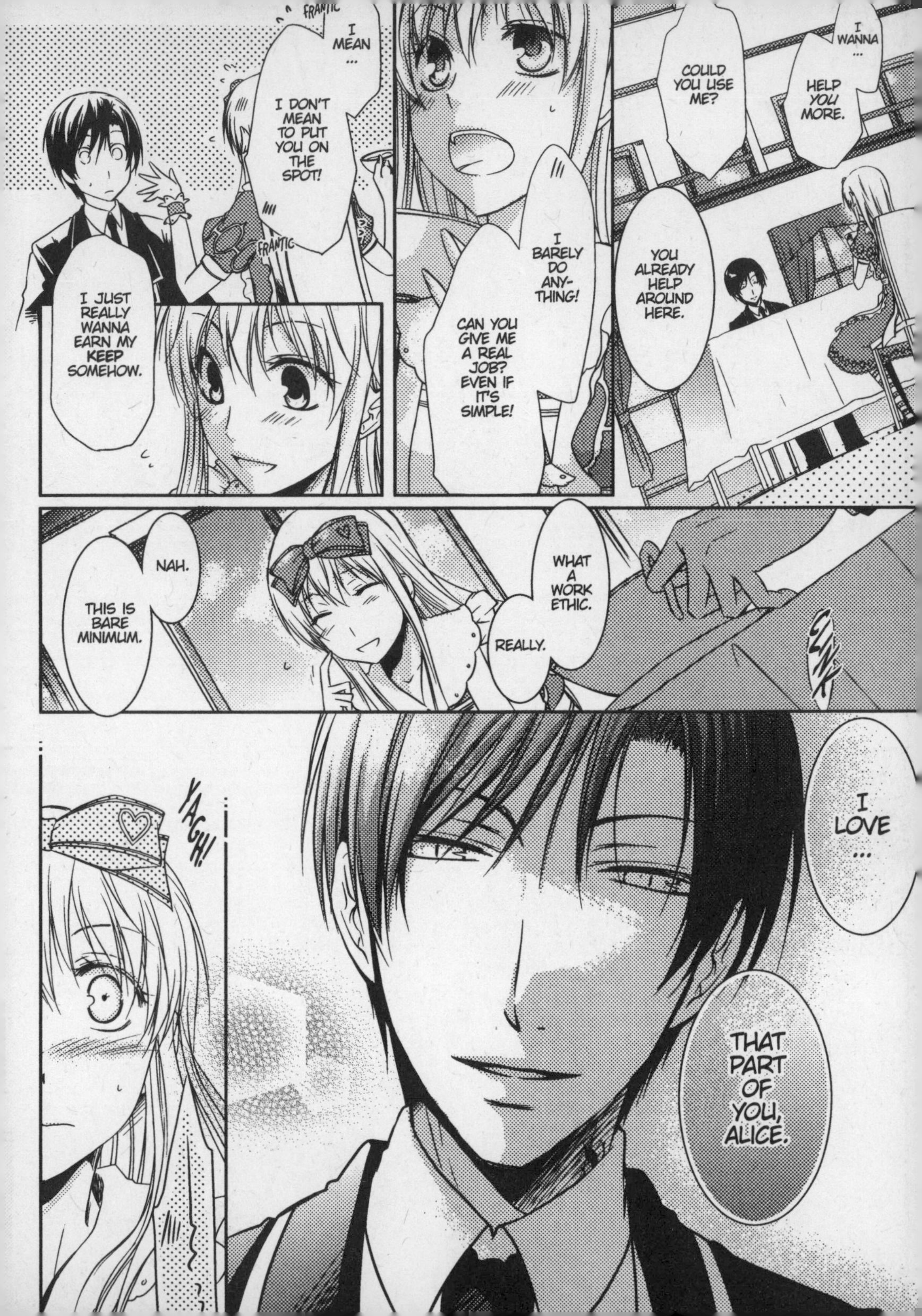
I WANNA ...
HELP YOU MORE.
COULD YOU USE ME?
YOU ALREADY HELP AROUND HERE.
I BARELY DO ANY-THING!
CAN YOU GIVE ME A REAL JOB? EVEN IF IT'S SIMPLE!
FRANTIC
I MEAN ...
I DON'T MEAN TO PUT YOU ON THE SPOT!
FRANTIC
I JUST REALLY WANNA EARN MY KEEP SOMEHOW.
CLINK
WHAT A WORK ETHIC.
REALLY.
NAH.
THIS IS BARE MINIMUM.
I LOVE ...
THAT PART OF YOU, ALICE.
YAGH!

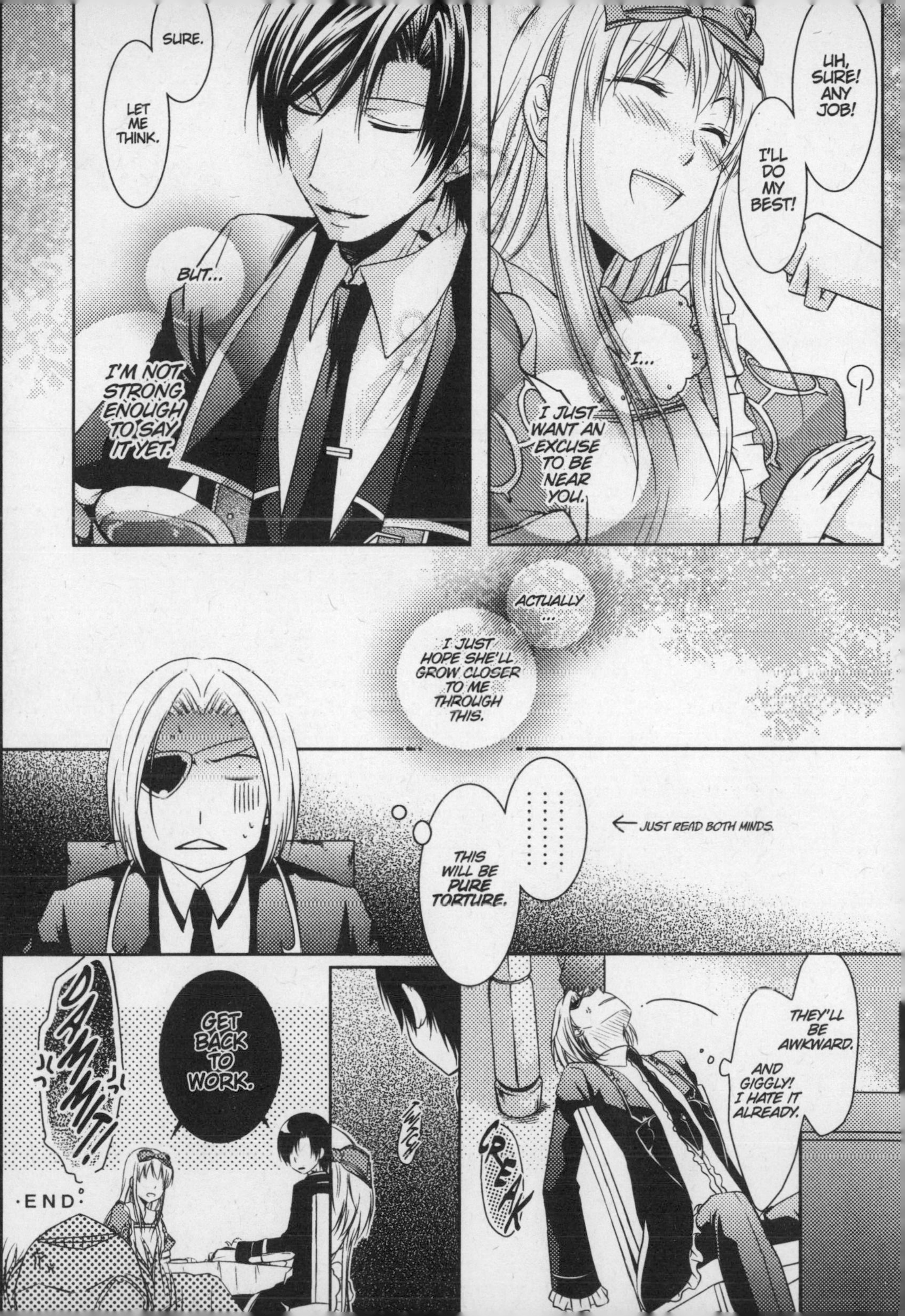
UH, SURE! ANY JOB!
I'LL DO MY BEST!
I...
I JUST WANT AN EXCUSE TO BE NEAR YOU.
SURE.
LET ME THINK.
BUT...
I'M NOT STRONG ENOUGH TO SAY IT YET.
ACTUALLY...
I JUST HOPE SHE'LL GROW CLOSER TO ME THROUGH THIS.
← JUST READ BOTH MINDS.
......
THIS WILL BE PURE TORTURE.
THEY'LL BE AWKWARD.
AND GIGGLY! I HATE IT ALREADY.
CREAK
TWITCH
GET BACK TO WORK.
DAMMIT!
·END·

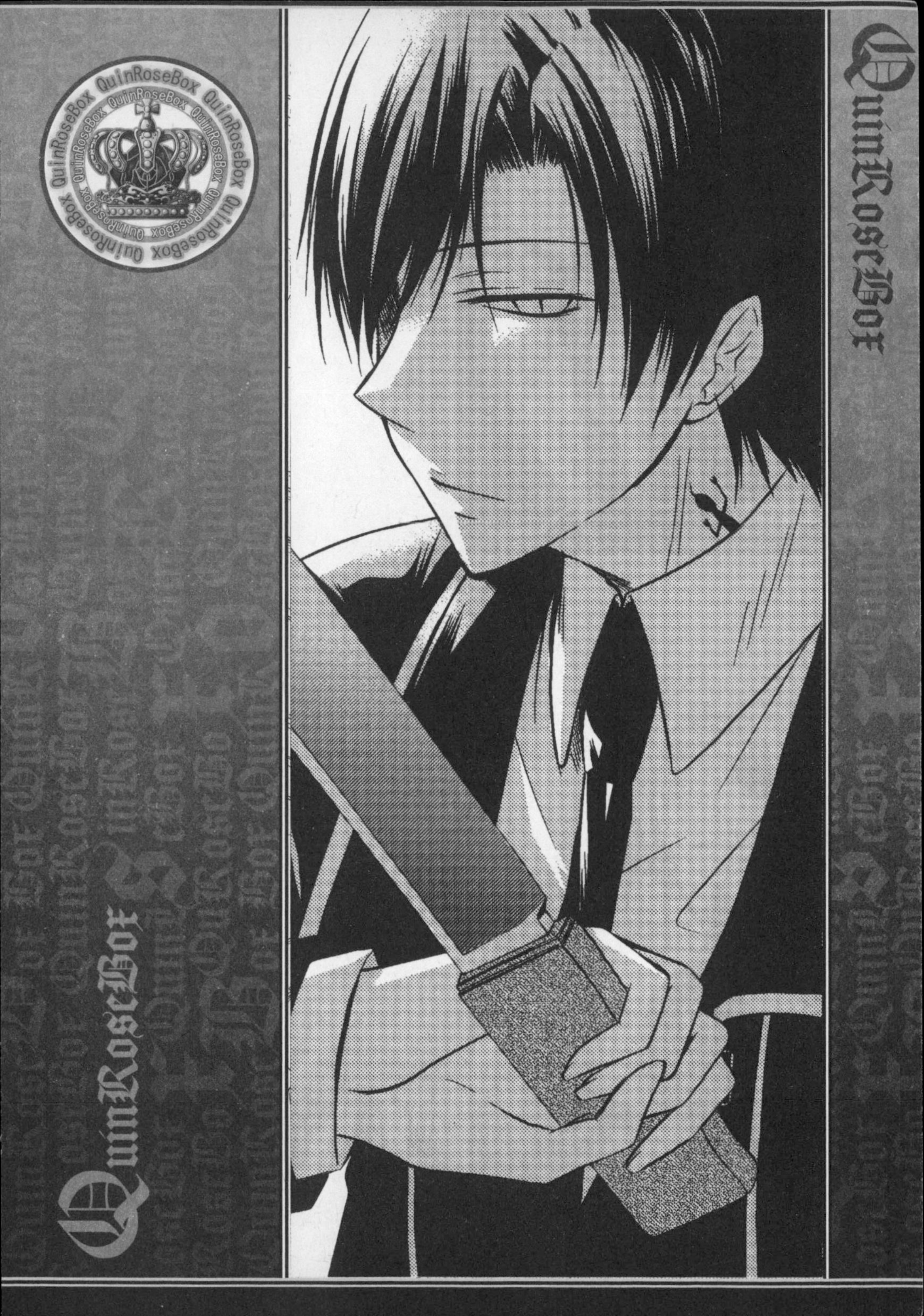
QuinRoseBox
QuinRoseBox
QuinRoseBox

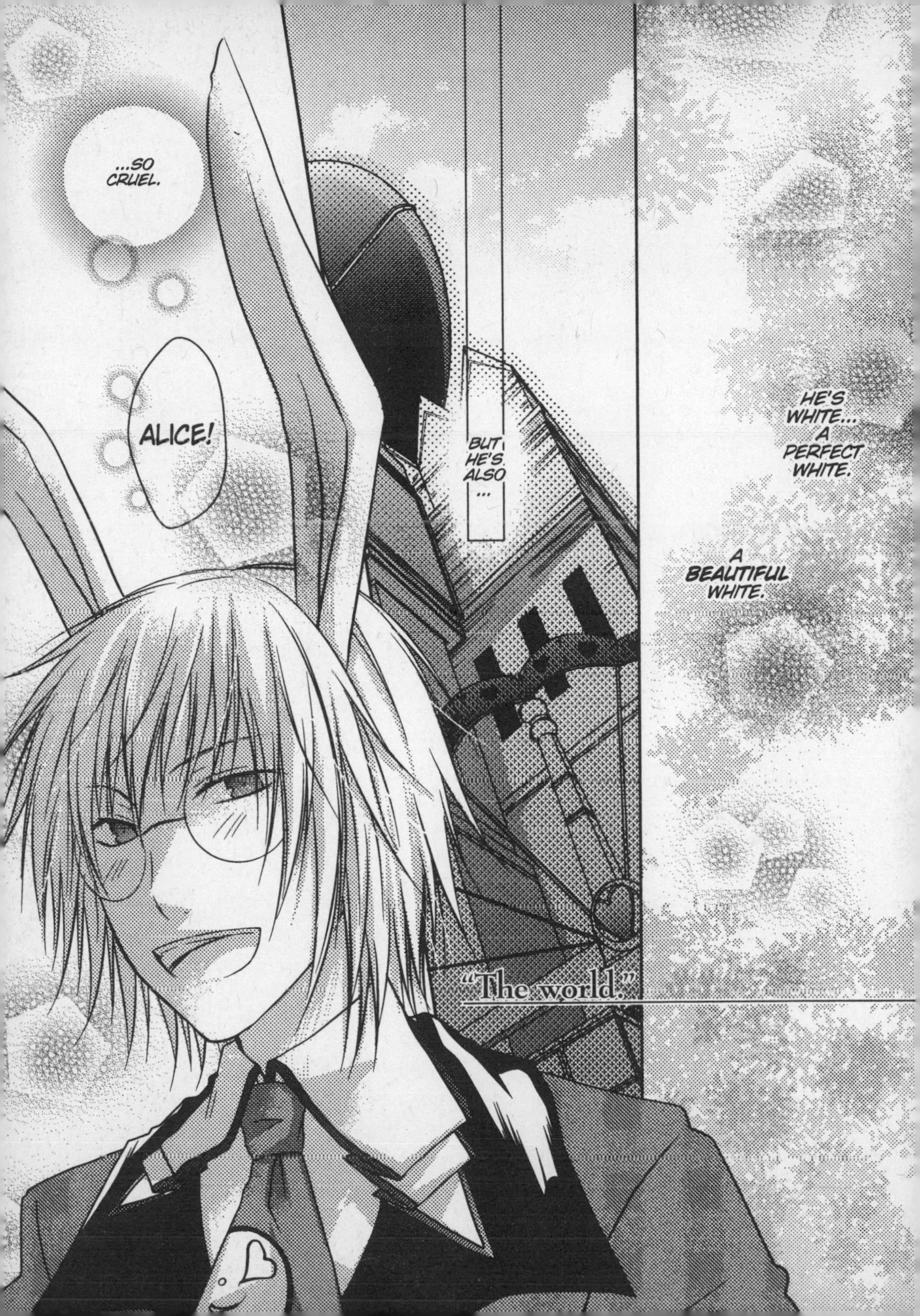
HE'S WHITE... A PERFECT WHITE.
A BEAUTIFUL WHITE.
BUT HE'S ALSO ...
"The world."
...SO CRUEL.
ALICE!

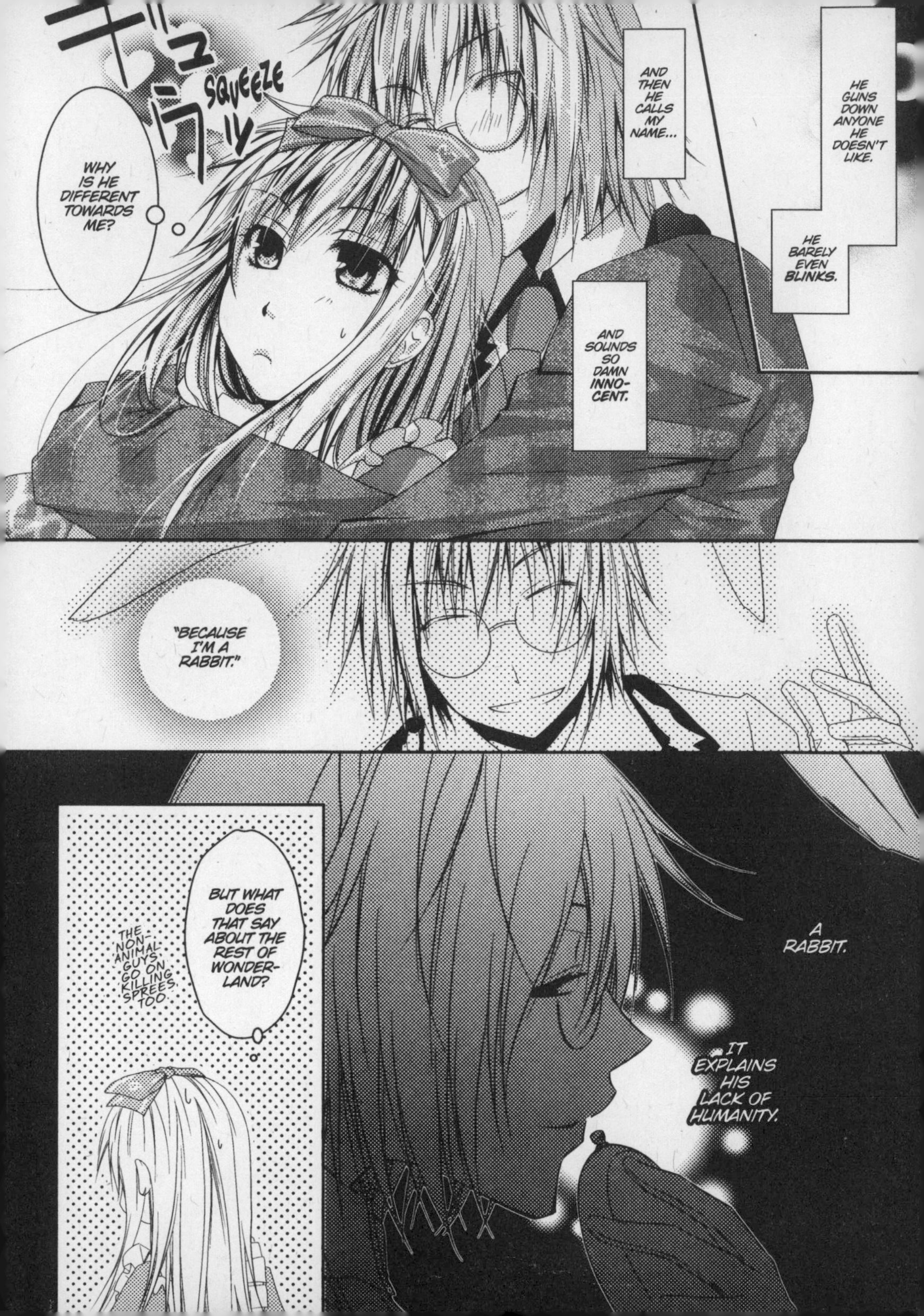
HE GUNS DOWN ANYONE HE DOESN'T LIKE.
HE BARELY EVEN BLINKS.
AND THEN HE CALLS MY NAME...
AND SOUNDS SO DAMN INNO-CENT.
SQUEEZE
WHY IS HE DIFFERENT TOWARDS ME?
"BECAUSE I'M A RABBIT."
A RABBIT.
IT EXPLAINS HIS LACK OF HUMANITY.
BUT WHAT DOES THAT SAY ABOUT THE REST OF WONDER-LAND?
THE NON-ANIMAL GUYS GO ON KILLING SPREES, TOO

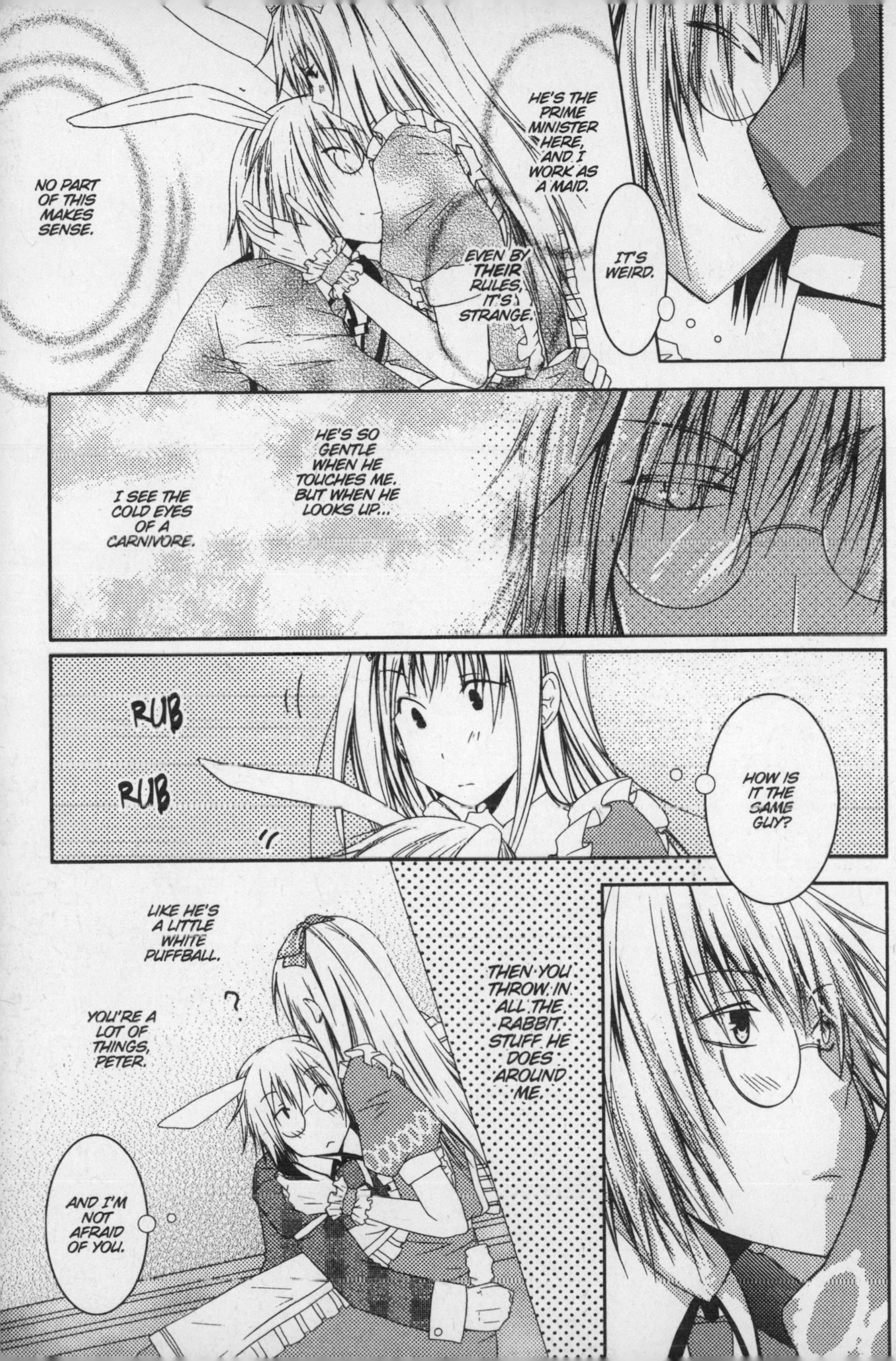
IT'S WEIRD.
HE'S THE PRIME MINISTER HERE, AND I WORK AS A MAID.
EVEN BY THEIR RULES, IT'S STRANGE.
NO PART OF THIS MAKES SENSE.
HE'S SO GENTLE WHEN HE TOUCHES ME. BUT WHEN HE LOOKS UP...
I SEE THE COLD EYES OF A CARNIVORE.
HOW IS IT THE SAME GUY?
RUB
RUB
THEN YOU THROW IN ALL THE RABBIT STUFF HE DOES AROUND ME.
LIKE HE'S A LITTLE WHITE PUFFBALL.
?
YOU'RE A LOT OF THINGS, PETER.
AND I'M NOT AFRAID OF YOU.

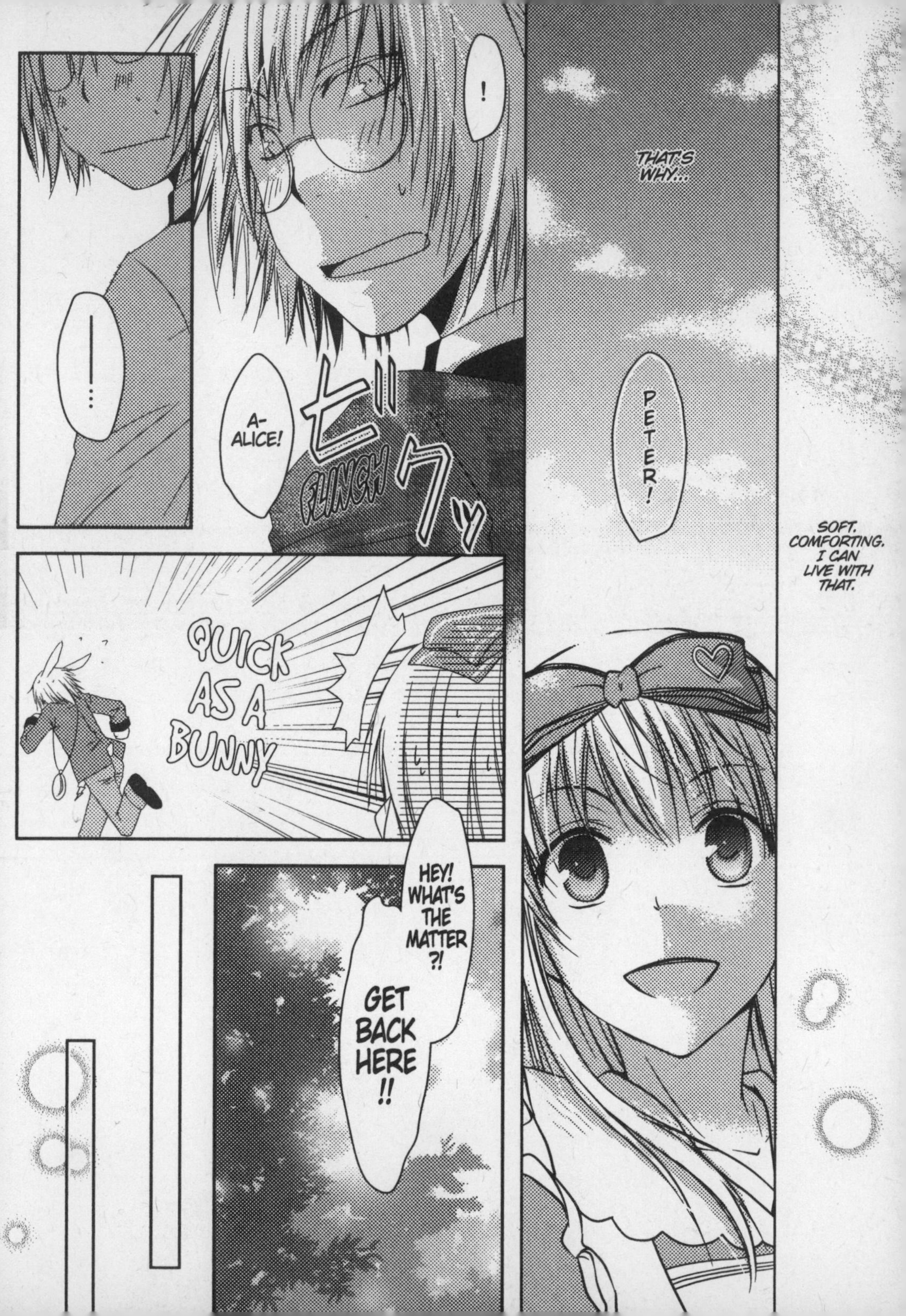
SOFT. COMFORTING. I CAN LIVE WITH THAT.
THAT'S WHY...
PETER!
!
A- ALICE!
FLINCH
!...
QUICK AS A BUNNY
HEY! WHAT'S THE MATTER ?!
GET BACK HERE !!

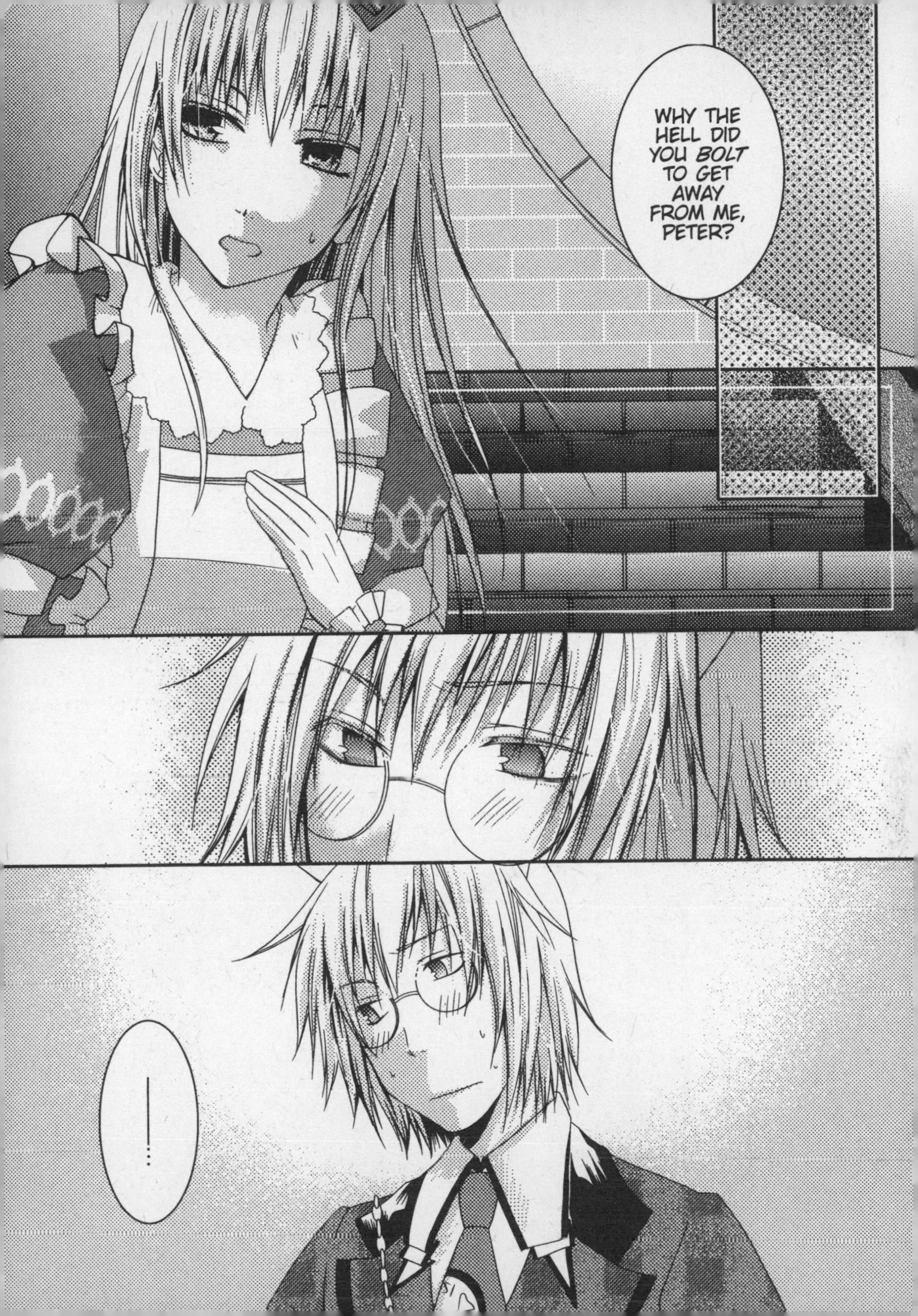
WHY THE HELL DID YOU *BOLT* TO GET AWAY FROM ME, PETER?
—……

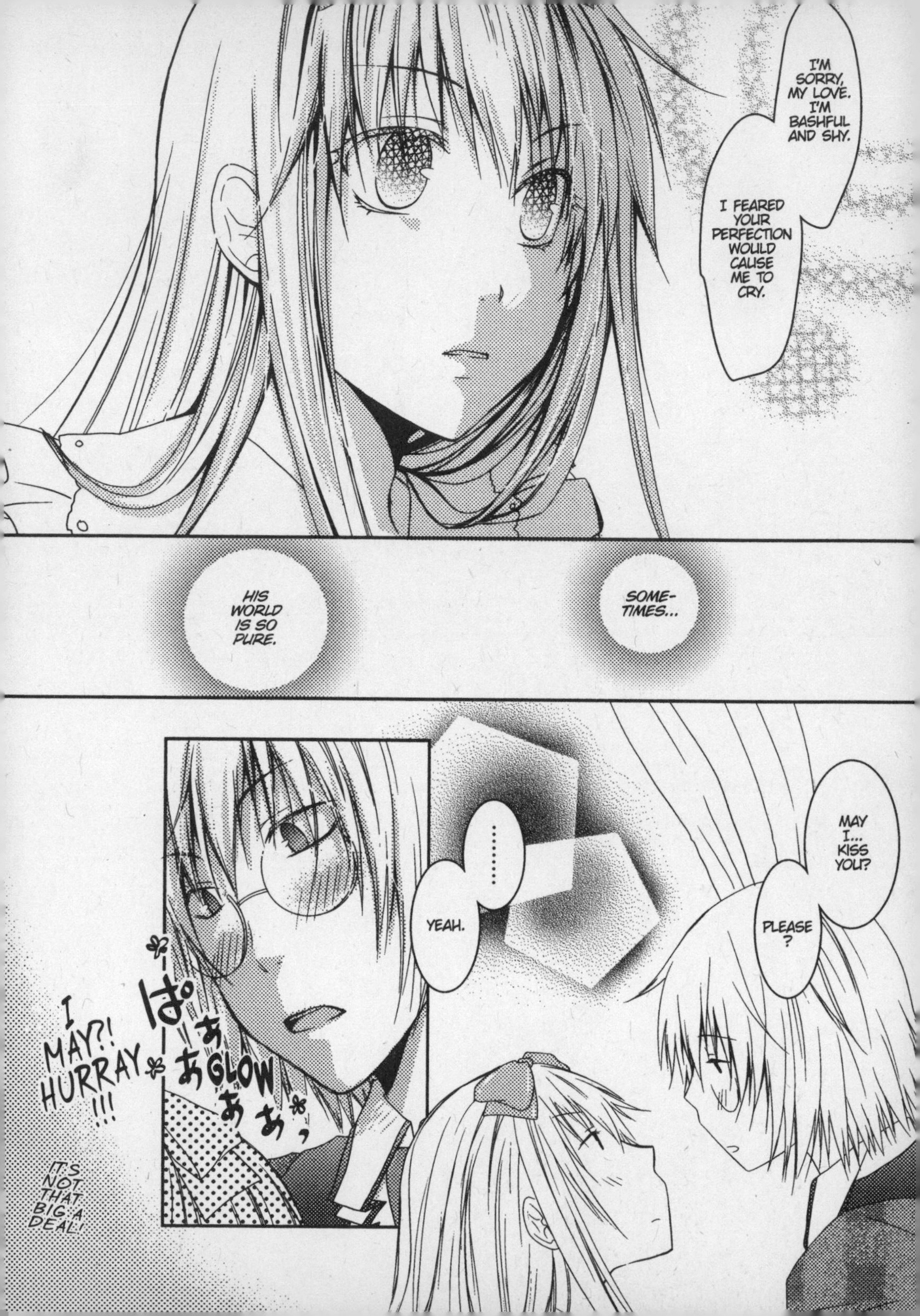
I'M SORRY, MY LOVE. I'M BASHFUL AND SHY.
I FEARED YOUR PERFECTION WOULD CAUSE ME TO CRY.
SOME-TIMES...
HIS WORLD IS SO PURE.
MAY I... KISS YOU?
PLEASE?
......
YEAH.
ぱーーああああ GLOW
I MAY?! HURRAY!!!
IT'S NOT THAT BIG A DEAL!

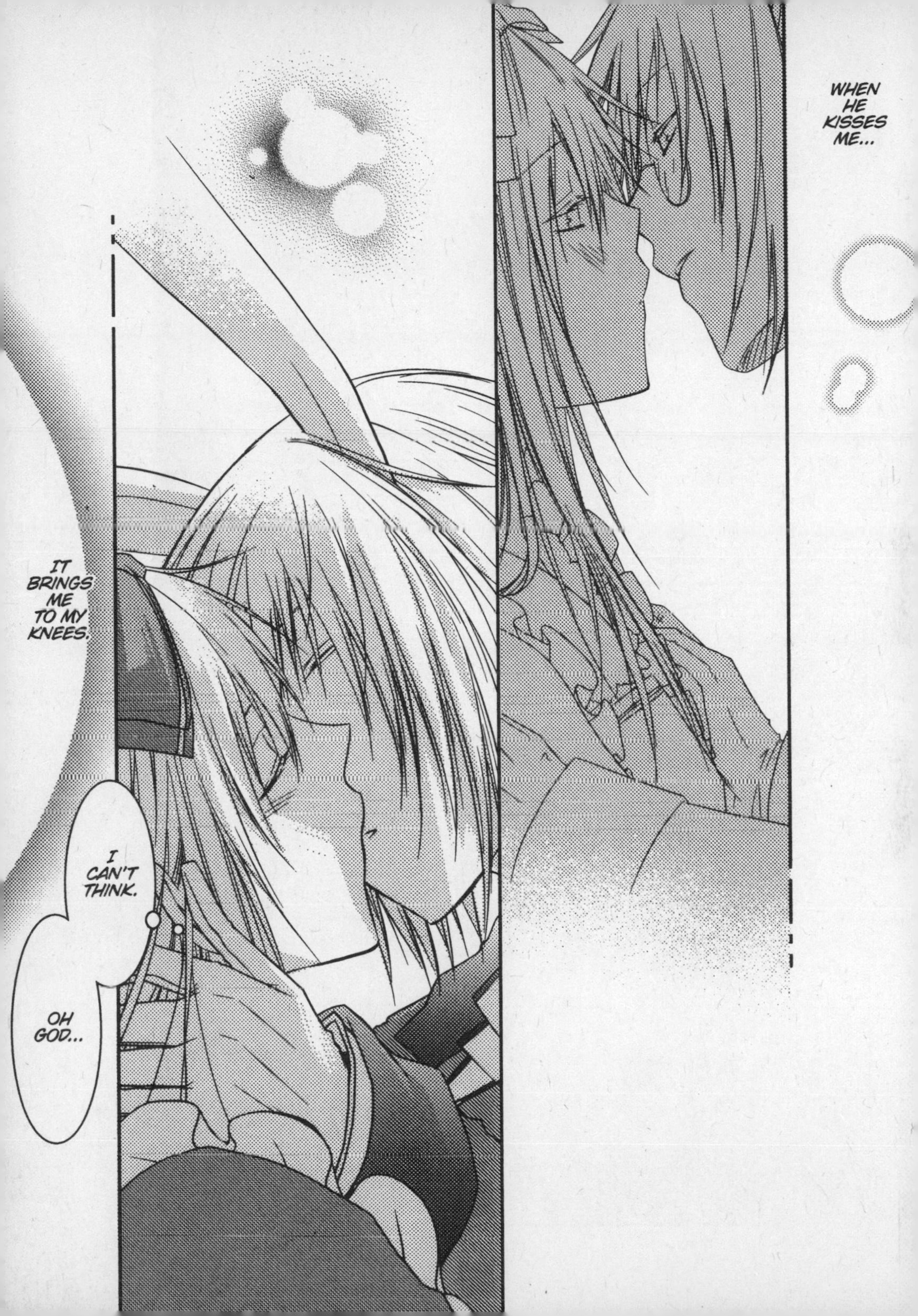
WHEN HE KISSES ME...
IT BRINGS ME TO MY KNEES.
I CAN'T THINK.
OH GOD...

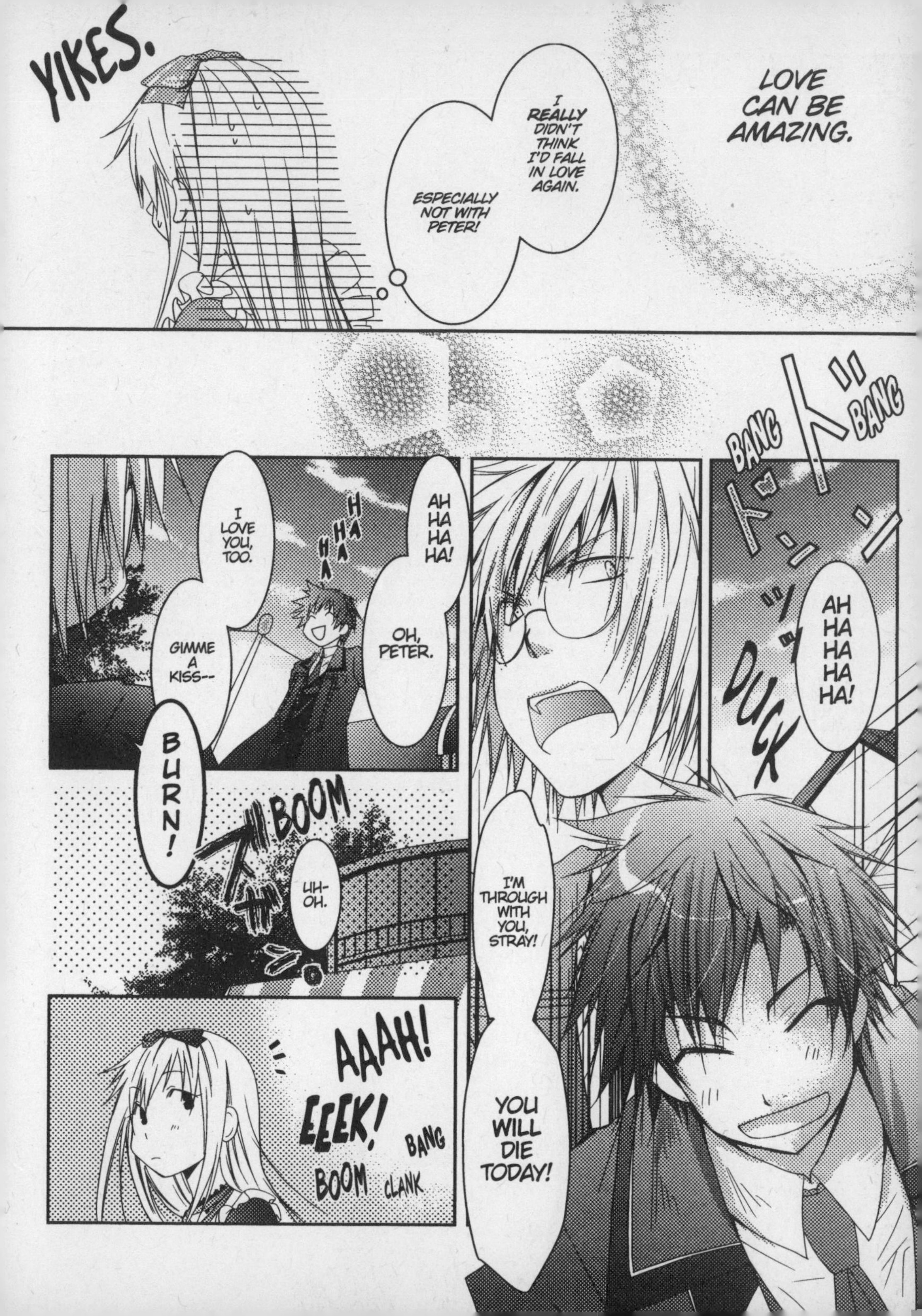
LOVE CAN BE AMAZING.
I REALLY DIDN'T THINK I'D FALL IN LOVE AGAIN.
ESPECIALLY NOT WITH PETER!
YIKES.
BANG
BANG
AH HA HA HA HA HA!
DUCK
I'M THROUGH WITH YOU, STRAY!
YOU WILL DIE TODAY!
AH HA HA HA HA!
OH, PETER.
HA HA HA HA
I LOVE YOU, TOO.
GIMME A KISS--
BURN!
BOOM
UH-OH.
AAAH!
EEEK!
BANG
BOOM
CLANK

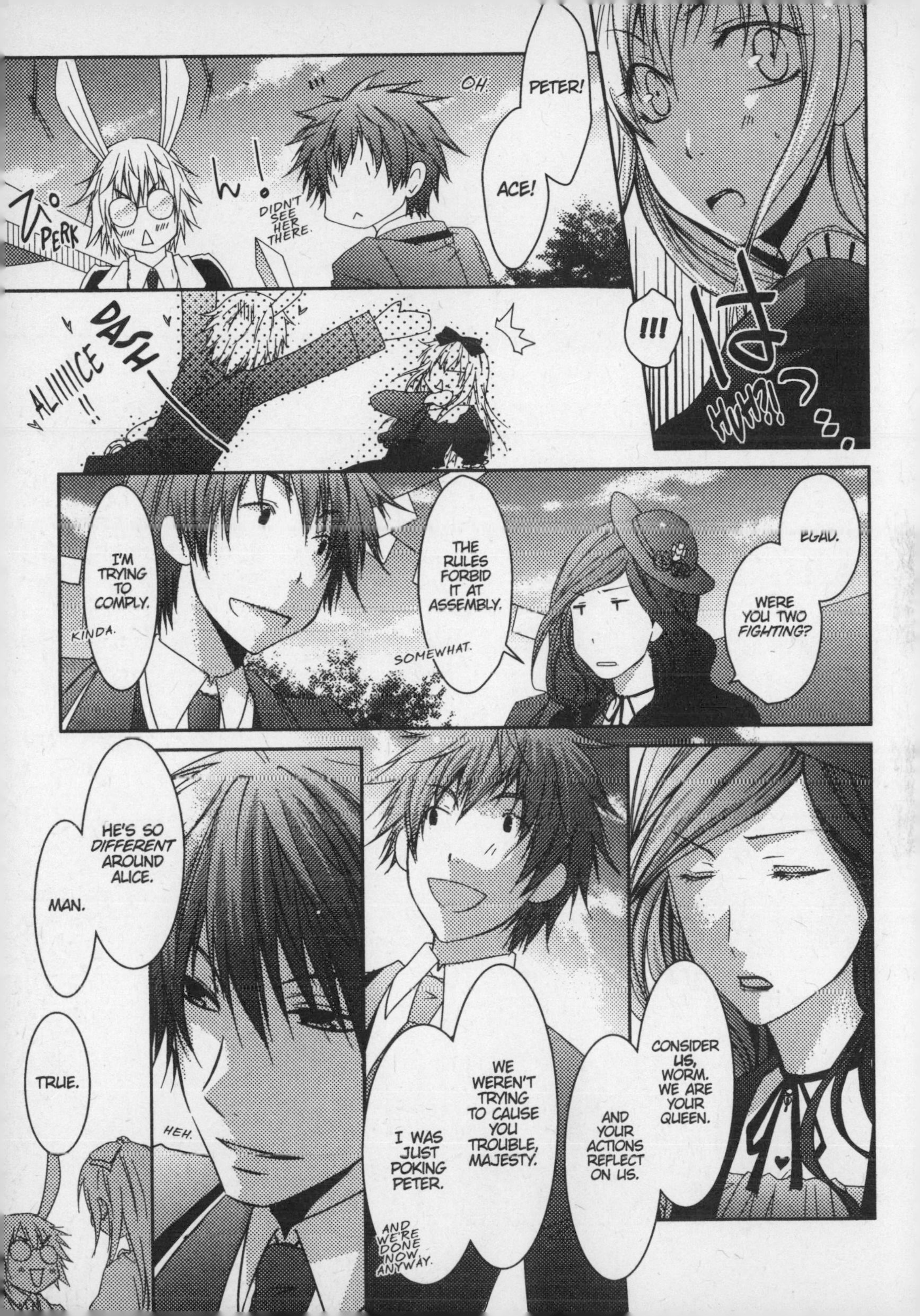
PETER!
ACE!
OH.
DIDN'T SEE HER THERE.
PERK
!!!
はっ
HUH?!
DASH
ALIIIIICE!!
EGAD.
WERE YOU TWO FIGHTING?
THE RULES FORBID IT AT ASSEMBLY.
SOMEWHAT.
I'M TRYING TO COMPLY.
KINDA.
CONSIDER US, WORM. WE ARE YOUR QUEEN.
AND YOUR ACTIONS REFLECT ON US.
WE WEREN'T TRYING TO CAUSE YOU TROUBLE, MAJESTY.
I WAS JUST POKING PETER.
AND WE'RE DONE NOW ANYWAY.
HE'S SO DIFFERENT AROUND ALICE.
MAN.
TRUE.
HEH.

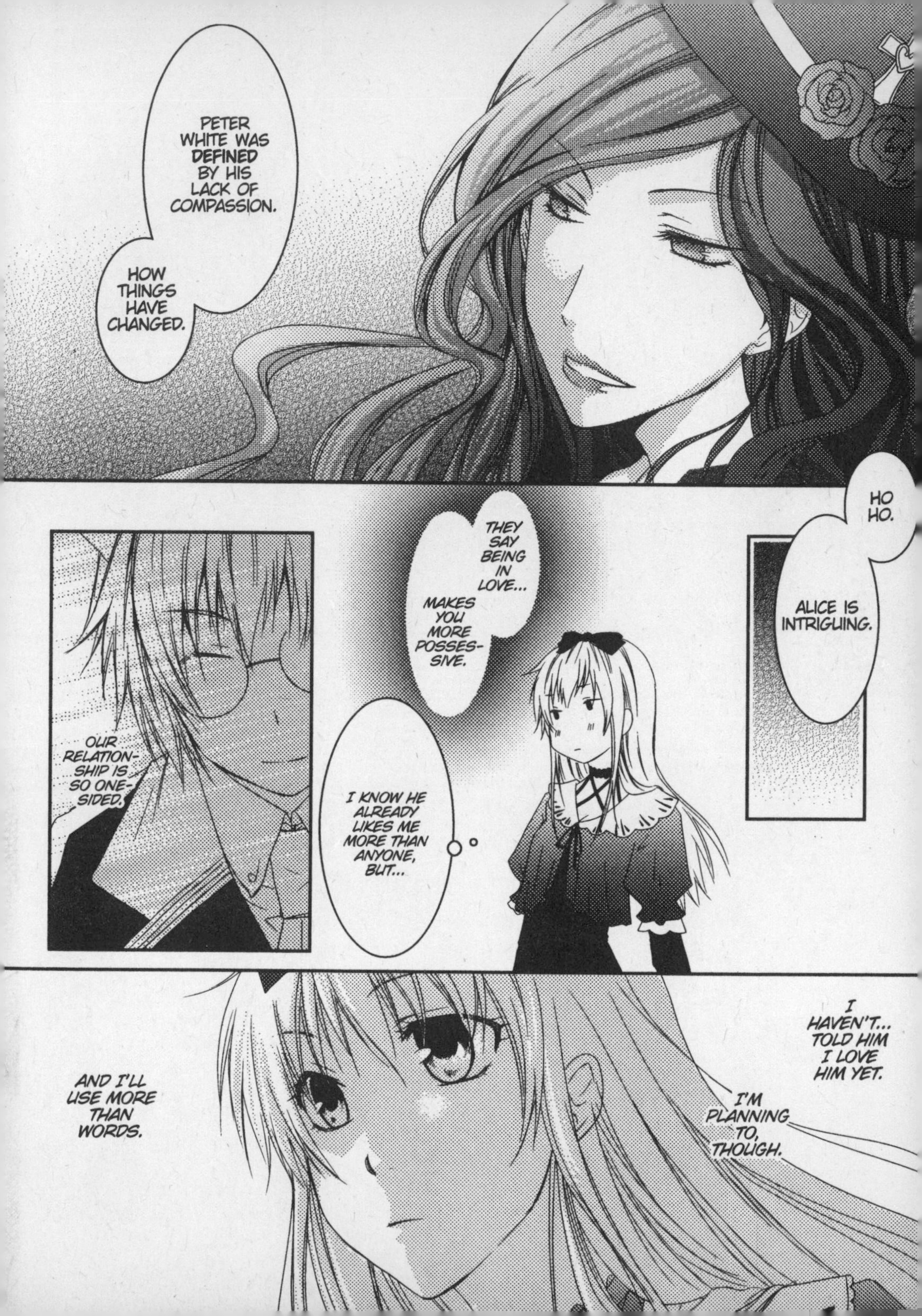
PETER WHITE WAS **DEFINED** BY HIS LACK OF COMPASSION.
HOW THINGS HAVE CHANGED.
HO HO.
ALICE IS INTRIGUING.
THEY SAY BEING IN LOVE... MAKES YOU MORE POSSES-SIVE.
I KNOW HE ALREADY LIKES ME MORE THAN ANYONE, BUT...
OUR RELATION-SHIP IS SO ONE-SIDED.
I HAVEN'T... TOLD HIM I LOVE HIM YET.
I'M PLANNING TO, THOUGH.
AND I'LL USE MORE THAN WORDS.

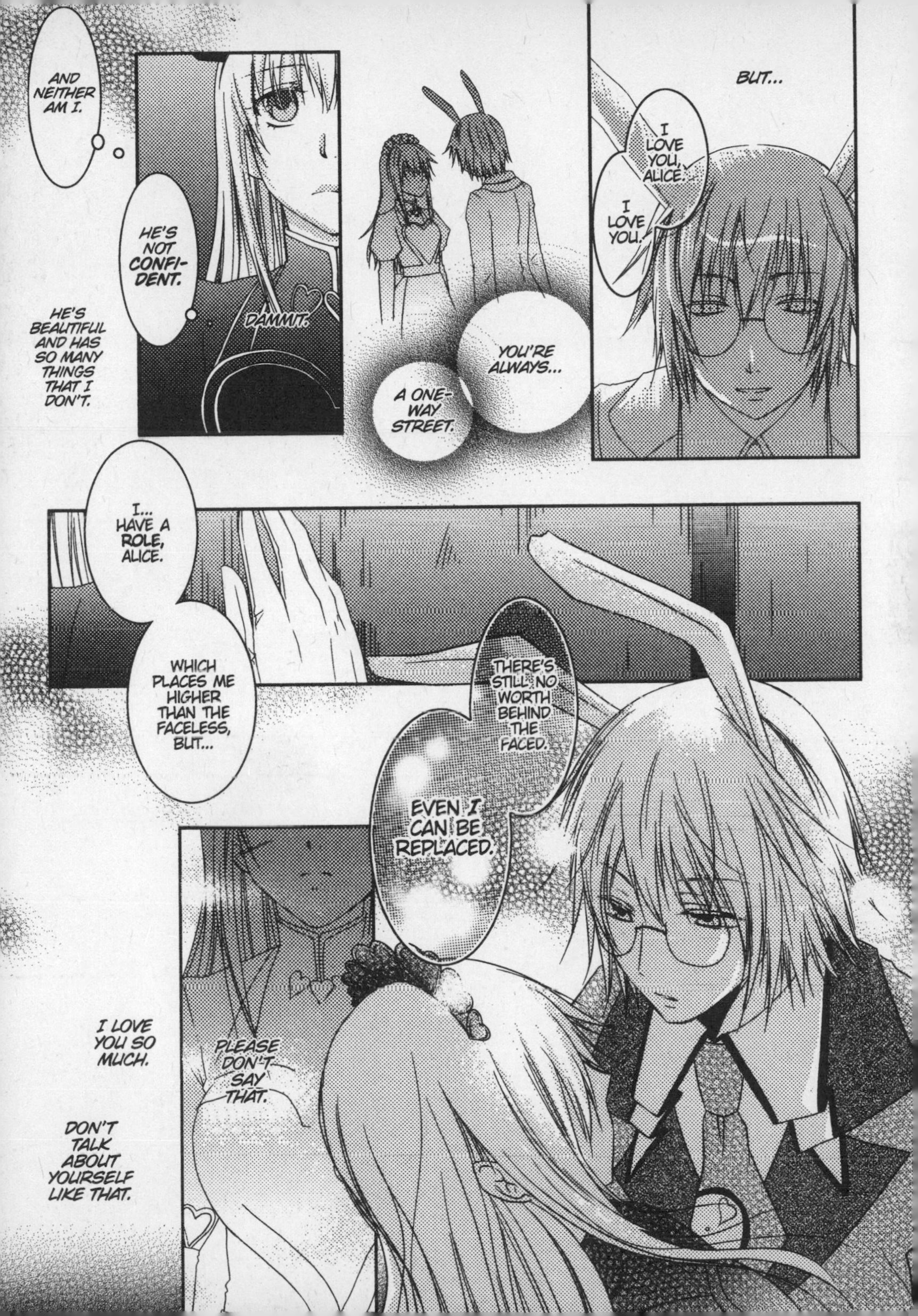
BUT...
I LOVE YOU, ALICE.
I LOVE YOU.
YOU'RE ALWAYS...
A ONE-WAY STREET.
HE'S NOT CONFIDENT.
AND NEITHER AM I.
DAMMIT.
HE'S BEAUTIFUL AND HAS SO MANY THINGS THAT I DON'T.
I... HAVE A ROLE, ALICE.
WHICH PLACES ME HIGHER THAN THE FACELESS, BUT...
THERE'S STILL NO WORTH BEHIND THE FACED.
EVEN I CAN BE REPLACED.
PLEASE DON'T SAY THAT.
I LOVE YOU SO MUCH.
DON'T TALK ABOUT YOURSELF LIKE THAT.

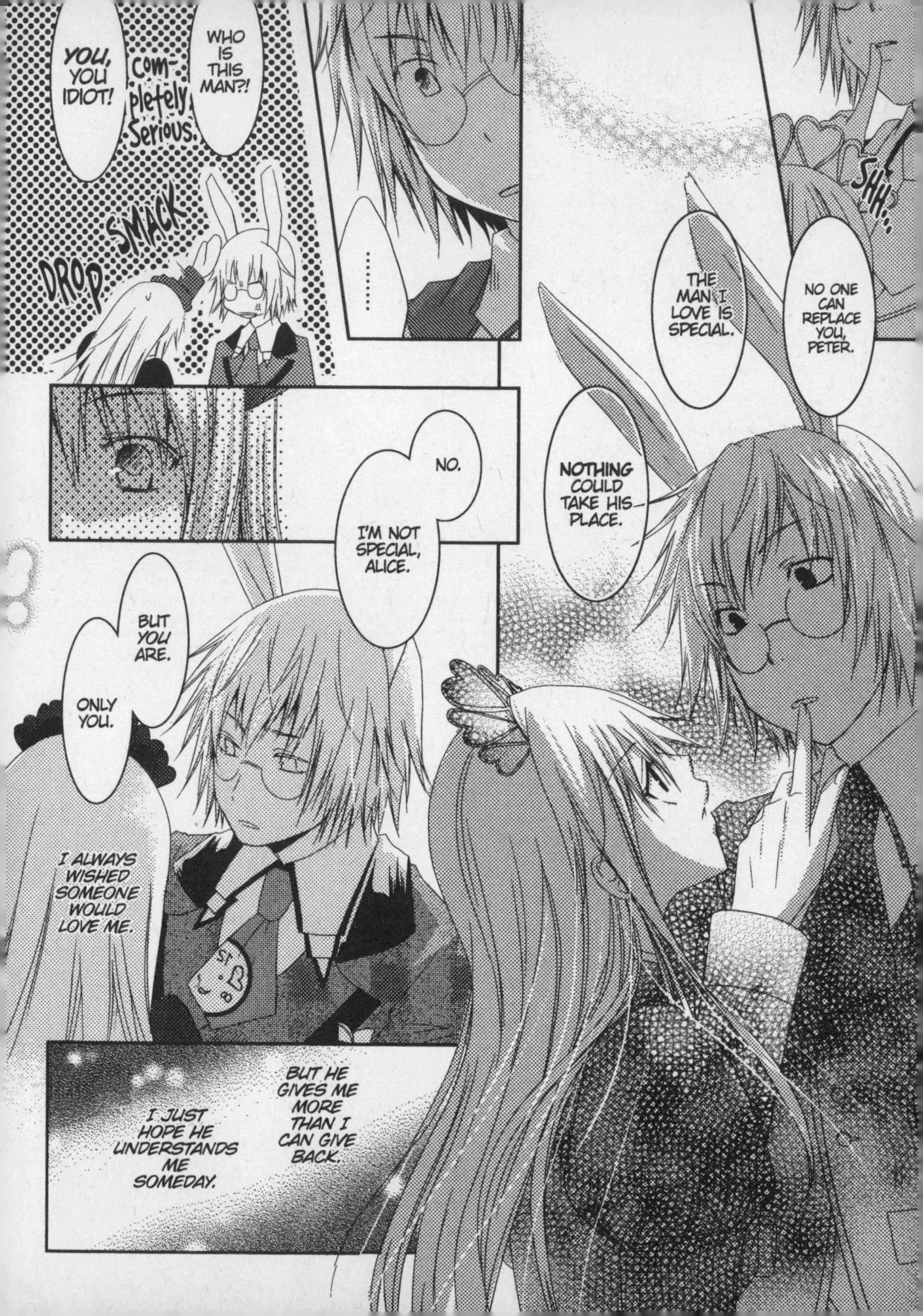
SHH...
NO ONE CAN REPLACE YOU, PETER.
THE MAN I LOVE IS SPECIAL.
NOTHING COULD TAKE HIS PLACE.
......
WHO IS THIS MAN?!
YOU, YOU IDIOT!
Completely Serious.
SMACK
DROP
NO.
I'M NOT SPECIAL, ALICE.
BUT YOU ARE.
ONLY YOU.
I ALWAYS WISHED SOMEONE WOULD LOVE ME.
BUT HE GIVES ME MORE THAN I CAN GIVE BACK.
I JUST HOPE HE UNDERSTANDS ME SOMEDAY.

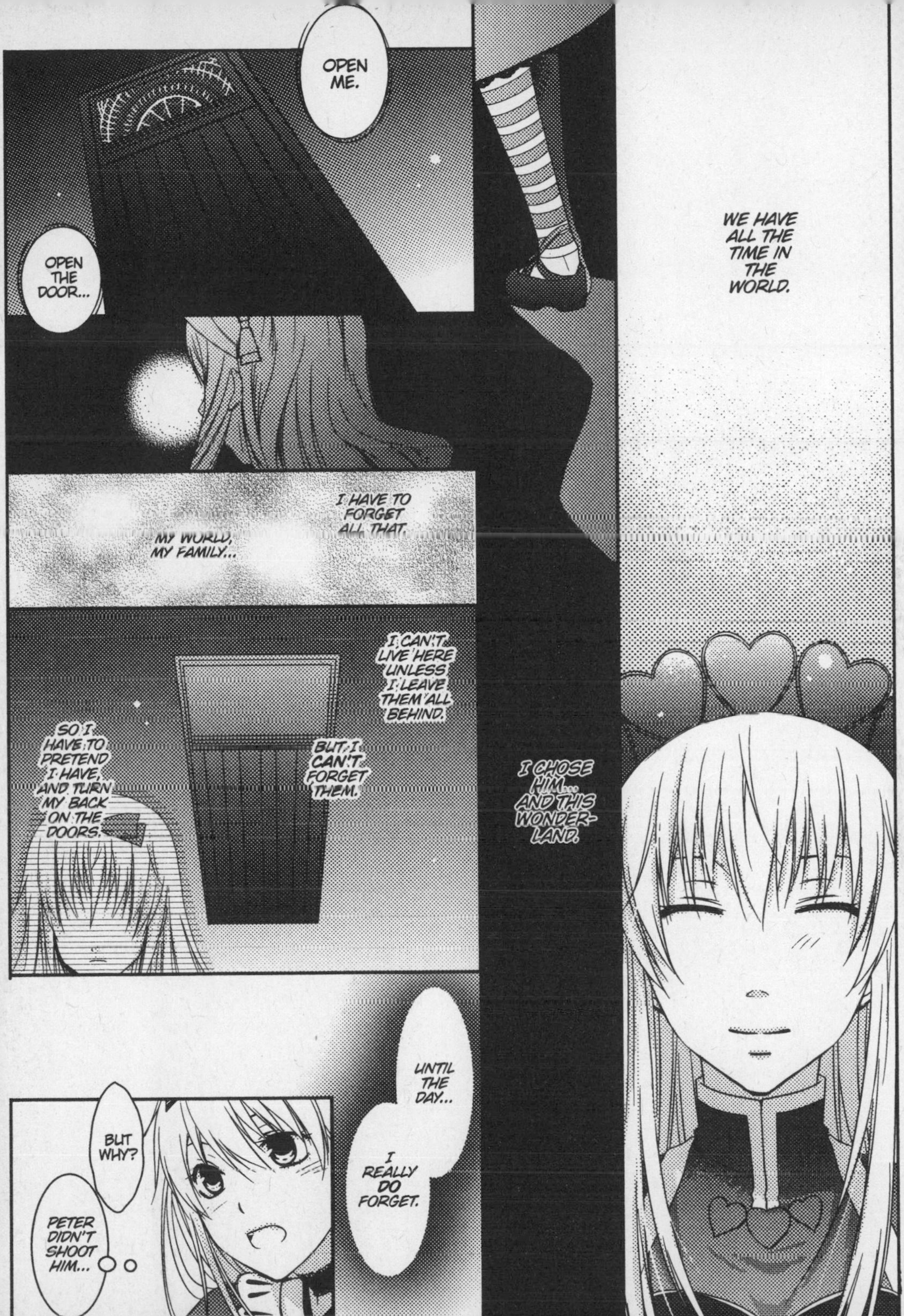
WE HAVE ALL THE TIME IN THE WORLD.
I CHOSE HIM... AND THIS WONDERLAND.
OPEN ME.
OPEN THE DOOR...
I HAVE TO FORGET ALL THAT.
MY WORLD, MY FAMILY...
I CAN'T LIVE HERE UNLESS I LEAVE THEM ALL BEHIND.
BUT I CAN'T FORGET THEM.
SO I HAVE TO PRETEND I HAVE, AND TURN MY BACK ON THE DOORS.
UNTIL THE DAY...
I REALLY DO FORGET.
BUT WHY?
PETER DIDN'T SHOOT HIM...

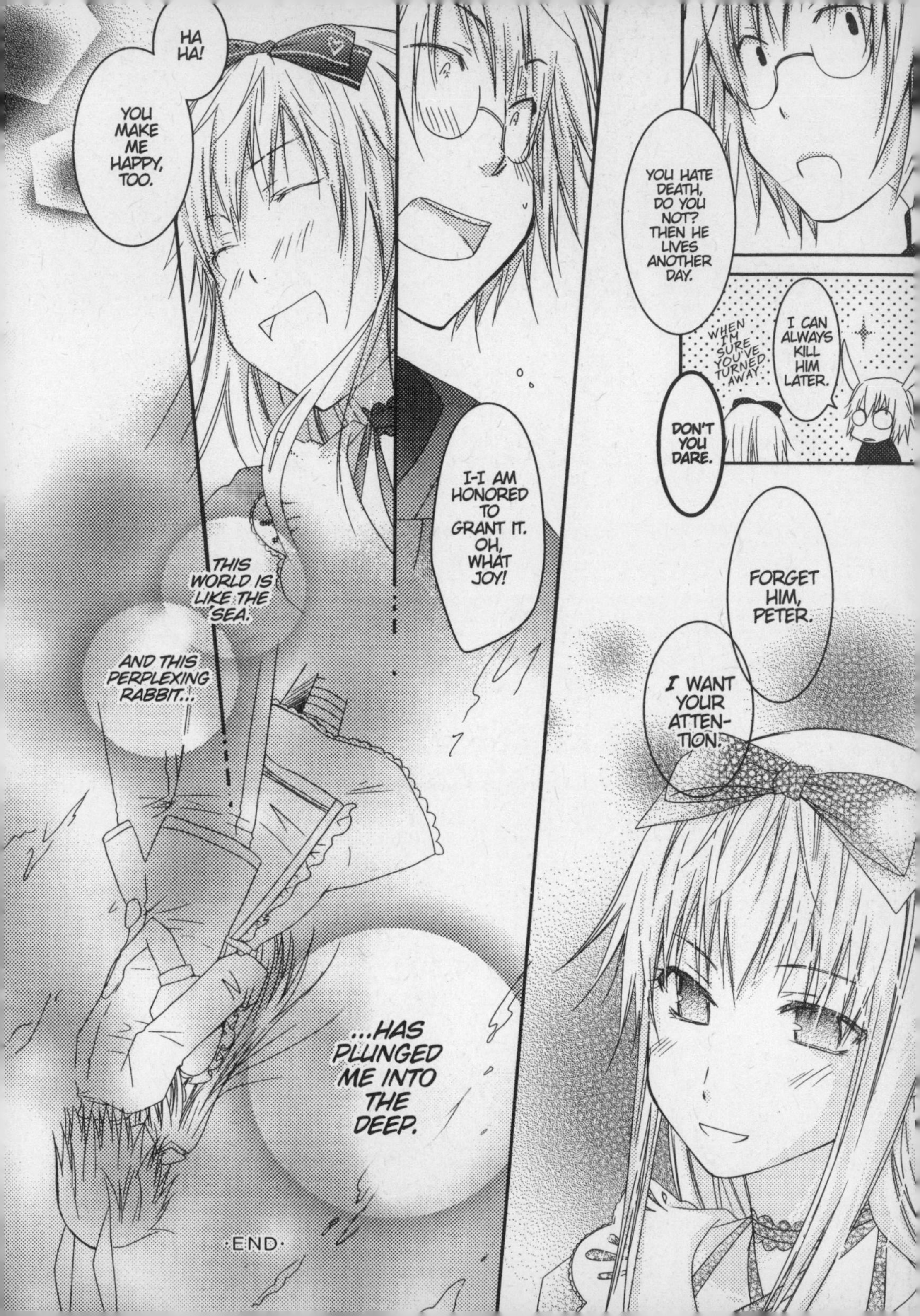

YOU HATE DEATH, DO YOU NOT? THEN HE LIVES ANOTHER DAY.
I CAN ALWAYS KILL HIM LATER.
WHEN I'M SURE YOU'VE TURNED AWAY.
DON'T YOU DARE.
FORGET HIM, PETER.
I WANT YOUR ATTENTION.
I-I AM HONORED TO GRANT IT. OH, WHAT JOY!
HA HA!
YOU MAKE ME HAPPY, TOO.
THIS WORLD IS LIKE THE SEA.
AND THIS PERPLEXING RABBIT...
...HAS PLUNGED ME INTO THE DEEP.
·END·

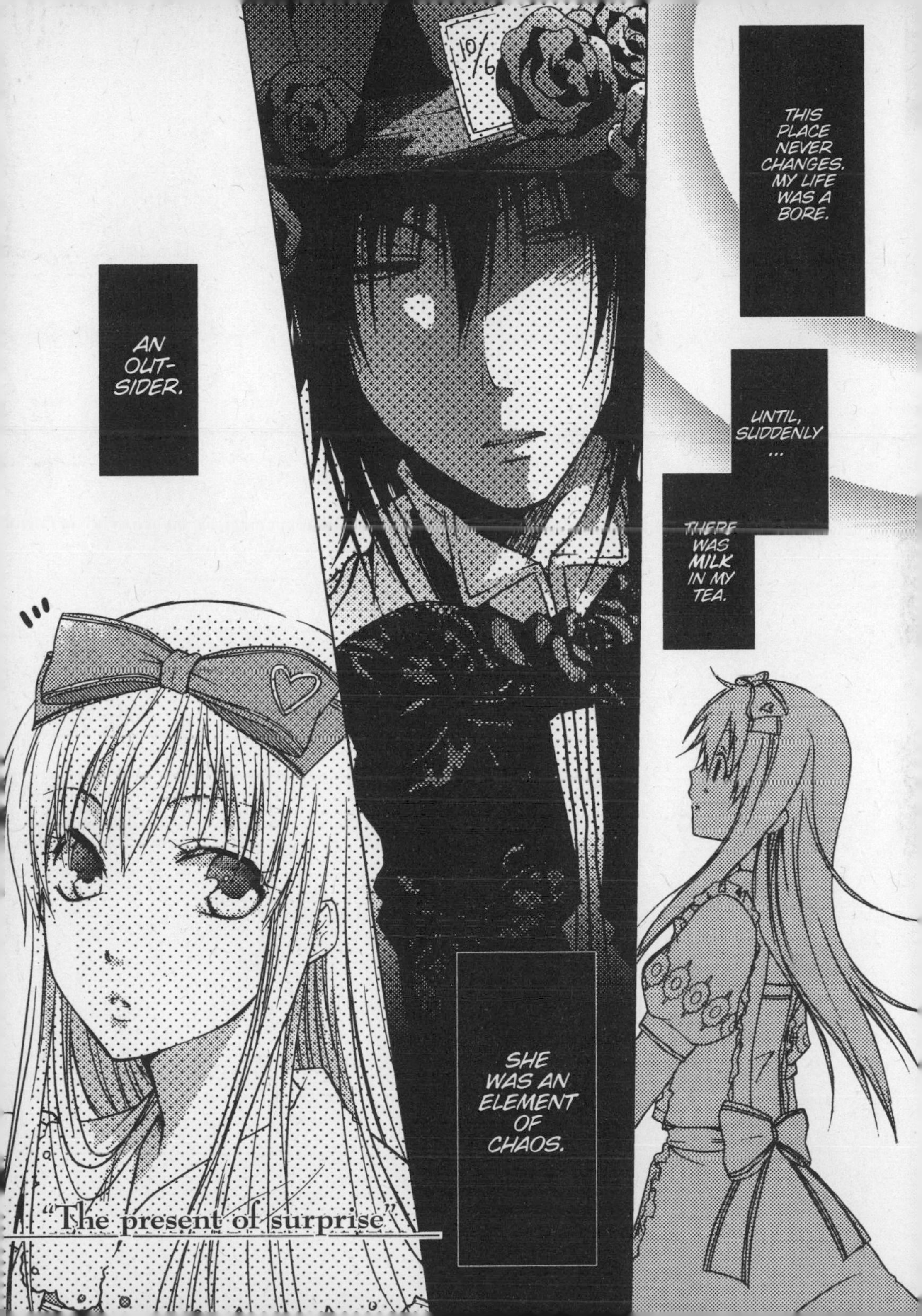
THIS PLACE NEVER CHANGES. MY LIFE WAS A BORE.
UNTIL, SUDDENLY ...
THERE WAS MILK IN MY TEA.
SHE WAS AN ELEMENT OF CHAOS.
AN OUTSIDER.
"The present of surprise"

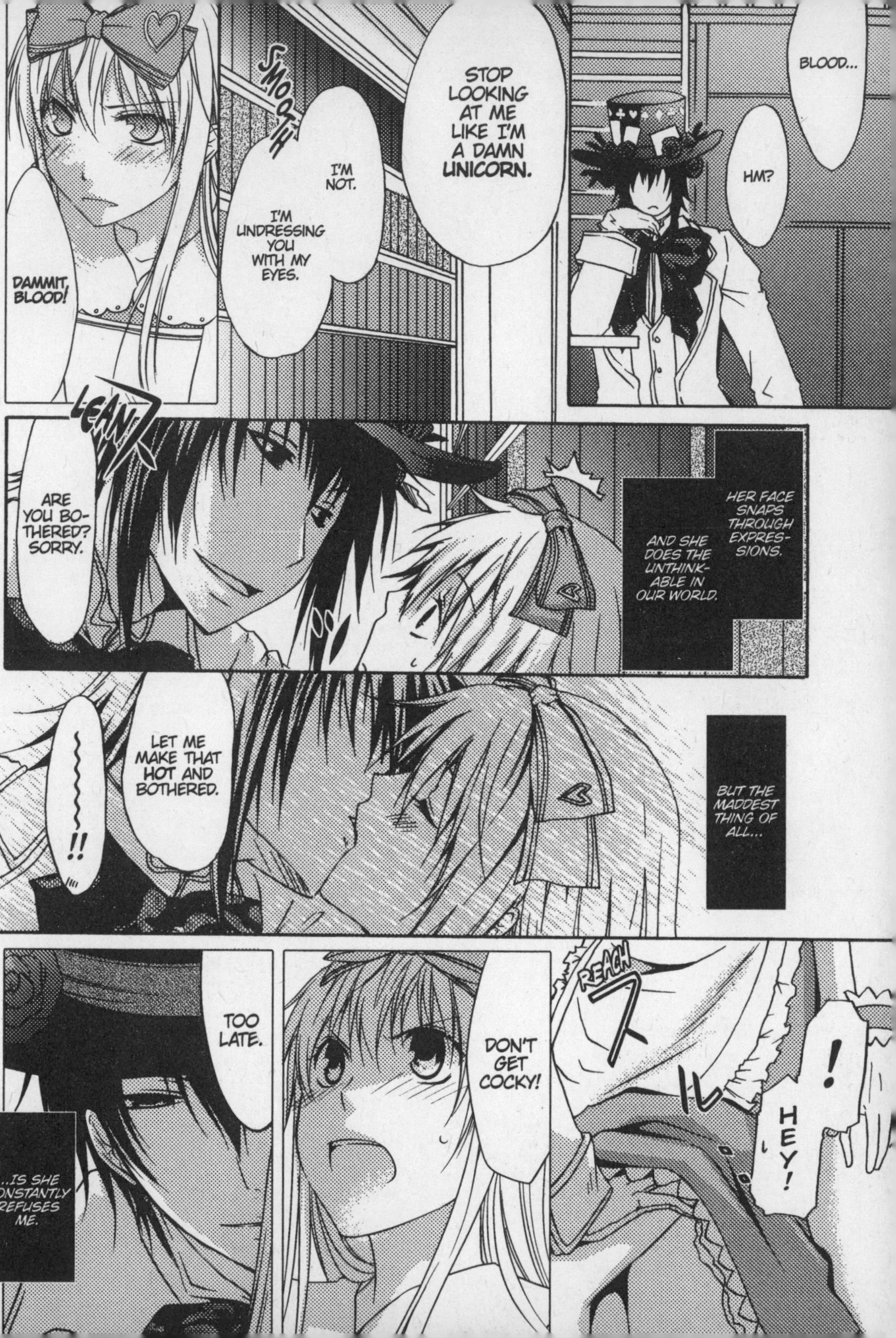
BLOOD...
HM?
STOP LOOKING AT ME LIKE I'M A DAMN UNICORN.
SMOOTH
I'M NOT.
I'M UNDRESSING YOU WITH MY EYES.
DAMMIT, BLOOD!
HER FACE SNAPS THROUGH EXPRES-SIONS.
AND SHE DOES THE UNTHINK-ABLE IN OUR WORLD.
ARE YOU BO-THERED? SORRY.
LEAN
BUT THE MADDEST THING OF ALL...
LET ME MAKE THAT HOT AND BOTHERED.
~~~~!!
REACH
!
HEY!
DON'T GET COCKY!
TOO LATE.
...IS SHE CONSTANTLY REFUSES ME.
~~~~

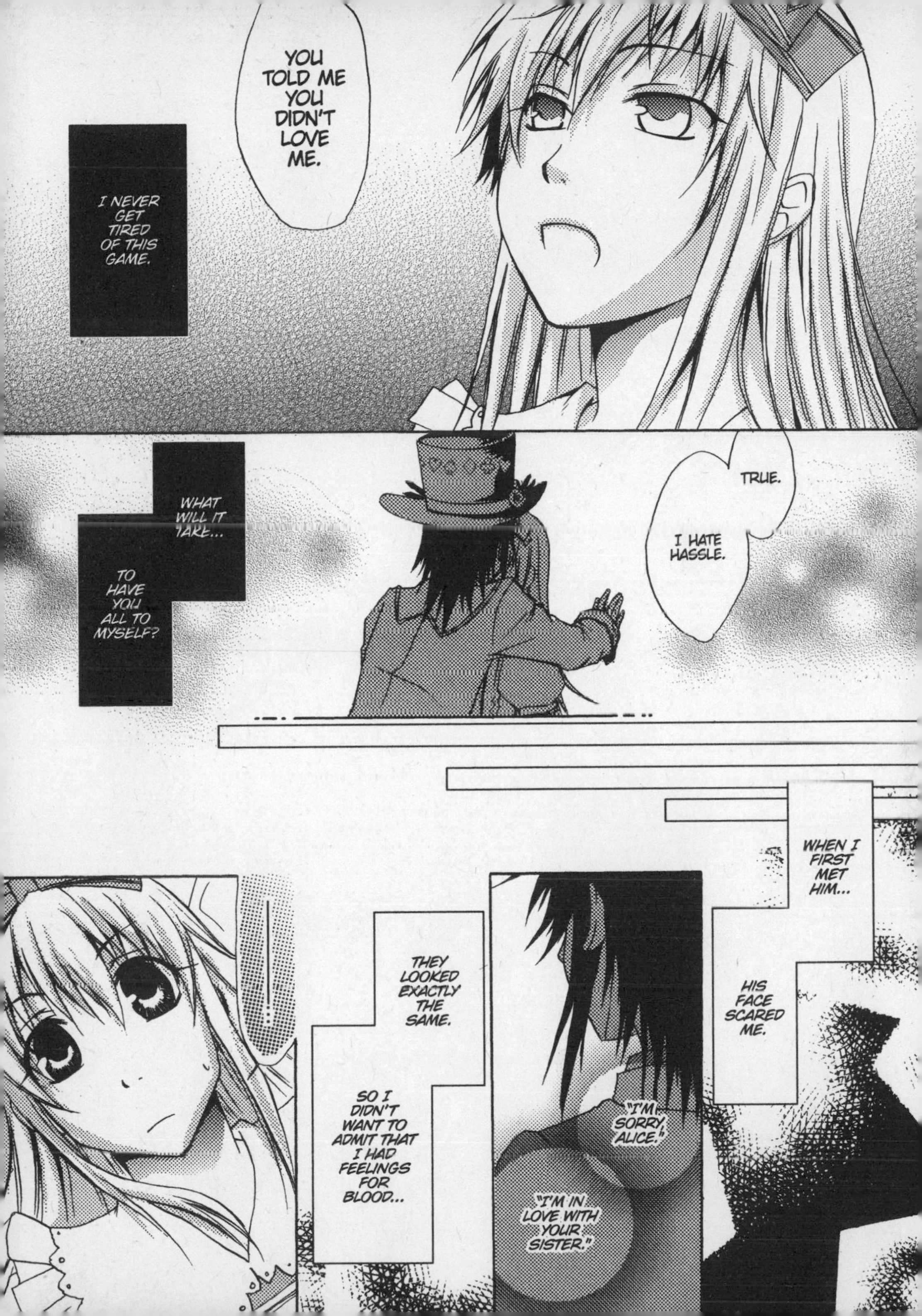
YOU TOLD ME YOU DIDN'T LOVE ME.
I NEVER GET TIRED OF THIS GAME.
TRUE.
I HATE HASSLE.
WHAT WILL IT TAKE...
TO HAVE YOU ALL TO MYSELF?
WHEN I FIRST MET HIM...
HIS FACE SCARED ME.
"I'M SORRY, ALICE."
"I'M IN LOVE WITH YOUR SISTER."
THEY LOOKED EXACTLY THE SAME.
SO I DIDN'T WANT TO ADMIT THAT I HAD FEELINGS FOR BLOOD...
!

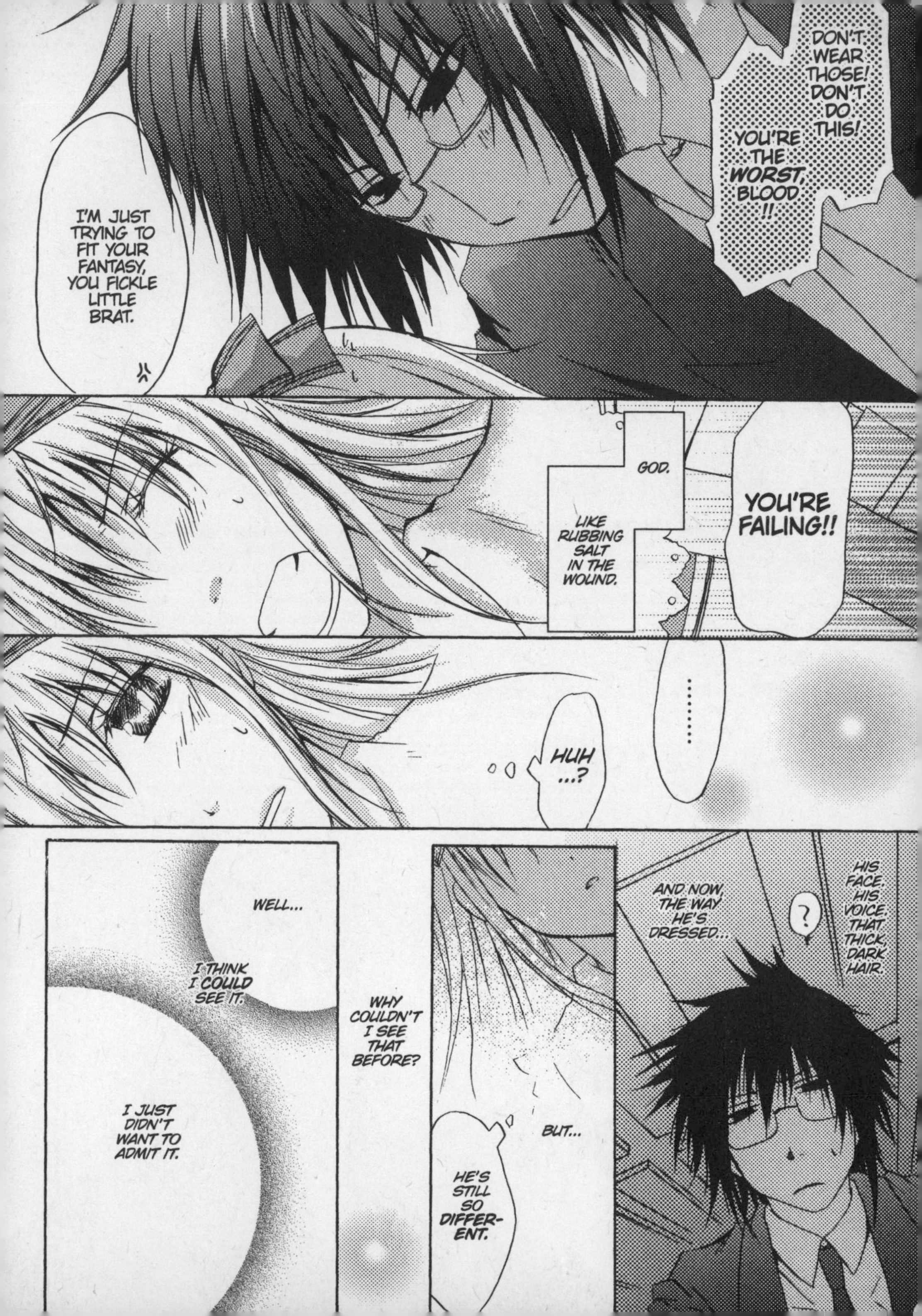
DON'T WEAR THOSE! DON'T DO THIS!
YOU'RE THE WORST, BLOOD!!
I'M JUST TRYING TO FIT YOUR FANTASY, YOU FICKLE LITTLE BRAT.
YOU'RE FAILING!!
GOD.
LIKE RUBBING SALT IN THE WOUND.
......
HUH ...?
HIS FACE. HIS VOICE. THAT THICK, DARK HAIR.
AND NOW, THE WAY HE'S DRESSED...
?
WHY COULDN'T I SEE THAT BEFORE?
BUT...
HE'S STILL SO DIFFER-ENT.
WELL...
I THINK I COULD SEE IT.
I JUST DIDN'T WANT TO ADMIT IT.

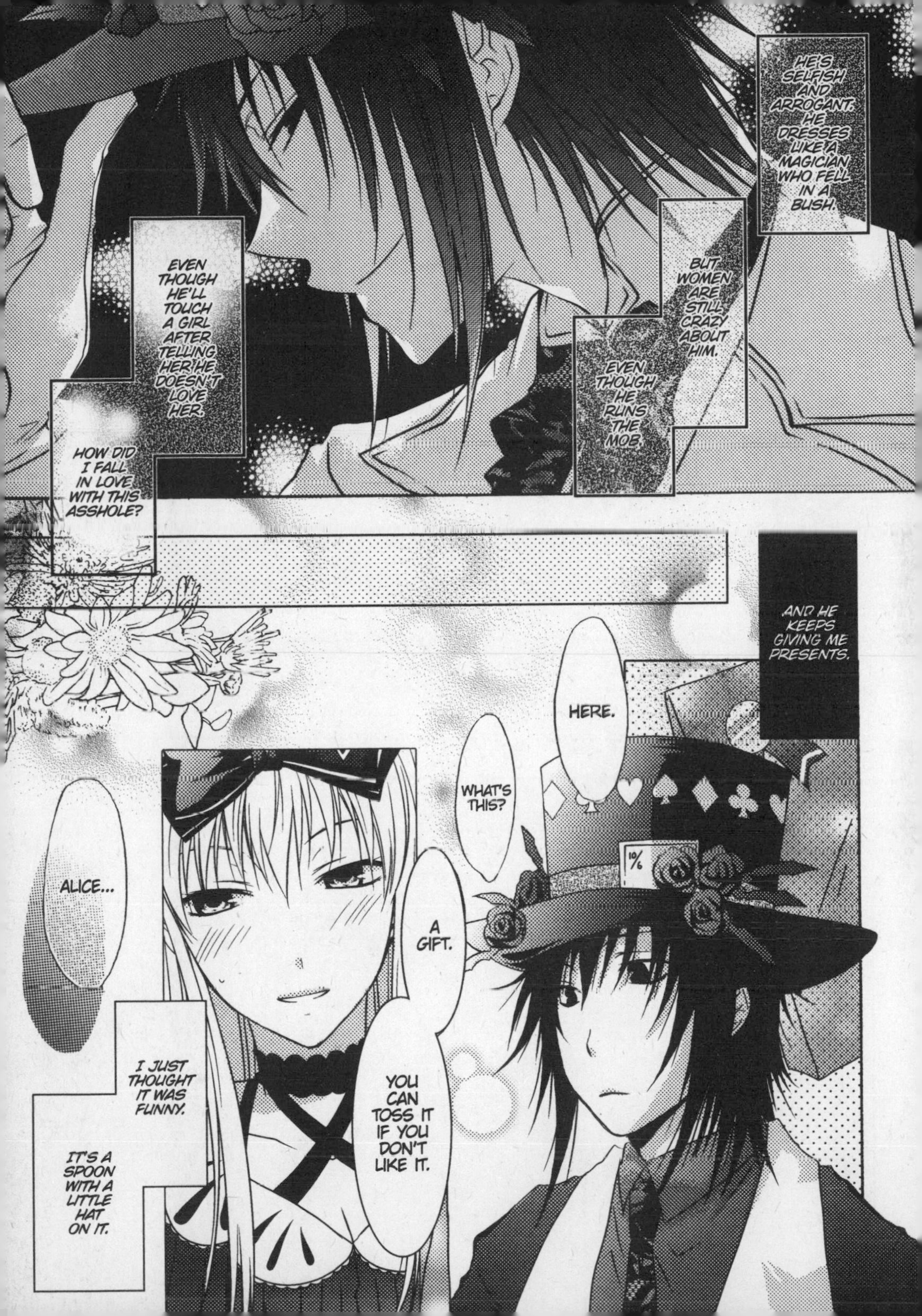
HE'S SELFISH AND ARROGANT. HE DRESSES LIKE A MAGICIAN WHO FELL IN A BUSH.
BUT WOMEN ARE STILL CRAZY ABOUT HIM.
EVEN THOUGH HE RUNS THE MOB.
EVEN THOUGH HE'LL TOUCH A GIRL AFTER TELLING HER HE DOESN'T LOVE HER.
HOW DID I FALL IN LOVE WITH THIS ASSHOLE?
AND HE KEEPS GIVING ME PRESENTS.
HERE.
WHAT'S THIS?
A GIFT.
YOU CAN TOSS IT IF YOU DON'T LIKE IT.
ALICE...
I JUST THOUGHT IT WAS FUNNY.
IT'S A SPOON WITH A LITTLE HAT ON IT.

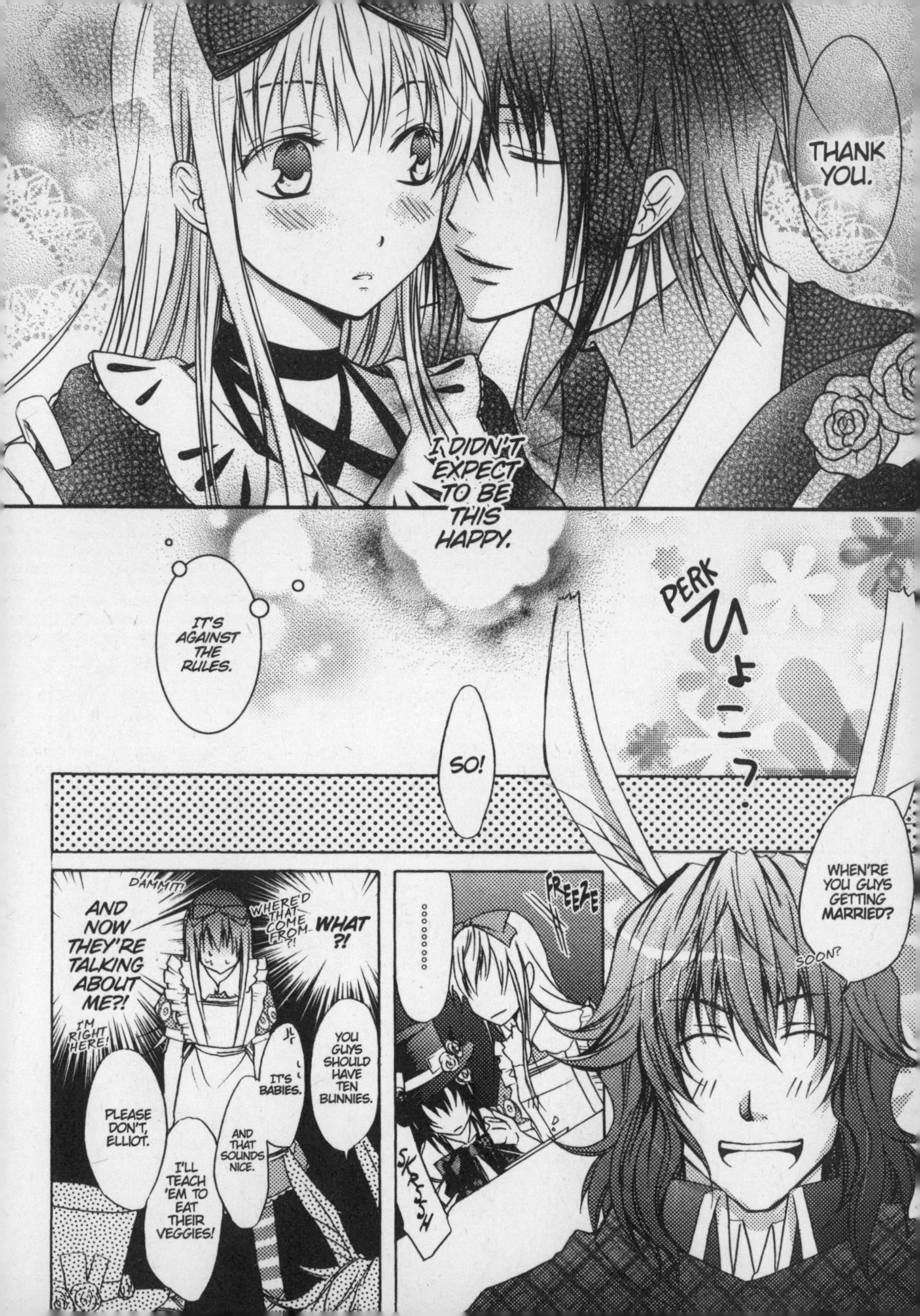
THANK YOU.
I DIDN'T EXPECT TO BE THIS HAPPY.
IT'S AGAINST THE RULES.
PERK
ひょこっ
SO!
WHEN'RE YOU GUYS GETTING MARRIED?
SOON?
FREEZE
....
SKRTSH
YOU GUYS SHOULD HAVE TEN BUNNIES.
IT'S BABIES.
WHAT?!
WHERE'D THAT COME FROM?!
DAMMIT!
AND NOW THEY'RE TALKING ABOUT ME?!
I'M RIGHT HERE!
AND THAT SOUNDS NICE.
PLEASE DON'T, ELLIOT.
I'LL TEACH 'EM TO EAT THEIR VEGGIES!

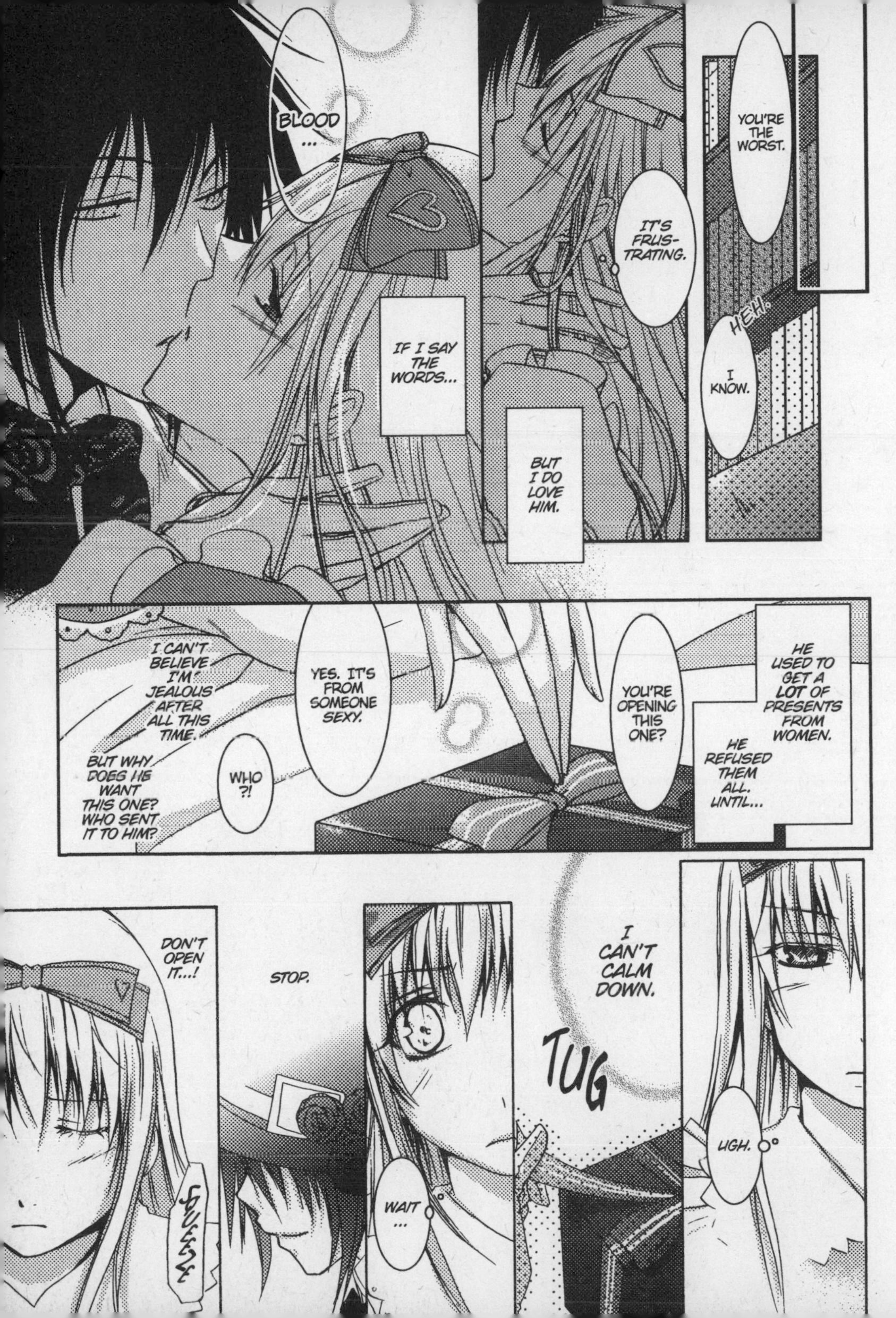
YOU'RE THE WORST.
HEH.
I KNOW.
IT'S FRUS-TRATING.
BUT I DO LOVE HIM.
BLOOD ...
IF I SAY THE WORDS...
HE USED TO GET A LOT OF PRESENTS FROM WOMEN.
HE REFUSED THEM ALL. UNTIL...
YOU'RE OPENING THIS ONE?
YES. IT'S FROM SOMEONE SEXY.
WHO ?!
I CAN'T BELIEVE I'M JEALOUS AFTER ALL THIS TIME.
BUT WHY DOES HE WANT THIS ONE? WHO SENT IT TO HIM?
UGH.
I CAN'T CALM DOWN.
TUG
WAIT ...
DON'T OPEN IT...!
STOP.
SQUEEZE

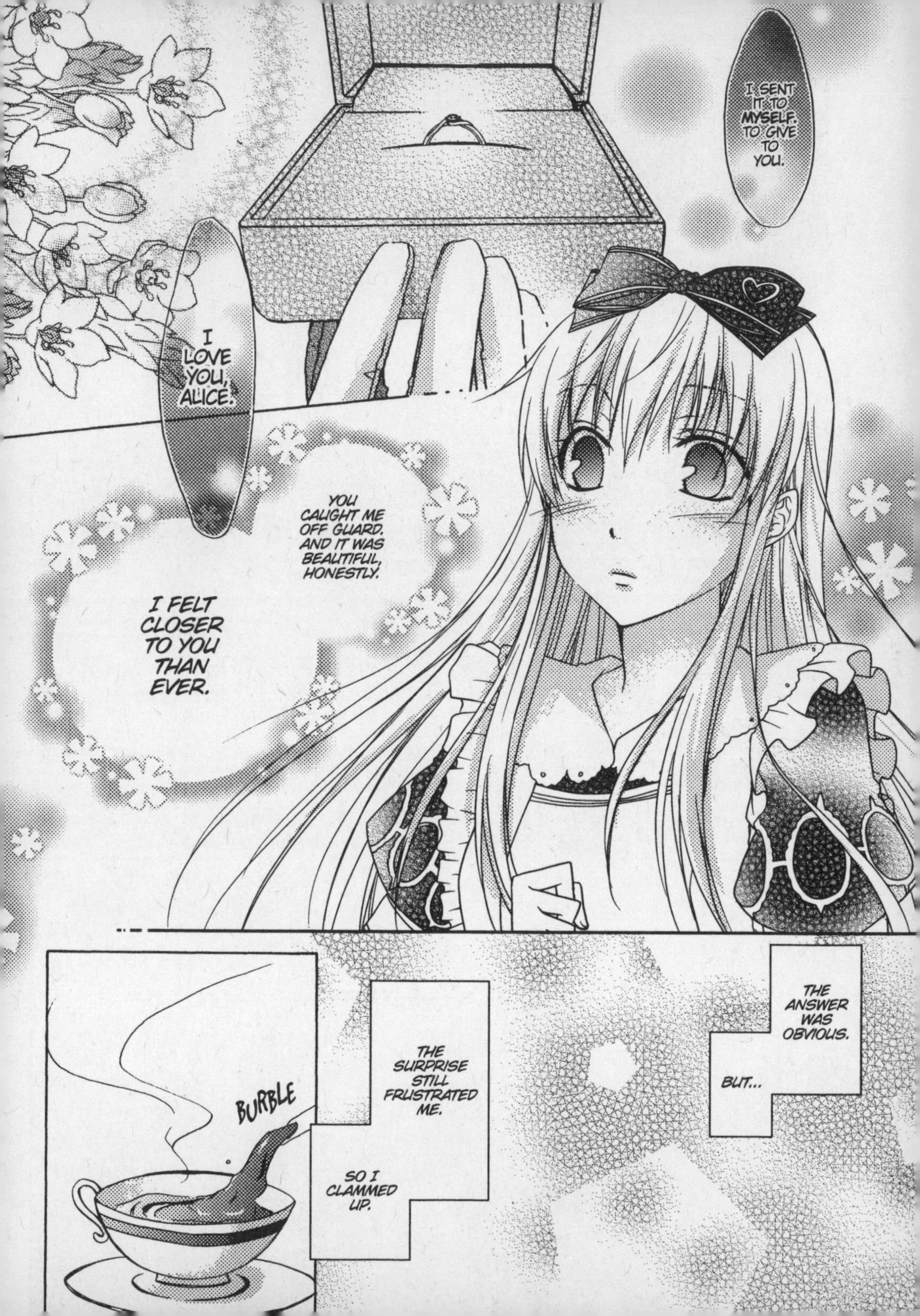
I SENT IT TO MYSELF. TO GIVE TO YOU.
I LOVE YOU, ALICE.
YOU CAUGHT ME OFF GUARD. AND IT WAS BEAUTIFUL, HONESTLY.
I FELT CLOSER TO YOU THAN EVER.
THE ANSWER WAS OBVIOUS.
BUT...
THE SURPRISE STILL FRUSTRATED ME.
SO I CLAMMED UP.
BURBLE

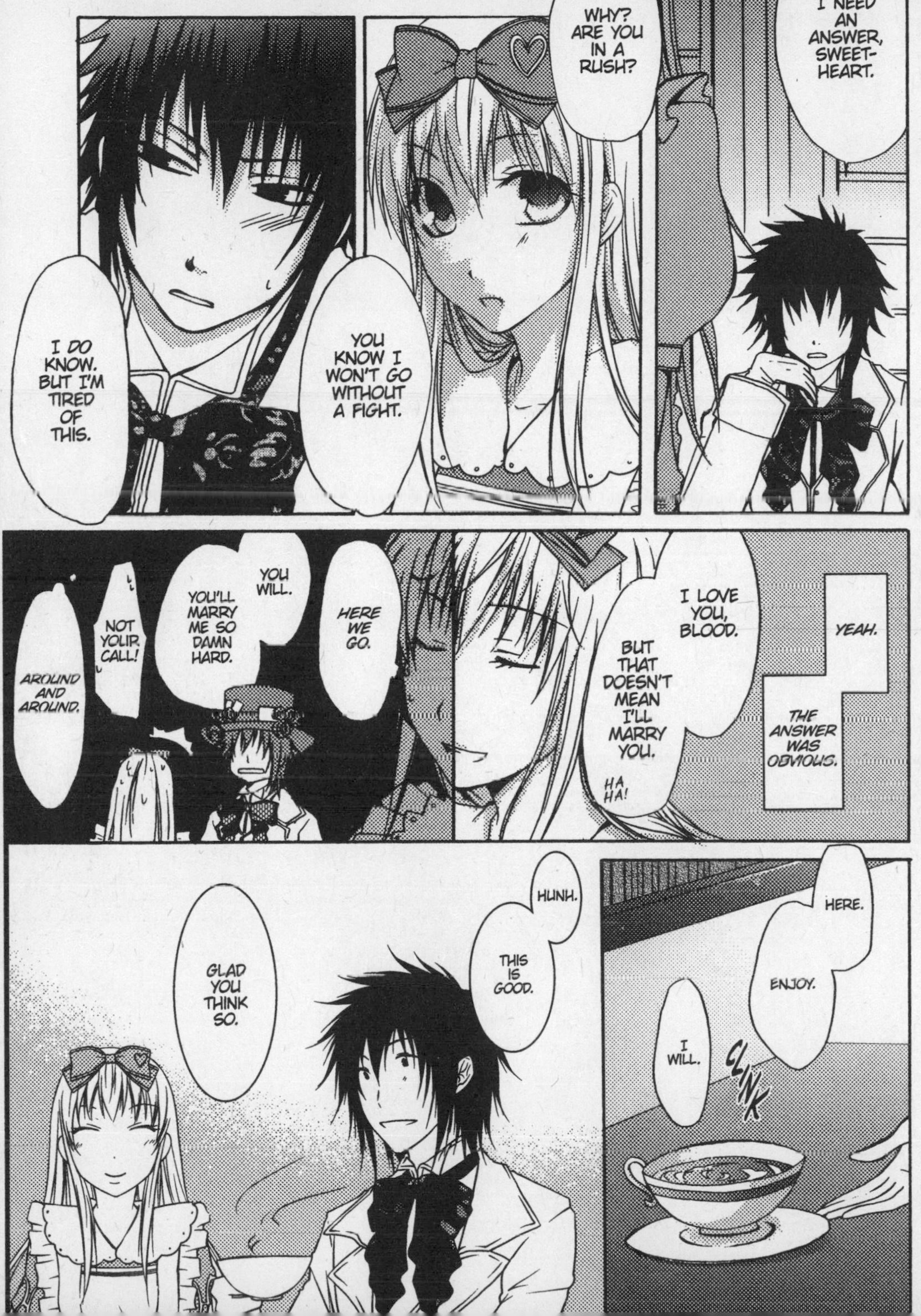
I NEED AN ANSWER, SWEET-HEART.
WHY? ARE YOU IN A RUSH?
YOU KNOW I WON'T GO WITHOUT A FIGHT.
I DO KNOW. BUT I'M TIRED OF THIS.
YEAH.
THE ANSWER WAS OBVIOUS.
I LOVE YOU, BLOOD.
BUT THAT DOESN'T MEAN I'LL MARRY YOU.
HA HA!
HERE WE GO.
YOU WILL.
YOU'LL MARRY ME SO DAMN HARD.
NOT YOUR CALL!
AROUND AND AROUND.
HERE.
ENJOY.
I WILL.
CLINK
HUNH.
THIS IS GOOD.
GLAD YOU THINK SO.

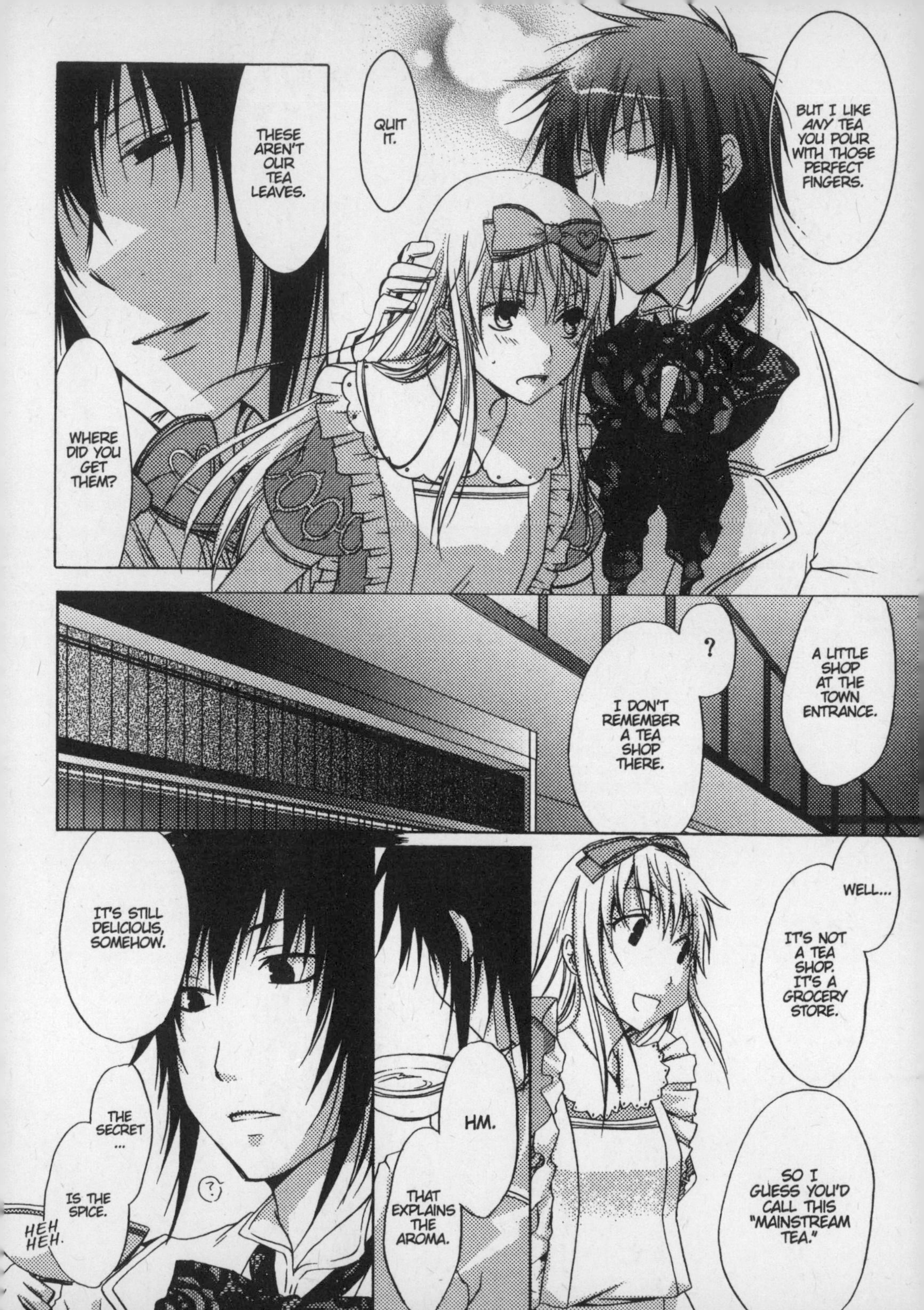
BUT I LIKE ANY TEA YOU POUR WITH THOSE PERFECT FINGERS.
QUIT IT.
THESE AREN'T OUR TEA LEAVES.
WHERE DID YOU GET THEM?
A LITTLE SHOP AT THE TOWN ENTRANCE.
?
I DON'T REMEMBER A TEA SHOP THERE.
WELL...
IT'S NOT A TEA SHOP. IT'S A GROCERY STORE.
SO I GUESS YOU'D CALL THIS "MAINSTREAM TEA."
HM.
THAT EXPLAINS THE AROMA.
IT'S STILL DELICIOUS, SOMEHOW.
THE SECRET...
IS THE SPICE.
HEH HEH.
?

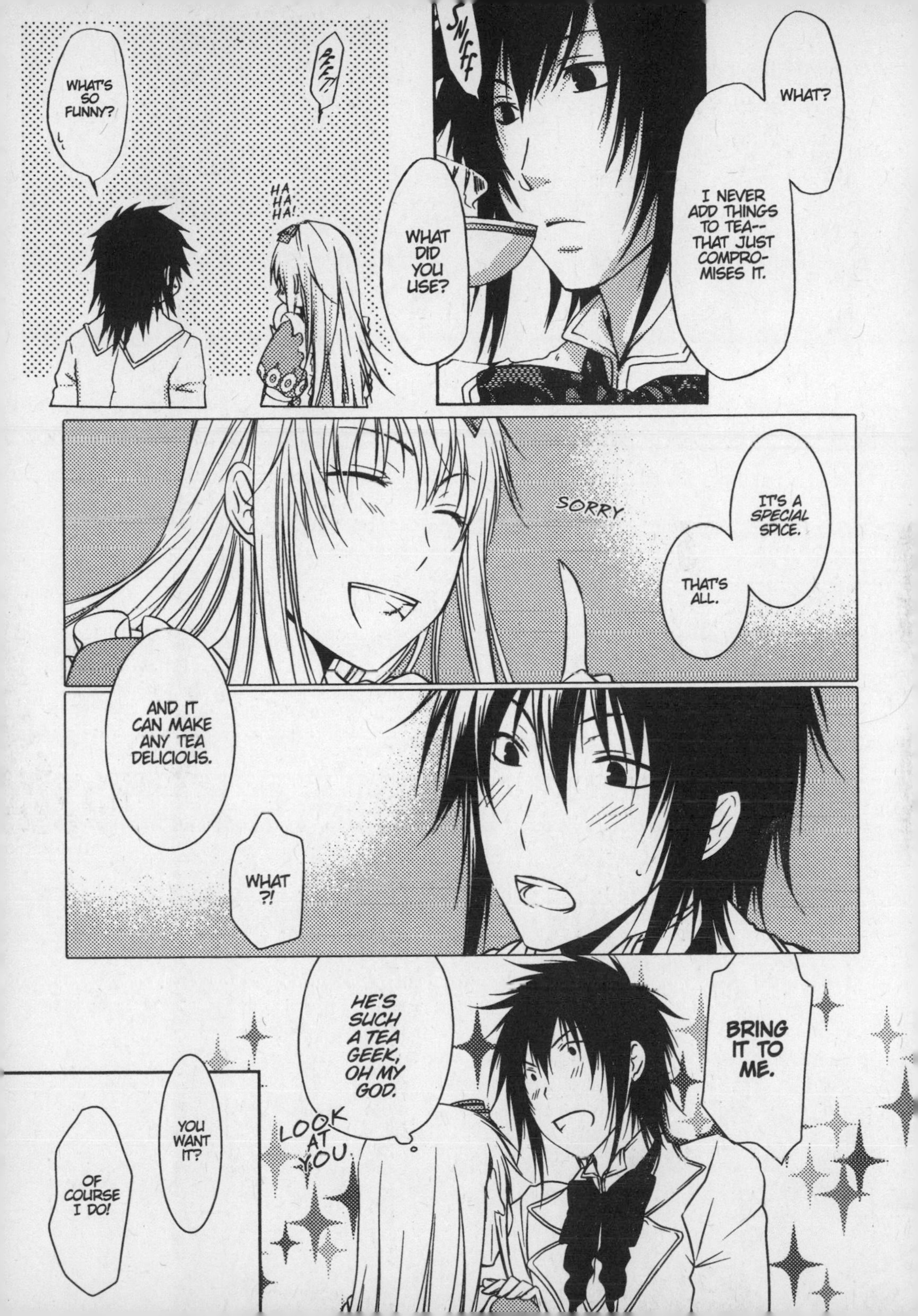
SNIFF
WHAT?
I NEVER ADD THINGS TO TEA--THAT JUST COMPROMISES IT.
WHAT DID YOU USE?
HA HA HA!
WHAT'S SO FUNNY?
IT'S A SPECIAL SPICE.
THAT'S ALL.
SORRY.
AND IT CAN MAKE ANY TEA DELICIOUS.
WHAT ?!
BRING IT TO ME.
HE'S SUCH A TEA GEEK, OH MY GOD.
LOOK AT YOU
YOU WANT IT?
OF COURSE I DO!

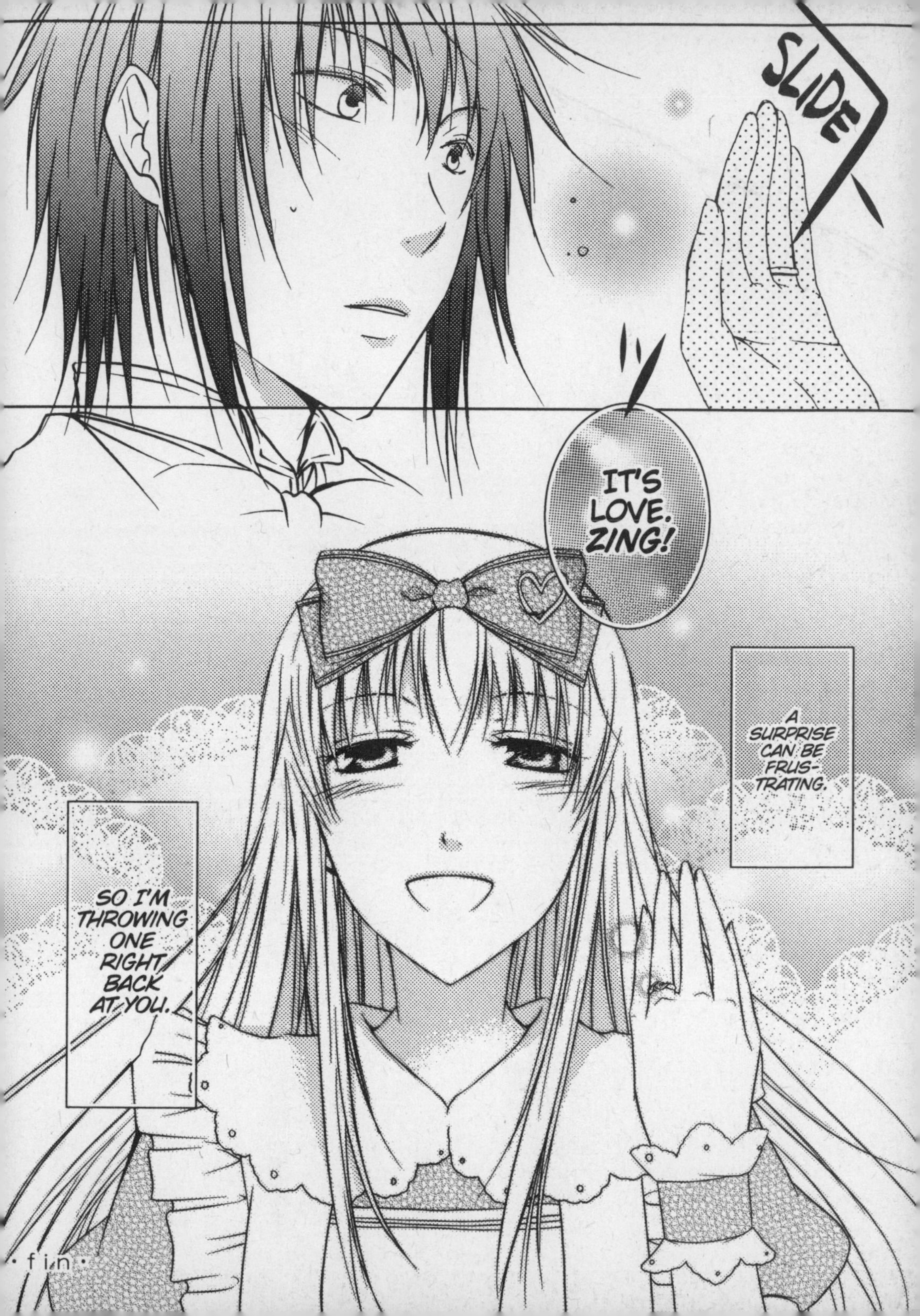
SLIDE
IT'S LOVE. ZING!
A SURPRISE CAN BE FRUS-TRATING.
SO I'M THROWING ONE RIGHT BACK AT YOU.
• fin •

CRIMSON EMPIRE
クリムゾン・エンパイア
~ Circumstances to serve a noble ~

We devote our life proudly.
my life for you. For all you.

Quin Rose 2008

- STORY -

The setting is a country of aristocrats: a tributary nation for Luxonne. *Crimson Empire* is a love adventure game about a maid, Sheila, who works in the luxurious royal castle. But behind the lavish façade, the castle is home to a savage—and bloody—political war.

Strong and skilled, Sheila uses her position as a maid to hide her true profession: bodyguard to Prince Edvard. Sheila carries a dark past of enslavement and murder. Now she survives day to day, with only a small wish in her heart.

While navigating the power struggle between Prince Edvard and his brother, the deceptive Prince Justin, Sheila must understand and use the dangerous people who surround her. But although a brilliant fighter and tactician, Sheila is unskilled when it comes to love and friendships. Such a gap between her power and her heart could lead to a dire ending indeed!

Crimson Empire Character Information

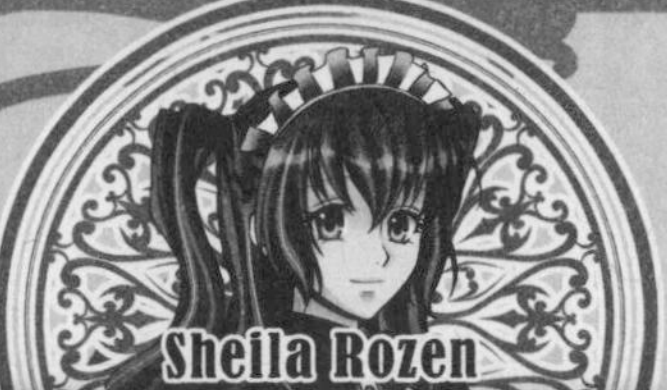

Sheila Rozen

The intensely loyal head maid to Prince Edvard—and his secret bodyguard. She's a skilled leader and shrewdly political, in addition to being fierce in combat. She doesn't hide her roots as a slave.

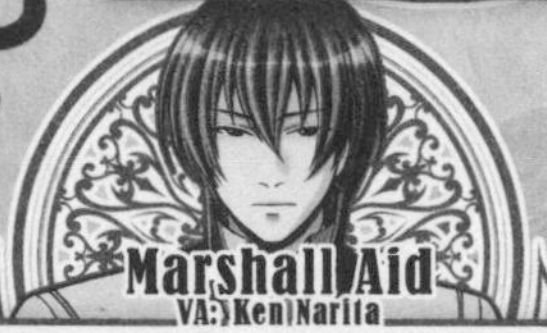

Marshall Aid
VA: Ken Narita

Prince Justin's head servant. He argues with Sheila in public but doesn't dislike her. In private, they're intimate enough to spar peacefully.

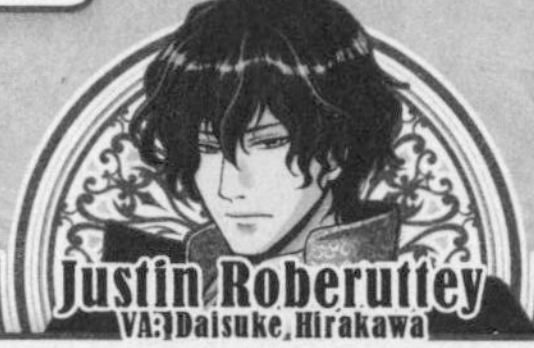

Justin Roberuttey
VA: Daisuke Hirakawa

The eldest prince, and Edvard's older half-brother. Since his mother is of lower status, Justin falls below his younger brother in line for the throne.

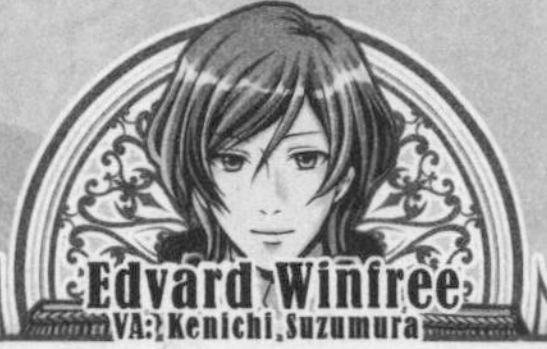

Edvard Winfree
VA: Kenichi Suzumura

Sheila's master. While friendly and regal on the surface, he's very condescending. He thinks of Sheila as more than a subordinate and loves her more than his own family... or so he *claims*.

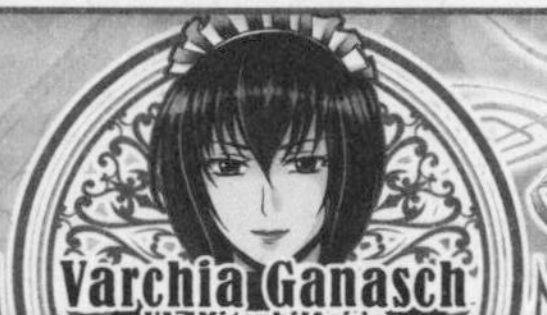

Varchia Ganasch
VA: Mitsuki Saiga

Varchia, the vice-maid, is a close friend of Sheila's, and is a former slave. Her actions and words are always painfully neutral. She's trustworthy and helps Sheila in both public and private.

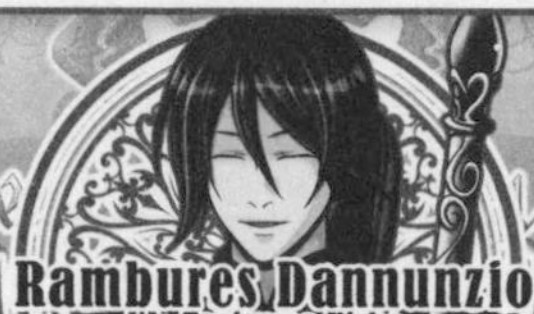

Rambures Dannunzio
VA: Taniyama Kisho

A commoner who was knighted after saving the king. He loves to lurk in his room and brew concoctions—which often stink and explode—instead of interacting with the nobility.

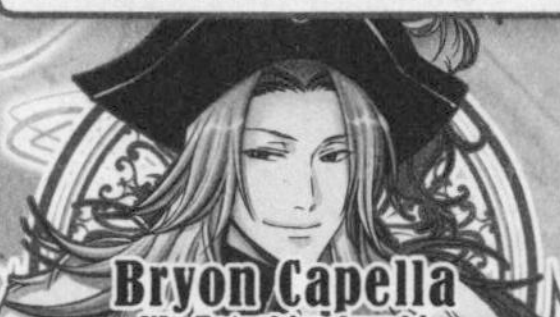

Bryon Capella
VA: Tatsuhisa Suzuki

Son of the marquis who one day will inherit the position and become an important pillar of the country. He seems cheerful and carefree, but rather guarded. Like his sister, he adores Sheila.

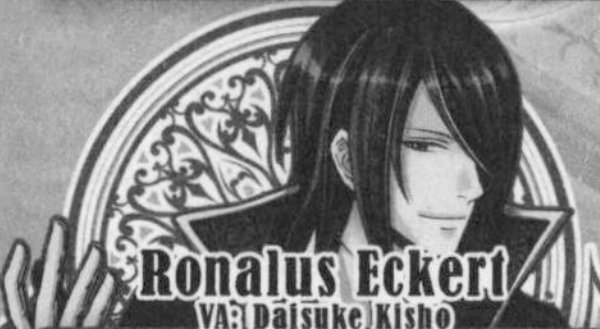

Ronalus Eckert
VA: Daisuke Kisho

Another guest in the royal castle, Ronalus is the servant to the Queen of Luxonne. Although he enjoys a higher status by serving the queen, he has a good relationship with other servants. His role is to monitor Meissen.

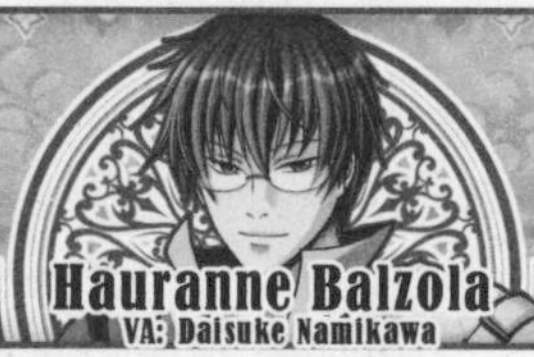

Hauranne Balzola
VA: Daisuke Namikawa

A wizard staying in the royal castle who is treated as a guest, but he's been in the castle longer than anyone. He's lived a *long* life...and his real age doesn't match his looks.

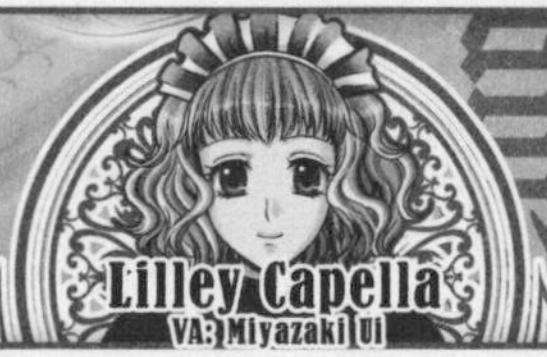

Lilley Capella
VA: Miyazaki Ui

Another battle maid, but of noble birth, Lilley is fiercely loyal to Sheila. She has innate skill, and her strength is second only to Sheila's. She and her brother Bryon are very close.

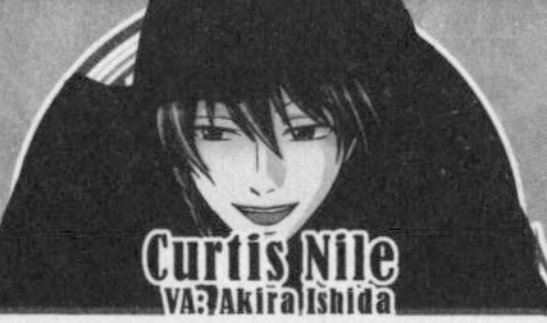

Curtis Nile
VA: Akira Ishida

A deadly assassin who specializes in poisons. He raised Sheila, and nearly killed her with his vicious training. Ever since, their relationship has been strained, to say the least.

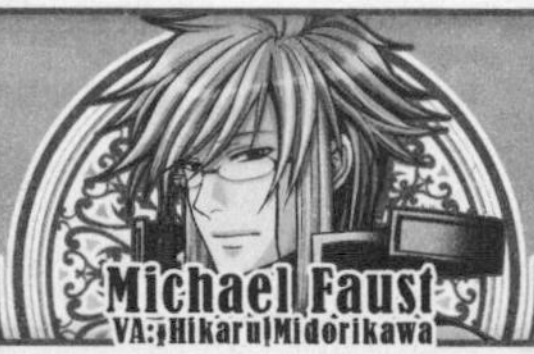

Michael Faust
VA: Hikaru Midorikawa

A demon who made a contract with Meissen. He's dangerously strong, monologues frequently, and is oddly nervous. His mental instability feeds his pessimism.

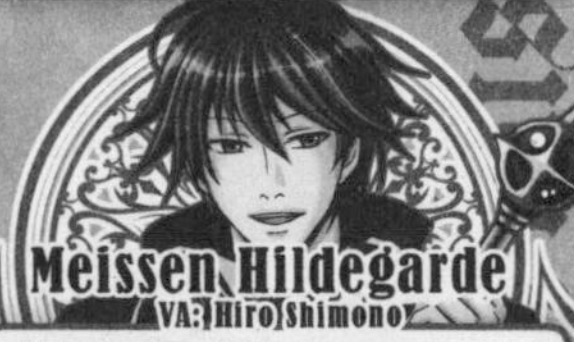

Meissen Hildegarde
VA: Hiro Shimono

Meissen has a tendency to wander, and he's traveled all over the world. His ladykiller persona hides a powerful wizard. He's searching for the truth and is trying to become a sage...supposedly.

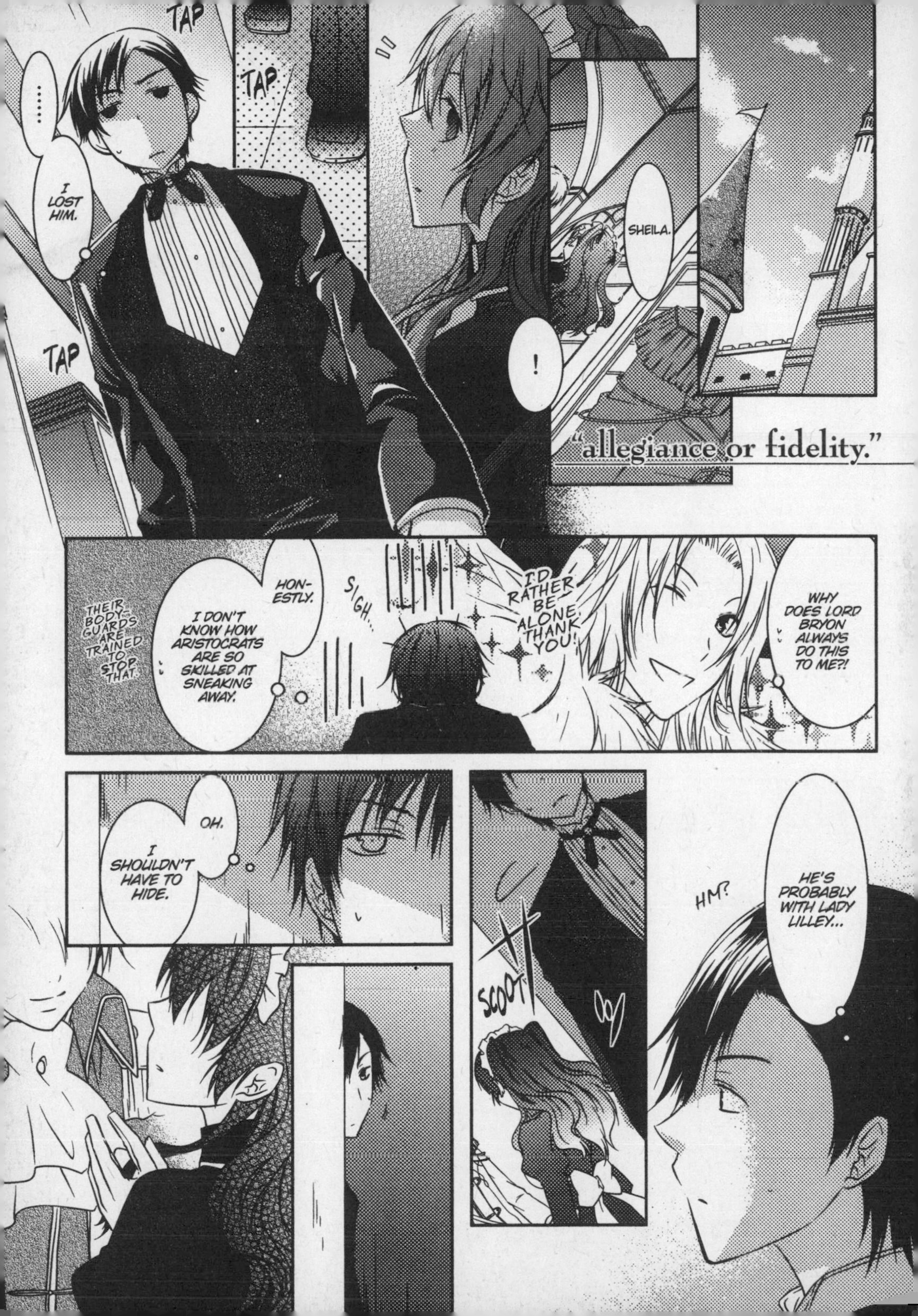

SHEILA.
!
"allegiance or fidelity."
TAP
......
I LOST HIM.
TAP
TAP
WHY DOES LORD BRYON ALWAYS DO THIS TO ME?!
I'D RATHER BE ALONE THANK YOU!
SIGH...
HON-ESTLY.
I DON'T KNOW HOW ARISTOCRATS ARE SO SKILLED AT SNEAKING AWAY.
THEIR BODY-GUARDS ARE TRAINED TO STOP THAT.
HE'S PROBABLY WITH LADY LILLEY...
HM?
SCOOT
OH.
I SHOULDN'T HAVE TO HIDE.

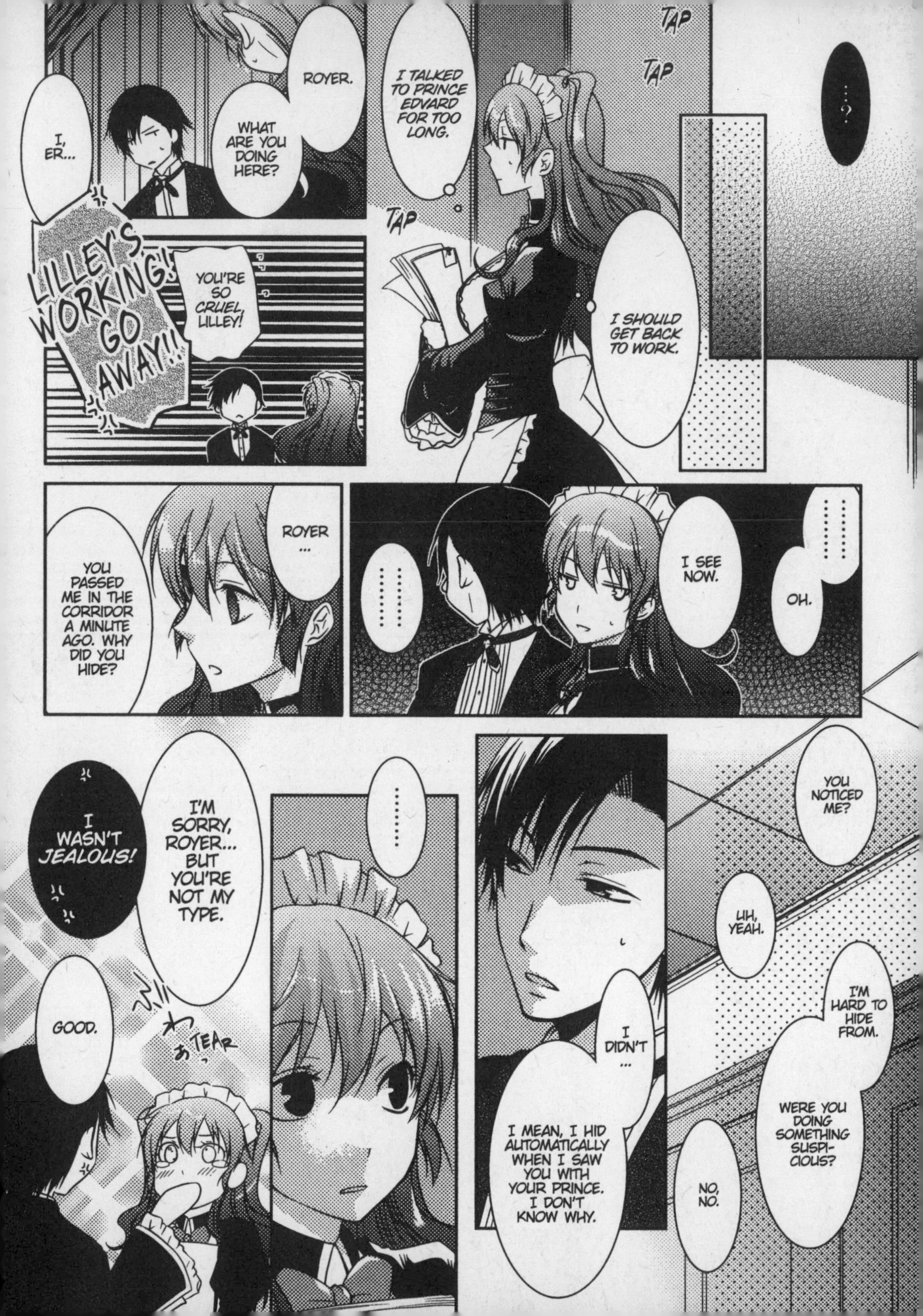

...?
TAP
TAP
I TALKED TO PRINCE EDVARD FOR TOO LONG.
TAP
I SHOULD GET BACK TO WORK.
ROYER.
WHAT ARE YOU DOING HERE?
I, ER...
LILLEY'S WORKING! GO AWAY!!
YOU'RE SO CRUEL, LILLEY!
......
OH.
I SEE NOW.
......
ROYER...
YOU PASSED ME IN THE CORRIDOR A MINUTE AGO. WHY DID YOU HIDE?
YOU NOTICED ME?
UH, YEAH.
I'M HARD TO HIDE FROM.
WERE YOU DOING SOMETHING SUSPICIOUS?
NO, NO.
I DIDN'T...
I MEAN, I HID AUTOMATICALLY WHEN I SAW YOU WITH YOUR PRINCE. I DON'T KNOW WHY.
......
I'M SORRY, ROYER... BUT YOU'RE NOT MY TYPE.
I WASN'T JEALOUS!
GOOD.
TEAR

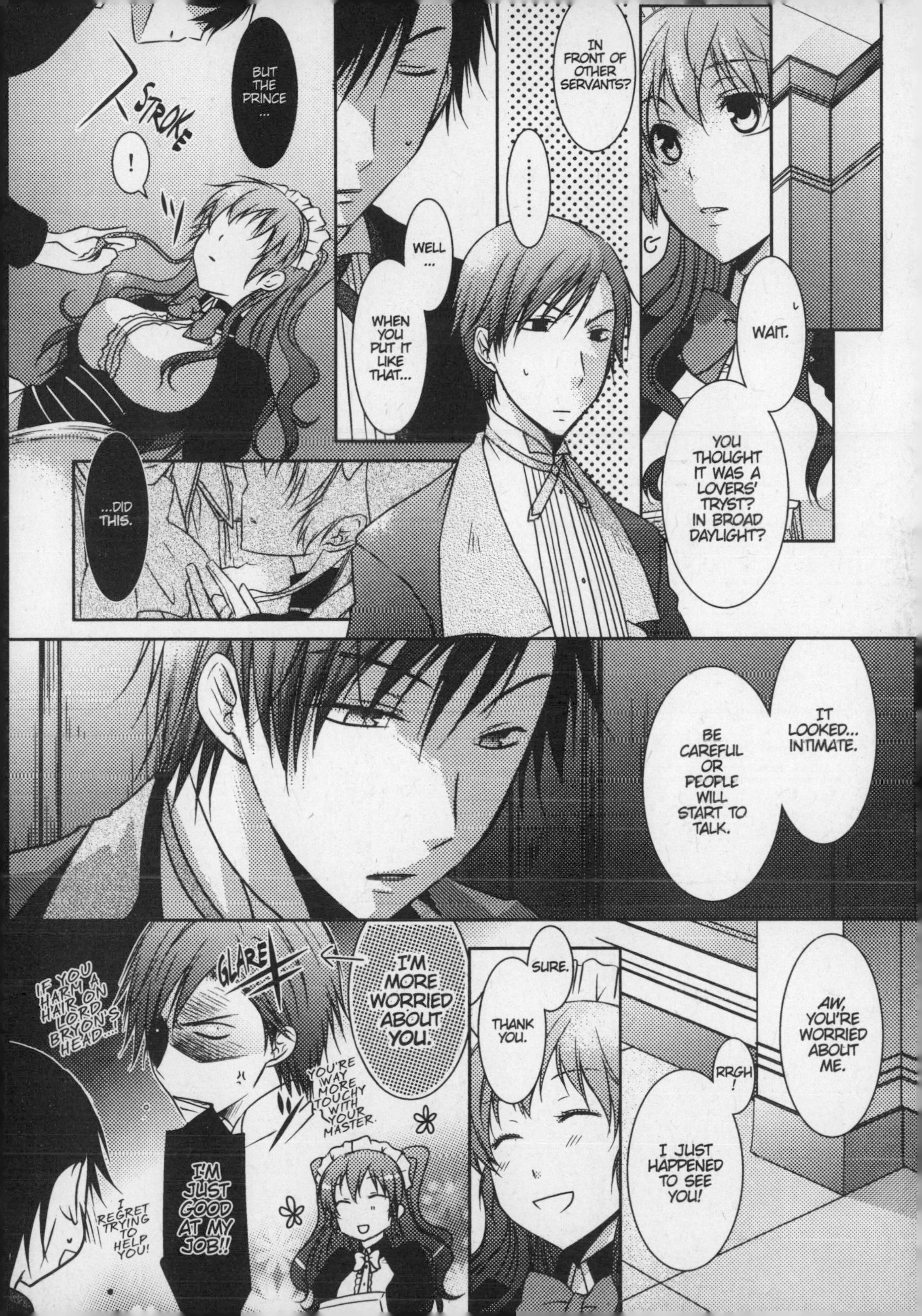
WAIT.
YOU THOUGHT IT WAS A LOVERS' TRYST? IN BROAD DAYLIGHT?
IN FRONT OF OTHER SERVANTS?
......
WELL ...
WHEN YOU PUT IT LIKE THAT...
BUT THE PRINCE ...
STROKE
!
...DID THIS.
IT LOOKED... INTIMATE.
BE CAREFUL OR PEOPLE WILL START TO TALK.
AW, YOU'RE WORRIED ABOUT ME.
SURE.
THANK YOU.
RRGH!
I JUST HAPPENED TO SEE YOU!
I'M MORE WORRIED ABOUT YOU.
GLARE
IF YOU HARM A HAIR ON LORD BRYON'S HEAD...!
YOU'RE WAY MORE TOUCHY WITH YOUR MASTER.
I'M JUST GOOD AT MY JOB!!
I REGRET TRYING TO HELP YOU!

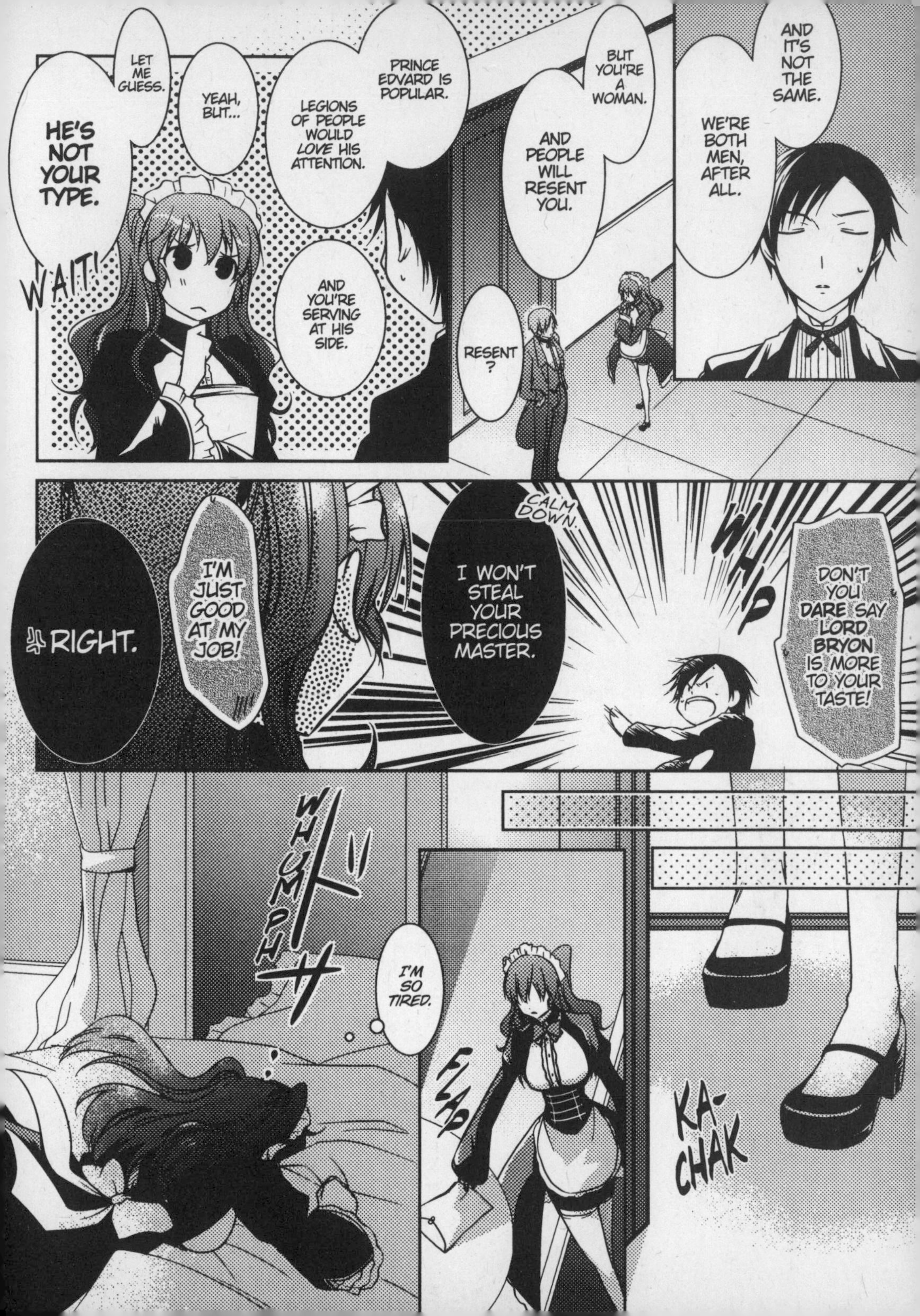
AND IT'S NOT THE SAME.
WE'RE BOTH MEN, AFTER ALL.
BUT YOU'RE A WOMAN.
AND PEOPLE WILL RESENT YOU.
RESENT?
PRINCE EDVARD IS POPULAR.
LEGIONS OF PEOPLE WOULD *LOVE* HIS ATTENTION.
AND YOU'RE SERVING AT HIS SIDE.
YEAH, BUT...
LET ME GUESS.
HE'S NOT YOUR TYPE.
WAIT!
WHIP
DON'T YOU DARE SAY LORD BRYON IS MORE TO YOUR TASTE!
CALM DOWN.
I WON'T STEAL YOUR PRECIOUS MASTER.
I'M JUST GOOD AT MY JOB!
RIGHT.
KA-CHAK
FLAP
I'M SO TIRED.
WHUMPH

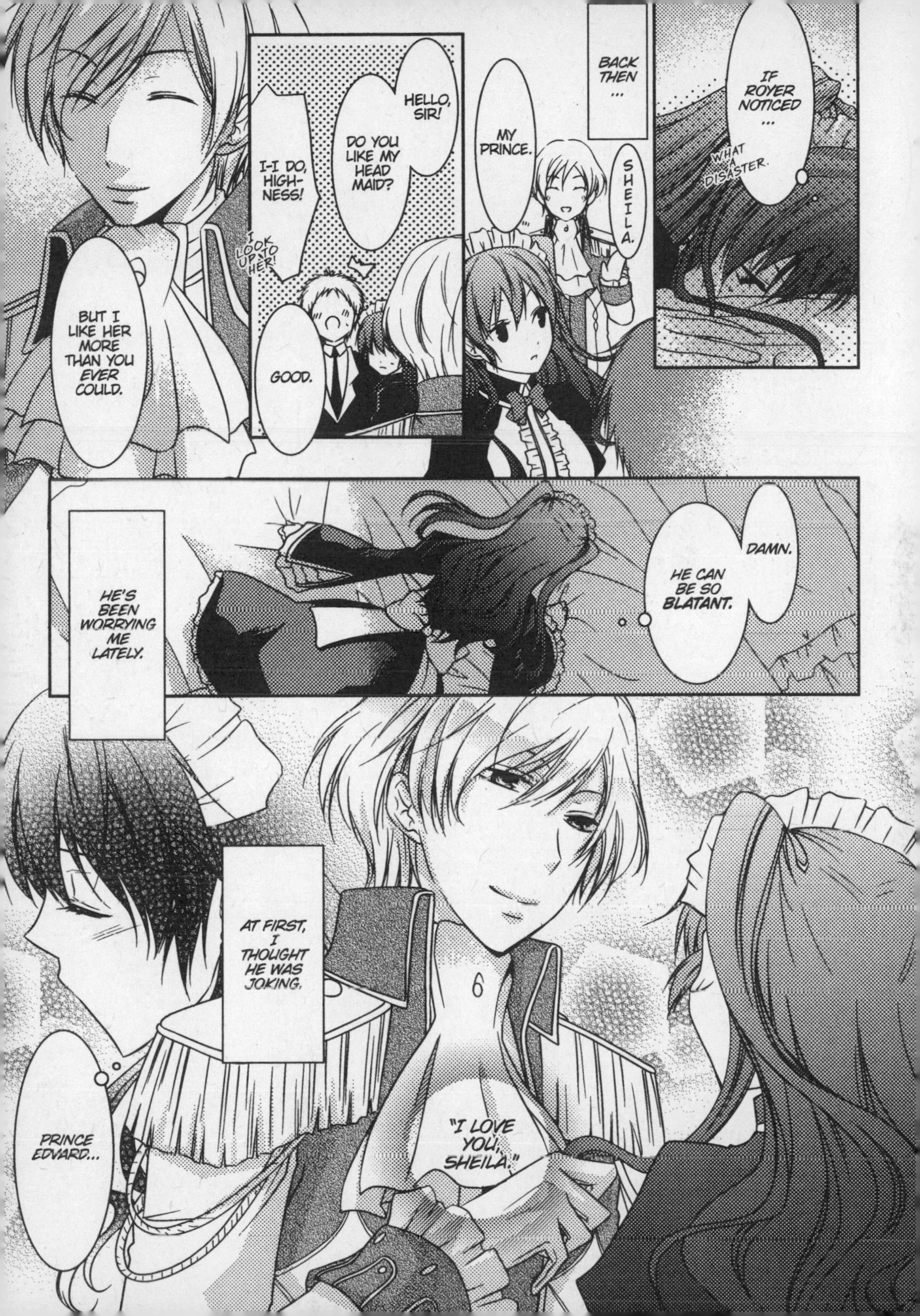
IF ROYER NOTICED ...
WHAT A DISASTER.
BACK THEN ...
MY PRINCE.
SHEILA.
HELLO, SIR!
DO YOU LIKE MY HEAD MAID?
I-I DO, HIGHNESS!
I LOOK UP TO HER!
GOOD.
BUT I LIKE HER MORE THAN YOU EVER COULD.
DAMN.
HE CAN BE SO BLATANT.
HE'S BEEN WORRYING ME LATELY.
AT FIRST, I THOUGHT HE WAS JOKING.
"I LOVE YOU, SHEILA."
PRINCE EDVARD...

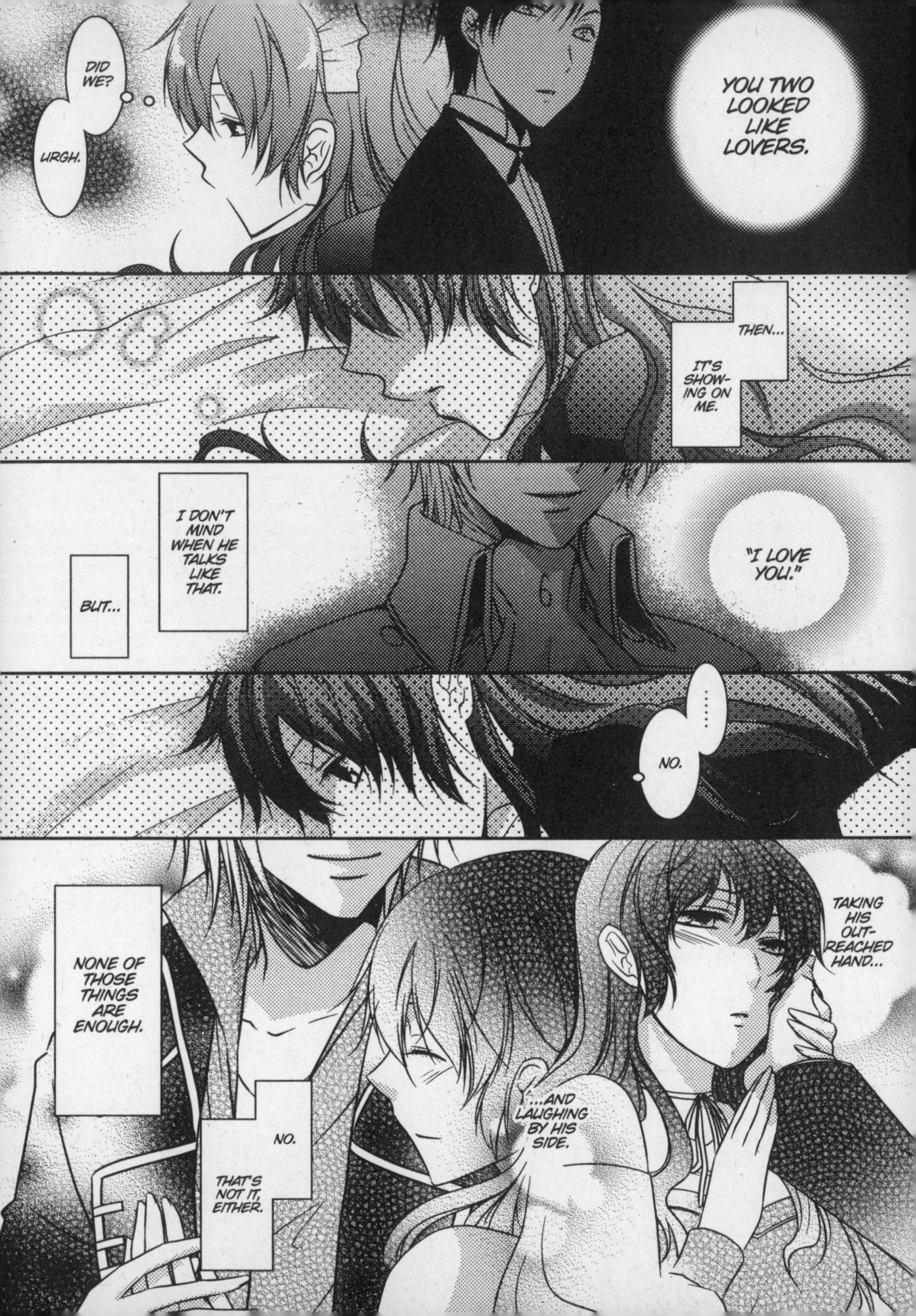
YOU TWO LOOKED LIKE LOVERS.
DID WE?
URGH.
THEN...
IT'S SHOWING ON ME.
"I LOVE YOU."
I DON'T MIND WHEN HE TALKS LIKE THAT.
BUT...
...
NO.
TAKING HIS OUT-REACHED HAND...
...AND LAUGHING BY HIS SIDE.
NONE OF THOSE THINGS ARE ENOUGH.
NO.
THAT'S NOT IT, EITHER.

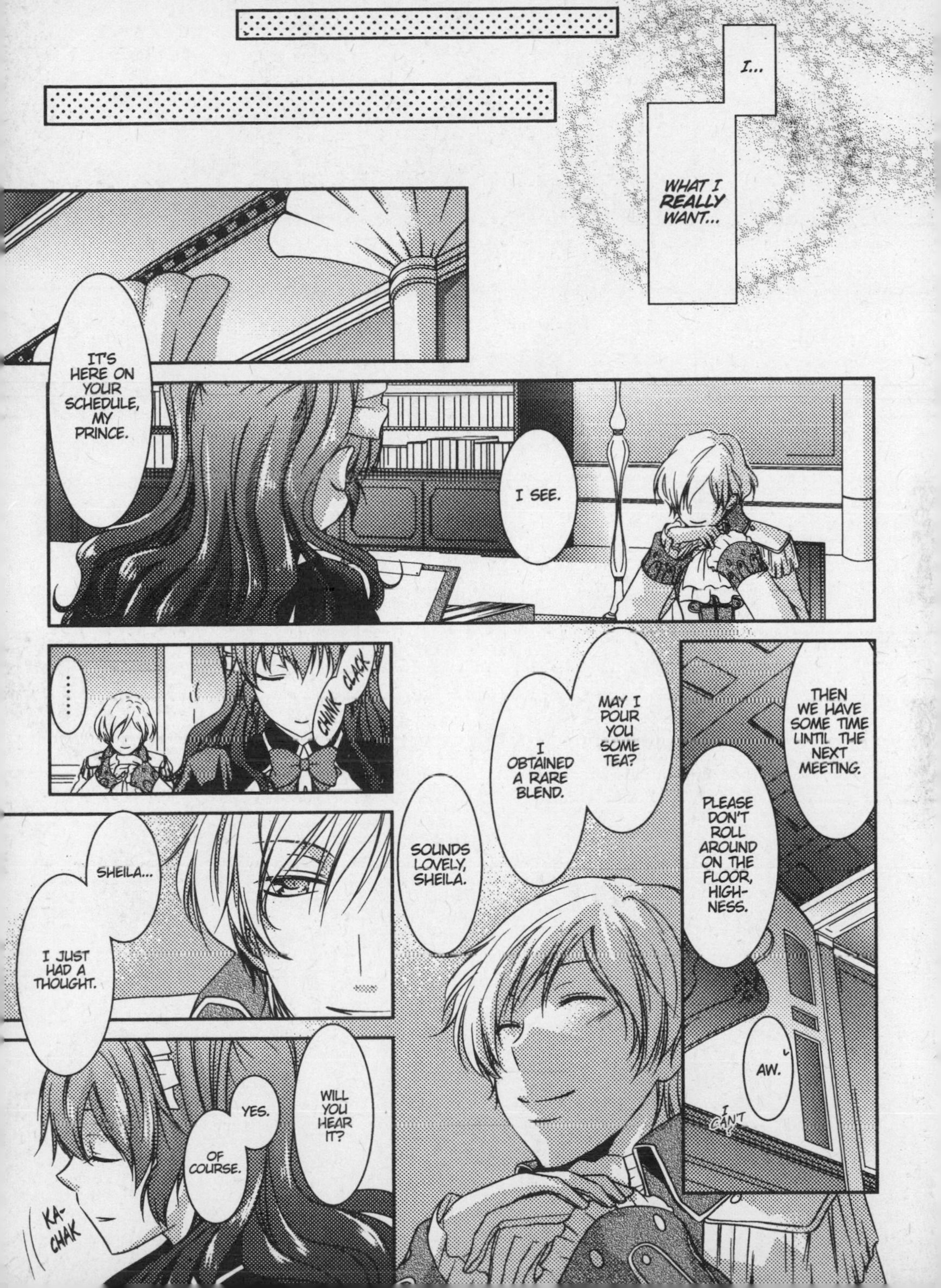
I...
WHAT I REALLY WANT...
IT'S HERE ON YOUR SCHEDULE, MY PRINCE.
I SEE.
THEN WE HAVE SOME TIME UNTIL THE NEXT MEETING.
PLEASE DON'T ROLL AROUND ON THE FLOOR, HIGHNESS.
AW.
I CAN'T
MAY I POUR YOU SOME TEA?
I OBTAINED A RARE BLEND.
SOUNDS LOVELY, SHEILA.
CHINK CLACK
......
SHEILA...
I JUST HAD A THOUGHT.
WILL YOU HEAR IT?
YES.
OF COURSE.
KA-CHAK

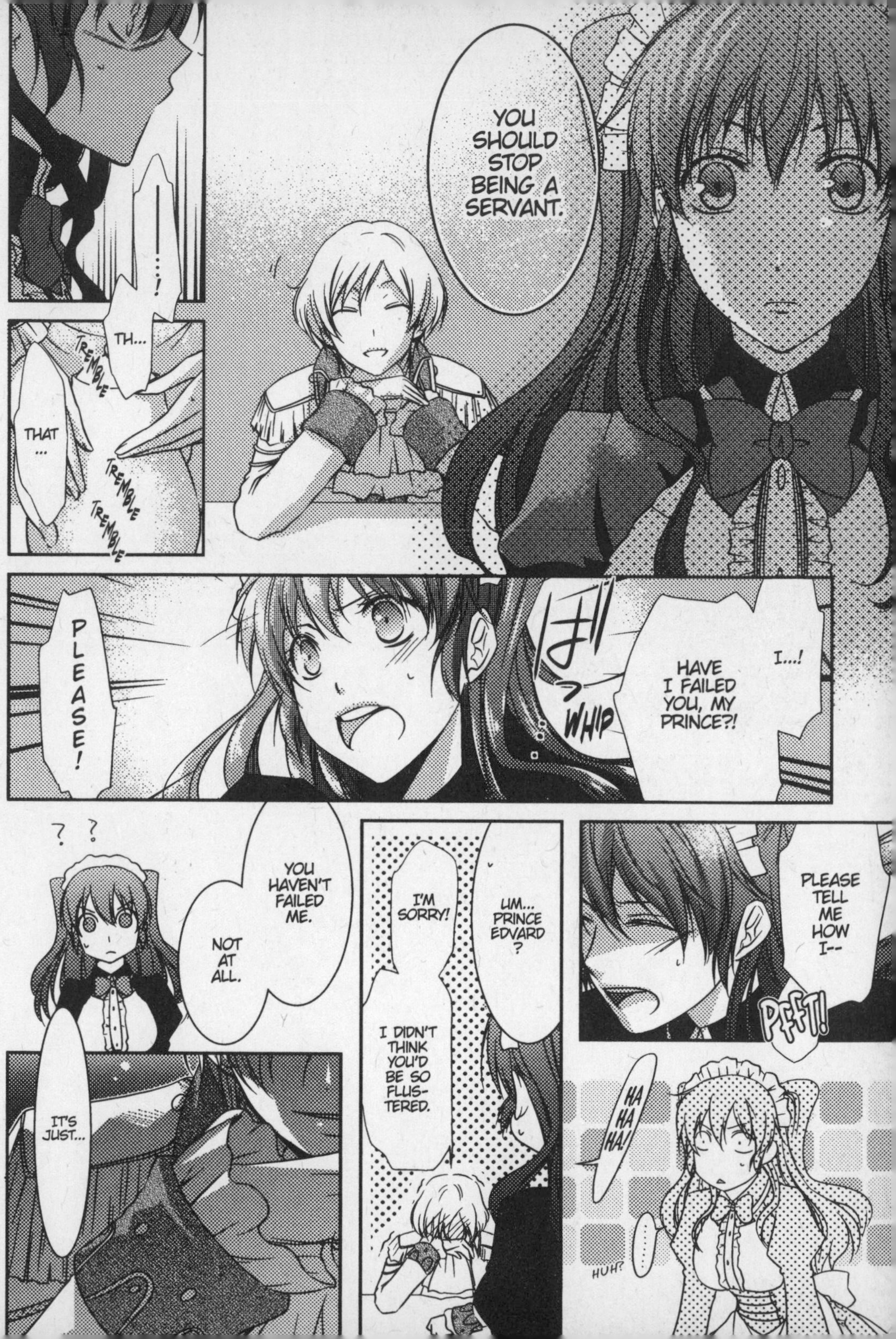
YOU SHOULD STOP BEING A SERVANT.
...!
TH...
TREMBLE
THAT...
TREMBLE
TREMBLE
I...!
HAVE I FAILED YOU, MY PRINCE?!
ばっ
WHIP
PLEASE!
PLEASE TELL ME HOW I--
PFFT!
UM... PRINCE EDVARD?
I'M SORRY!
? ?
YOU HAVEN'T FAILED ME.
NOT AT ALL.
HA HA HA!
...
HUH?
I DIDN'T THINK YOU'D BE SO FLUS-TERED.
IT'S JUST...

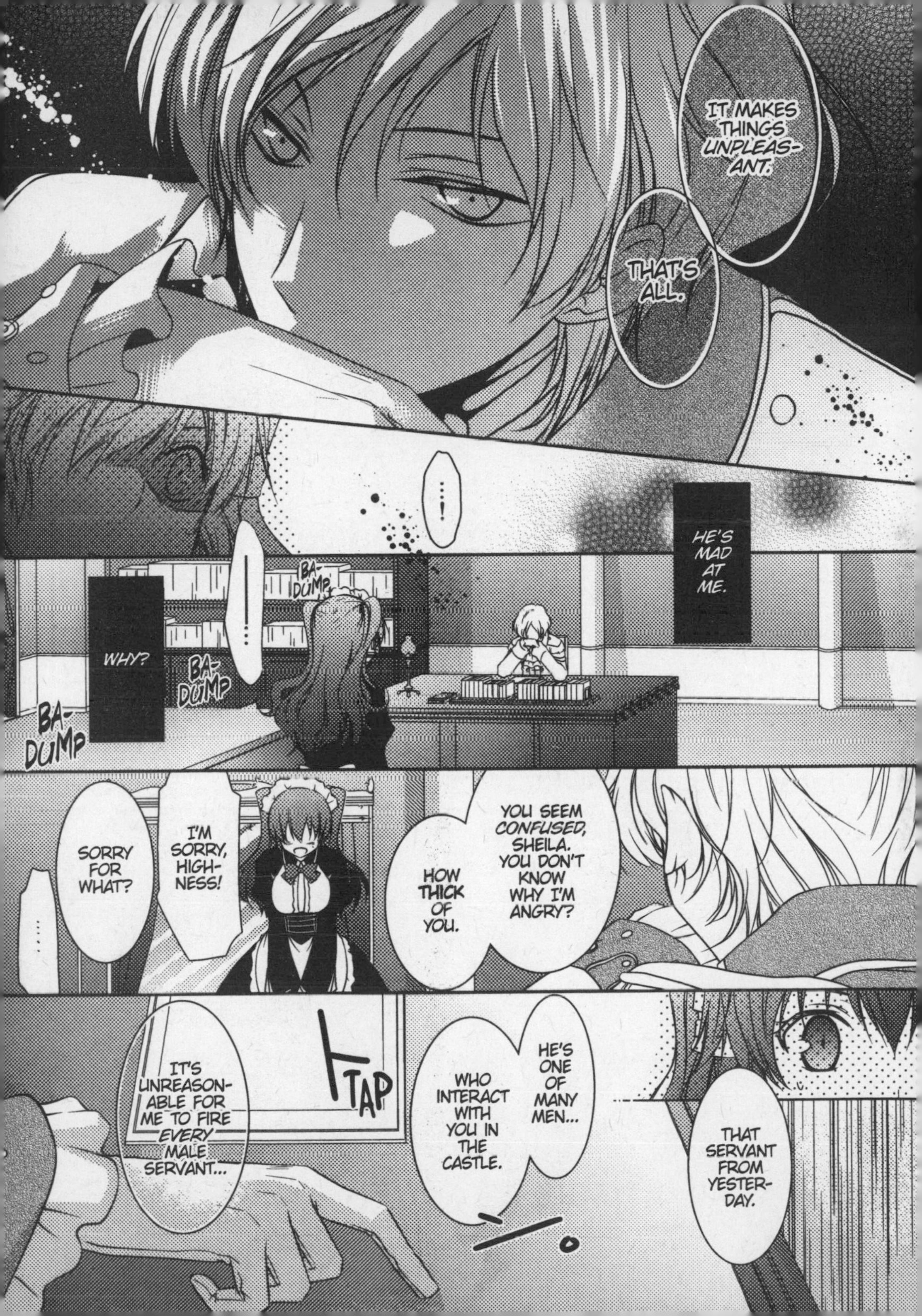
IT MAKES THINGS UNPLEAS-ANT.
THAT'S ALL.
...!
HE'S MAD AT ME.
BA-DUMP
...!
WHY?
BA-DUMP
BA-DUMP
YOU SEEM CONFUSED, SHEILA. YOU DON'T KNOW WHY I'M ANGRY?
HOW THICK OF YOU.
I'M SORRY, HIGHNESS!
SORRY FOR WHAT?
......
THAT SERVANT FROM YESTER-DAY.
HE'S ONE OF MANY MEN...
WHO INTERACT WITH YOU IN THE CASTLE.
TAP
IT'S UNREASON-ABLE FOR ME TO FIRE EVERY MALE SERVANT...

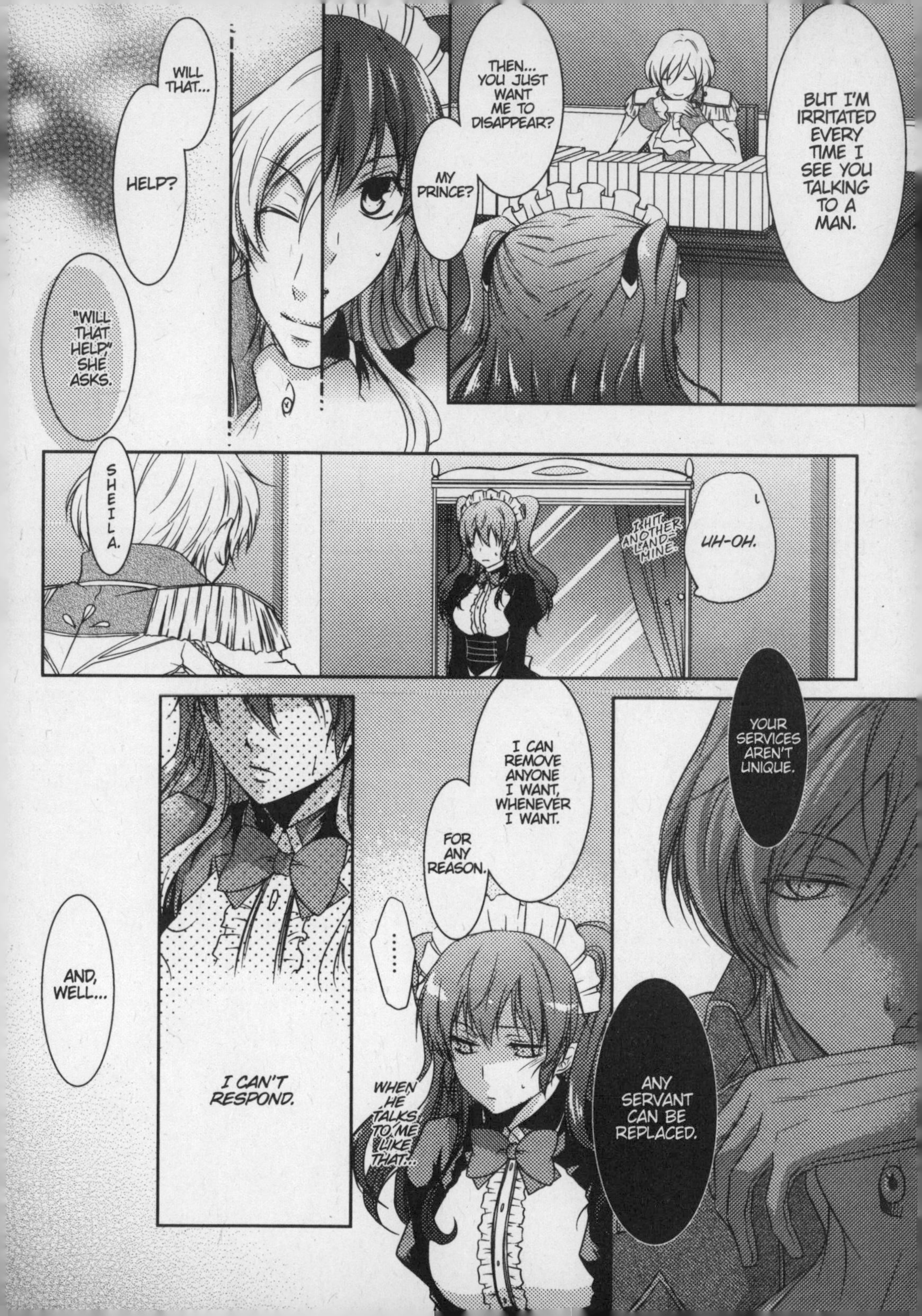
BUT I'M IRRITATED EVERY TIME I SEE YOU TALKING TO A MAN.
THEN... YOU JUST WANT ME TO DISAPPEAR?
MY PRINCE?
WILL THAT...
HELP?
"WILL THAT HELP," SHE ASKS.
UH-OH.
I HIT ANOTHER LANDMINE.
SHEILA.
YOUR SERVICES AREN'T UNIQUE.
ANY SERVANT CAN BE REPLACED.
I CAN REMOVE ANYONE I WANT, WHENEVER I WANT.
FOR ANY REASON.
......
WHEN HE TALKS TO ME LIKE THAT...
I CAN'T RESPOND.
AND, WELL...

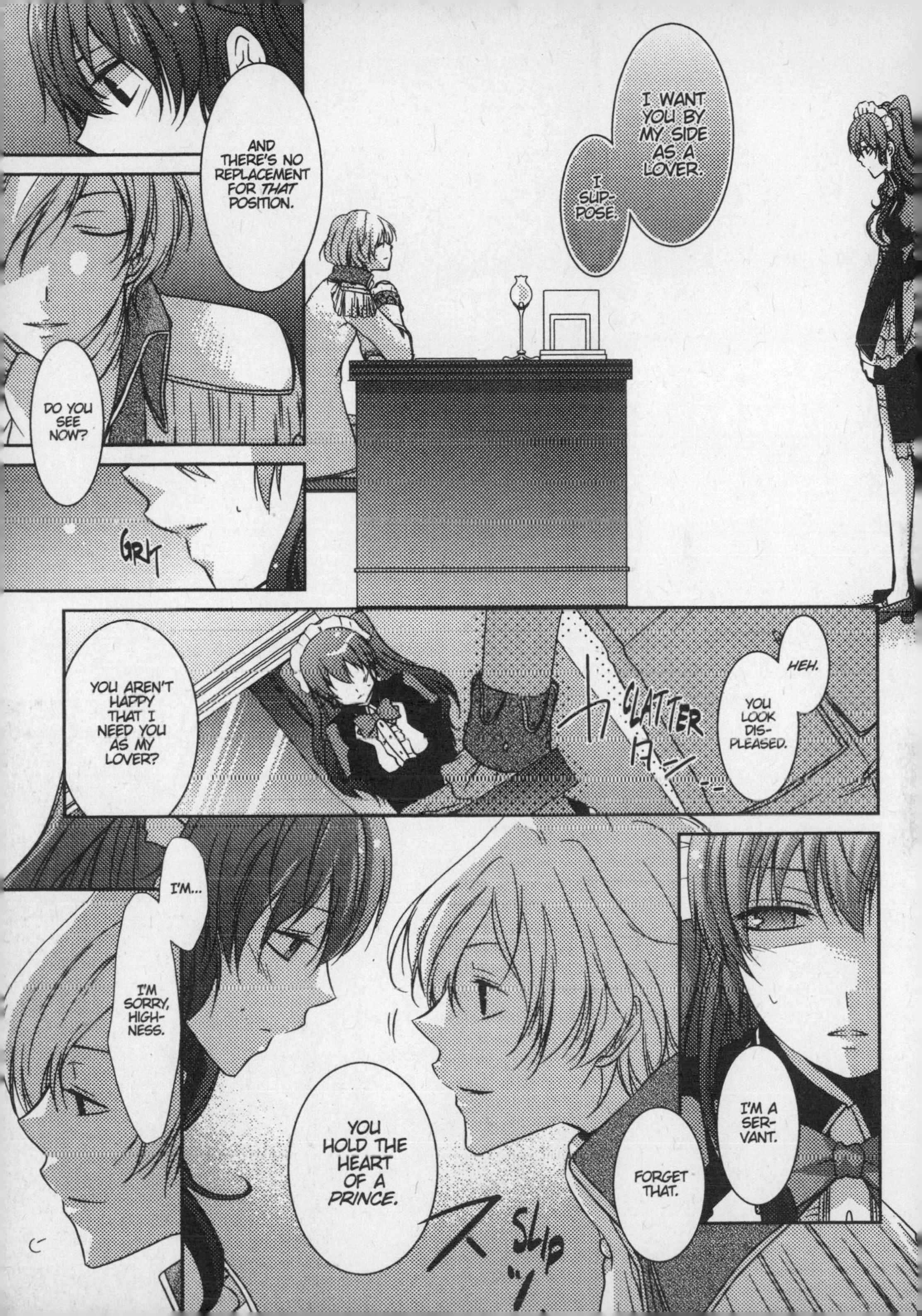
I WANT YOU BY MY SIDE AS A LOVER.
I SUPPOSE.
AND THERE'S NO REPLACEMENT FOR *THAT* POSITION.
DO YOU SEE NOW?
GRK
HEH.
YOU LOOK DISPLEASED.
CLATTER
YOU AREN'T HAPPY THAT I NEED YOU AS MY LOVER?
I'M A SERVANT.
FORGET THAT.
I'M...
I'M SORRY, HIGHNESS.
YOU HOLD THE HEART OF A *PRINCE*.
SLIP

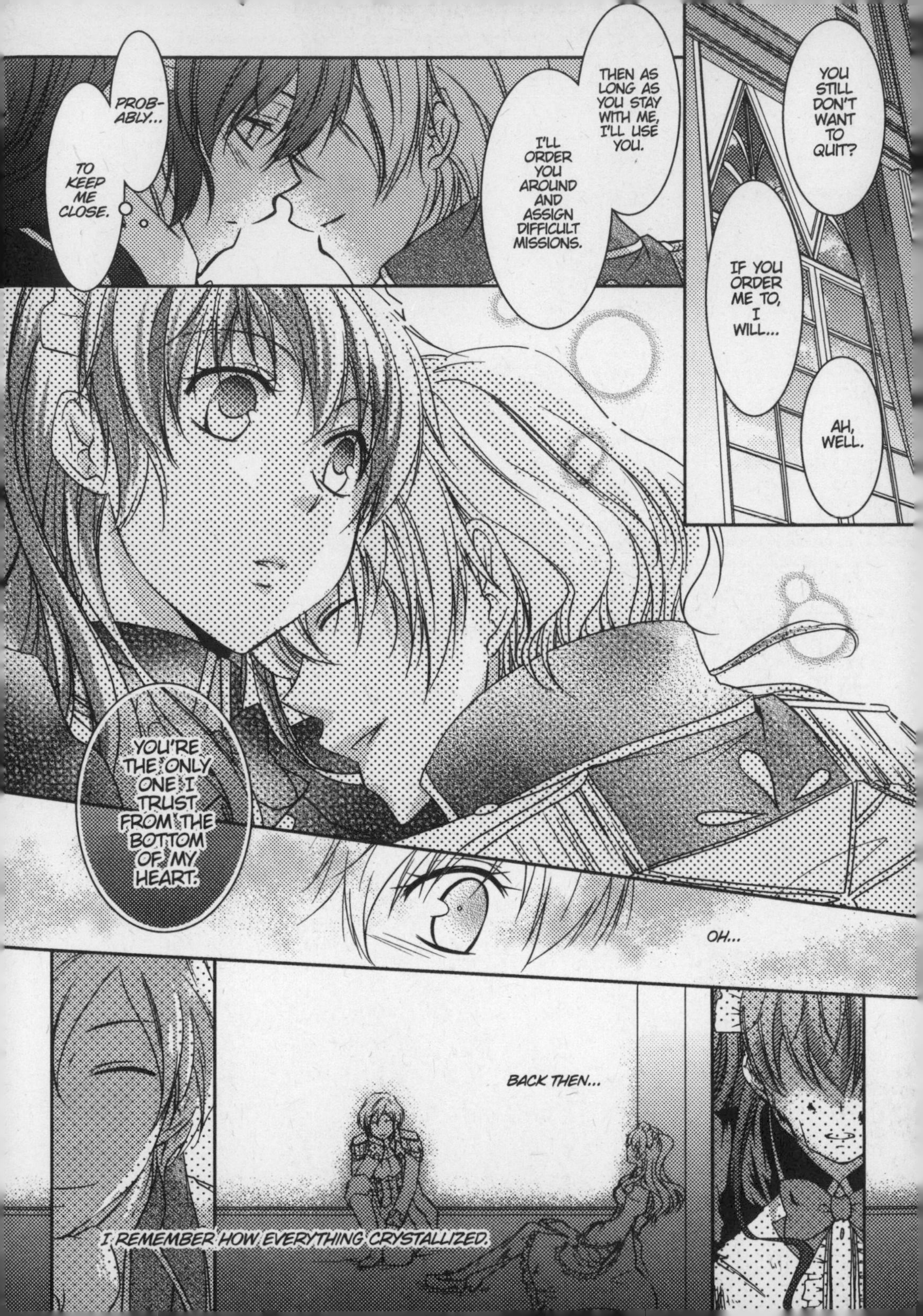
YOU STILL DON'T WANT TO QUIT?
IF YOU ORDER ME TO, I WILL...
AH, WELL.
THEN AS LONG AS YOU STAY WITH ME, I'LL USE YOU.
I'LL ORDER YOU AROUND AND ASSIGN DIFFICULT MISSIONS.
PROB-ABLY...
TO KEEP ME CLOSE.
YOU'RE THE ONLY ONE I TRUST FROM THE BOTTOM OF MY HEART.
OH...
BACK THEN...
I REMEMBER HOW EVERYTHING CRYSTALLIZED.

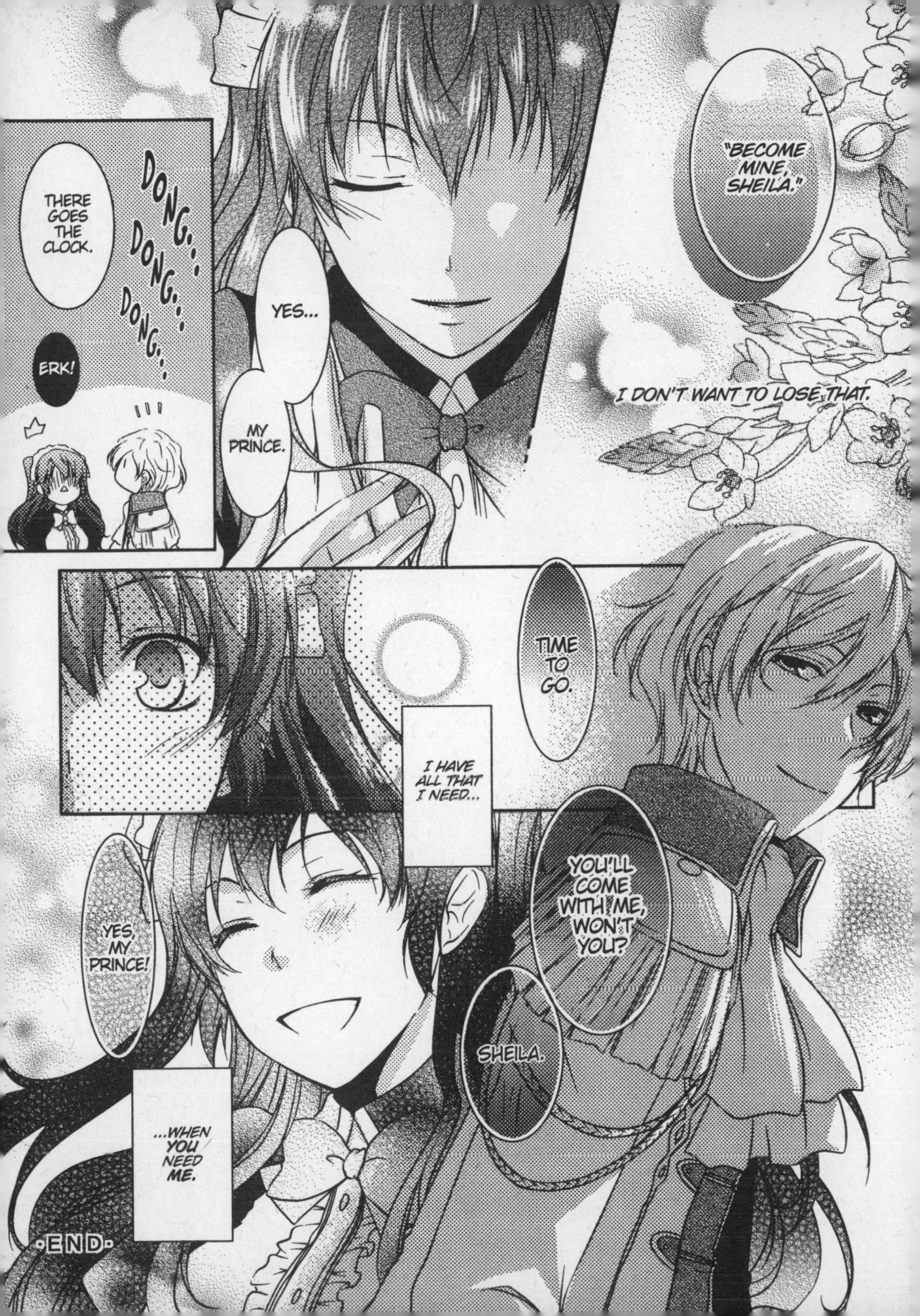
"BECOME MINE, SHEILA."
I DON'T WANT TO LOSE THAT.
YES...
MY PRINCE.
DONG... DONG... DONG...
THERE GOES THE CLOCK.
ERK!
TIME TO GO.
I HAVE ALL THAT I NEED...
YOU'LL COME WITH ME, WON'T YOU?
SHEILA.
YES, MY PRINCE!
...WHEN YOU NEED ME.
•END•

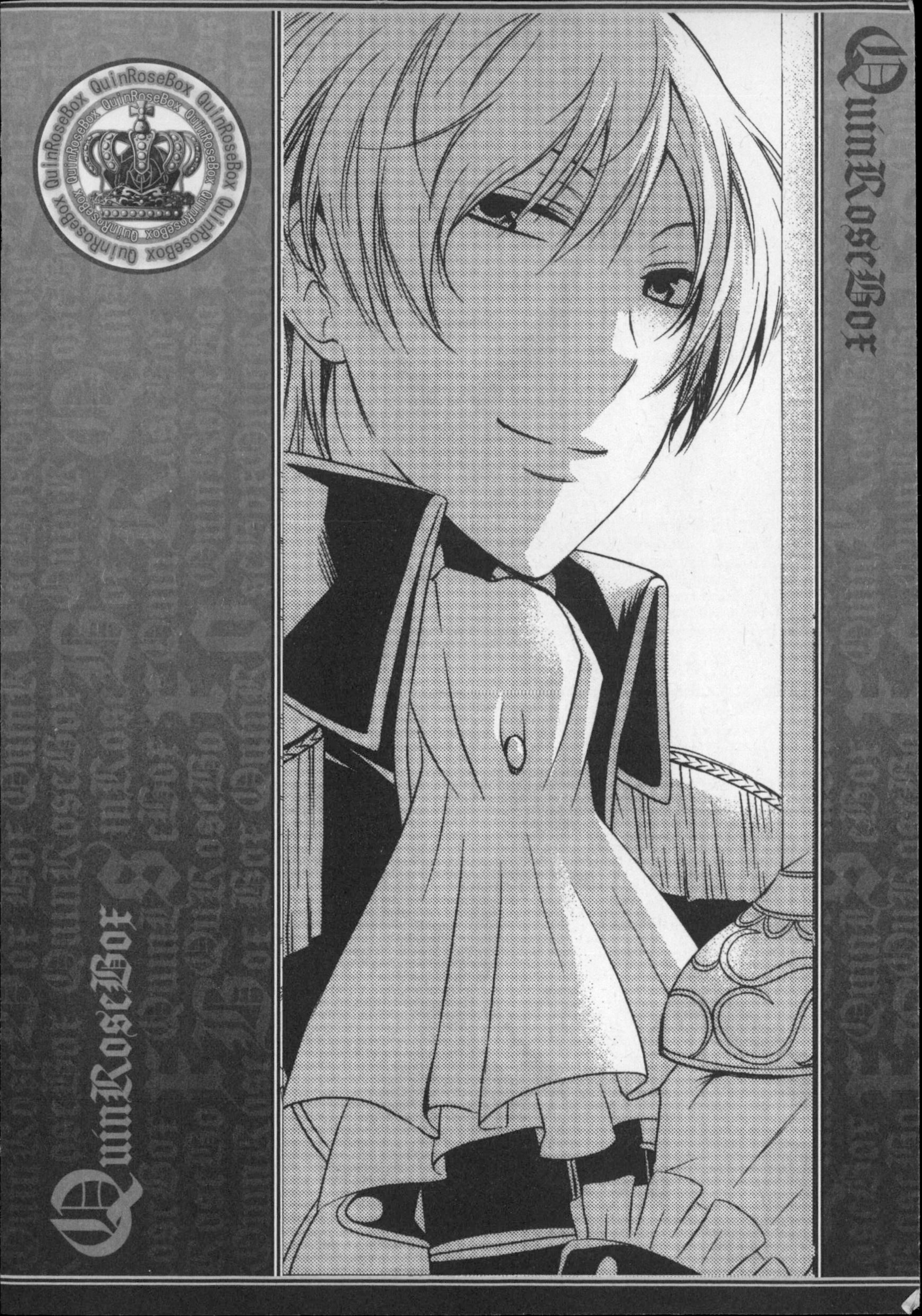
QuinRoseBox
QuinRoseBox
QuinRoseBox

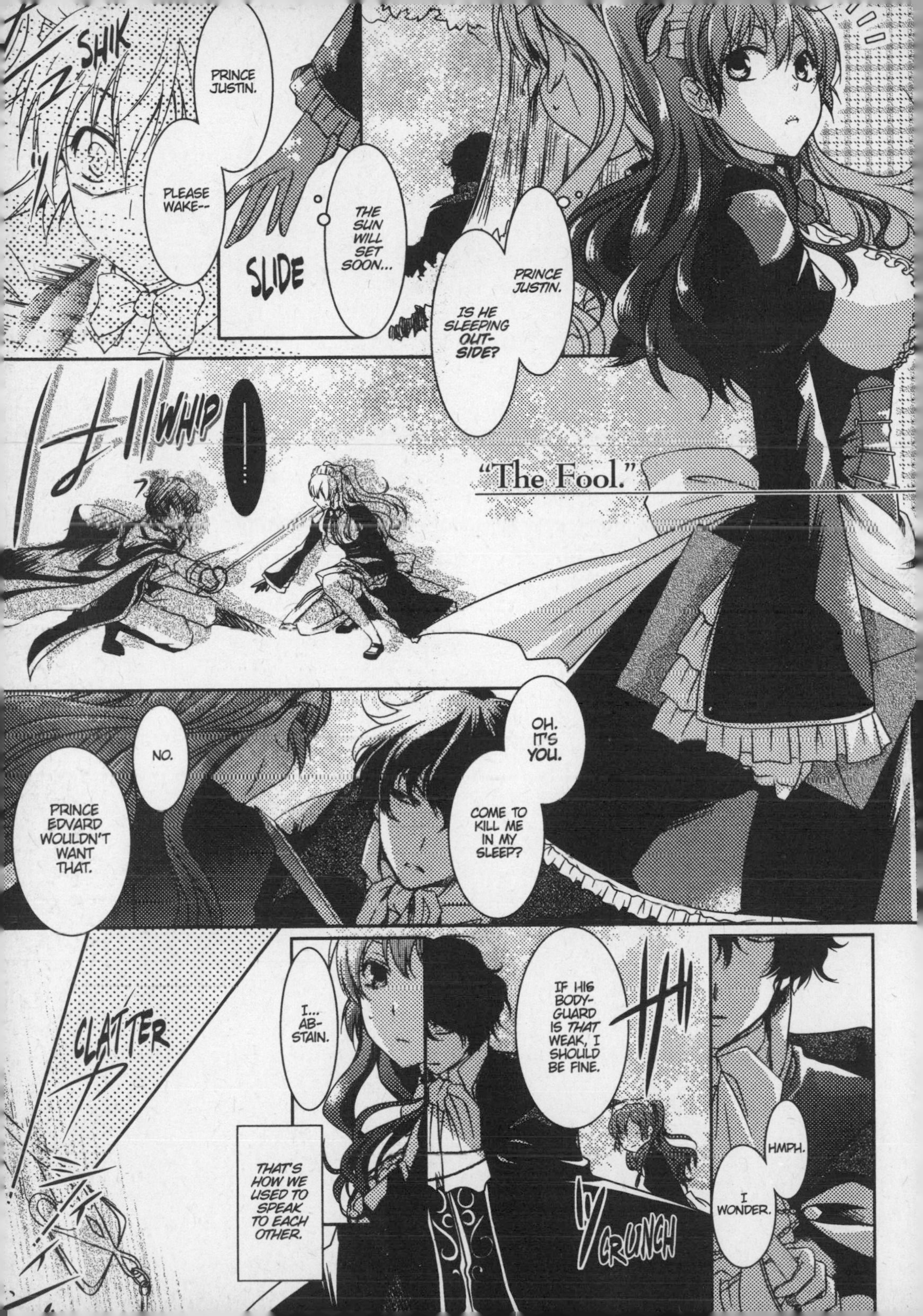
PRINCE JUSTIN.
IS HE SLEEPING OUT-SIDE?
"The Fool."
THE SUN WILL SET SOON...
SLIDE
PRINCE JUSTIN.
PLEASE WAKE--
SHIK
...!
WHIP
OH. IT'S YOU.
COME TO KILL ME IN MY SLEEP?
NO.
PRINCE EDVARD WOULDN'T WANT THAT.
HMPH.
I WONDER.
IF HIS BODY-GUARD IS THAT WEAK, I SHOULD BE FINE.
CRUNCH
I... AB-STAIN.
THAT'S HOW WE USED TO SPEAK TO EACH OTHER.
CLATTER

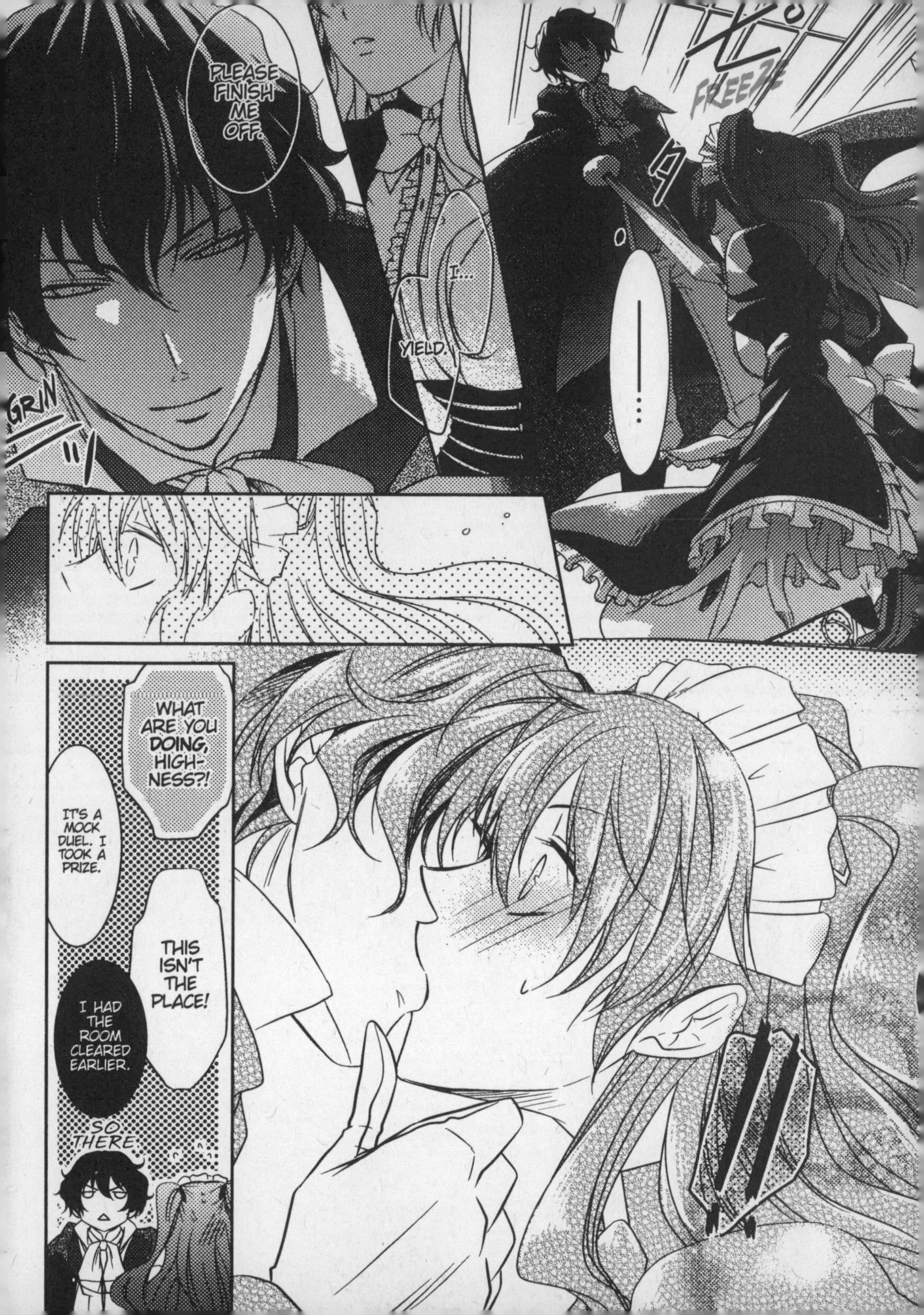
FREEZE
I...
YIELD.
PLEASE FINISH ME OFF.
GRIN
WHAT ARE YOU DOING, HIGHNESS?!
IT'S A MOCK DUEL. I TOOK A PRIZE.
THIS ISN'T THE PLACE!
I HAD THE ROOM CLEARED EARLIER.
SO THERE.

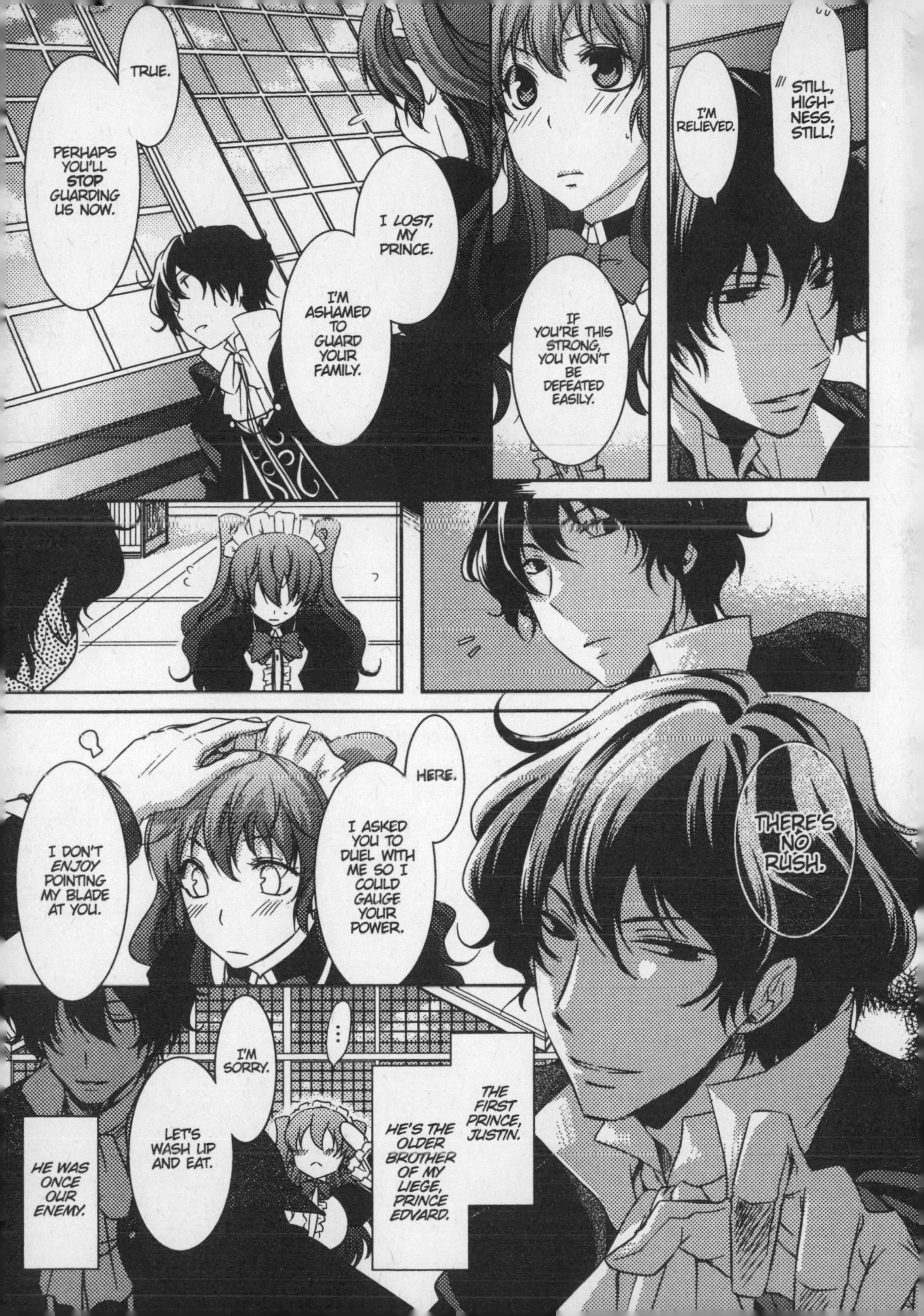
STILL, HIGHNESS. STILL!
I'M RELIEVED.
I LOST, MY PRINCE.
I'M ASHAMED TO GUARD YOUR FAMILY.
IF YOU'RE THIS STRONG, YOU WON'T BE DEFEATED EASILY.
TRUE.
PERHAPS YOU'LL STOP GUARDING US NOW.
THERE'S NO RUSH.
HERE.
I ASKED YOU TO DUEL WITH ME SO I COULD GAUGE YOUR POWER.
I DON'T ENJOY POINTING MY BLADE AT YOU.
...
I'M SORRY.
THE FIRST PRINCE, JUSTIN.
HE'S THE OLDER BROTHER OF MY LIEGE, PRINCE EDVARD.
LET'S WASH UP AND EAT.
HE WAS ONCE OUR ENEMY.

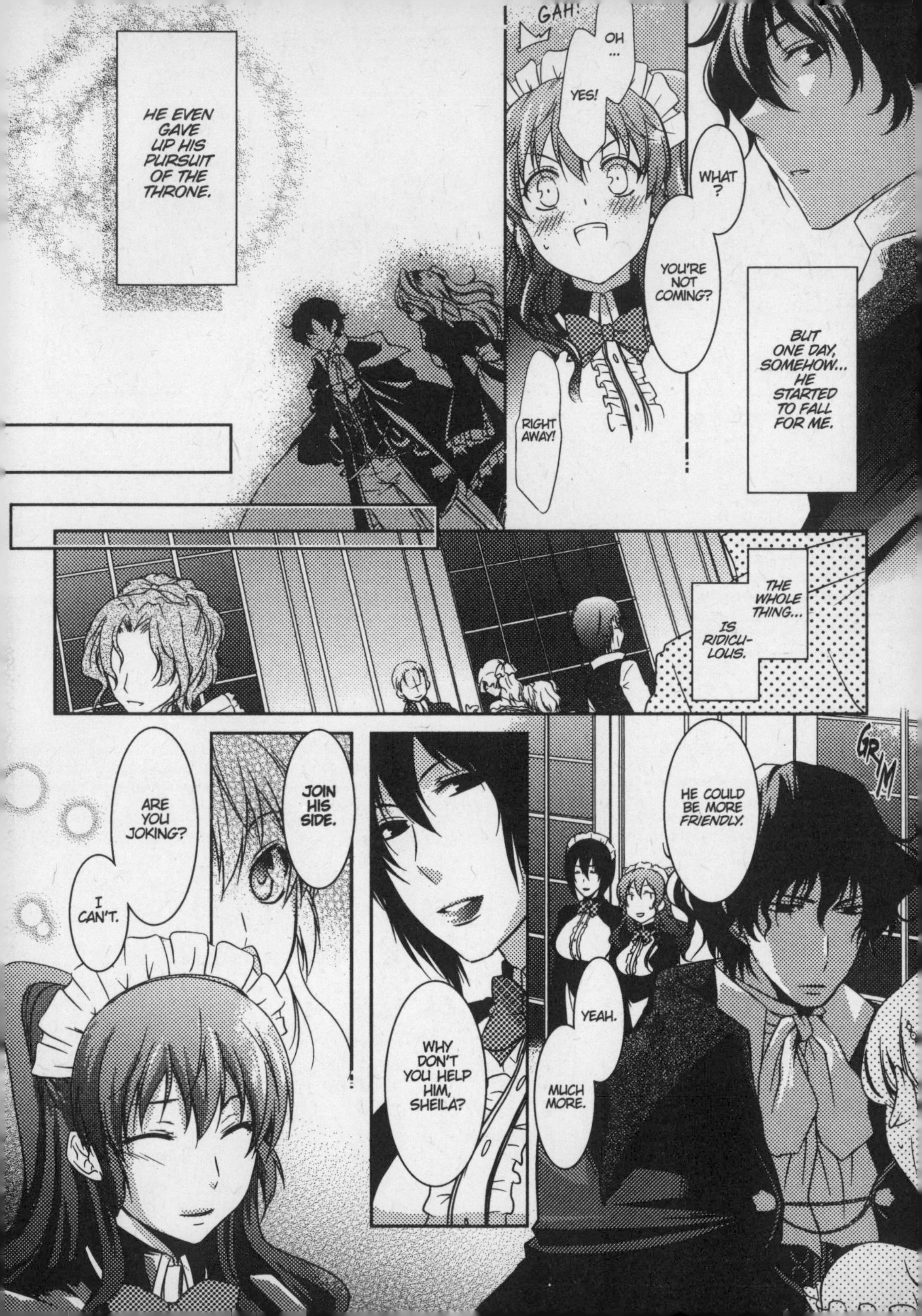
BUT ONE DAY, SOMEHOW... HE STARTED TO FALL FOR ME.
GAH!
OH ... YES!
WHAT?
YOU'RE NOT COMING?
RIGHT AWAY!
HE EVEN GAVE UP HIS PURSUIT OF THE THRONE.
THE WHOLE THING... IS RIDICULOUS.
GRUM
HE COULD BE MORE FRIENDLY.
YEAH.
MUCH MORE.
WHY DON'T YOU HELP HIM, SHEILA?
JOIN HIS SIDE.
ARE YOU JOKING?
I CAN'T.

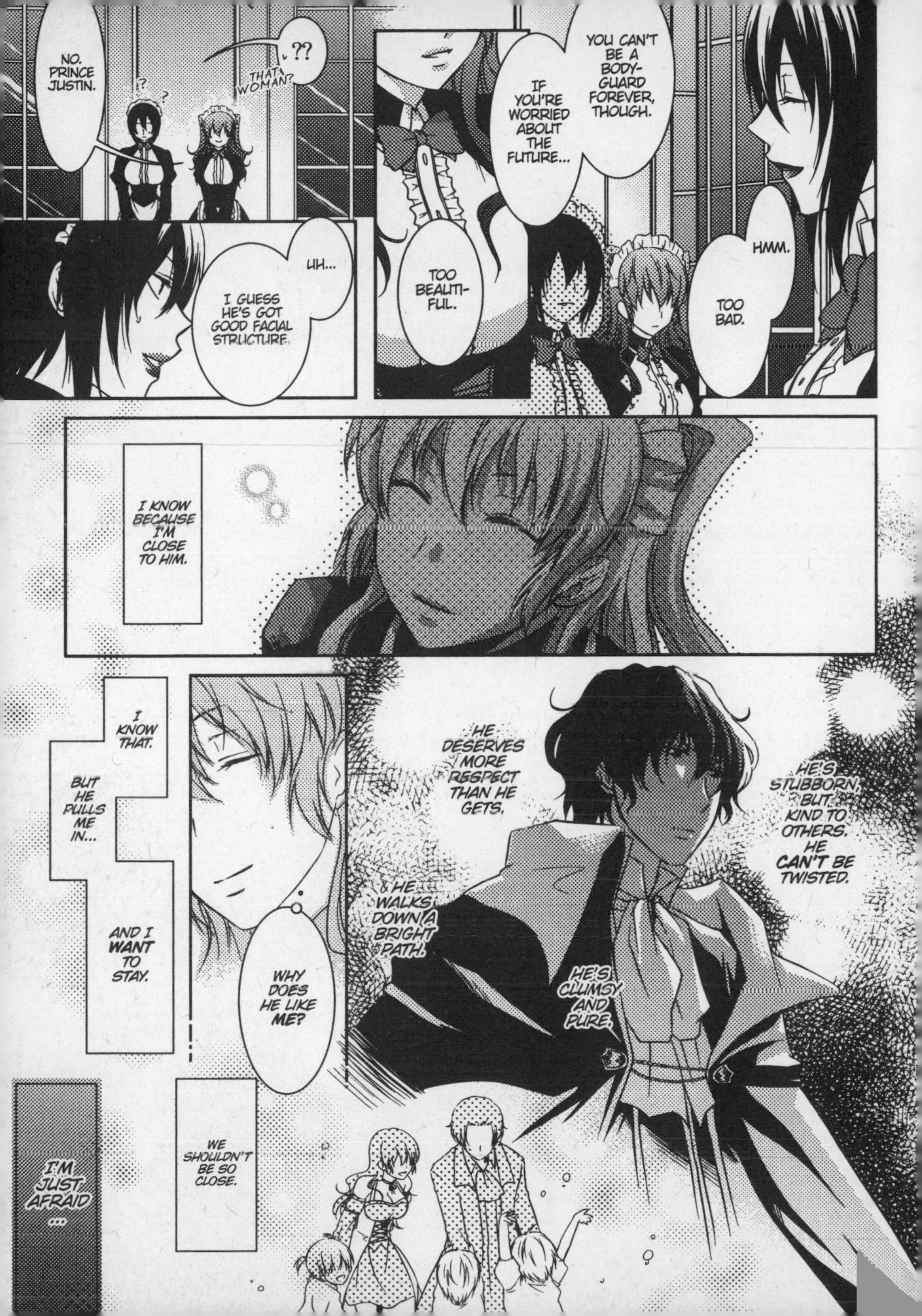
YOU CAN'T BE A BODY-GUARD FOREVER, THOUGH.
IF YOU'RE WORRIED ABOUT THE FUTURE...
HMM.
TOO BAD.
TOO BEAUTIFUL.
??
THAT WOMAN?
NO. PRINCE JUSTIN.
UH...
I GUESS HE'S GOT GOOD FACIAL STRUCTURE.
I KNOW BECAUSE I'M CLOSE TO HIM.
HE'S STUBBORN, BUT KIND TO OTHERS. HE CAN'T BE TWISTED.
HE DESERVES MORE RESPECT THAN HE GETS.
& HE WALKS DOWN A BRIGHT PATH.
HE'S CLUMSY AND PURE.
WHY DOES HE LIKE ME?
I KNOW THAT.
BUT HE PULLS ME IN...
AND I WANT TO STAY.
WE SHOULDN'T BE SO CLOSE.
I'M JUST AFRAID...

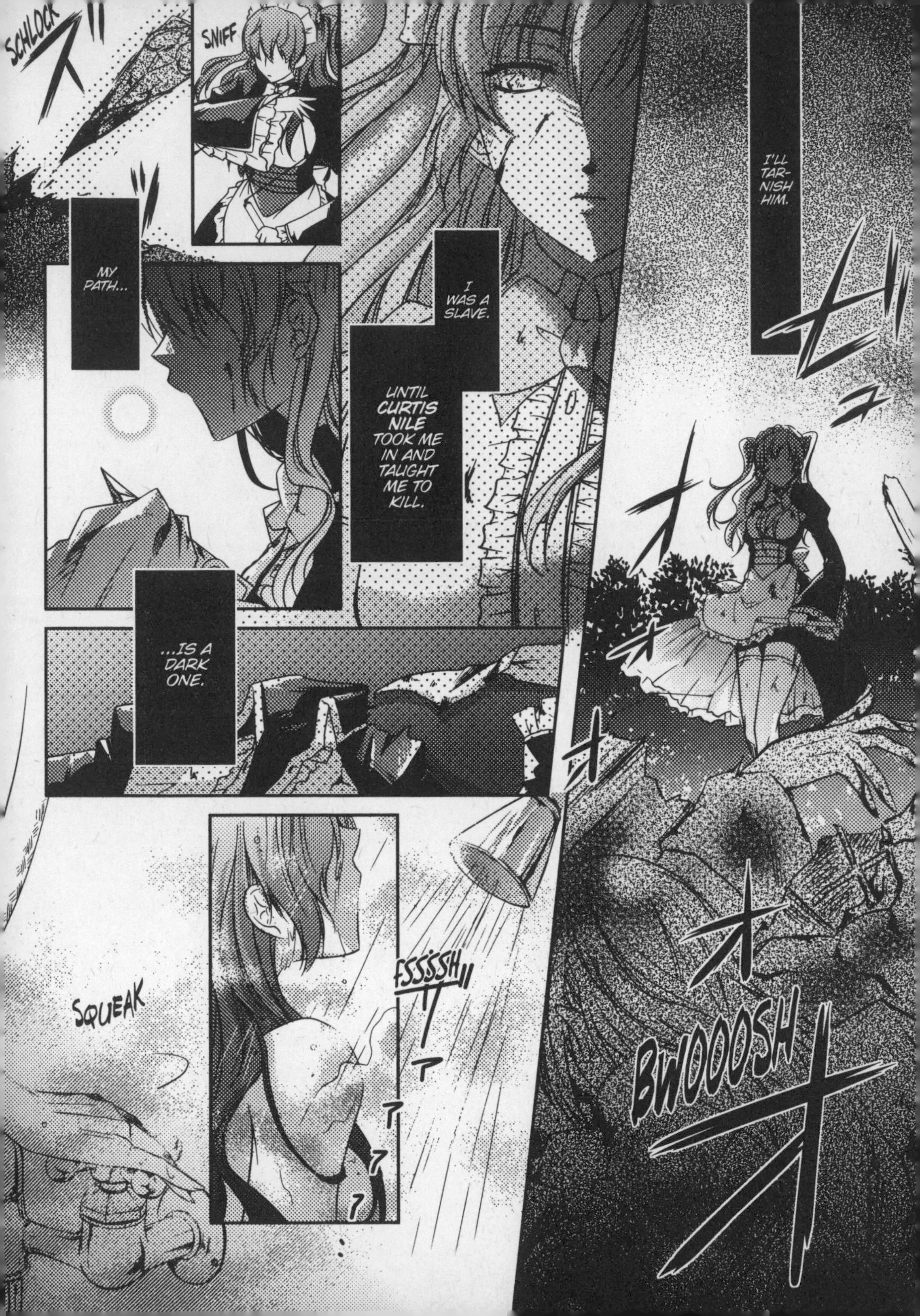
I'LL TAR-NISH HIM.
BWOOOSH
I WAS A SLAVE.
UNTIL CURTIS NILE TOOK ME IN AND TAUGHT ME TO KILL.
SNIFF
SCHLOCK
MY PATH...
...IS A DARK ONE.
FSSSSH
SQUEAK

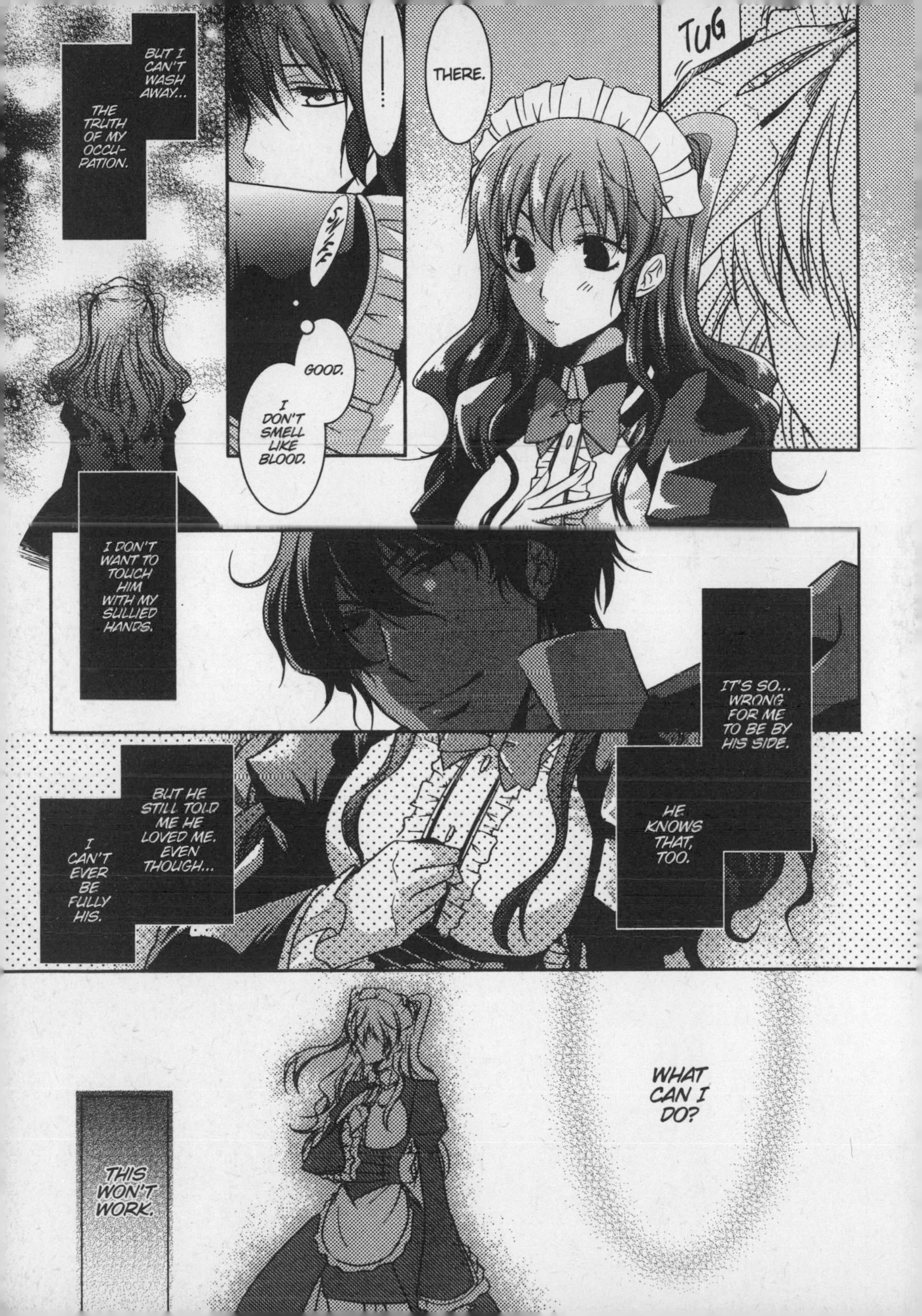
TUG
THERE.
...!
SNIFF
GOOD.
I DON'T SMELL LIKE BLOOD.
BUT I CAN'T WASH AWAY...
THE TRUTH OF MY OCCUPATION.
I DON'T WANT TO TOUCH HIM WITH MY SULLIED HANDS.
IT'S SO... WRONG FOR ME TO BE BY HIS SIDE.
HE KNOWS THAT, TOO.
BUT HE STILL TOLD ME HE LOVED ME. EVEN THOUGH...
I CAN'T EVER BE FULLY HIS.
WHAT CAN I DO?
THIS WON'T WORK.

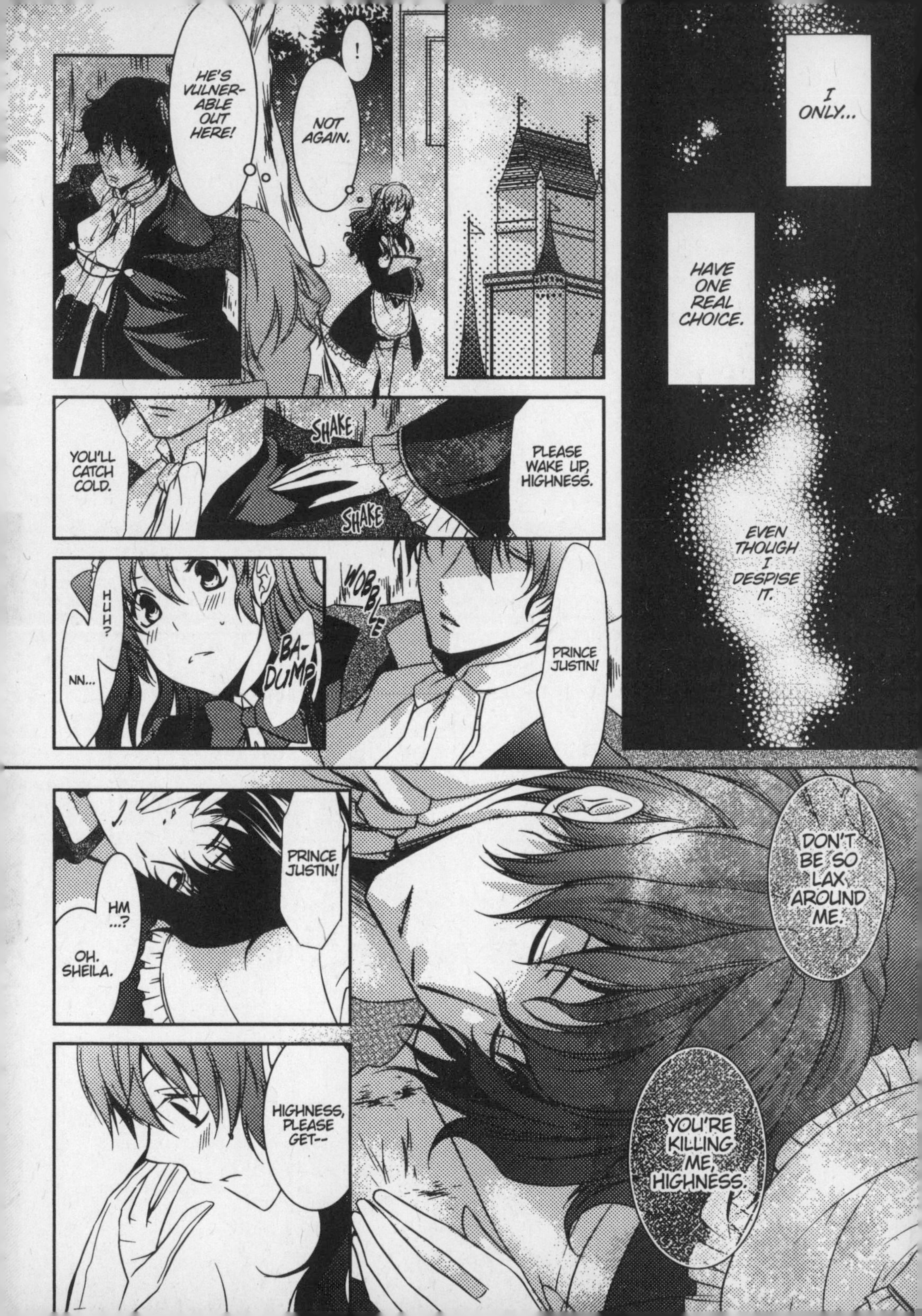
I ONLY...
HAVE ONE REAL CHOICE.
EVEN THOUGH I DESPISE IT.
!
NOT AGAIN.
HE'S VULNER-ABLE OUT HERE!
PLEASE WAKE UP, HIGHNESS.
SHAKE
SHAKE
YOU'LL CATCH COLD.
PRINCE JUSTIN!
WOBBLE
BA-DUMP
HUH?
NN...
DON'T BE SO LAX AROUND ME.
YOU'RE KILLING ME, HIGHNESS.
PRINCE JUSTIN!
HM ...?
OH. SHEILA.
HIGHNESS, PLEASE GET--

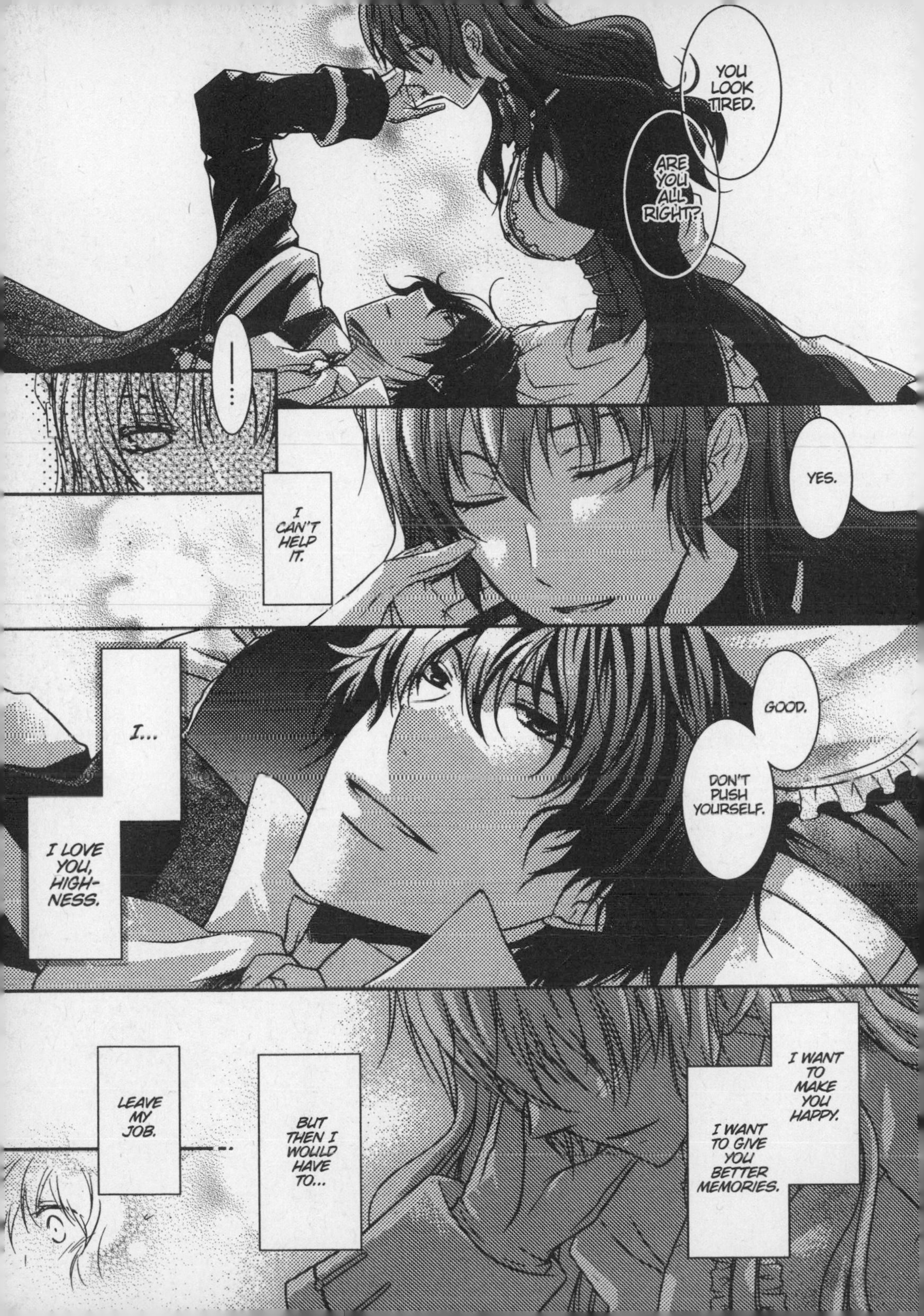
YOU LOOK TIRED.
ARE YOU ALL RIGHT?
!......
YES.
I CAN'T HELP IT.
GOOD.
DON'T PUSH YOURSELF.
I...
I LOVE YOU, HIGH-NESS.
I WANT TO MAKE YOU HAPPY.
I WANT TO GIVE YOU BETTER MEMORIES.
BUT THEN I WOULD HAVE TO...
LEAVE MY JOB.

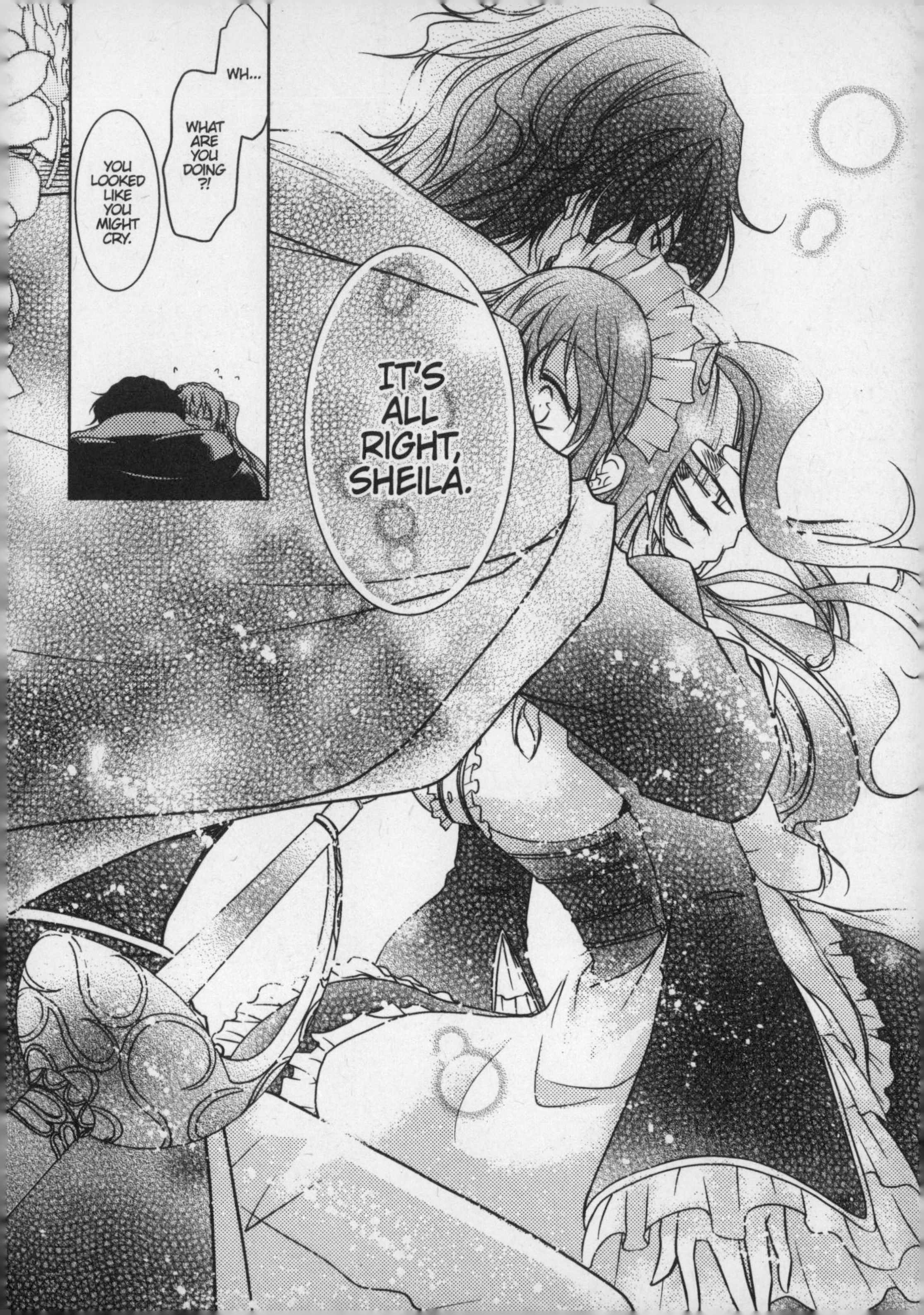
IT'S ALL RIGHT, SHEILA.
WH...
WHAT ARE YOU DOING ?!
YOU LOOKED LIKE YOU MIGHT CRY.

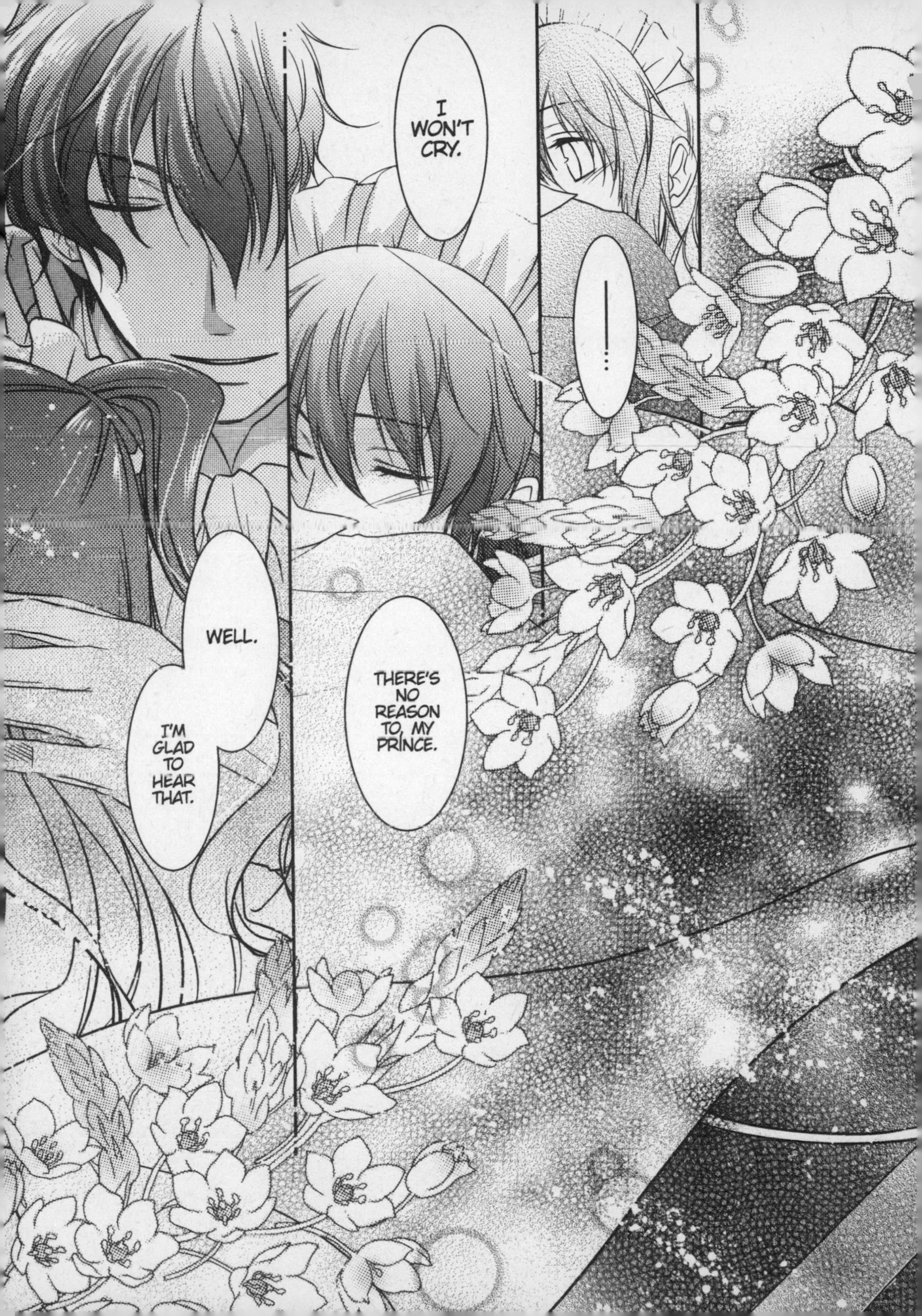
—......
I WON'T CRY.
THERE'S NO REASON TO, MY PRINCE.
WELL.
I'M GLAD TO HEAR THAT.

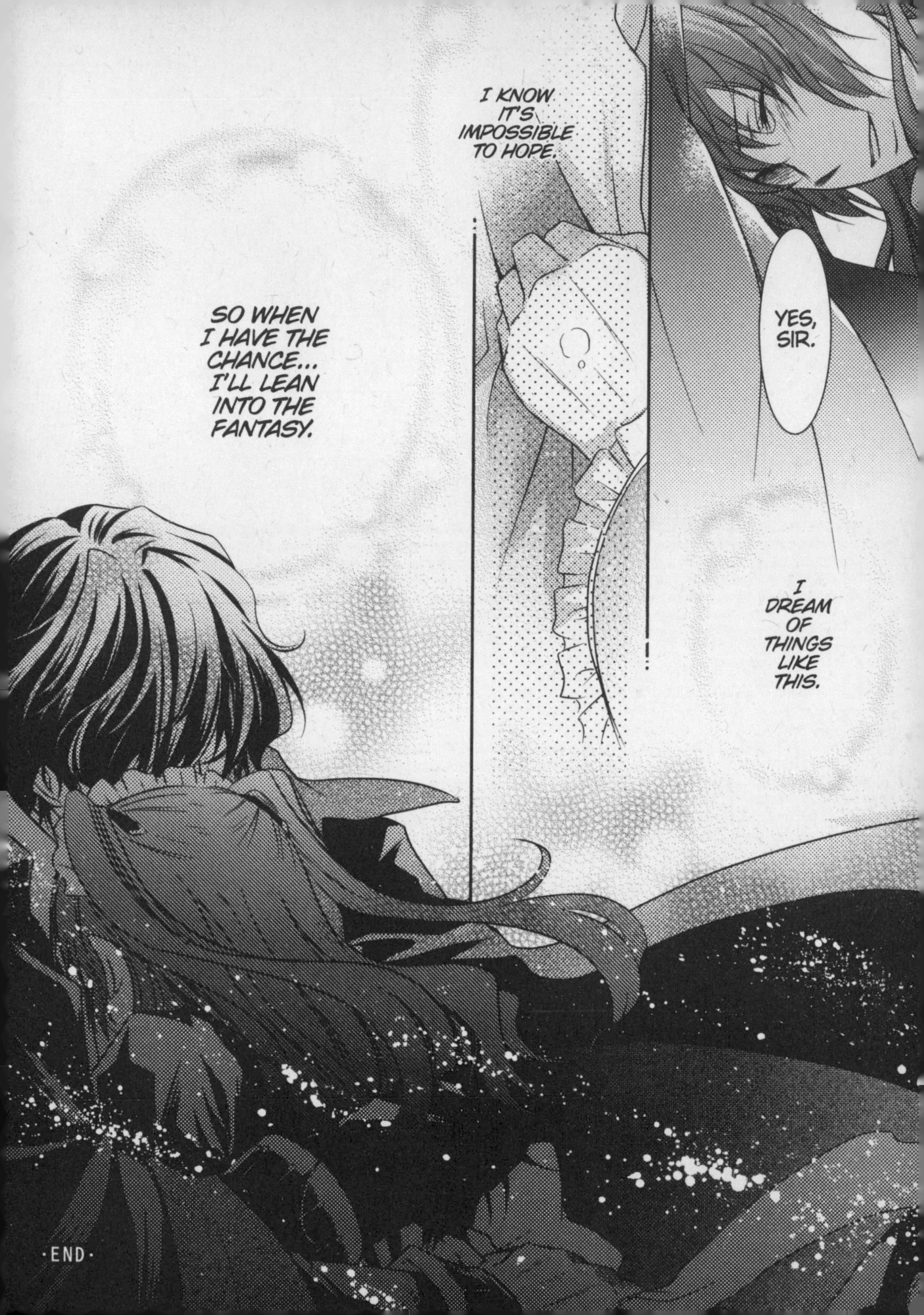
YES, SIR.
I DREAM OF THINGS LIKE THIS.
I KNOW IT'S IMPOSSIBLE TO HOPE.
SO WHEN I HAVE THE CHANCE... I'LL LEAN INTO THE FANTASY.
·END·

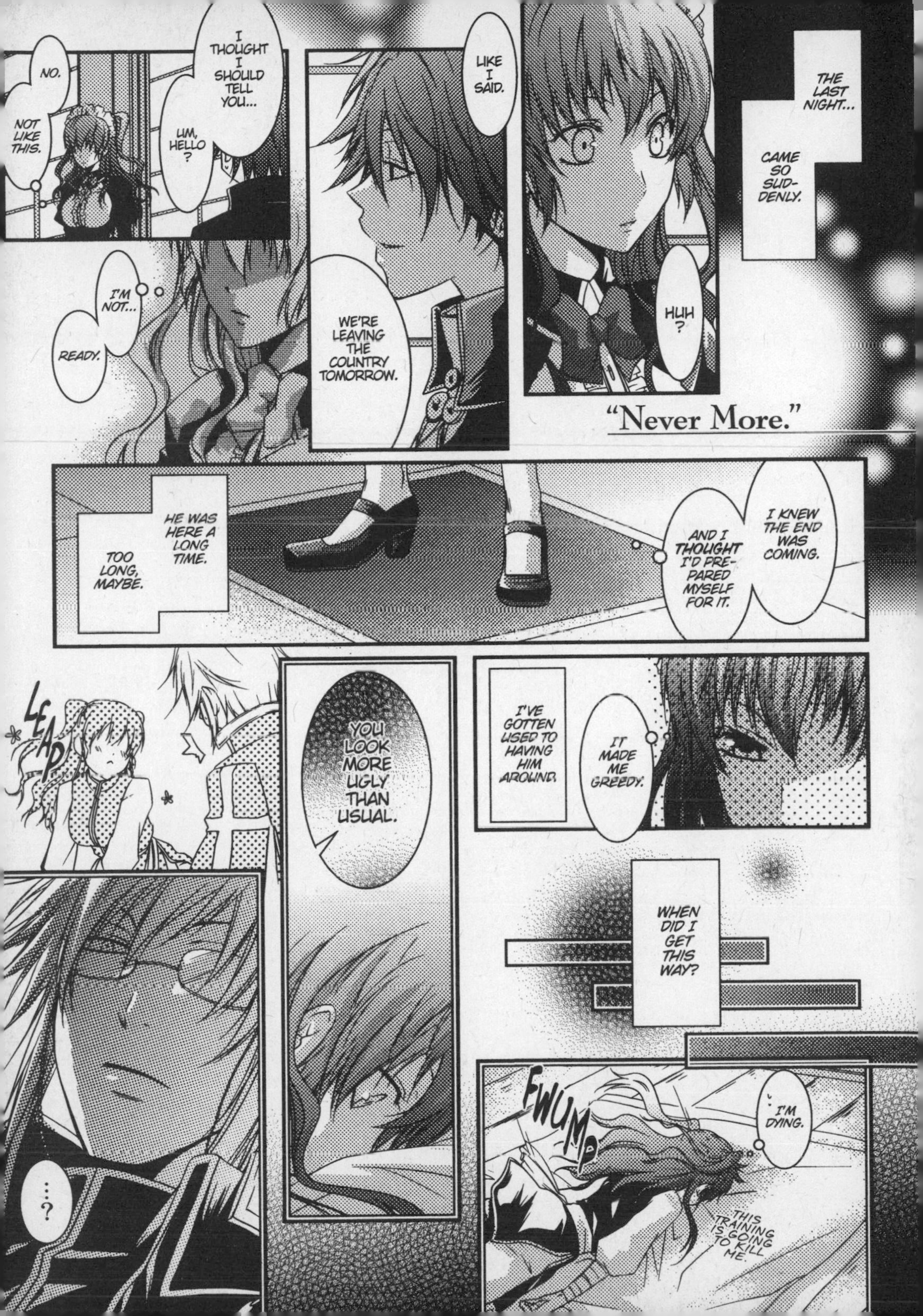
THE LAST NIGHT...
CAME SO SUD-DENLY.
HUH?
LIKE I SAID.
WE'RE LEAVING THE COUNTRY TOMORROW.
I THOUGHT I SHOULD TELL YOU...
UM, HELLO?
NO.
NOT LIKE THIS.
I'M NOT...
READY.
"Never More."
I KNEW THE END WAS COMING.
AND I THOUGHT I'D PRE-PARED MYSELF FOR IT.
HE WAS HERE A LONG TIME.
TOO LONG, MAYBE.
IT MADE ME GREEDY.
I'VE GOTTEN USED TO HAVING HIM AROUND.
YOU LOOK MORE UGLY THAN USUAL.
LEAP
WHEN DID I GET THIS WAY?
...I'M DYING.
FWUMP
THIS TRAINING IS GOING TO KILL ME.
...?

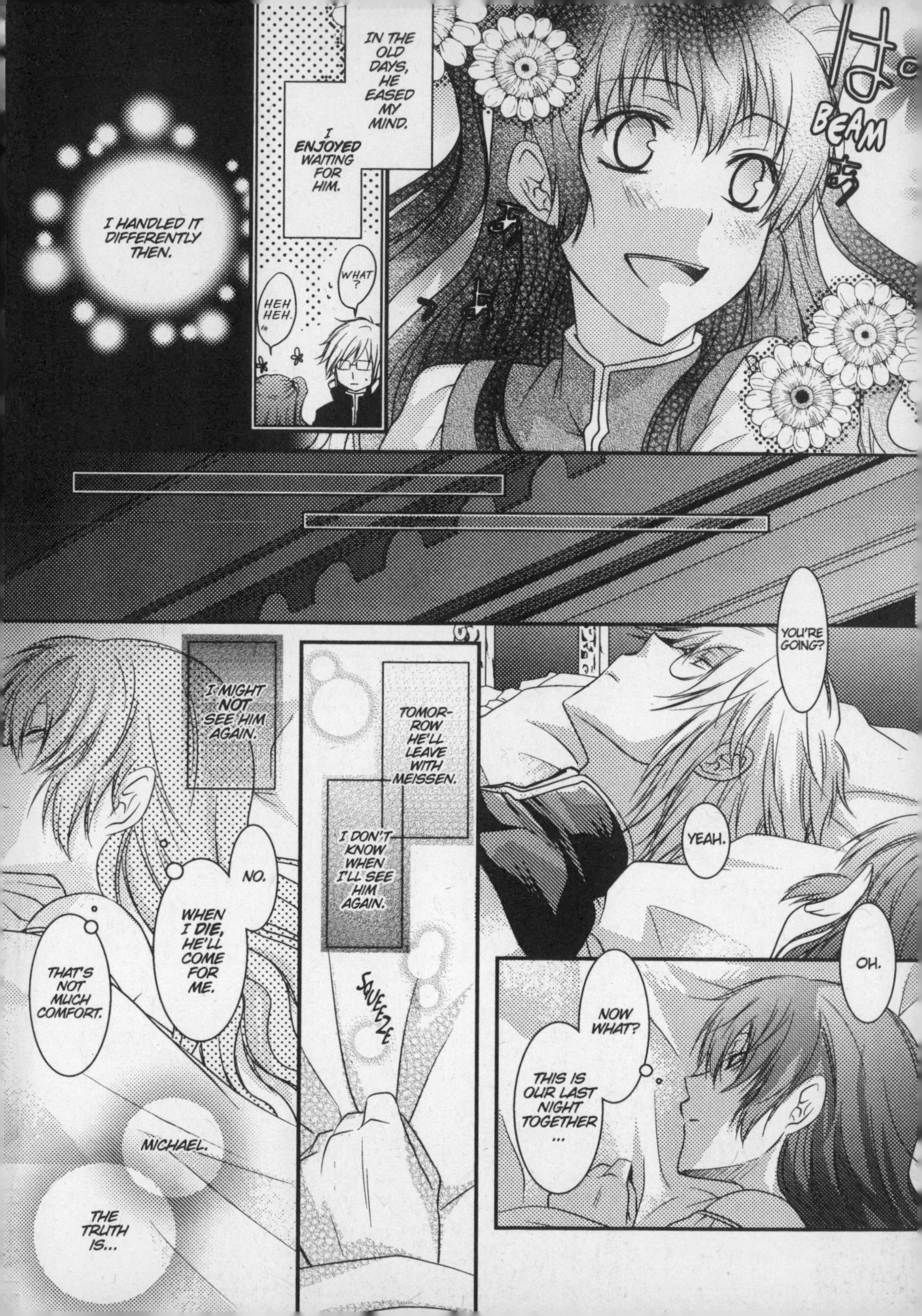
BEAM
IN THE OLD DAYS, HE EASED MY MIND.
I ENJOYED WAITING FOR HIM.
WHAT?
HEH HEH.
I HANDLED IT DIFFERENTLY THEN.
YOU'RE GOING?
YEAH.
OH.
NOW WHAT?
THIS IS OUR LAST NIGHT TOGETHER...
TOMOR-ROW HE'LL LEAVE WITH MEISSEN.
I DON'T KNOW WHEN I'LL SEE HIM AGAIN.
SQUEEZE
I MIGHT NOT SEE HIM AGAIN.
NO.
WHEN I DIE, HE'LL COME FOR ME.
THAT'S NOT MUCH COMFORT.
MICHAEL.
THE TRUTH IS...

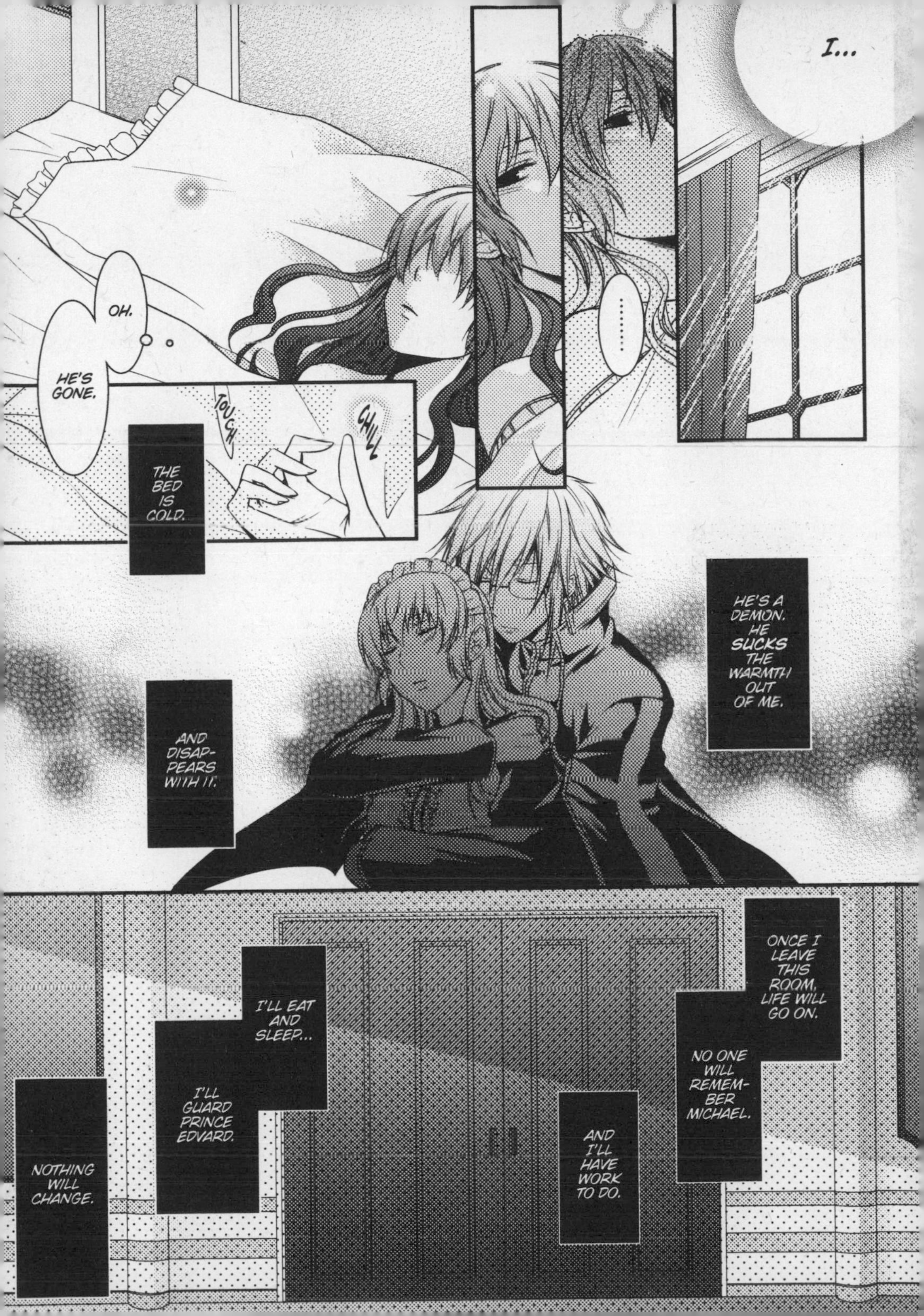
I...
......
OH.
HE'S GONE.
TOUCH
CHILL
THE BED IS COLD.
HE'S A DEMON. HE **SUCKS** THE WARMTH OUT OF ME.
AND DISAPPEARS WITH IT.
ONCE I LEAVE THIS ROOM, LIFE WILL GO ON.
NO ONE WILL REMEMBER MICHAEL.
AND I'LL HAVE WORK TO DO.
I'LL EAT AND SLEEP...
I'LL GUARD PRINCE EDVARD.
NOTHING WILL CHANGE.

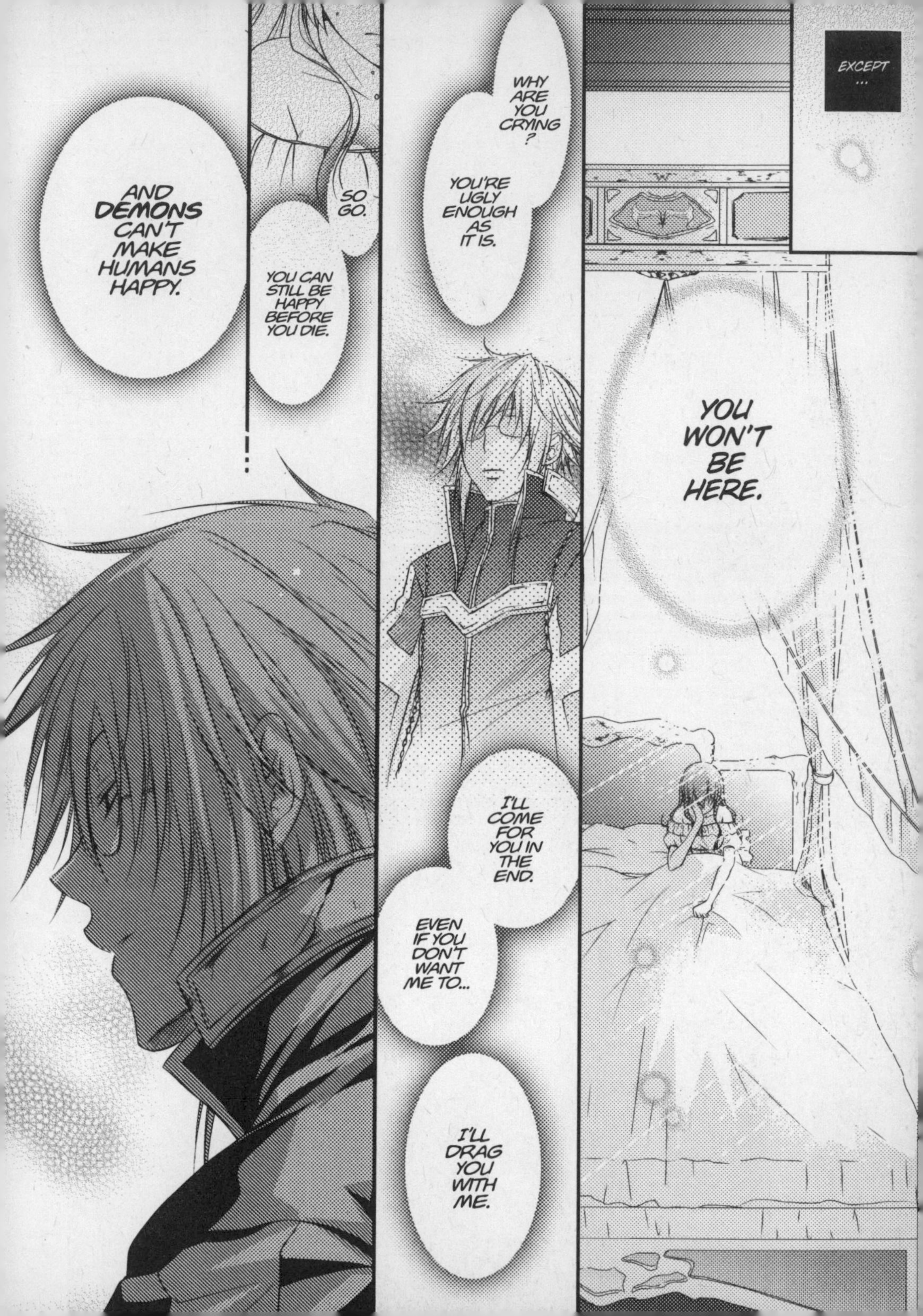
EXCEPT ...
YOU WON'T BE HERE.
WHY ARE YOU CRYING?
YOU'RE UGLY ENOUGH AS IT IS.
I'LL COME FOR YOU IN THE END.
EVEN IF YOU DON'T WANT ME TO...
I'LL DRAG YOU WITH ME.
SO GO.
YOU CAN STILL BE HAPPY BEFORE YOU DIE.
AND DEMONS CAN'T MAKE HUMANS HAPPY.

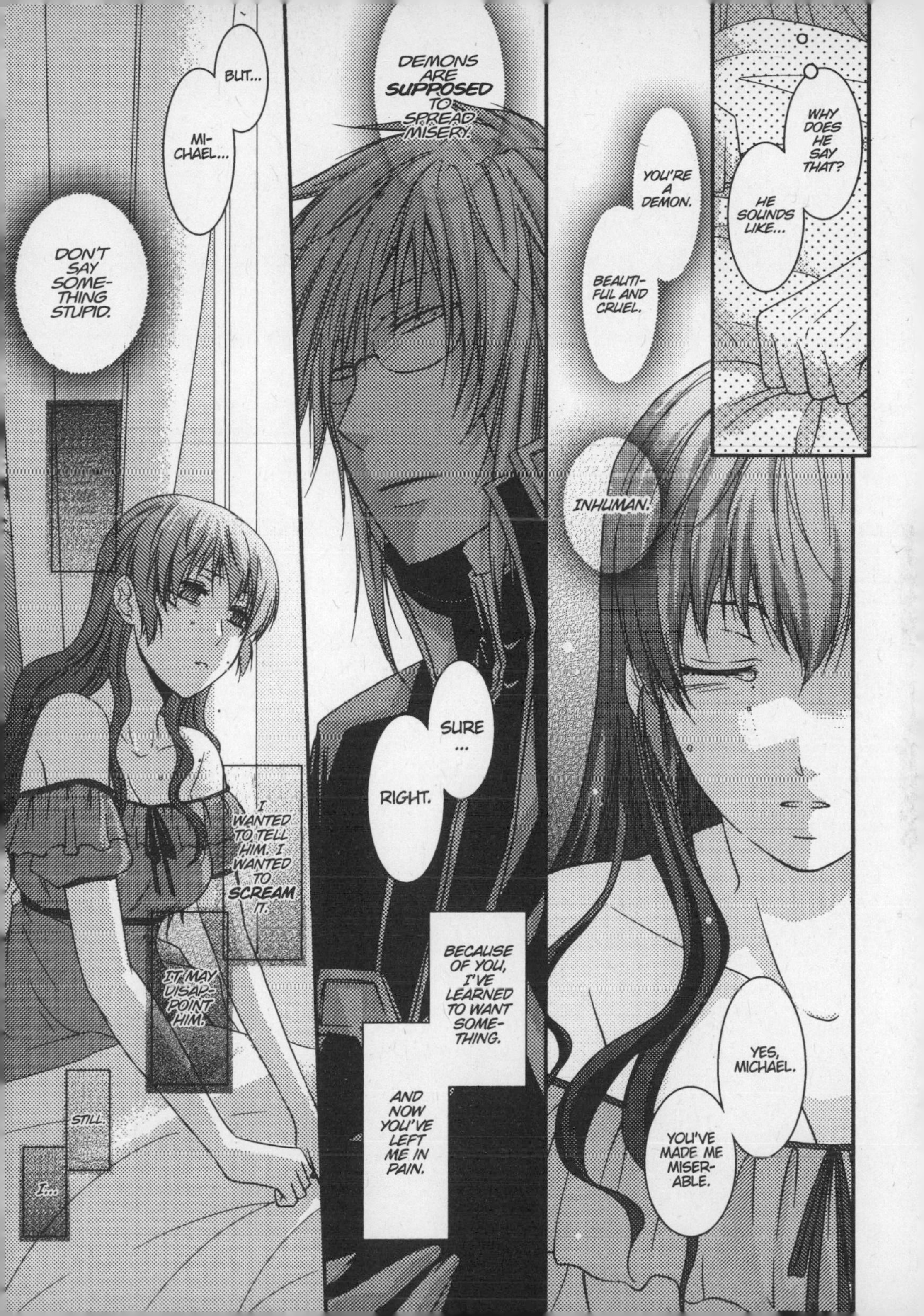
WHY DOES HE SAY THAT?
HE SOUNDS LIKE...
YOU'RE A DEMON.
BEAUTIFUL AND CRUEL.
INHUMAN.
YES, MICHAEL.
YOU'VE MADE ME MISERABLE.
DEMONS ARE **SUPPOSED** TO SPREAD MISERY.
SURE...
RIGHT.
BECAUSE OF YOU, I'VE LEARNED TO WANT SOMETHING.
AND NOW YOU'VE LEFT ME IN PAIN.
BUT...
MICHAEL...
DON'T SAY SOMETHING STUPID.
I WANTED TO TELL HIM. I WANTED TO **SCREAM** IT.
IT MAY DISAPPOINT HIM.
STILL.
I...

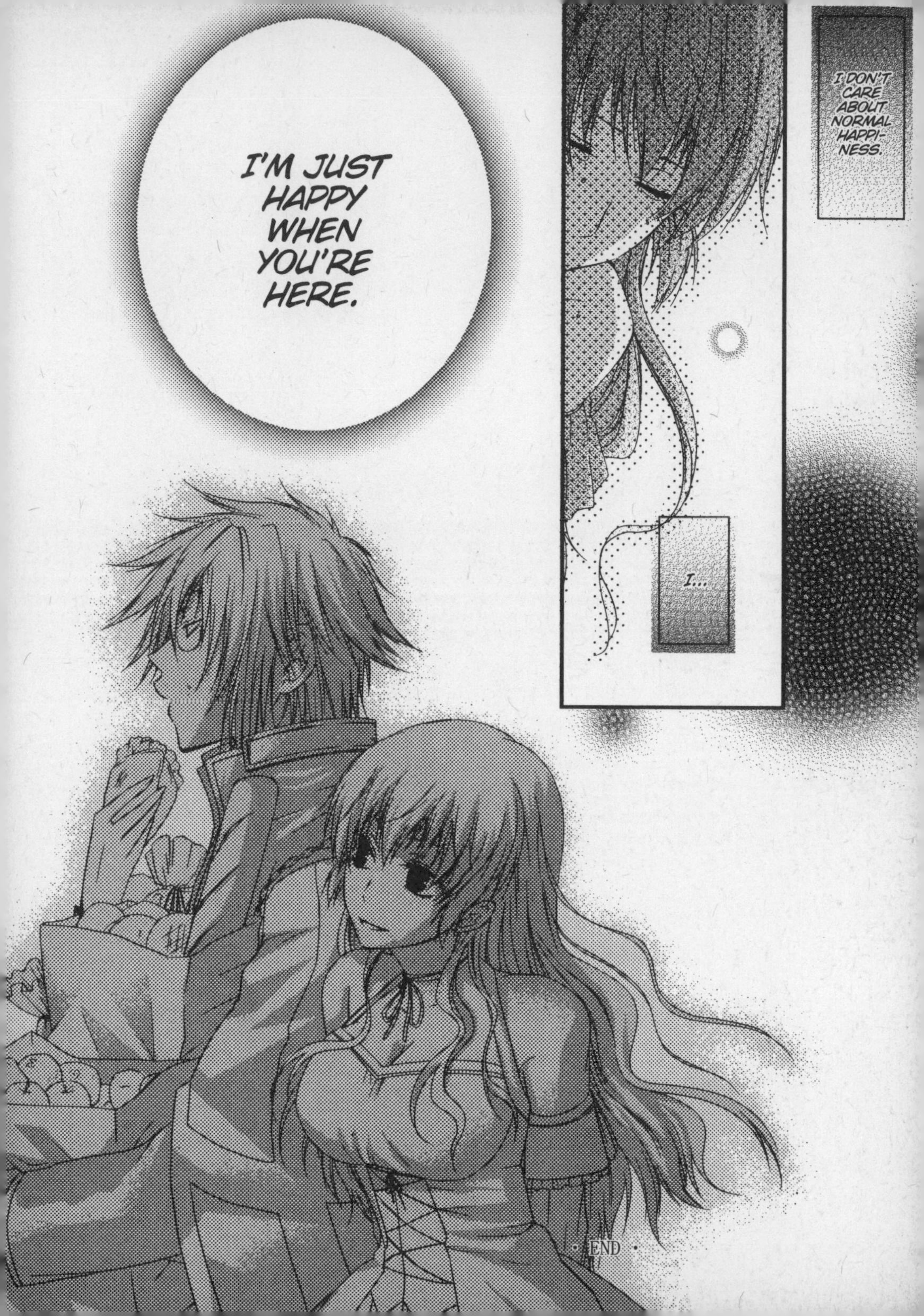
I DON'T CARE ABOUT NORMAL HAPPINESS.
I...
I'M JUST HAPPY WHEN YOU'RE HERE.
• END •

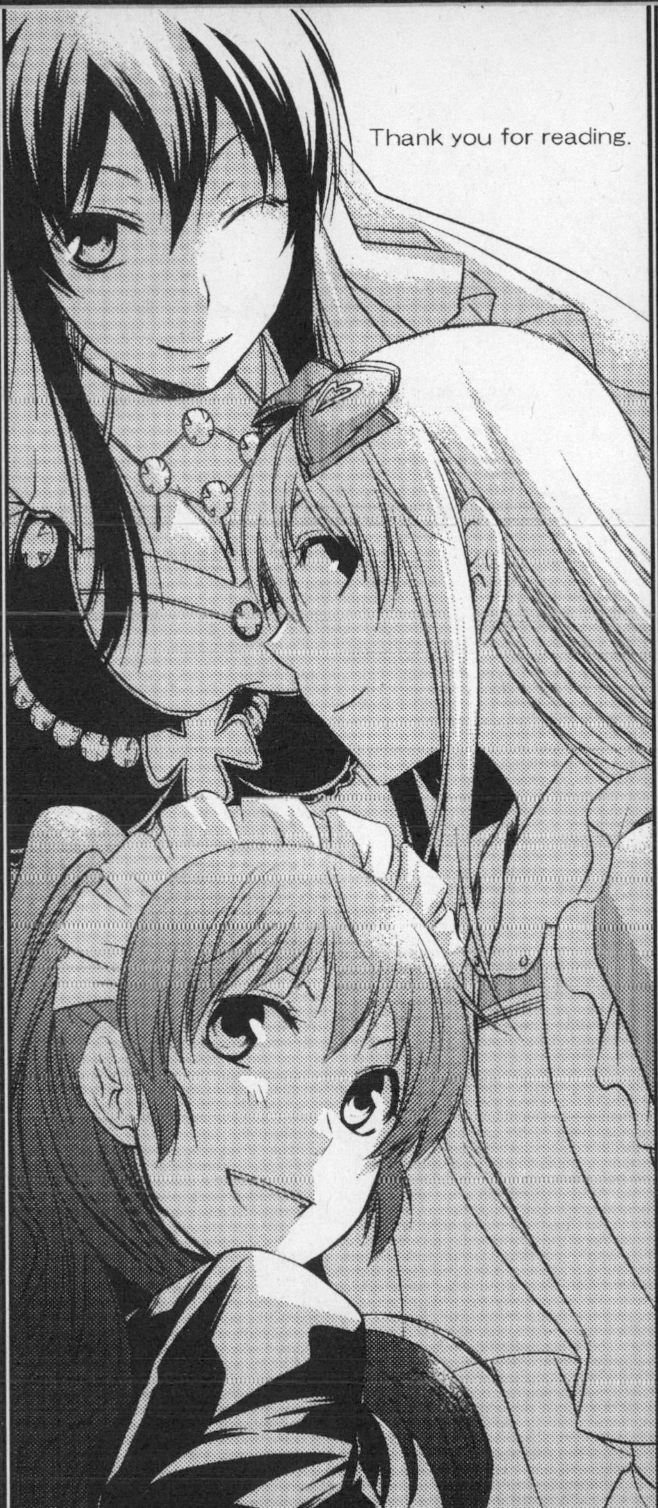
Thank you for reading.

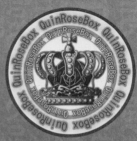

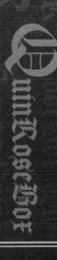

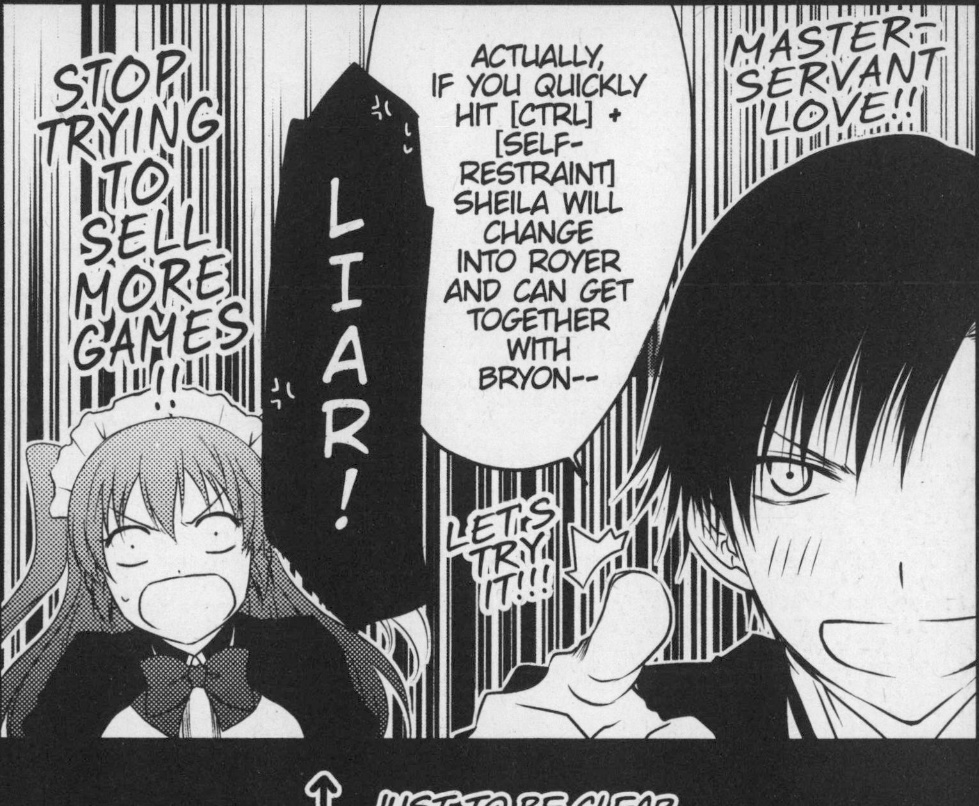
MASTER-SERVANT LOVE!!
ACTUALLY, IF YOU QUICKLY HIT [CTRL] + [SELF-RESTRAINT] SHEILA WILL CHANGE INTO ROYER AND CAN GET TOGETHER WITH BRYON--
LET'S TRY IT!!!
LIAR!
STOP TRYING TO SELL MORE GAMES!!

↑ JUST TO BE CLEAR, THIS IS A JOKE.

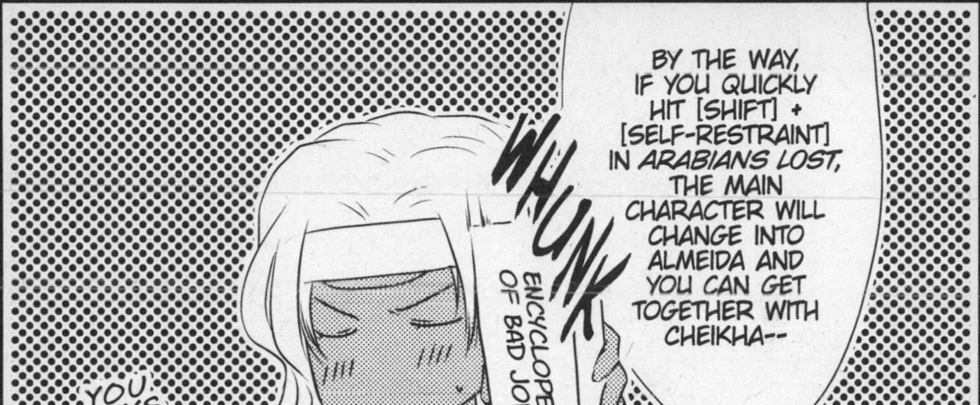
BY THE WAY, IF YOU QUICKLY HIT [SHIFT] + [SELF-RESTRAINT] IN *ARABIANS LOST*, THE MAIN CHARACTER WILL CHANGE INTO ALMEIDA AND YOU CAN GET TOGETHER WITH CHEIKHA--
WHUNK
ENCYCLOPEDIA OF BAD JOKES
YOU GUYS HAVING FUN?

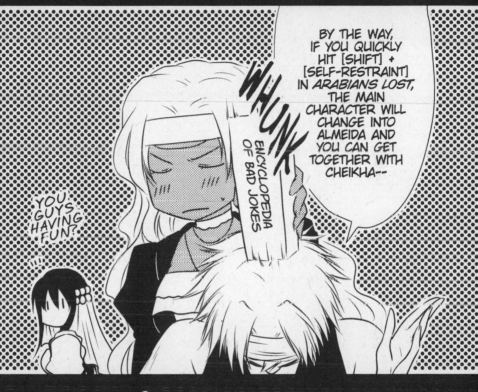

↑ ALSO A BLATANT LIE.

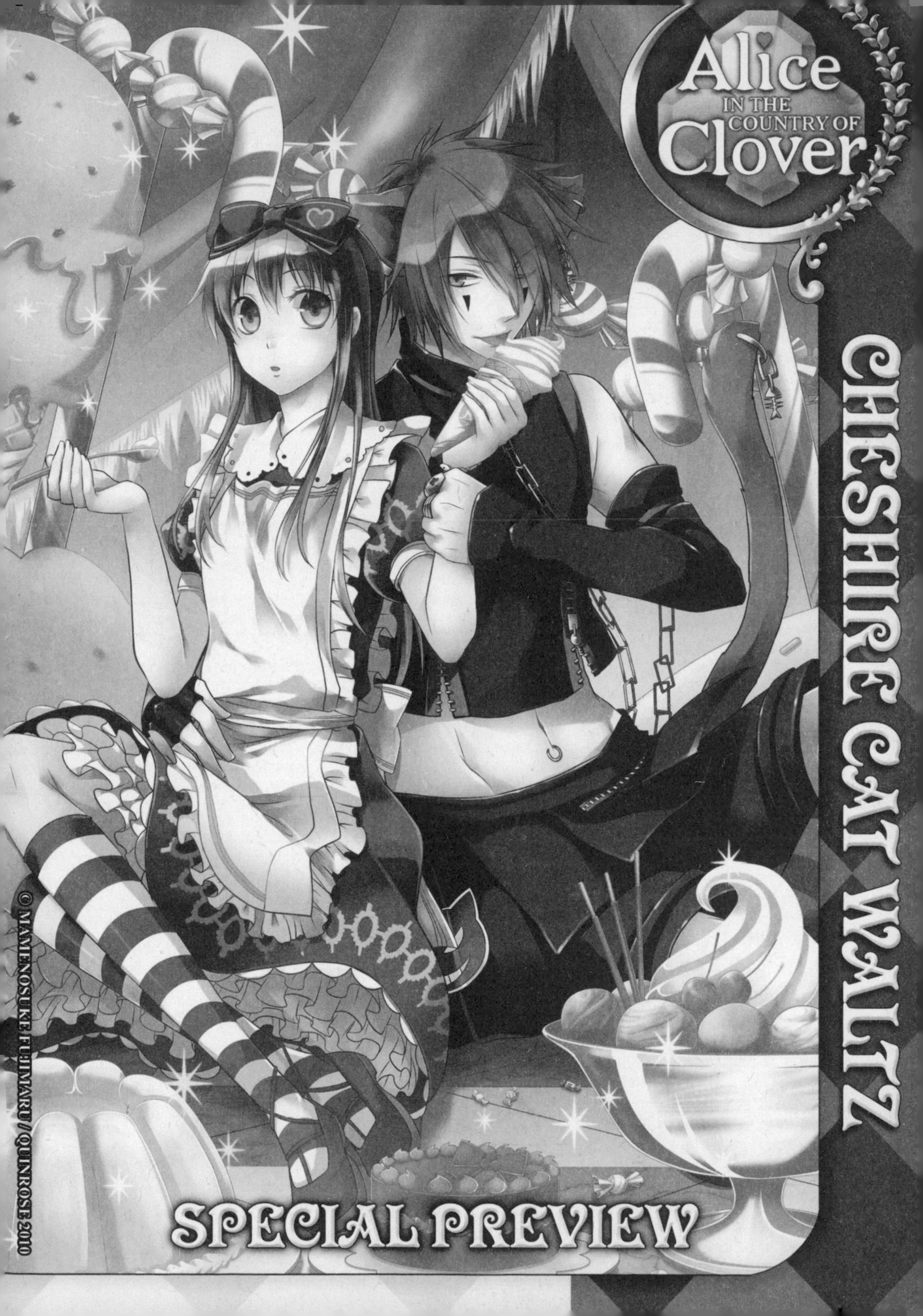
Alice IN THE COUNTRY OF Clover
CHESHIRE CAT WALTZ
SPECIAL PREVIEW
© MAMENOSUKE FUJIMARU / QUINROSE 2010

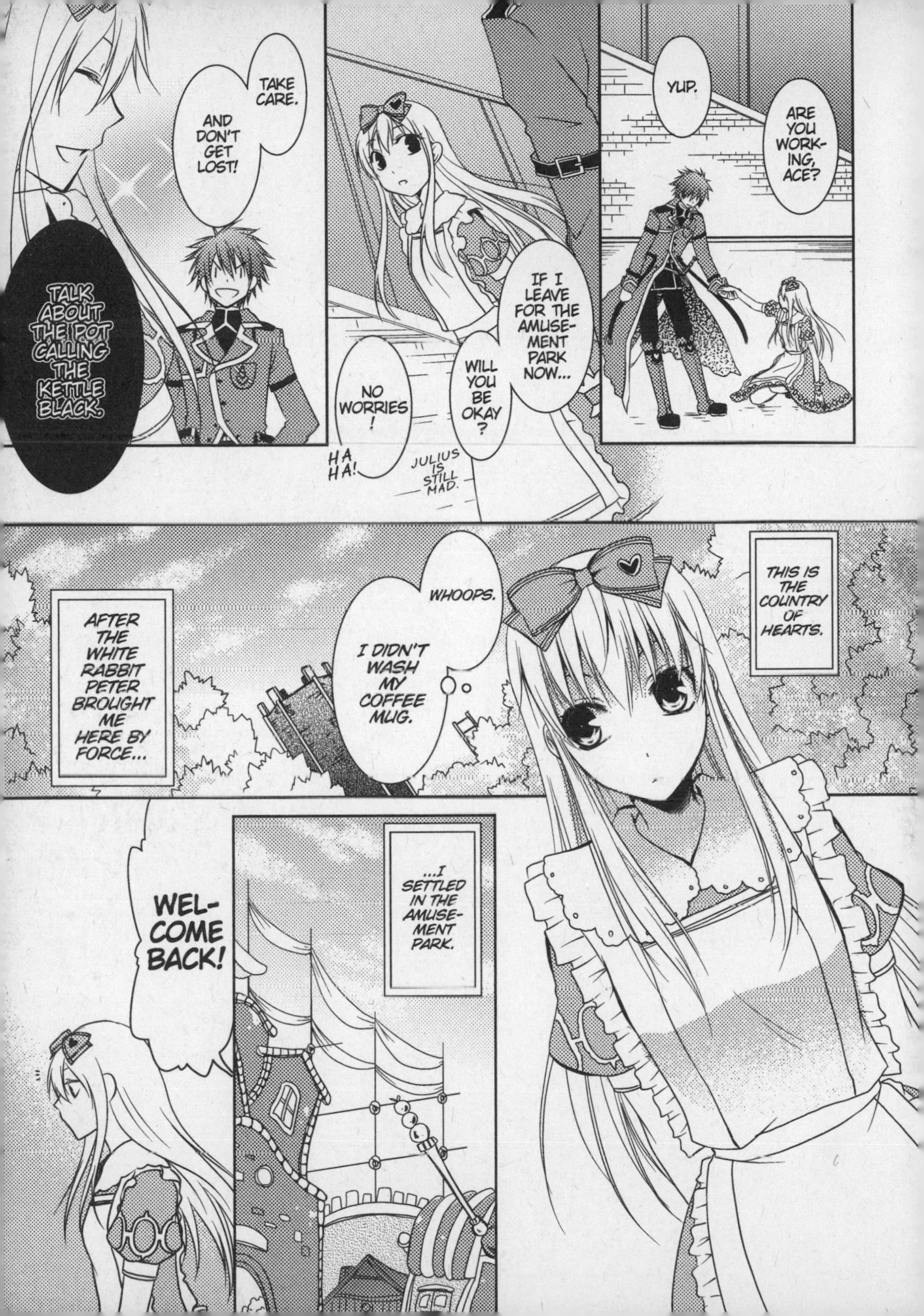
ARE YOU WORKING, ACE?
YUP.
IF I LEAVE FOR THE AMUSEMENT PARK NOW...
WILL YOU BE OKAY?
NO WORRIES!
HA HA!
JULIUS IS STILL MAD.
TAKE CARE.
AND DON'T GET LOST!
TALK ABOUT THE POT CALLING THE KETTLE BLACK.
THIS IS THE COUNTRY OF HEARTS.
WHOOPS.
I DIDN'T WASH MY COFFEE MUG.
AFTER THE WHITE RABBIT PETER BROUGHT ME HERE BY FORCE...
...I SETTLED IN THE AMUSEMENT PARK.
WEL-COME BACK!

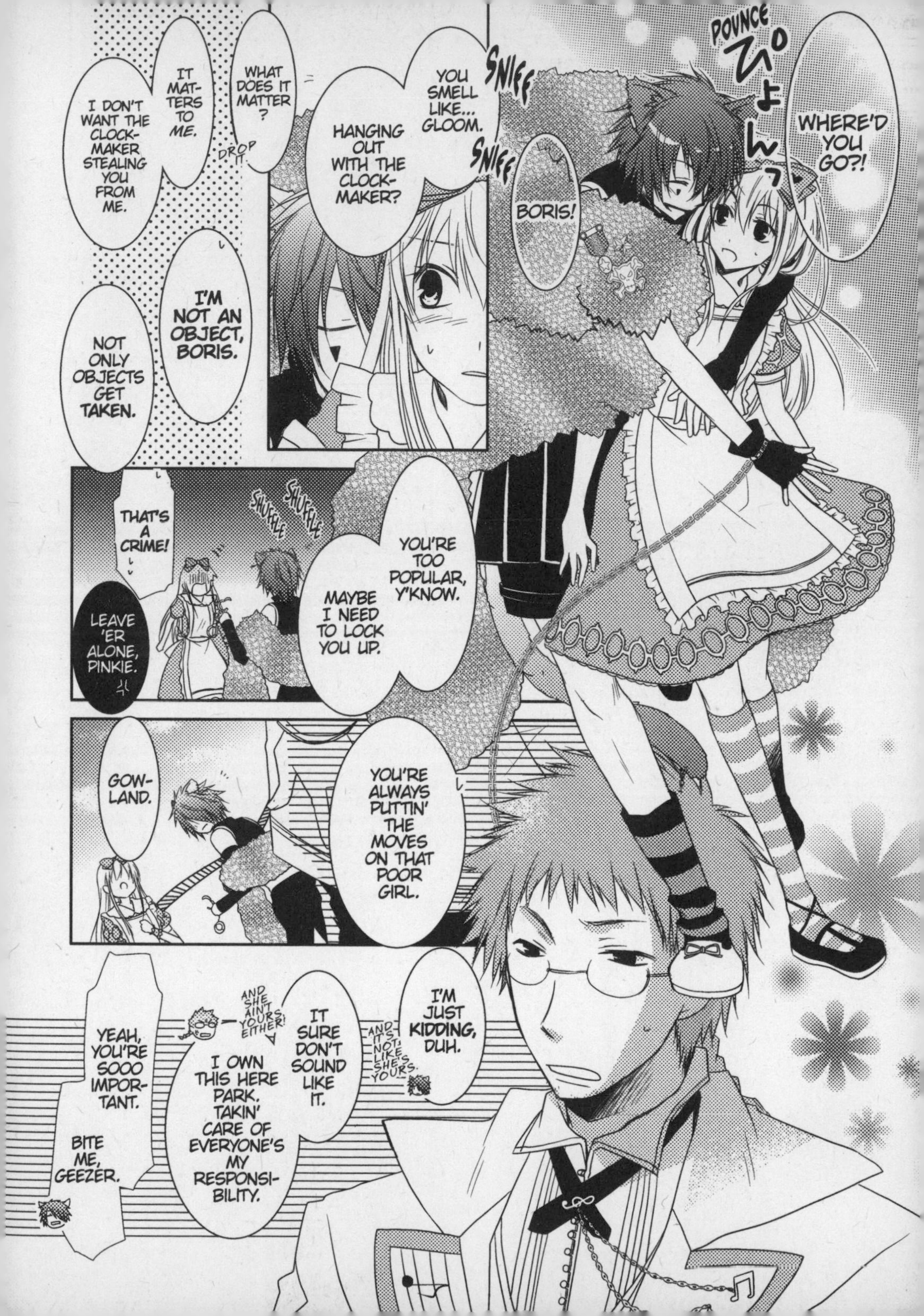
POUNCE
ぴょんっ
WHERE'D YOU GO?!
SNIFF
SNIFF
BORIS!
YOU SMELL LIKE... GLOOM.
HANGING OUT WITH THE CLOCK-MAKER?
WHAT DOES IT MATTER?
DROP IT.
IT MATTERS TO ME.
I DON'T WANT THE CLOCK-MAKER STEALING YOU FROM ME.
I'M NOT AN OBJECT, BORIS.
NOT ONLY OBJECTS GET TAKEN.
YOU'RE TOO POPULAR, Y'KNOW.
MAYBE I NEED TO LOCK YOU UP.
SHUFFLE
SHUFFLE
THAT'S A CRIME!
LEAVE 'ER ALONE, PINKIE.
YOU'RE ALWAYS PUTTIN' THE MOVES ON THAT POOR GIRL.
GOW-LAND.
I'M JUST KIDDING, DUH.
AND IT'S NOT LIKE SHE'S YOURS.
IT SURE DON'T SOUND LIKE IT.
AND SHE AIN'T YOURS EITHER!
I OWN THIS HERE PARK. TAKIN' CARE OF EVERYONE'S MY RESPONSI-BILITY.
YEAH, YOU'RE SOOO IMPOR-TANT.
BITE ME, GEEZER.

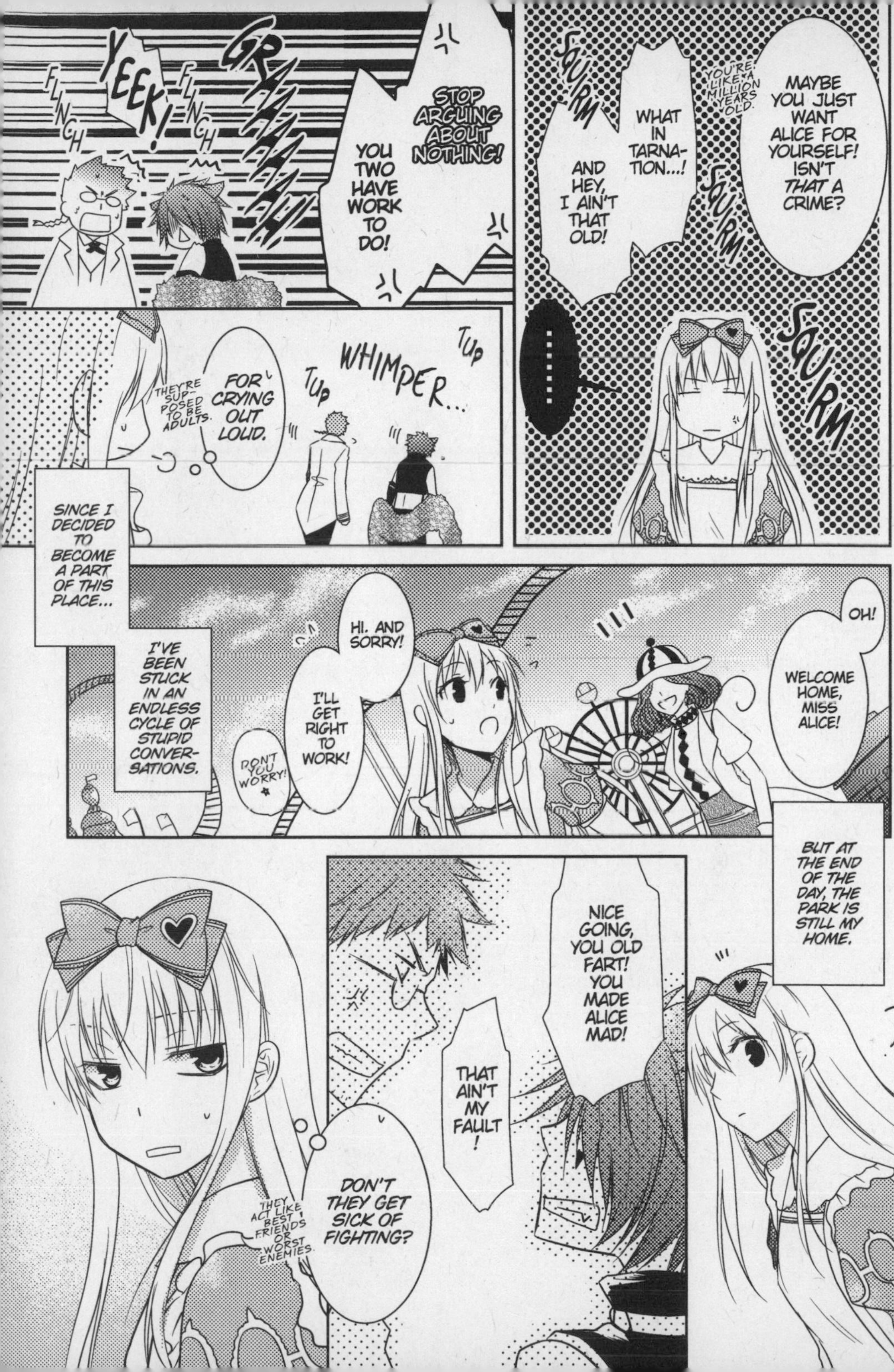
MAYBE YOU JUST WANT ALICE FOR YOURSELF! ISN'T THAT A CRIME?
YOU'RE LIKE A MILLION YEARS OLD.
SQUIRM
WHAT IN TARNATION...!
AND HEY, I AIN'T THAT OLD!
SQUIRM
SQUIRM
......
STOP ARGUING ABOUT NOTHING!
YOU TWO HAVE WORK TO DO!
GRAAAAAAH!!
YEEK!
FLINCH
FLINCH
WHIMPER...
TUP
TUP
FOR CRYING OUT LOUD.
THEY'RE SUPPOSED TO BE ADULTS.
SINCE I DECIDED TO BECOME A PART OF THIS PLACE...
OH!
WELCOME HOME, MISS ALICE!
HI. AND SORRY!
I'LL GET RIGHT TO WORK!
DON'T YOU WORRY!
I'VE BEEN STUCK IN AN ENDLESS CYCLE OF STUPID CONVERSATIONS.
BUT AT THE END OF THE DAY, THE PARK IS STILL MY HOME.
NICE GOING, YOU OLD FART! YOU MADE ALICE MAD!
THAT AIN'T MY FAULT!
DON'T THEY GET SICK OF FIGHTING?
THEY ACT LIKE BEST FRIENDS OR WORST ENEMIES.

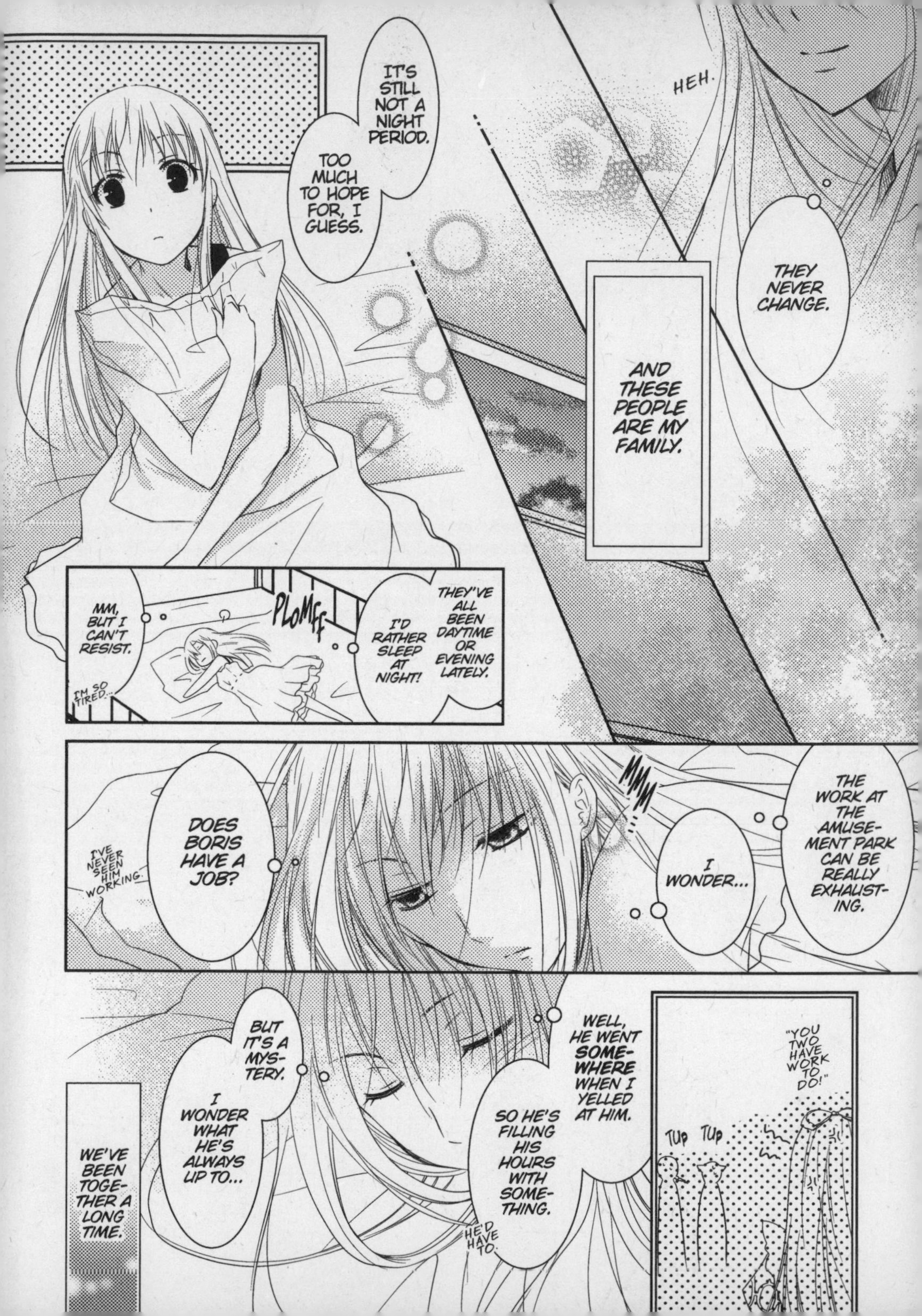
HEH.
THEY NEVER CHANGE.
AND THESE PEOPLE ARE MY FAMILY.
IT'S STILL NOT A NIGHT PERIOD.
TOO MUCH TO HOPE FOR, I GUESS.
THEY'VE ALL BEEN DAYTIME OR EVENING LATELY.
I'D RATHER SLEEP AT NIGHT!
PLOMFF
MM, BUT I CAN'T RESIST.
I'M SO TIRED...
THE WORK AT THE AMUSEMENT PARK CAN BE REALLY EXHAUSTING.
MMM...
I WONDER...
DOES BORIS HAVE A JOB?
I'VE NEVER SEEN HIM WORKING.
"YOU TWO HAVE WORK TO DO!"
TUP TUP
WELL, HE WENT SOMEWHERE WHEN I YELLED AT HIM.
SO HE'S FILLING HIS HOURS WITH SOMETHING.
HE'D HAVE TO.
BUT IT'S A MYSTERY.
I WONDER WHAT HE'S ALWAYS UP TO...
WE'VE BEEN TOGETHER A LONG TIME.

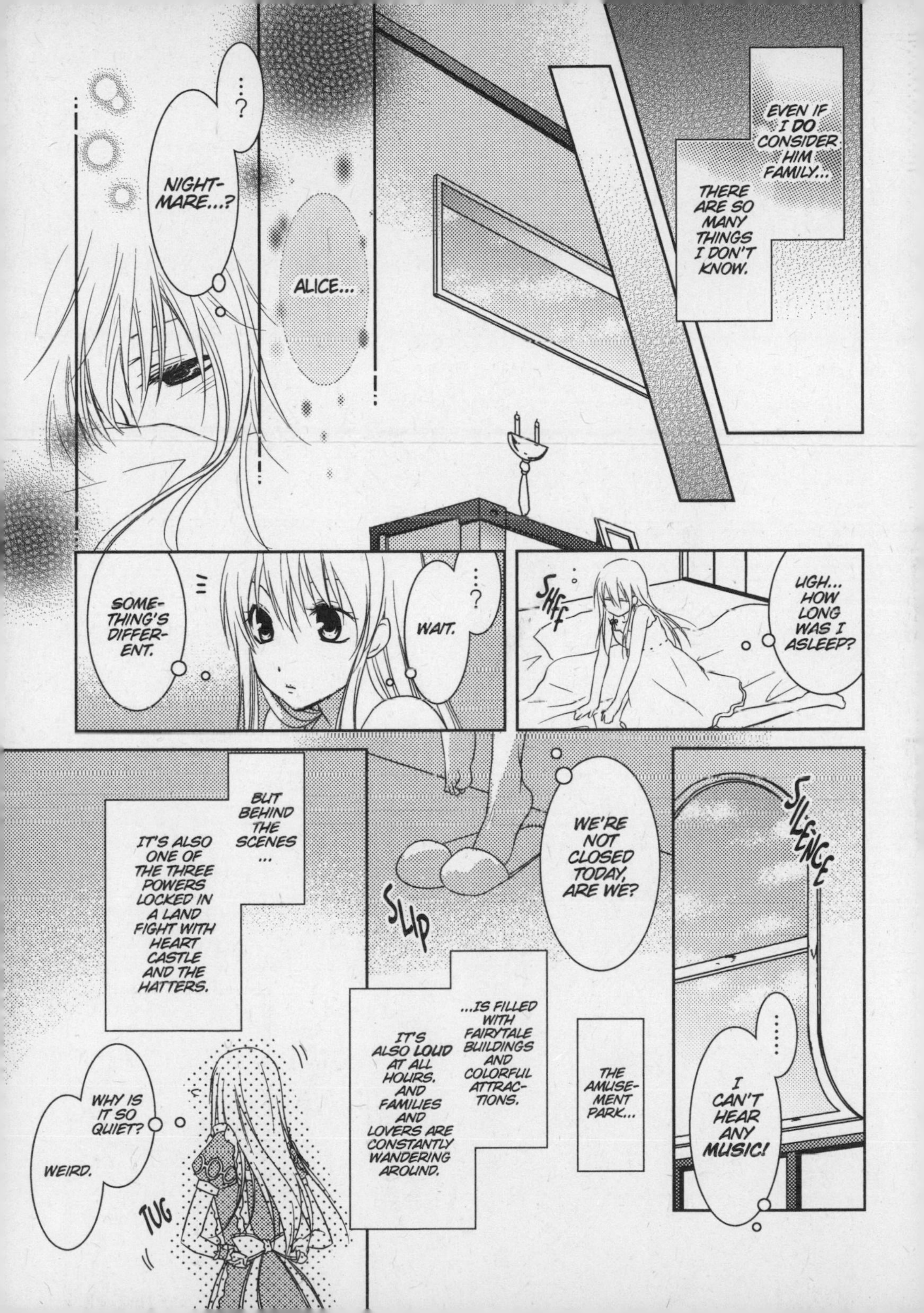
EVEN IF I DO CONSIDER HIM FAMILY...
THERE ARE SO MANY THINGS I DON'T KNOW.
ALICE...
...?
NIGHT-MARE...?
SHFF
UGH... HOW LONG WAS I ASLEEP?
...?
WAIT.
SOME-THING'S DIFFER-ENT.
SILENCE
......
I CAN'T HEAR ANY MUSIC!
WE'RE NOT CLOSED TODAY, ARE WE?
SLIP
THE AMUSE-MENT PARK...
...IS FILLED WITH FAIRYTALE BUILDINGS AND COLORFUL ATTRAC-TIONS.
IT'S ALSO LOUD AT ALL HOURS, AND FAMILIES AND LOVERS ARE CONSTANTLY WANDERING AROUND.
BUT BEHIND THE SCENES...
IT'S ALSO ONE OF THE THREE POWERS LOCKED IN A LAND FIGHT WITH HEART CASTLE AND THE HATTERS.
WHY IS IT SO QUIET?
WEIRD.
TUG

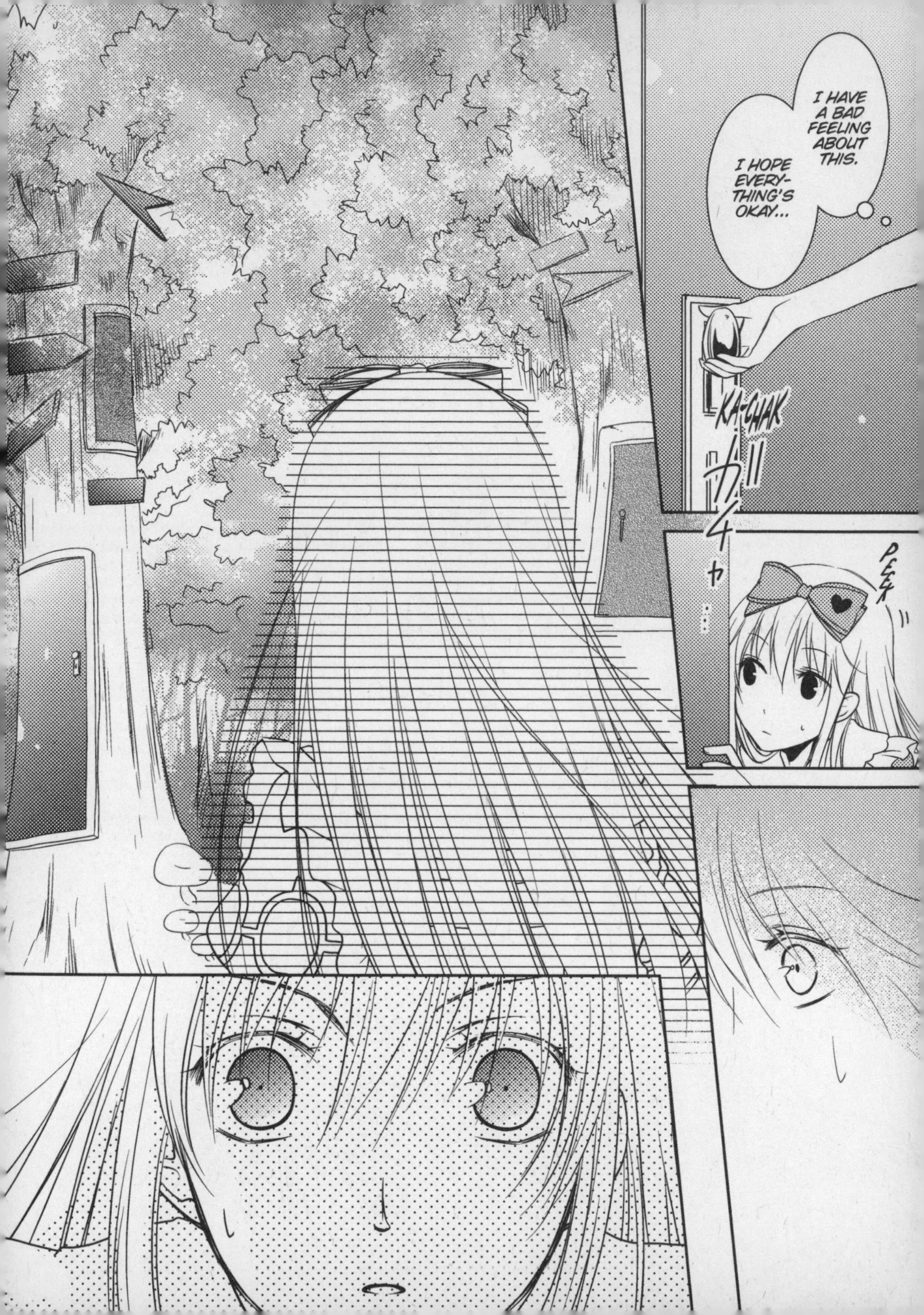
I HAVE A BAD FEELING ABOUT THIS.
I HOPE EVERYTHING'S OKAY...
KA-CHAK
PEEK

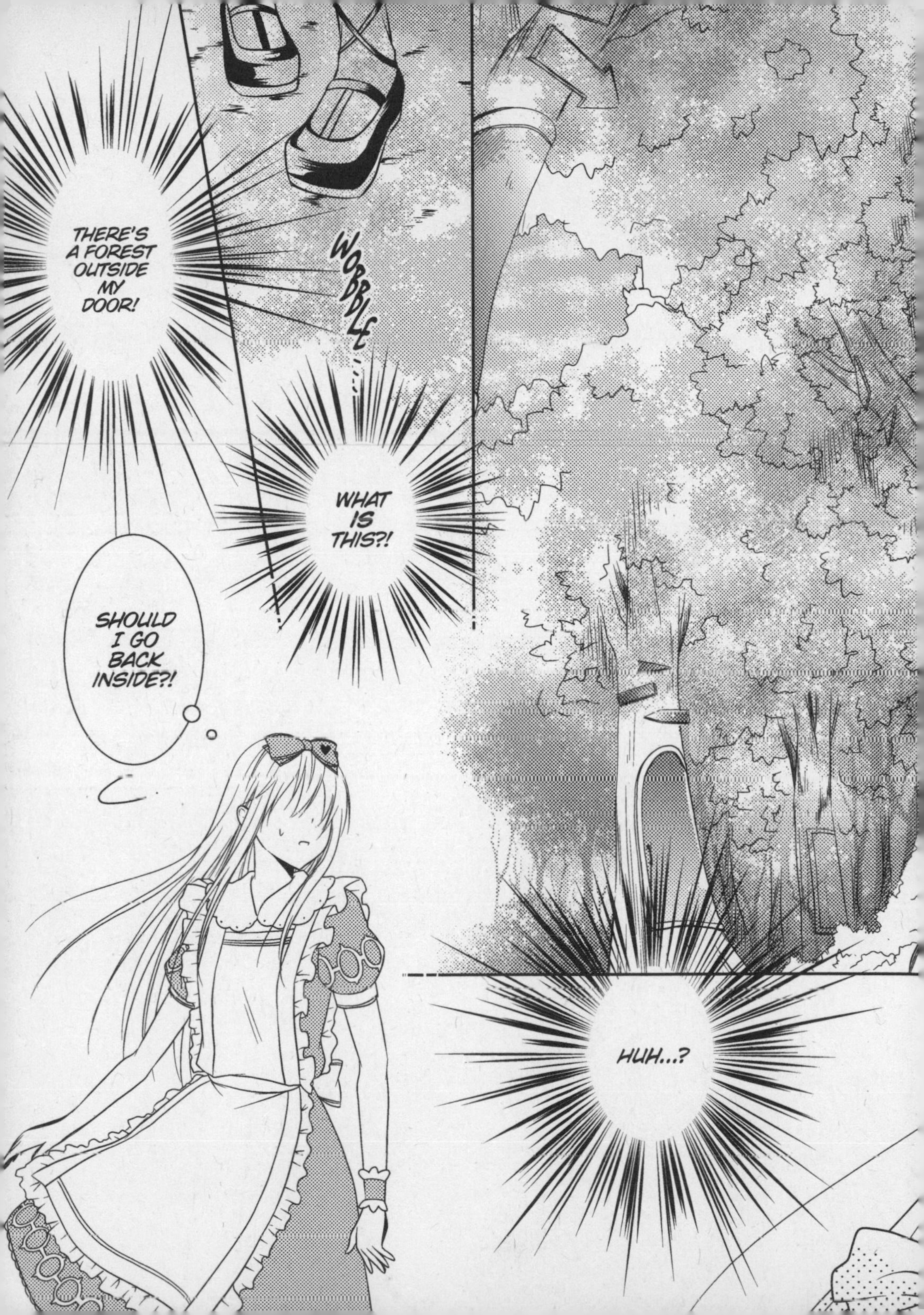
WOBBLE...
THERE'S A FOREST OUTSIDE MY DOOR!
WHAT IS THIS?!
HUH...?
SHOULD I GO BACK INSIDE?!

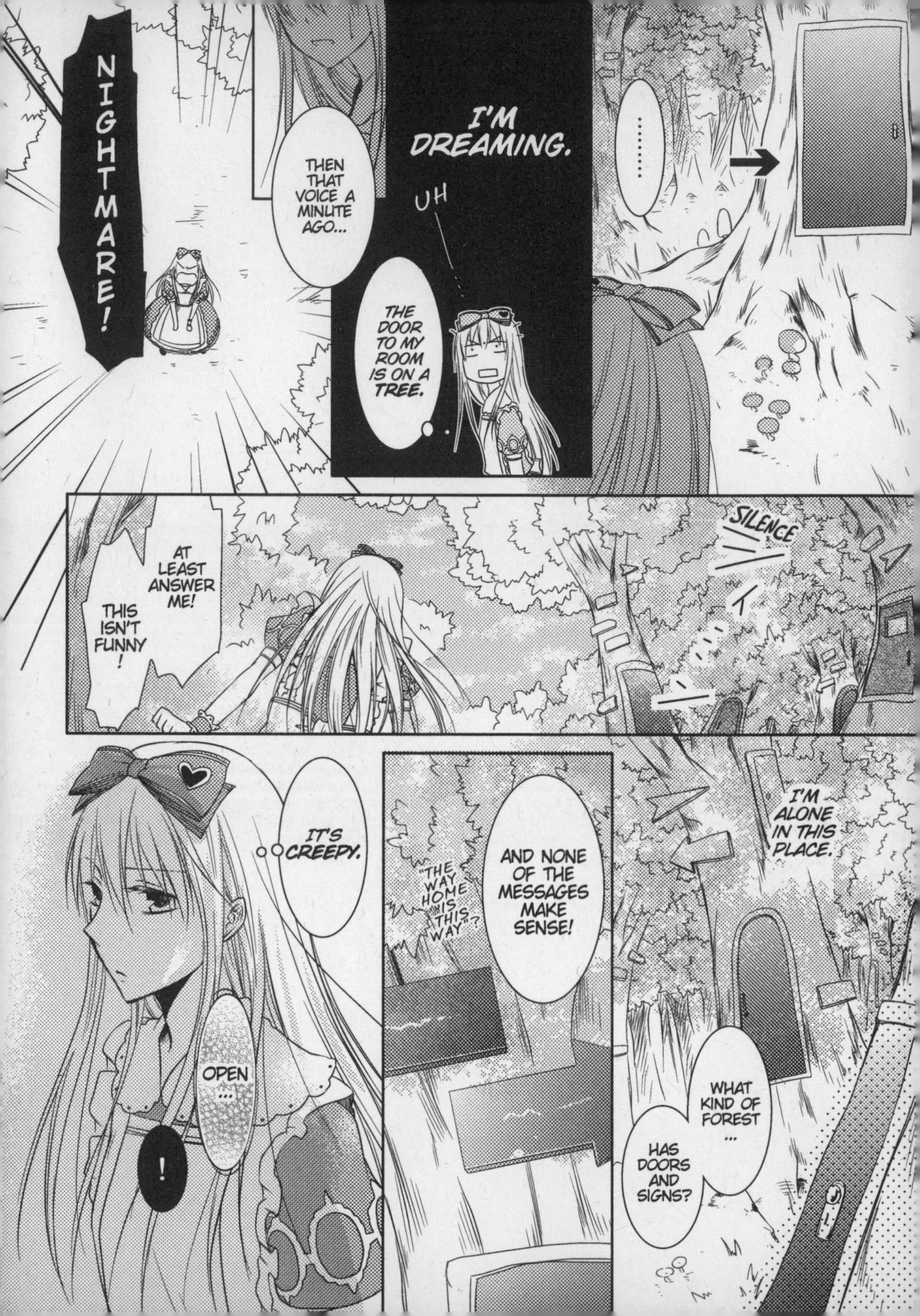
......
I'M DREAMING.
THEN THAT VOICE A MINUTE AGO...
UH
THE DOOR TO MY ROOM IS ON A TREE.
NIGHTMARE!
SILENCE
AT LEAST ANSWER ME!
THIS ISN'T FUNNY!
I'M ALONE IN THIS PLACE.
WHAT KIND OF FOREST...
HAS DOORS AND SIGNS?
AND NONE OF THE MESSAGES MAKE SENSE!
"THE WAY HOME IS THIS WAY"?
IT'S CREEPY.
OPEN...
!

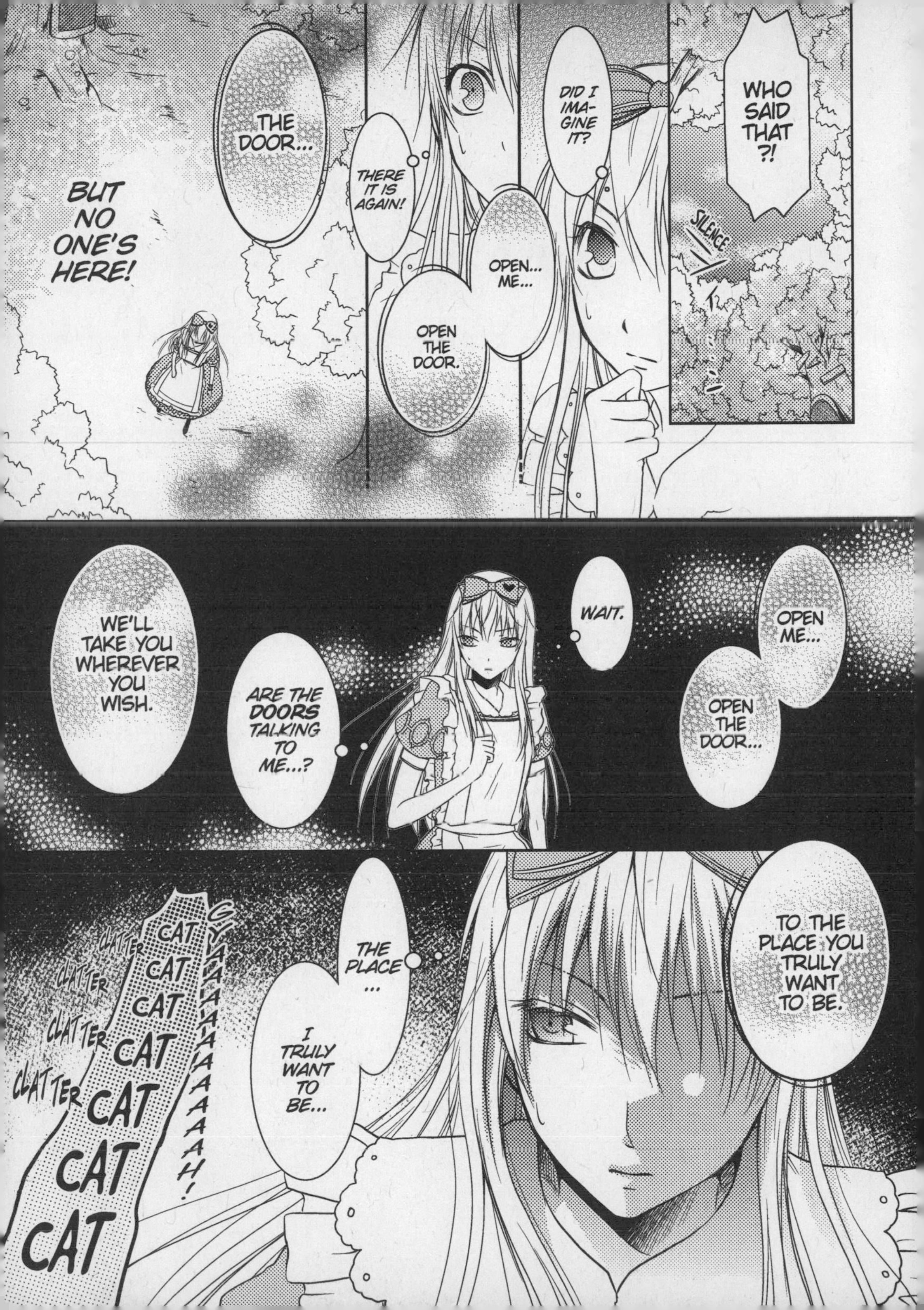
WHO SAID THAT?!
SILENCE
DID I IMAGINE IT?
THERE IT IS AGAIN!
OPEN... ME...
OPEN THE DOOR.
THE DOOR...
BUT NO ONE'S HERE!
OPEN ME...
OPEN THE DOOR...
WAIT.
ARE THE DOORS TALKING TO ME...?
WE'LL TAKE YOU WHEREVER YOU WISH.
TO THE PLACE YOU TRULY WANT TO BE.
THE PLACE...
I TRULY WANT TO BE...
GYAAAAAAAAAAAAAAAH!
CLATTER CAT CLATTER CAT CAT CLATTER CAT CLATTER CAT CAT CAT CAT

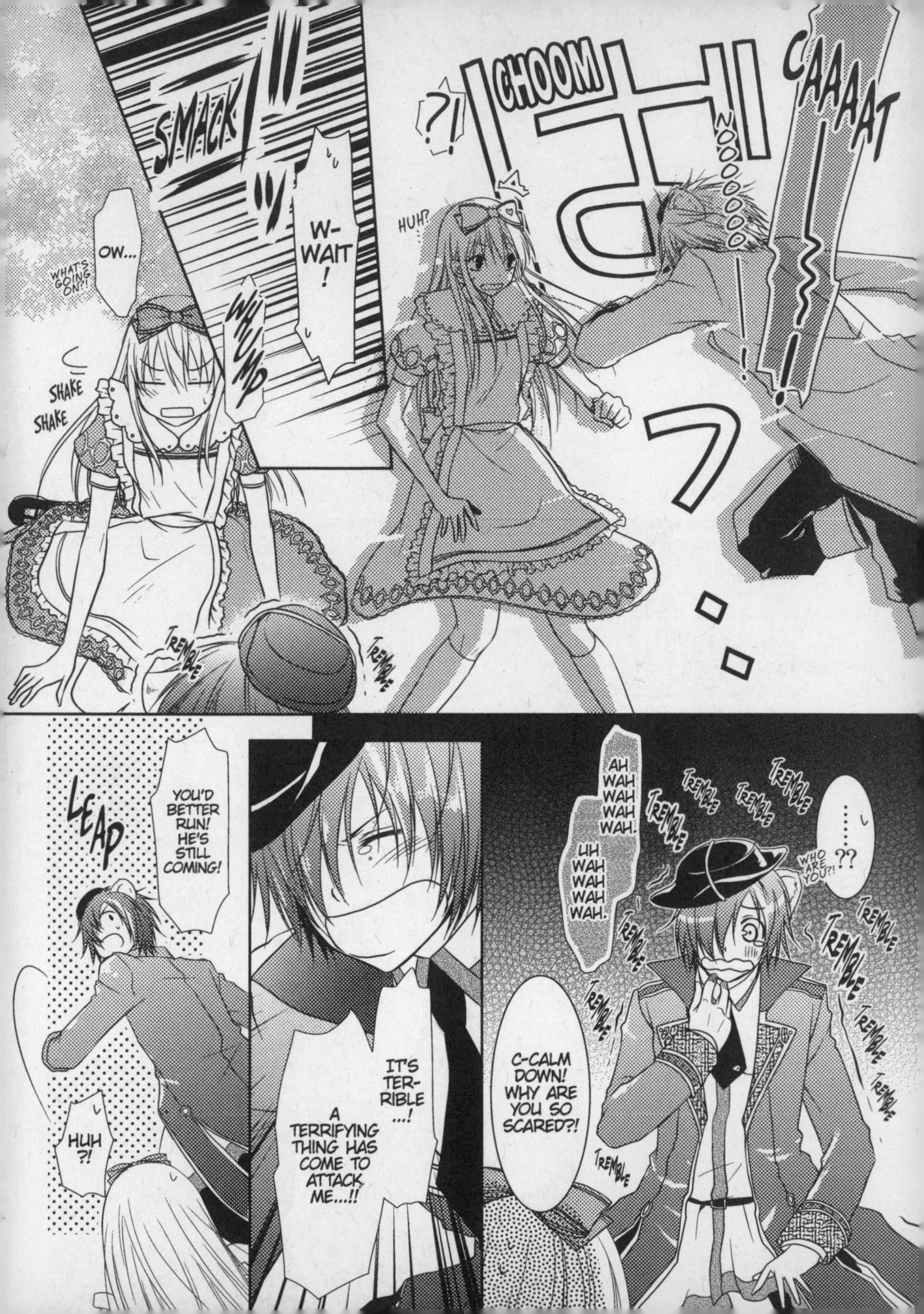
CAAAAT!!
NOOOOOOOO!!
CHOOM
?!
HUH?
W-WAIT!
SMACK!!
WHUMP
OW...
WHAT'S GOING ON?!
SHAKE SHAKE
TREMBLE
TREMBLE
......
WHO ARE YOU?!
??
AH WAH WAH WAH WAH.
UH WAH WAH WAH WAH WAH.
TREMBLE TREMBLE TREMBLE TREMBLE TREMBLE TREMBLE TREMBLE TREMBLE TREMBLE TREMBLE
C-CALM DOWN! WHY ARE YOU SO SCARED?!
IT'S TERRIBLE...!
A TERRIFYING THING HAS COME TO ATTACK ME...!!
YOU'D BETTER RUN! HE'S STILL COMING!
LEAP
HUH?!

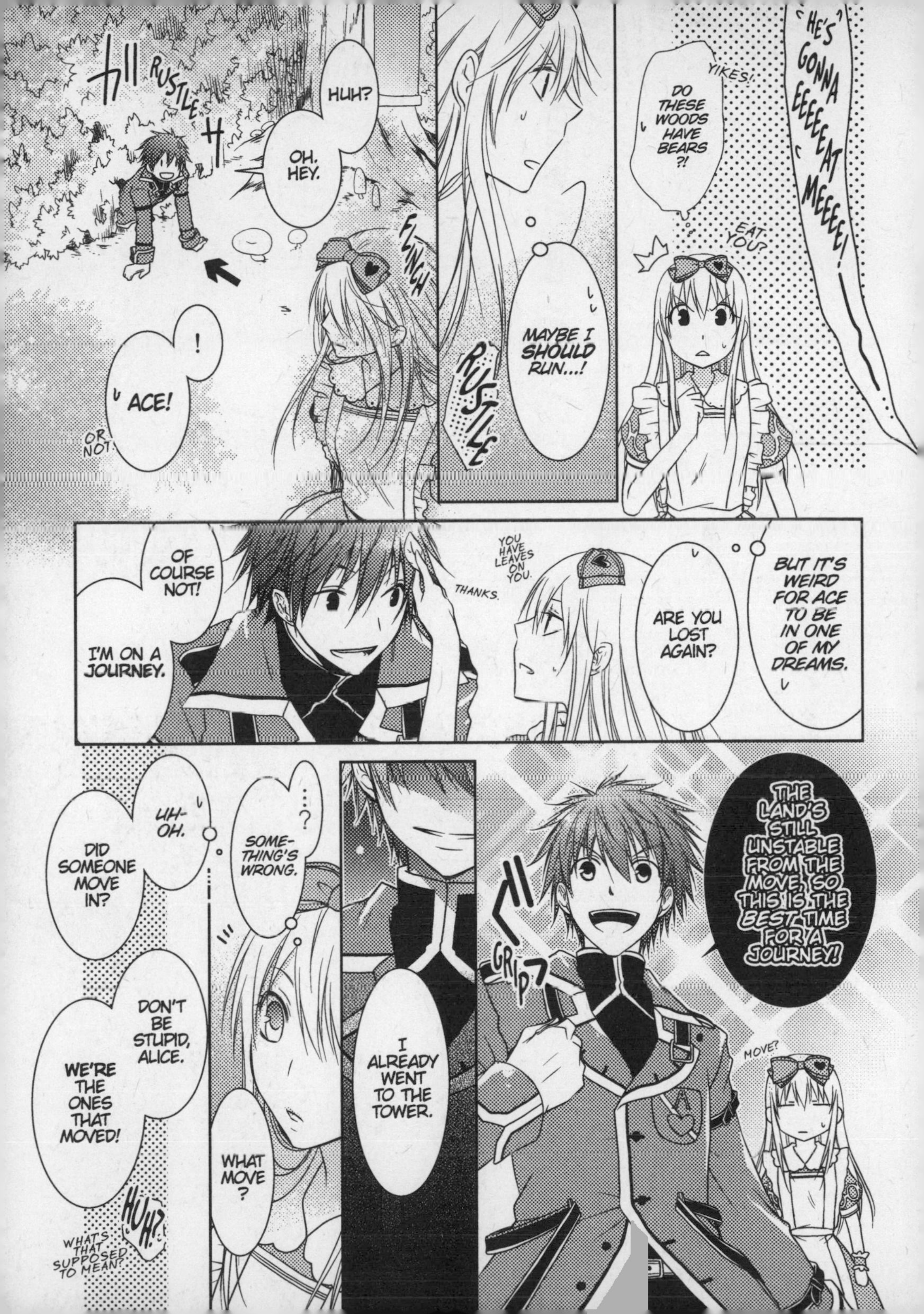
HE'S GONNA EEEEEAT MEEEEE!
YIKES!
DO THESE WOODS HAVE BEARS?!
EAT YOU?
MAYBE I SHOULD RUN...!
RUSTLE
RUSTLE
HUH?
OH. HEY.
FLINCH
!
ACE!
OR NOT.
BUT IT'S WEIRD FOR ACE TO BE IN ONE OF MY DREAMS.
ARE YOU LOST AGAIN?
YOU HAVE LEAVES ON YOU.
THANKS.
OF COURSE NOT!
I'M ON A JOURNEY.
THE LAND'S STILL UNSTABLE FROM THE MOVE, SO THIS IS THE BEST TIME FOR A JOURNEY!
GRIP
MOVE?
I ALREADY WENT TO THE TOWER.
...?
SOMETHING'S WRONG.
UH-OH.
DID SOMEONE MOVE IN?
DON'T BE STUPID, ALICE.
WE'RE THE ONES THAT MOVED!
WHAT MOVE?
HUH?
WHAT'S THAT SUPPOSED TO MEAN?

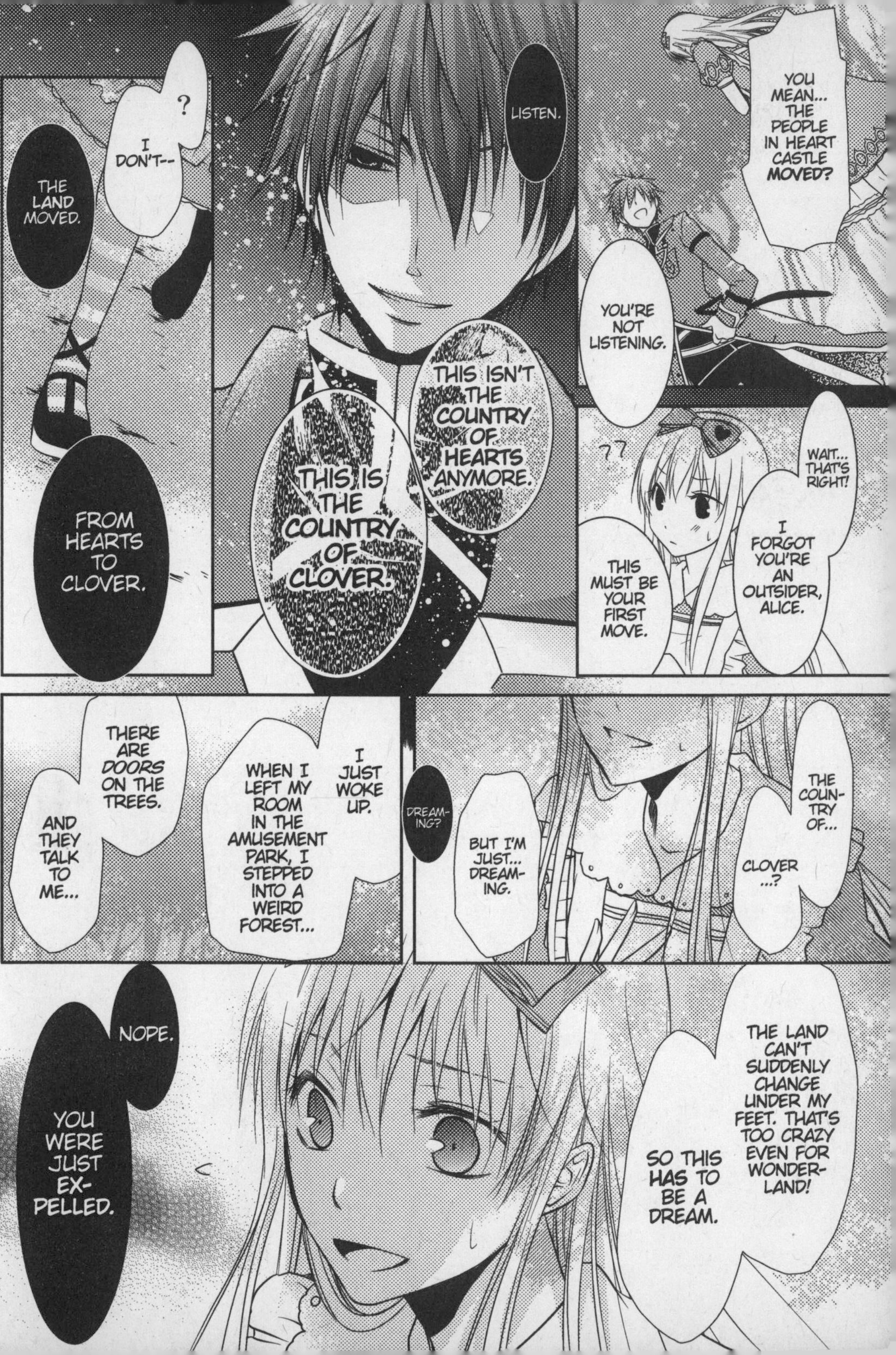
YOU MEAN... THE PEOPLE IN HEART CASTLE MOVED?
YOU'RE NOT LISTENING.
??
WAIT... THAT'S RIGHT!
I FORGOT YOU'RE AN OUTSIDER, ALICE.
THIS MUST BE YOUR FIRST MOVE.
LISTEN.
THIS ISN'T THE COUNTRY OF HEARTS ANYMORE.
THIS IS THE COUNTRY OF CLOVER.
?
I DON'T--
THE LAND MOVED.
FROM HEARTS TO CLOVER.
THE COUNTRY OF...
CLOVER ...?
BUT I'M JUST... DREAMING.
DREAMING?
I JUST WOKE UP.
WHEN I LEFT MY ROOM IN THE AMUSEMENT PARK, I STEPPED INTO A WEIRD FOREST...
THERE ARE DOORS ON THE TREES.
AND THEY TALK TO ME...
THE LAND CAN'T SUDDENLY CHANGE UNDER MY FEET. THAT'S TOO CRAZY EVEN FOR WONDER-LAND!
SO THIS HAS TO BE A DREAM.
NOPE.
YOU WERE JUST EX-PELLED.

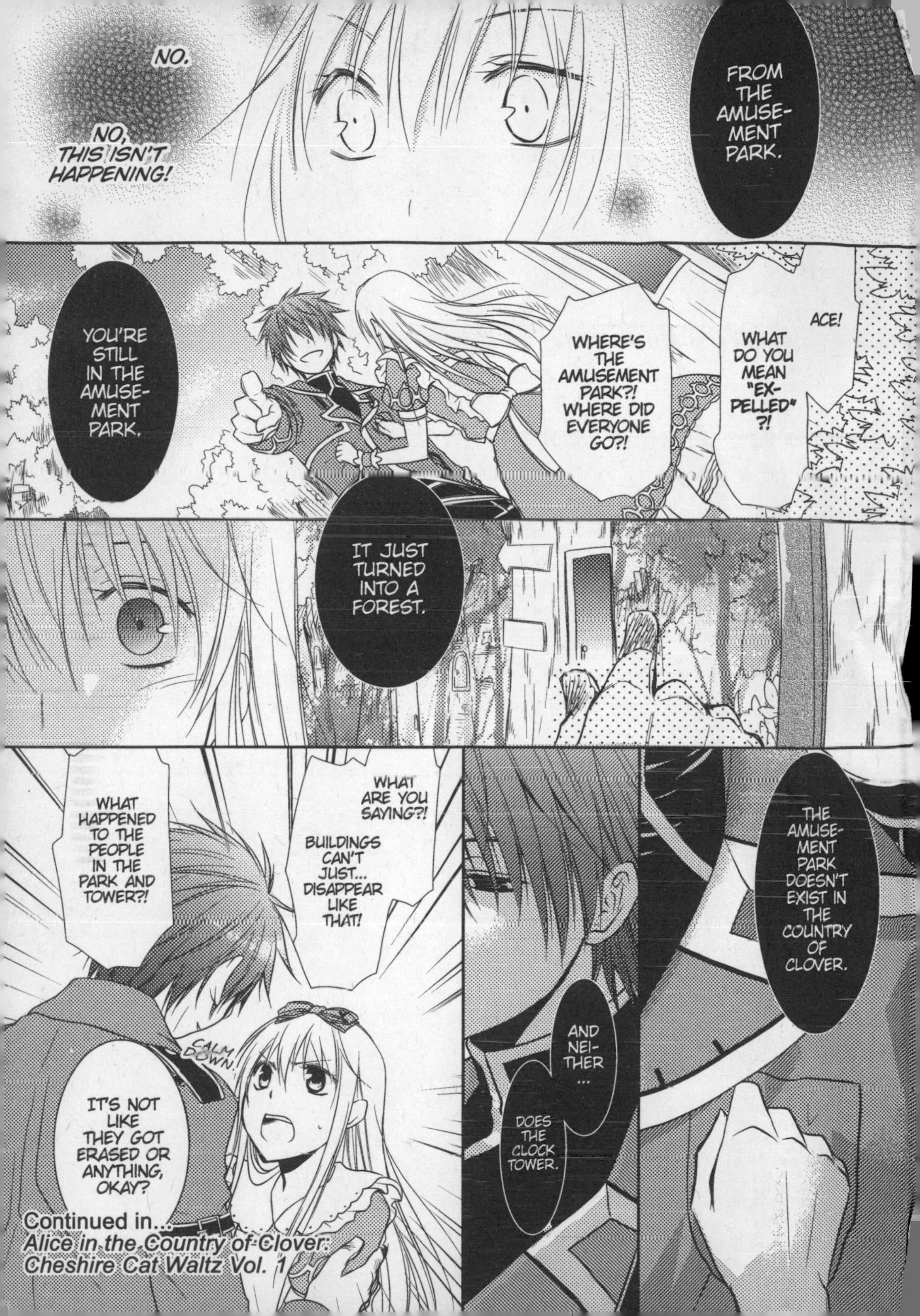
FROM THE AMUSEMENT PARK.
NO.
NO, THIS ISN'T HAPPENING!
ACE! WHAT DO YOU MEAN "EXPELLED"?!
WHERE'S THE AMUSEMENT PARK?! WHERE DID EVERYONE GO?!
YOU'RE STILL IN THE AMUSEMENT PARK.
IT JUST TURNED INTO A FOREST.
THE AMUSEMENT PARK DOESN'T EXIST IN THE COUNTRY OF CLOVER.
AND NEITHER...
DOES THE CLOCK TOWER.
WHAT ARE YOU SAYING?! BUILDINGS CAN'T JUST... DISAPPEAR LIKE THAT!
WHAT HAPPENED TO THE PEOPLE IN THE PARK AND TOWER?!
CALM DOWN.
IT'S NOT LIKE THEY GOT ERASED OR ANYTHING, OKAY?

Continued in...
Alice in the Country of Clover: Cheshire Cat Waltz Vol. 1

COMING SOON

DECEMBER 2013
Crimson Empire Vol. 3

JANUARY 2014
Alice in the Country of Hearts:
The Mad Hatter's Late Night
Tea Party Vol. 2

FEBRUARY 2014
Alice in the Country of Joker:
Circus and Liars Game Vol. 4

MARCH 2014
Alice in the Country of Clover:
March's Hare